TEACHER RESOURCE BOOK

Ready®
New York CCLS

6 English Language Arts
INSTRUCTION
Teacher Resource Book

Advisors

Crystal Bailey, Math Impact Teacher, Eastern Guilford Middle School, Guilford County Schools, Gibsonville, NC

Leslie Blauman, Classroom Teacher, Cherry Hills Village Elementary, Cherry Creek School District, Cherry Hills Village, CO

Max Brand, Reading Specialist, Indian Run Elementary, Dublin City School District, Dublin, OH

Kathy Briguet, Retired Curriculum Coordinator for K-12 Literacy, Forest Lake Area Schools, Forest Lake, MN; Adjunct Instructor, Reading Instruction in the Elementary Grades, University of Minnesota, Minneapolis, MN

Helen Comba, Supervisor of Basic Skills & Language Arts, School District of the Chathams, Chatham, NJ

Cindy Dean, Classroom Teacher, Mt. Diablo Unified School District, Concord, CA

Randall E. Groth, Ph.D., Associate Professor of Mathematics Education, Salisbury University, Salisbury, MD

Jennifer Geaber, Kingston Hill Academy Charter School, South Kingstown, RI

Bill Laraway, Classroom Teacher, Silver Oak Elementary, Evergreen School District, San Jose, CA

Susie Legg, Elementary Curriculum Coordinator, Kansas City Public Schools, Kansas City, KS

Sarah Levine, Classroom Teacher, Springhurst Elementary School, Dobbs Ferry School District, Dobbs Ferry, NY

Nicole Peirce, Classroom Teacher, Eleanor Roosevelt Elementary, Pennsbury School District, Morrisville, PA

Donna Phillips, Classroom Teacher, Farmington R-7 School District, Farmington, MO

Kari Ross, Reading Specialist, MN

Sunita Sangari, Math Coach, PS/MS 29, New York City Public Schools, New York, NY

Shannon Tsuruda, Classroom Teacher, Mt. Diablo Unified School District, Concord, CA

Mark Hoover Thames, Research Scientist, University of Michigan, Ann Arbor, MI

Acknowledgments

Project Manager: Susan James
Revising Editors: Rob Hill, Nick Caster
Cover Designer and Illustrator: Julia Bourque
Book Designer: Mark Nodland

Managing Editor: Nicole VanderLinden
Director–Product Development: Daniel J. Smith
Vice President–Product Development: Adam Berkin

Table of Contents

Unit 2: Key Ideas and Details in Literature

Unit 3: Craft and Structure in Informational Text

Unit 4: Craft and Structure in Literature

Unit 5: Integration of Knowledge and Ideas in Informational Text

Unit 6: Integration of Knowledge and Ideas in Literature

Language Handbook

Conventions of Standard English

Knowledge of Language

Vocabulary Acquisition and Use

Ready® New York CCLS Program Overview

Ready® New York CCLS is an integrated program of assessment and data-driven instruction designed to teach your classroom the Common Core Learning Standards (CCLS) for English Language Arts. The program teaches and assesses all the tested CCLS in the Reading, Writing, and Language strands. You can use the program in a supplemental way to address specific standards where your students need instruction and practice, or in a more comprehensive way to engage students in all the CCLS.

Built for the Common Core. Not just aligned.

Differentiated Instruction and Assessments

Ready New York CCLS Instruction—provides differentiated instruction and independent practice of key concepts and skills that builds student confidence. Interim reading assessments give frequent opportunities to monitor progress. A Language Handbook gives instruction and practice on the Common Core Language standards.

Ready New York CCLS Assessments provides extensive practice on the high-rigor items required by the Common Core, giving you a measure of student growth. The two full-length assessments will strengthen students' skills, build their confidence, and ensure that they are ready to show their mastery of the Common Core.

Teacher Resource Book and Teacher Toolbox

Ready New York CCLS Teacher Resource Books support teachers with strong professional development, step-by-step lesson plans, and best practices for implementing the CCLS.

Ready New York CCLS Teacher Toolbox (Toolbox sold separately) provides online lessons, prerequisite lessons from previous grades, and targeted best-practice teaching strategies.

i-Ready® Diagnostic

Built on the Common Core and integrated with the **Ready** program, **i-Ready Diagnostic** helps teachers track student growth, pointing teachers toward the correct **Ready** lessons to use for remediation. See page A22 for details. (**i-Ready** sold separately.)

Features

 Built with brand-new content

 Uses a research-based gradual-release instructional model

 Employs higher-rigor test questions, requiring students to cite text-based evidence to support answers

 Includes complex, authentic texts from a wide range of genres

 Embeds thoughtful professional development

 Integrates teaching of language arts standards at point of use

 Engages students with high-interest themes for passages, drawing in commonly studied science and social studies topics

NEW 2014 Edition

- More high-rigor test items reflecting latest guidance from EngageNY and PARCC
- New Language Handbook covering the CCLS Language strand
- Updated item Depth of Knowledge (DOK) levels based on latest guidance

The Common Core Learning Standards (CCLS) were developed to make sure that by the time students graduate from high school, they are college- and career-ready. Therefore, the creators of the standards started with the expectations they had for students at the end of 12th grade and worked down to kindergarten. As a result of this backward design approach, the CCLS are more rigorous than most current standards. The creators of the standards want students at every grade to be creative and critical readers and writers. At the end of each grade, students are expected to independently read and comprehend increasingly complex text. Not only are most current textbooks lacking alignment to the CCLS, they also lack the levels of complex text identified in the CCLS. *Ready® New York CCLS* is here to help.

Because every Common Core reading standard has been addressed with a clear, thoughtful pedagogy, you can use the *Ready* program as the main structure of a year-long program. Any other materials aligned to the CCLS can be easily woven into the curriculum.

Each *Ready* lesson covers the entirety of a particular skill, so classrooms can work through any lesson independently from the rest of the book. This gives teachers in states transitioning to the CCLS enormous flexibility, knowing that *Ready* lessons can be pulled out and applied to any implementation plan.

Keep Up to Date with *Ready®* Teacher Toolbox

The online *Ready* Teacher Toolbox gives you access to a host of multilevel resources, such as instructional support, online lessons, and lessons for prerequisite skills. (See pages A20 and A21 for more.) You can access the latest version of *Ready Assessments* there, as well.

Smarter Balanced Assessment Consortium (SBAC) and the Partnership for Assessment of Readiness for College and Career (PARCC) are state-led consortia developing assessments aligned to the Common Core. They are creating higher-rigor, innovative item types and assessments that can measure a student's mastery of the Common Core. (See page A14 to see the higher-level DOK items in *Ready*, matching the consortia approach.) To match the differing approaches of the two consortia, we have created custom versions of *Ready Assessments*, one for PARCC and one for SBAC.

The situation will be changing rapidly as the consortia complete their work. We will make sure that *Ready Assessments* addresses the most recent information released by the consortia. You can ensure you have access to the latest updates by visiting the *Ready* Teacher Toolbox (*www.teacher-toolbox.com*).

Helpful Resources for the Transition to the Common Core

In New York, the Common Core are called the Common Core Learning Standards, or CCLS. Since the 2012–13 school year, New York instructors have been required to teach the Common Core in their classroom curriculum. The Common Core have been assessed in the classroom and by New York assessments in grades 3–8 in English Language Arts and Mathematics since the 2012–13 school year.

Key Websites:

New York State Department of Education: *http://www.nysed.gov/*
New York State P–12 Common Core Learning Standards:
   http://www.p12.nysed.gov/ciai/common_core_standards/
EngageNY: *http://engageny.org*
The main website for the Common Core: *http://www.corestandards.org/*
PARCC, the testing consortium developing for New York's 2014–15 assessment: *http://www.parcconline.org*
ASCD's resources on the Common Core: *http://www.ascd.org/common-core-state-standards/common-core.aspx*
Reading Today Online's resources on the Common Core:
   http://www.reading.org/resources/ResourcesByTopic/CommonCore-resourcetype/CommonCore-rt-resources.aspx

THE DEMANDS OF THE COMMON CORE	HOW *READY*® DELIVERS
Text Complexity: Students must engage with texts of sufficient complexity to prepare them for college and career.	All texts in **Ready** have been carefully leveled to meet Common Core requirements for complexity. See more on page A11.
Intentional, Close Reading: Careful, close readings of complex texts teach students how to gather evidence and build knowledge.	All **Ready** lessons contain activities requiring close reading, re-reading, and frequent interactions with text. On-page guidance models the good habits that successful readers employ. See more on page A12.
Text-based Evidence: Students' interpretations and comprehension of the text must be supported by the words in the text.	All the questions and activities in **Ready** lessons require students to cite evidence directly from the text. Instruction and hints throughout the lesson reinforce the importance of quoting from the text to substantiate interpretations.
Wide Range of Genres, Emphasis on Nonfiction: Students must read a true balance of authentic literary and informational texts. Success in college and the real world requires that students master the skills needed to read a wide range of genres.	**Ready** passages encompass the range of genres and text types cited in the Common Core, including articles, poems, historical text, technical text, scientific text, and dramas. 50% of **Ready** lessons focus on informational texts. See more on page A13.
Building Content Knowledge: Students should view reading as an opportunity to learn new information. As much as possible, therefore, have students read text on related topics that allow them to deepen their understanding.	All passages in a **Ready** lesson are thematically linked. Many of the themes relate to grade-appropriate science and social studies content, others to high-interest, appealing topics. Theme activities provide opportunities for students to see relationships between topics and deepen their content knowledge.
High-Quality Texts: It's important that students are exposed to well-crafted texts that are worth reading closely and exhibit exceptional craft and thought or provide useful information.	**Ready** lessons include authentic texts that students will see in the real world, including text and images from websites, and newspaper and magazine articles from such publications as *The New York Times*, *National Geographic*, and *Highlights*.
Integrated ELA Instruction: Use the texts as a source of rich language arts instruction, as opposed to isolated skill instruction.	**Ready** integrates Speaking & Listening, Writing, and Language activities with every Reading lesson.
Use of Technology and Digital Media: Students learn to use technology thoughtfully and efficiently to enhance their reading.	Specific **Ready** Media Features and lessons allow students to integrate audio and visual media into their reading experience. They learn to evaluate the pros and cons of various media and to employ the best medium to achieve a particular purpose.

The Importance of Text Complexity

Research has shown that the complexity levels of the texts in current classrooms are far below what is required for college- and career-readiness. A major emphasis of the Common Core Learning Standards is for students to encounter appropriately complex texts at each grade level in order to develop the mature language skills and conceptual knowledge they need for success in school and life. Instructional materials should meet this challenge with texts of appropriate complexity at each grade level.

A Three-Part Model for Measuring Text Complexity

No single formula can provide an accurate measure of text complexity. For that reason, the CCLS has developed a balanced three-part model that takes into account the following three ways of assessing text complexity:

Qualitative Measures:
The purpose of the text, the structure and clarity of the language, and background knowledge demands

Quantitative Measures:
Standard readability formulas, such as Lexile and Flesch-Kincaid

Reader–Task Consideration:
Including the reader's motivation and experience, as well as the complexity of the task assigned and questions posed

Text Complexity in *Ready®*

All passages in **Ready** conform to the leveling criteria outlined by the CCLS. We used quantitative formulas to place texts within the grade-level bands recommended by the Standards, which are more rigorous than those of the past. We also had an experienced team of teachers and literacy specialists apply the qualitative and reader–task measures described above. Through the scaffolded instruction in **Ready**, students develop the strategies they will need to comprehend this challenging text.

Academic Vocabulary

The CCLS categorize types of vocabulary in a three-tier model similar to the one developed by Beck, McKeown, & Kucan in *Bringing Words to Life*. (Beck, McKeown, & Kucan, 2002) Tier One Vocabulary are the words of everyday speech. Tier Two (which CCLS calls "general academic vocabulary") are the words a reader encounters in rich, complex texts of all types. Tier Three (which CCLS calls "domain specific") are the words particular to a field of study, such as science or history. While Tier Three words are often explicitly defined in a subject-area text, this is not the case with Tier Two words. Their meanings are often subtle, yet they are the most important words for students to learn, since they are generalizable, or applicable to a wide variety of texts.

Unlike reading programs of the past, in which difficult vocabulary was "pretaught" before reading, CCLS emphasizes the use of text-based strategies, such as context and word structure, to determine word meaning. **Ready** provides this type of instruction in the Teacher Resource Book lessons by identifying challenging Tier Two words in a passage and giving the teacher explicit text-based strategies to support students in unlocking their meanings.

What Is Close Reading?

The purpose of a close reading is to unlock the meanings of a text and to probe an author's motivations for writing it. To achieve these goals, readers must

- reread the text (in whole or in part),
- write down questions and observations relevant to the text's meaning and purpose, and
- mark up the text to identify details that help answer those questions and develop those observations.

Internalizing and mastering such close-reading strategies prepares students for college and careers, which is a key goal of the Common Core: "[Research] links the close reading of complex text—whether the student is a struggling reader or advanced—to significant gains in reading proficiency." (PARCC, 2011)

How Do We Apply Close Reading Instruction in *Ready® New York CCLS*?

Short, rich, complex text: Readers use close-reading strategies with challenging text that are hard to fully comprehend on a first reading. It's this type of complex text you'll find in **Ready**. **Ready** uses short text because we agree with reading experts that "When students are introduced to a . . . strategy through close reading, it's wise to use a short piece of text. Constraining the amount of text under investigation helps students see how to apply that . . . strategy and limits the amount of time required to teach [it]." (Fisher, Frey, & Lapp, 2012)

Multiple readings: In Guided Practice, we explicitly emphasize multiple readings (see page A28). For the first reading, students focus on literal comprehension. In the second reading, students apply close-reading strategies to unlock meaning and practice the lesson's featured standard. Fisher, Frey, & Lapp describe the value of multiple readings: "Sophisticated readers understand that the nature of some text requires that they be read more than once. . . . First and foremost, close reading requires a willingness to return to the text to read part or even all of it more than once." (Fisher, Frey, & Lapp, 2012)

Marking up the text: Our Close Reading activities guide students to mark up the text, helping them remember and make sense of what they read. We prompt students to mark specific evidence in the text that provide answers to the text-dependent questions they will need to answer. As Fisher, Frey, & Lapp describe it, "[b]y annotating texts . . . students learn to slow down their reading to mine the depths of the concepts, arguments, and metaphors used by the writer." (Fisher, Frey, & Lapp, 2012)

Teaching for transfer: Students must take what they learn from the study of one text and apply it to the next. To encourage this transfer, we remove the scaffolds in our Common Core Practice section. See page A30 for a tip activating these metacognitive strategies.

Monitoring Student Progress in *Ready® Instruction*

These ongoing assessment features in the **Ready** program keep you informed about student progress:

Student Lesson

- **Common Core Practice:** Each lesson ends with Common Core Practice. Use these results to identify how well students mastered the specific standard. If students scored poorly, review the lesson and use reteaching support in the Teacher Resource Book.

- **Interim Assessment:** Use the Interim Assessments and Performance Tasks at the end of each unit to see how well students can integrate the skills and strategies covered in that unit.

Full-Length Assessments

- **Ready Assessments:** Three full-length assessments allow you to benchmark student progress on each CCLS throughout the year.

Teacher Resource Book

- **Error Alerts:** This easy-to-use feature allows you to quickly identify and address common misconceptions students experience when applying the targeted standard.

Genres and Themes in *Ready*®

To succeed in college and the world outside the classroom, students must master reading a wide range of genres. *Ready*® ensures students read rich texts linked in meaningful ways by including a variety of genres and by organizing each lesson under a theme. The following chart shows the themes and genres for grade 6 lessons.

Lesson	Theme	Genres
1: Determining Central Idea and Details	Extraordinary Plants	Science
2: Summarizing Informational Texts	Links in the Food Chain	Science
3: Citing Evidence to Make Inferences	Mysterious Creatures	Science
4: Analyzing Key Ideas in a Text	Legendary Places	History
5: Citing Evidence to Make Inferences	Passing Wisdom Down Through the Ages	Myth, Native American Legend, Realistic Fiction
6: Describing Plot	Adventure and Conflict	Adventure, Drama, Historical Fiction
7: Analyzing Character Development	Recognizing Potential	Drama, Realistic Fiction
8: Determining Theme or Central Idea	A Time to Change	Realistic Fiction
9: Summarizing Literary Texts	Puzzles and Mysteries	Mystery
10: Determining Word Meanings: Figurative, Connotative & Technical	The Power of Music	History, Science
11: Analyzing Text Structures	Ancient Civilizations	History
12: Determining Point of View	Extreme Sports	Editorial, Essay
13: Determining Word Meanings: Figurative and Connotative	Out in the Elements	Adventure, Lyric Poem, Realistic Fiction
14: Analyzing Word Choice	Surprise Endings	Mystery, Narrative Poem, Realistic Fiction
15: Analyzing the Structure of a Poem	Capturing Memories	Ballad, Lyric Poem
16: Analyzing the Structure of Stories	Wilderness Adventures	Adventure
17: Explaining Point of View	Culture Shock	Historical Fiction, Realistic Fiction
18: Evaluating an Argument	Weighing the Evidence	Editorial, Persuasive Essay
19: Comparing and Contrasting Texts	American Icons	Biography, Memoir
20: Comparing and Contrasting Genres	Courage	Fantasy, Lyric Poem, Historical Fiction, Realistic Fiction, Science Fiction

Depth of Knowledge Level 3 Items in *Ready® New York CCLS*

The following table shows the **Ready®** lessons and sections with higher-complexity items, as measured by Webb's Depth of Knowledge index.

Lesson	Section	Item	Lesson	Section	Item
1	Guided Practice	3	13	Common Core Practice	5
1	Common Core Practice	5	14	Guided Practice	1
3	Guided Practice	2	14	Guided Practice	3
3	Guided Practice	3	14	Common Core Practice	1
3	Common Core Practice	4	14	Common Core Practice	2
3	Common Core Practice	5	14	Common Core Practice	4
4	Guided Practice	3	15	Guided Practice	3
4	Common Core Practice	3	15	Common Core Practice	4
4	Common Core Practice	4	15	Common Core Practice	5
Unit 1	Interim Assessment	2A	16	Guided Practice	3
Unit 1	Interim Assessment	2B	16	Common Core Practice	4
Unit 1	Interim Assessment	4	17	Guided Instruction	–
Unit 1	Interim Assessment	7	17	Guided Practice	3
Unit 1	Interim Assessment	8	17	Common Core Practice	1
Unit 1	Interim Assessment	9	17	Common Core Practice	3
5	Guided Practice	3	Unit 4	Interim Assessment	2
5	Common Core Practice	5	Unit 4	Interim Assessment	4
6	Guided Practice	3	Unit 4	Interim Assessment	6
6	Common Core Practice	4	Unit 4	Interim Assessment	7
7	Guided Practice	3	Unit 4	Interim Assessment	8
7	Common Core Practice	3	Unit 4	Interim Assessment	9
7	Common Core Practice	4	18	Guided Instruction	–
8	Guided Practice	3	18	Guided Practice	3
8	Common Core Practice	4	18	Common Core Practice	2
9	Common Core Practice	2	18	Common Core Practice	4
Unit 2	Interim Assessment	3	19	Guided Instruction	–
Unit 2	Interim Assessment	4	19	Guided Practice	1
Unit 2	Interim Assessment	6	19	Guided Practice	2
Unit 2	Interim Assessment	8	19	Guided Practice	3
Unit 2	Interim Assessment	9	19	Common Core Practice	1
10	Guided Instruction	–	19	Common Core Practice	2
10	Guided Practice	2	19	Common Core Practice	3
10	Guided Practice	3	Unit 5	Interim Assessment	2
10	Common Core Practice	1	Unit 5	Interim Assessment	4
10	Common Core Practice	2	Unit 5	Interim Assessment	5A
11	Guided Practice	1	Unit 5	Interim Assessment	5B
11	Guided Practice	3	Unit 5	Interim Assessment	6
11	Common Core Practice	5	Unit 5	Interim Assessment	7
12	Guided Instruction	–	Unit 5	Interim Assessment	8
12	Guided Practice	1	20	Guided Practice	1
12	Guided Practice	2	20	Guided Practice	2
12	Guided Practice	3	20	Guided Practice	3
12	Common Core Practice	1	20	Common Core Practice	1
12	Common Core Practice	2	20	Common Core Practice	2
12	Common Core Practice	3	20	Common Core Practice	3
12	Common Core Practice	5	20	Common Core Practice	4
Unit 3	Interim Assessment	4	Unit 6	Interim Assessment	1
Unit 3	Interim Assessment	5	Unit 6	Interim Assessment	2
Unit 3	Interim Assessment	7	Unit 6	Interim Assessment	3
Unit 3	Interim Assessment	8	Unit 6	Interim Assessment	4
Unit 3	Interim Assessment	9	Unit 6	Interim Assessment	5A
Unit 3	Interim Assessment	10	Unit 6	Interim Assessment	5B
13	Guided Practice	2	Unit 6	Interim Assessment	6
13	Guided Practice	3	Unit 6	Interim Assessment	7
13	Common Core Practice	2	Unit 6	Interim Assessment	8
13	Common Core Practice	4	Unit 6	Interim Assessment	9

Cognitive Rigor Matrix

The following table combines the hierarchies of learning from both Webb and Bloom. For each level of hierarchy, descriptions of student behaviors that would fulfill expectations at each of the four DOK levels are given. For example, students can show how they evaluate by citing evidence or checking multiple sources, but there isn't a lower-rigor (DOK 1 or 2) way of truly assessing this skill.

Depth of Thinking (Webb) + Type of Thinking (Revised Bloom)	DOK Level 1 Recall & Reproduction	DOK Level 2 Basic Skills & Concepts	DOK Level 3 Strategic Thinking & Reasoning	DOK Level 4 Extended Thinking
Remember	• Recall, locate basic facts, definitions, details, events			
Understand	• Select appropriate words for use when intended meaning is clearly evident	• Specify, explain relationships • Summarize • Identify central ideas	• Explain, generalize, or connect ideas using supporting evidence (quote, text evidence, example . . .)	• Explain how concepts or ideas specifically relate to other content domains or concepts
Apply	• Use language structure (pre/suffix) or word relationships (synonym/antonym) to determine meaning	• Use content to identify word meanings • Obtain and interpret information using text features	• Use concepts to solve non-routine problems	• Devise an approach among many alternatives to research a novel problem
Analyze	• Identify the kind of information contained in a graphic, table, visual, etc.	• Compare literary elements, facts, terms, events • Analyze format, organization, & text structures	• Analyze or interpret author's craft (e.g., literary devices, viewpoint, or potential bias) to critique a text	• Analyze multiple sources or texts • Analyze complex/abstract themes
Evaluate			• Cite evidence and develop a logical argument for conjectures based on one text or problem	• Evaluate relevancy, accuracy, & completeness of information across texts/sources
Create	• Brainstorm ideas, concepts, problems, or perspectives related to a topic or concept	• Generate conjectures or hypotheses based on observations or prior knowledge and experience	• Develop a complex model for a given situation • Develop an alternative solution	• Synthesize information across multiple sources or texts • Articulate a new voice, alternate theme, new knowledge or perspective

SBAC, 2012; adapted from Hess et al., 2009

Using *Ready® New York CCLS*

The **Ready®** program provides rigorous instruction on the Common Core State Standards using a proven-effective gradual-release approach that builds student confidence. It also prepares students for more complex assessment items with full-length assessments and interim assessments. With the Teacher Resource Book, you get strong support, step-by-step lesson plans, and best-practice tips to learn new approaches to teaching the Common Core. The Teacher Toolbox gives you access to invaluable, easy-to-use resources to differentiate instruction with a host of online materials, all in one place.

Using as a Supplement to a Textbook

The textbook you use in your classroom may not have been developed for the Common Core. It may not have all the resources you'll need to meet these challenging standards. In addition, the passages in textbooks don't reflect the levels of text complexity required by the Common Core, and the activities and questions don't reflect their rigor. By supplementing with **Ready**, you'll be able to address all of these gaps and deficiencies.

Using with a Balanced Literacy/Reading Workshop Curriculum

Because every standard in **Ready New York CCLS** has been addressed with a clear, thoughtful pedagogy, you can use the **Ready** program as the main structure of a year-long English language arts program. Any other materials aligned to the Common Core can be woven into the curriculum, using the four easy steps on this page as your map.

Using with *i-Ready® Diagnostic*

If you are an **i-Ready** subscriber, you can administer the **i-Ready Diagnostic** as a cross-grade-level assessment to pinpoint instructional needs and address them with **Ready New York CCLS Instruction**. For more on this, see page A22.

1 Measure Growth

- Use Assessment 1 from **Ready New York CCLS Assessments** to establish a baseline for measurement and to focus instructional plans. Use Assessment 2 to measure growth as students work through the program. These tests give students practice and build the stamina students need to prepare for the New York State English Language Arts Test.

2 Instruct

- Administer each **Ready New York CCLS Instruction** lesson, using the Pacing Guide on page A17 as a guide. Language Handbook lessons are also listed to show how the Reading and Language lessons can be used together.

- At any time during the instructional program, refer to the Teacher Toolbox to review prerequisite skills and access lessons from previous grades for remediation.

3 Monitor Progress

- Use the Interim Assessments at the end of each **Ready Instruction** unit to pinpoint student progress on the standards they have most recently learned and diagnose problem areas.

4 Differentiate Instruction

Provide differentiated instruction for your students using the rich and varied resources in the Teacher Toolbox. Here you'll find links to prerequisite skills from earlier grades of **Ready**, as well as links to highly interactive animated modules that will deepen students' understanding of skills and strategies. See page A20 for more on using the Teacher Toolbox.

Year-Long Pacing Guide for Grade 6

Week	Ready® New York CCLS Instruction Lesson	Days	Minutes per Day	Language Handbook Lesson (allow 20 minutes per lesson)
1	Assessment 1	3	60	
2	Lesson 1: Determining Central Idea and Details	5	30–45	11
3	Lesson 2: Summarizing Informational Texts	5	30–45	12
4	Lesson 3: Citing Evidence to Make Inferences	5	30–45	13
5	Lesson 4: Analyzing Key Ideas in a Text	5	30–45	14
	Unit 1 Interim Assessment	1	30–45	
6	Lesson 5: Citing Evidence to Make Inferences	5	30–45	—
7	Lesson 6: Describing Plot	5	30–45	—
8	Lesson 7: Analyzing Character Development	5	30–45	9
9	Lesson 8: Determining Theme or Central Idea	5	30–45	10
10	Lesson 9: Summarizing Literary Texts	5	30–45	—
	Unit 2 Interim Assessment	1	30–45	
11	Lesson 10: Determining Word Meanings: Figurative, Connotative & Technical	5	30–45	15
12	Lesson 11: Analyzing Text Structures	5	30–45	16
13	Lesson 12: Determining Point of View	5	30–45	17
	Unit 3 Interim Assessment	1	30–45	
14	Lesson 13: Determining Word Meanings: Figurative and Connotative	5	30–45	1
15	Lesson 14: Analyzing Word Choice	5	30–45	2
16	Lesson 15: Analyzing the Structure of a Poem	5	30–45	3
17	Lesson 16: Analyzing the Structure of Stories	5	30–45	4
18	Lesson 17: Explaining Point of View	5	30–45	—
	Unit 4 Interim Assessment	1	30–45	
19	Lesson 18: Evaluating an Argument	5	30–45	5
20	Lesson 19: Comparing and Contrasting Texts	5	30–45	6
21	Lesson 19W: Writing an Extended-Response Essay	5	30–45	—
	Unit 5 Interim Assessment	1	30–45	
	Media Feature 1: Integrating Information	5	30–45	7
22	Lesson 20: Comparing and Contrasting Genres	5	30–45	—
	Unit 6 Interim Assessment	1	30–45	
	Media Feature 2: Comparing and Contrasting Reading to Viewing	5	30–45	8
23	Assessment 2	3	60	

Ready® New York CCLS Instruction was created to help students develop proficiency with the Common Core Learning Standards (CCLS). Each lesson uses scaffolded instruction, beginning with modeled and guided instruction, and then gradually releasing the student into fully independent practice of the skills and strategies behind the Common Core. Use in conjunction with the Teacher Toolbox, which allows you to access additional resources—see page A20 for more information.

Weekly Pacing

Year-Long Program: Use *Ready New York CCLS Instruction* as the foundation of a year-long English language arts program or a year-long supplement to your basal program. The Year-Long Sample Week (below) shows a model schedule for teaching one Reading lesson per week. The Year-Long Sample Week, *Ready New York CCLS* Language Handbook table on page A19 shows a model schedule for teaching five Language lessons per week. Use the Year-Long Pacing Guide on page A17 for a specific week-to-week schedule integrating Reading and Language instruction.

Intensive Test Preparation: Target *Ready New York CCLS Instruction* lessons based on *Ready New York CCLS Assessments* results to focus learning during test-preparation. The Intensive Test Preparation chart on page A19 models teaching two Reading lessons (lessons A and B here) per week.

Year-Long Sample Week, *Ready New York CCLS Instruction*

	Day 1		Day 2	Day 3	Day 4	Day 5
Core	**Part 1: Introduction** (20 minutes, includes Tap Students' Prior Knowledge from TRB)	**Part 2: Modeled Instruction** (25 minutes)	**Part 3: Guided Instruction** (45 minutes, includes Answer Analysis discussion from TRB)	**Part 4: Guided Practice** (45 minutes, includes Answer Analysis discussion and Integrating Standards activities from TRB)	**Part 5: Common Core Practice** (45 minutes)	**Part 5: Common Core Practice** Answer Analysis: discussion of test results (20 minutes, from TRB) Integrating Standards activities (25 minutes, from TRB)
Optional		Genre Focus (TRB)	Tier Two Vocabulary (TRB)	ELL Support (TRB)	Theme Connection (TRB)	Additional Activities (TRB)

Key:

Whole Class/Small Group

Individual

Lessons Built for the Common Core

Each grade level in *Ready® New York CCLS Instruction* provides targeted instruction on the Common Core Learning Standards for ELA.

Ready Instruction, covers the following strands:

- Reading Standards for Literature: Key Ideas and Details, Craft and Structure, Integration of Knowledge and Ideas

- Reading Standards for Informational Text: Key Ideas and Details, Craft and Structure, Integration of Knowledge and Ideas

The Ready Language Handbook covers the following strands within the CCLS Language Standards:

- Conventions of Standard English

- Knowledge of Language

- Vocabulary Acquisition and Use

The correlations chart beginning on page A39 provides an in-depth look at how *Ready New York CCLS Instruction* correlates to the CCLS. The passages and questions in *Ready Instruction* reflect the rigor and complexity required by the Common Core.

Intensive Test Preparation, *Ready New York CCLS Instruction*

	Day 1	Day 2	Day 3	Day 4	Day 5
In Class	**Lesson A** Introduction (15 minutes) Modeled Instruction (30 minutes)	**Lesson A** Guided Instruction (15 minutes) Guided Practice (30 minutes)	**Lesson B** Introduction (15 minutes) Modeled Instruction (30 minutes)	**Lesson B** Guided Instruction (15 minutes) Guided Practice (30 minutes)	**Lesson A** Review concepts and skills (20 minutes) **Lesson B** Review concepts and skills (20 minutes)
Homework (optional)		**Lesson A** Common Core Practice		**Lesson B** Common Core Practice	

Year-Long Sample Week, *Ready New York CCLS* Language Handbook

Day 1	Day 2	Day 3	Day 4	Day 5
Introduction (10–15 minutes)	**Introduction** (10–15 minutes)	**Introduction** (10–15 minutes)	**Introduction** (10–15 minutes)	**Introduction** (10–15 minutes)
Guided Practice (10–15 minutes)	**Guided Practice** (10–15 minutes)	**Guided Practice** (10–15 minutes)	**Guided Practice** (10–15 minutes)	**Guided Practice** (10–15 minutes)
Common Core Practice (10–15 minutes)	**Common Core Practice** (10–15 minutes)	**Common Core Practice** (10–15 minutes)	**Common Core Practice** (10–15 minutes)	**Common Core Practice** (10–15 minutes)

Connecting with the *Ready*® Teacher Toolbox

Designed for use with the **Ready® New York CCLS Instruction**, the Teacher Toolbox provides a host of multilevel resources teachers can use to differentiate instruction. If you purchased the Teacher Toolbox, you should have received an insert with access codes and information. Please contact Customer Service at (800)-225-0248 if you need this information. Visit *www.teacher-toolbox.com* to get started.

The Common Core builds on skills covered in the previous year's standards. Of course, many students will not have mastered those standards, and most students could use a review. **Ready New York CCLS** allows you to access lessons from previous **Ready** grades through the Teacher Toolbox.

How Do I Use the Teacher Toolbox?

Lessons are conveniently organized to match your print materials, making it easy to find additional resources for teaching the skills and standards associated with each lesson. All of these resources are perfect for use with any interactive whiteboard or other computer projection screen.

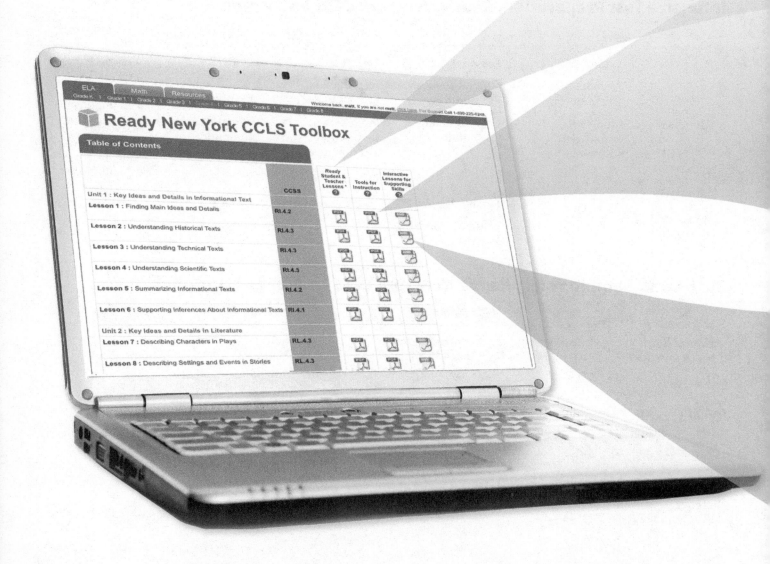

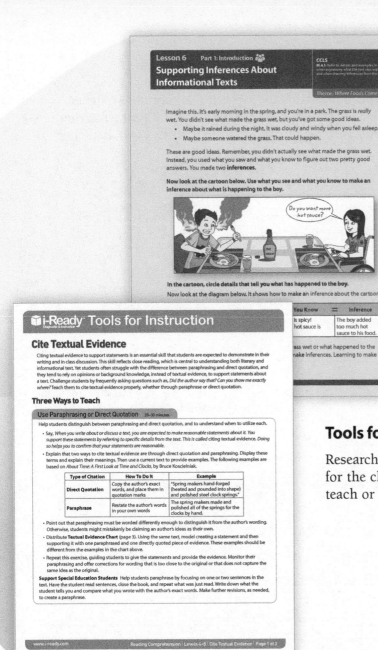

Ready® Lessons and Assessments

Ready® lessons make it easy for teachers to focus on particular skills, or even reteach skills that students may not have mastered at earlier grade levels. What you get:

- Every lesson in this book is available as an individual PDF file, which you can project for whole-class and small-group use.

- Prerequisite student lesson PDFs—and the accompanying Teacher Resource Book lesson—from prior grades are available to administer as remediation.

- Two full-length *Ready Assessments* are available for easy measurement of student growth.

Tools for Instruction

Research-based, best-practice routines and activities for the classroom and small groups provide ways to teach or review standards and prerequisite skills.

Guided Interactive Tutorials

Guided interactive tutorials give teachers another engaging way to provide whole-class or small-group instruction. Lessons follow a consistent structure of explicit instruction and guided practice. Immediate corrective feedback continuously supports students.

A21

Using *i-Ready® Diagnostic* with *Ready® New York CCLS*

If you have already purchased *i-Ready® Diagnostic*, you can use its robust reporting to monitor students' overall and domain-specific reading proficiency as they move through **Ready® New York CCLS Instruction**. Specifically, use the Student Profile report and the Instructional Grouping report to identify Next Step skills for student instruction.

Available for Grades K–8

Student Profile Report

The **Student Profile** report shows teachers students' performance levels for each strand and why they are struggling. Plus, it provides detailed recommendations and resources to support teacher-led instruction.

Jasmine Wells – Reading – Grade 5
Overall Performance

✔ On or Above Level   ◇ 1 Level Below   ✖ 2 or more Levels Below

Test	Placement	Scale Score		Standard Error
Test 3 – 04/12/2013	✔ Early 5		585	+/- 13.2
Test 2 – 01/12/2013	◇ Level 4		575	+/- 14.0
Test 1 – 09/12/2012	◇ Level 4		545	+/- 13.0

Scale Score 400 425 450 475 500 525 550 575 600 625 650 675 700 725 750 775 800

> Use the Overall Performance scores to measure growth over time.

Detail for Test 1 - 09/12/12

Domain	Placement	Scale Score	
Foundational Skills — Phonological Awareness	✔ Tested Out		
Phonics	✖ Level 3	565	
High-Frequency Words	✔ Tested Out		
Vocabulary	✖ Level 3	515	
Comprehension: Literature	◇ Level 4	565	
Comprehension: Informational Text	✖ Level 3	522	

Scale Score 400 425 450 475 500 525 550 575 600 625 650 675 700 725 750

> Drill down to see the performance details for each domain.

	Placement	Developmental Analysis
Overall Reading Performance	◇ Level 4	Results in Phonics indicate that Jasmine Wells has difficulty decoding words accurately. Vocabulary is another ca... indicates that Jasmine Wells has gaps in grade-level word knowledge. Targeting Phonics and Vocabulary Instruct... this student's growth as a reader. Taken together, this information places Jasmine Wells in Instructional Grouping...
Phonological Awareness	✔ Tested Out	This domain is focused on how students distinguish the sounds (or phonemes) in spoken words. Based on testing... demonstrated the ability to distinguish individual sounds in spoken words and is exempt from taking the Phonologi... Max Score: Above Level 1
Phonics	✖ Level 3	This domain focuses on how accurately students decode written words. Jasmine Wells needs instruction and prac... closed syllable patterns and in decoding multisyllabic words with a VV pattern such as *meteor*. Max Score: Above Level 3
High-Frequency Words	✔ Tested Out	This domain addresses how well students recognize frequently occurring words. Jasmine Wells has demonstrated... from taking this subtest. Max Score: Above Level 2
Vocabulary	✖ Level 3	Both word knowledge and word-learning strategies are addressed in this domain. Jasmine Wells needs instructio... typical of third-grade literature as well as science and social studies texts at that level. This student should also re... in prefixes *in-*, *dis-*, *mis-*, *non-*.
Comprehension: Literature	◇ Level 4	This domain addresses Jasmine Wells's understanding of literary text. Results indicate that Jasmine Wells needs... skills and strategies such as describing how a plot unfolds or how characters change. Teach these skills in a varie... poetry and plays. Jasmine Wells should also be reading fables and myths.
Comprehension: Informational Text	✖ Level 3	This domain addresses Jasmine Wells's understanding of informational text. Results indicate that Jasmine Wells... informational skills and strategies such as identifying and analyzing the author's point of view, purpose, or opinion... genres, including biographies, autobiographies, and newspaper or magazine articles.

> Detailed analysis of student needs provides the same information that a reading specialist would, but with **i-Ready Diagnostic**, it's completely automated.

Jasmine Wells – Reading – Grade 5

Test 1-09/12/2012	Placement	Scale Score	
Comprehension: Informational Text	✖ Level 3		522

Scale Score 0 50 100 150 200 250 300 350 400 450 500 550 600 650 700 750 800

Building Comprehension: Informational Text Skills

The CCSS expect students at this level to engage closely and actively with the details of informational text and to begin drawing inferences out of these textual details. A prerequisite to success with these standards is a strong base in comprehension skills and strategies. This subtest measures these prerequisite skills as they apply to informational text.

What Jasmine Can Do
Results indicate that Jasmine can likely do the skills shown below.

Results show that this student is developing proficiency in reading comprehension skills such as sequencing events, identifying cause-and-effect relationships, comparing and contrasting, and sorting information into categories.

🔵 **Answer questions about key ideas and details.** Answer such questions as *who*, *what*, *where*, *when*, *why*, and *how* to demonstrate understanding of key details in literary or informational text.

🔵 **Connect text and visuals in informational text.** Use details from illustrations and from text to describe key ideas.

🔵 **Identify sequence of events.** Identify the sequence of events (beginning, middle, end) in literary or informational text.

🔵 **Identify cause-and-effect relationships.** Identify cause and effect relationships in literary or informational text.

🔵 **Categorize and classify information in informational text.** Categorize or classify individuals, ideas, events, or facts.

🔵 **Compare and contrast informational text.** Compare or contrast key details about people and/or events in informational text.

Next Steps for Instruction
Results indicate that Jasmine will benefit from instruction and practice in the skills shown below.

Teach text features.
· Use informational texts to point out the functions of headings, graphics, captions, and boldfaced or italicized print.
· Discuss how these features make it easier for readers to locate key facts or information.

Teach making inferences based on textual evidence.
· Using the text, demonstrate how readers use evidence to support their inferences. Explain that evidence includes words or phrases from the text, details from pictures and illustrations, and one's own knowledge and experience.
· Point out that readers often revise inferences as they read and gather more information. They consider new details and ask themselves, "Does my previous inference still make sense with what I know now?"

Teach identifying author's purpose. When reading the text, model the following:
· Determining an author's purpose for writing an informational text, including to inform, to persuade, and to entertain.
· Determining an author's point of view in an informational text by looking for stated opinions.
· Distinguishing one's own point of view from that of the author of the text.

Teach retelling.
· Explain that a good retelling of an informational text includes a brief description of the key details such as people, places, and events. It also includes a brief description of these details in the order in which the author presents them.
· After reading the informational text, ask Jasmine: "What is the text mostly about?" "What is an important detail that tells more about a key idea?"
· Guide the student to retell the text orally, using a sequence graphic organizer as an aid in the retelling.

Teach interpreting figurative language. Guide Jasmine to apply these skills to the text:
· Interpret similes and metaphors. Use the clue words like and as to identify similes.
· Analyze the impact of figurative language on mood. Examine how the images created by the language choices convey a certain feeling.

Tools for Instruction

Use Text Features	Make Inferences	Determine Author's Purpose	Retell Details and Events

Recommended Products from Curriculum Associates

If you have this product...	Use...	
Ready New York CCLS	**Grade 3** **Unit 1: Key Ideas & Details in Informational Text:** Lesson 1: Asking Questions About Key Ideas, p. 3 **Unit 2: Craft and Structure in Informational Text:** Lesson 9: Unfamiliar Words, p. 87 Lesson 10: Text Features, p. 95 Lesson 11: Author's Point of View, p. 103 Lesson 12: Words in Context, p. 121 Unit 5: Integration of Knowledge and Ideas in Informational Text:	Learn More

> Recommends specific lessons in **Ready New York CCLS**.

©Curriculum Associates, LLC   Copying is not permitted.

Instructional Grouping Profile

The **Instructional Grouping Profile** report shows teachers exactly how to group students so that students who are struggling with the same skills get the most out of small-group instruction. The report also gives effective instructional recommendations and resources for each group profile.

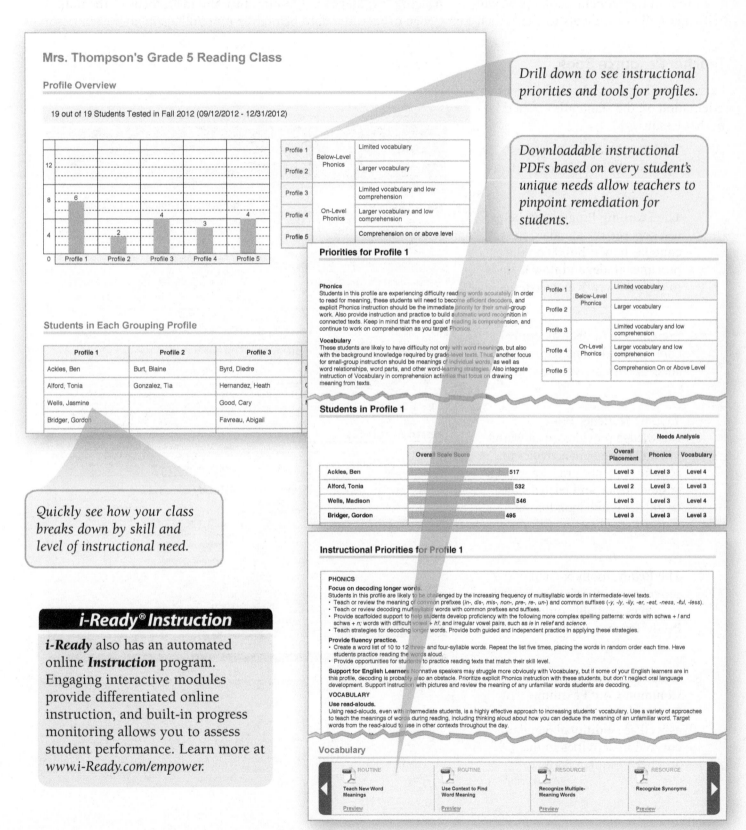

Drill down to see instructional priorities and tools for profiles.

Downloadable instructional PDFs based on every student's unique needs allow teachers to pinpoint remediation for students.

Quickly see how your class breaks down by skill and level of instructional need.

i-Ready® Instruction

i-Ready also has an automated online **Instruction** program. Engaging interactive modules provide differentiated online instruction, and built-in progress monitoring allows you to assess student performance. Learn more at *www.i-Ready.com/empower.*

A23

Features of *Ready® New York CCLS Instruction*

This section guides teachers to the key features of the Student Book and Teacher Resource Book. Numbered boxes call out and describe the key features. Use this section to familiarize yourself with the overall structure of a *Ready® New York CCLS Instruction* lesson.

Each unit in the Student Book opens with an engaging text and visual to introduce the main focus of the unit. A Self-Check allows students to check their knowledge of each standard before the unit and again after each lesson.

Teacher Resource Book

Each lesson begins with a full page of orientation on the standards covered in that lesson.

1 Lesson Objectives identifies specific skills goals for students.

2 The Learning Progression helps teachers see the standard in context, how it builds on the previous grade, and how it leads to the next year's expectations.

3 Prerequisite Skills lists critical concepts and skills required for success with a given lesson.

4 Tapping Students' Prior Knowledge provides quick warmups and discussion activities to activate students' prior knowledge of prerequisite and related skills, laying the foundation for the featured standard.

5 The *Ready* Toolbox chart provides an overview of related resources available online in the *Ready* Teacher Toolbox.

6 CCLS Focus identifies the Common Core Learning Standard featured in the lesson, as well as Additional Standards covered in activities in the Teacher Resource Book.

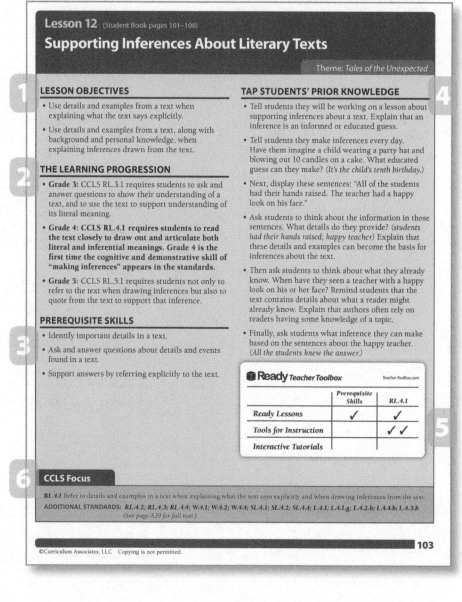

Lesson 12 (Student Book pages 101–108)

Supporting Inferences About Literary Texts

Theme: *Tales of the Unexpected*

1 LESSON OBJECTIVES

- Use details and examples from a text when explaining what the text says explicitly.
- Use details and examples from a text, along with background and personal knowledge, when explaining inferences drawn from the text.

2 THE LEARNING PROGRESSION

- **Grade 3:** CCLS RL.3.1 requires students to ask and answer questions to show their understanding of a text, and to use the text to support understanding of its literal meaning.
- **Grade 4:** CCLS RL.4.1 requires students to read the text closely to draw out and articulate both literal and inferential meanings. Grade 4 is the first time the cognitive and demonstrative skill of "making inferences" appears in the standards.
- **Grade 5:** CCLS RL.5.1 requires students not only to refer to the text when drawing inferences but also to quote from the text to support that inference.

3 PREREQUISITE SKILLS

- Identify important details in a text.
- Ask and answer questions about details and events found in a text.
- Support answers by referring explicitly to the text.

4 TAP STUDENTS' PRIOR KNOWLEDGE

- Tell students they will be working on a lesson about supporting inferences about a text. Explain that an inference is an informed or educated guess.
- Tell students they make inferences every day. Have them imagine a child wearing a party hat and blowing out 10 candles on a cake. What educated guess can they make? (*It's the child's tenth birthday.*)
- Next, display these sentences: "All of the students had their hands raised. The teacher had a happy look on his face."
- Ask students to think about the information in those sentences. What details do they provide? (*students had their hands raised; happy teacher*) Explain that these details and examples can become the basis for inferences about the text.
- Then ask students to think about what they already know. When have they seen a teacher with a happy look on his or her face? Remind students that the text contains details about what a reader might already know. Explain that authors often rely on readers having some knowledge of a topic.
- Finally, ask students what inference they can make based on the sentences about the happy teacher. (*All the students knew the answer.*)

5

📖 Ready *Teacher Toolbox*   *Teacher-Toolbox.com*

	Prerequisite Skills	RL.4.1
Ready Lessons	✓	✓
Tools for Instruction		✓ ✓
Interactive Tutorials		

6 CCLS Focus

RL.4.1 Refer to details and examples in a text when explaining what the text says explicitly and when drawing inferences from the text.
ADDITIONAL STANDARDS: RL.4.2; RL.4.3; RI.4.4; W.4.1; W.4.2; W.4.4; SL.4.1; SL.4.2; SL.4.4; L.4.1; L.4.1.g; L.4.2.b; L.4.4.b; L.4.5.b
(See page A39 for full text.)

103

©Curriculum Associates, LLC   Copying is not permitted.

Introduction

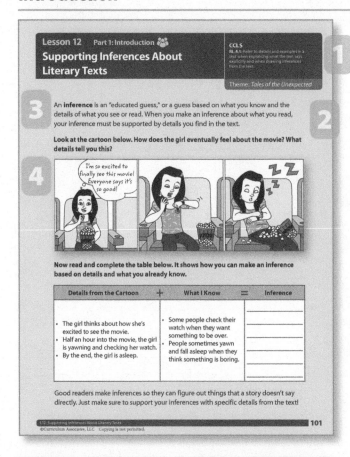

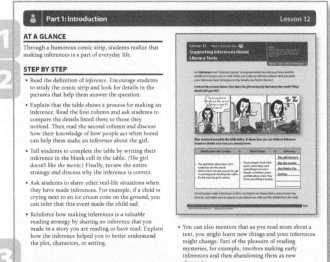

The Introduction builds student confidence and motivation by gradually introducing students to the lesson standard. Most pages begin by having students explore how they apply the strategy in non-text based ways. This page is meant to be teacher directed.

Student Book

1 The CCLS covered in the lesson are given, and the theme for the lesson is identified.

2 This page gives a student-friendly overview of the skills, concepts, strategies, and vocabulary of the covered standard(s).

3 Key vocabulary appears in boldface.

4 Visual aids—such as cartoons, tables, charts, and graphic organizers—engage struggling readers and visual learners.

Teacher Resource Book

1 At a Glance provides a brief overview of what students do in each lesson part.

2 Step by Step provides an explicit walk-through of the steps for guiding students through each lesson part.

3 Genre Focus provides a student-friendly introduction to one of the genres featured in the lesson.

Modeled Instruction

The teacher models how a good reader goes about the process of answering a question. The teacher begins by reading the passage aloud, and then, using the think-aloud support in the Teacher Resource Book, guides students through answering the question. Depending on the support your students need, you may choose to do this page together with the class or first have students independently complete the activity, and then review it together.

Student Book

1 The genre for each passage is identified by the Genre tab.

2 Students begin by applying the strategy to a short piece of text.

3 Clearly stated steps walk students through the thought process for responding to the question.

Teacher Resource Book

1 A detailed Think Aloud models the thought process for answering the question.

2 The ELL Support feature targets language concepts that students who are learning English may need reinforcement on, including compound words, prefixes, suffixes, contractions, homophones, multiple-meaning words, and regular and irregular verbs.

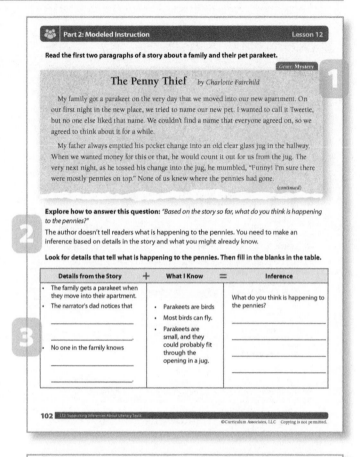

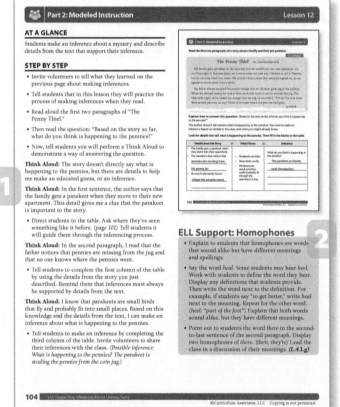

Guided Instruction

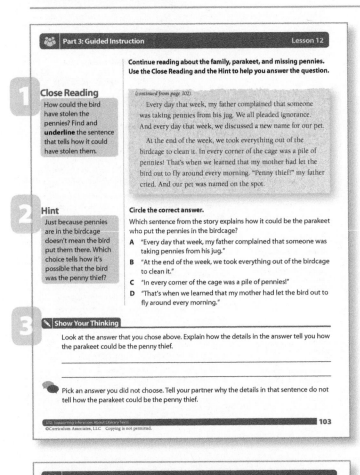

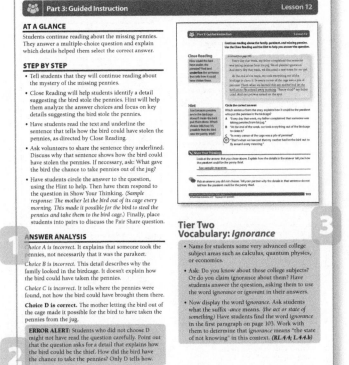

Students work through a sample question. The Close Reading and Hint provide strong guidance. After students respond to the question independently and respond to the Show Your Thinking prompt, partners discuss the reasons for their answers. Finally, the teacher discusses the steps leading to the correct answer, and discusses why the other choices are not correct.

Student Book

1 Close Reading encourages students to interact with the text, often directing them to mark up the text by underlining, circling, or note-taking.

2 The Hint provides clues to help students respond to a specific question.

3 Show Your Thinking challenges students to explain why the answer they chose is correct. A thoughtful open-ended question is posed for discussion.

Teacher Resource Book

1 Answer Analysis explains why an answer is correct and identifies the types of errors students commonly make in choosing incorrect answer choices.

2 Error Alert addresses common errors or misconceptions that lead students to an incorrect answer.

3 Tier Two Vocabulary gives guidance on helping students use text-based strategies to understand a given word. Tier Two (or general academic) words are more common in complex texts than in speech. Since they occur in many types of reading, a knowledge of Tier Two words is a powerful aid to comprehension.

Guided Practice

The Study Buddy, Close Reading, and Hints provide guidance as students read a longer passage and answer several questions. After an initial reading with students, the teacher checks literal comprehension by asking the questions in the Teacher Resource Book. After the second reading, students and teacher discuss the Study Buddy and Close Reading activities, then students use the Hints to answer the questions.

Student Book

1 Students apply the targeted reading strategy to a longer piece of text.

2 The Study Buddy is the student's reading coach, modeling strategies proficient readers use to access text.

3 Close Reading activities continue to guide students.

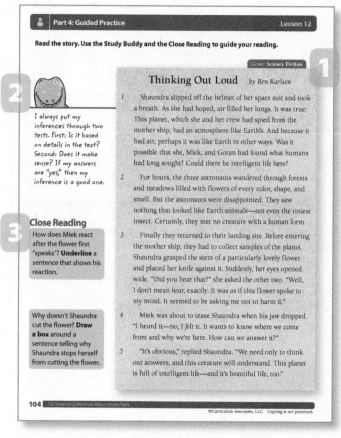

Teacher Resource Book

1 Written by experienced teachers, Tips provide thoughtful and practical suggestions on how to deepen students' understanding and appreciation of the target strategy.

2 ELL Support continues to appear at point of use.

3 Multi-paragraph, full-page passages are read and then reread, enforcing the good habits of close reading.

Teaching Tip: Read the Study Buddy prompt together with students and discuss how it relates to the text.

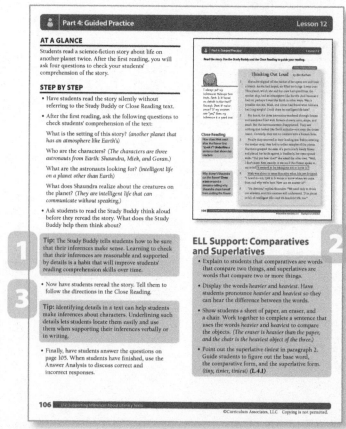

A28

Guided Practice

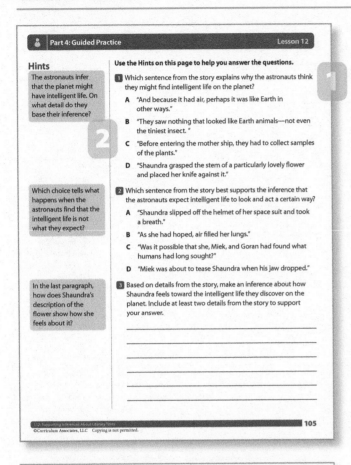

Student Book

1 Students answer a series of multiple-choice and/or short-response questions on the targeted skill.

2 Clues in the Hints draw students back to the text to find text-based evidence.

Teaching Tip: As you review the answers to each question in the Guided Practice, ask students how the Close Reading activity helps them answer the question. Probe how and why the parts of the text they marked up are evidence that they can cite in their answer.

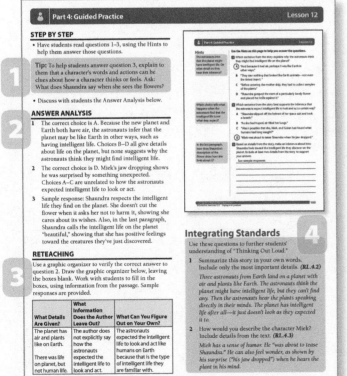

Teacher Resource Book

1 The Tip helps teachers extend one or more of the Hints.

2 Answer Analysis provides detailed discussion of why each answer choice is correct or incorrect, as well as a sample answer for the open-ended questions.

3 Reteaching reinforces and deepens students' learning by using a graphic organizer to visually depict and verify the correct answer to one of the questions.

4 Integrating Standards helps teachers integrate standard instruction by providing specific questions and short activities that apply standards in addition to the targeted one. Standard codes are provided at point of use.

Common Core Practice

Scaffolding is removed. Students work independently to read a longer passage and answer a series of multiple-choice and short-response questions. Students mark their answers directly in the Student Book by filling in bubbles in an Answer Form. After students have completed the questions, they record the number of questions they answered correctly in the scoring box on the right side of the Answer Form. The teacher can use the Answer Analysis to review correct and incorrect answers, encouraging students to discuss the thought process they used in their responses.

Student Book

Students apply the targeted strategy to a longer and more difficult text.

Teaching Tip: To encourage students to transfer the skills they've learned, have students ask themselves the following four questions, formulated by reading expert Nancy Boyles, as they reflect on the Common Core Practice passage. (Boyles, 2012/13)

- What is the author telling me here?
- Are there any hard or important words?
- What does the author want me to understand?
- How does the author play with language to add to meaning?

Teacher Resource Book

The Answer Form on the facsimile of the Student Book pages has the bubbles filled in for easy scoring.

Theme Connection provides short questions and activities that help students make connections among the lesson passages and build content knowledge about the lesson theme.

Answer Analysis provides detailed discussion of why each answer choice is correct or incorrect, as well as a sample answer for the open-ended questions.

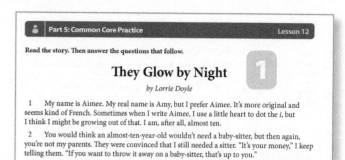

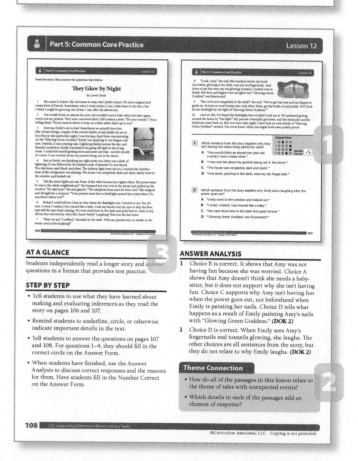

Common Core Practice

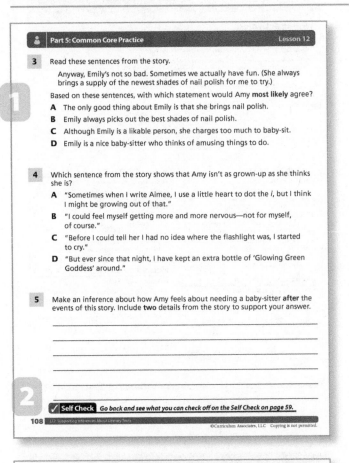

Student Book

Students answer multiple-choice and open-ended questions on the Common Core Practice passage.

Students are reminded to update their Self Check, located at the beginning of every unit, to reflect the learning accomplished in the lesson.

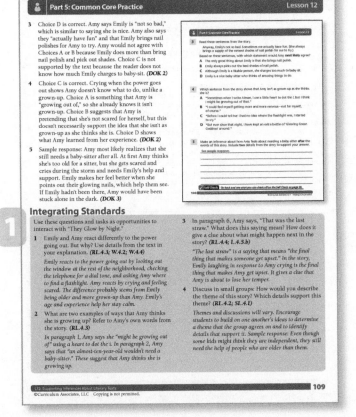

Teacher Resource Book

Integrating Standards helps teachers integrate all ELA standards instruction, including appropriate Language, Speaking & Listening, and Writing standards by providing specific questions and short activities that apply to the Common Core Practice passage. Standard codes are provided at point of use.

Additional Activities

Additional Activities provides short activities that allow you to expand on the passages in the lesson with meaningful standards-based Writing, Language, and Speaking & Listening activities. Standards codes are identified at point of use next to each activity, allowing you to easily integrate standards instruction.

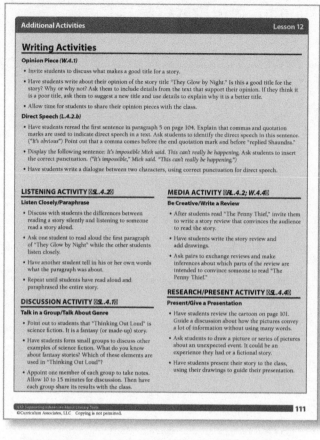

Interim Assessments

Interim Assessments are given at the end of each unit to assess students' understanding of the unit standards and to measure progress.

- Questions include both multiple-choice and short-response items that assess all of the unit's standards.

- A Performance Task—Extended Response asks students to write a longer essay about some aspect of the passage, citing evidence from the text to support their response. This item reflects how the testing consortia apply extended-response essays as a part of their performance-based events.

- In the Teacher Resource Book, correct answers are indicated on the Answer Form. Correct and incorrect answers are fully explained in Answer Analysis.

- Rubrics for the short-response items and Performance Task guide teachers in assigning a score to these items. Sample Responses provide examples of what a top-scoring response should include.

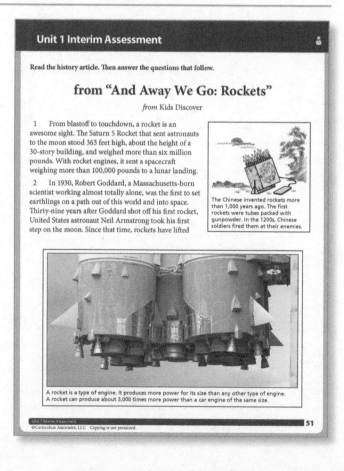

Features of the *Ready® New York CCLS* Language Handbook

The **Ready New York CCLS** Language Handbook was created to help students develop proficiency with the Common Core Learning Standards for Language. Each lesson uses scaffolded instruction, beginning with an introduction and guided practice and then moving students into fully independent practice of the skills and strategies behind the Common Core. This section shows the key features of the Student Book and Teacher Guide.

Student Book

Introduction

The Introduction builds student confidence and motivation by introducing students to the lesson standard. This part of the lesson is meant to be teacher directed.

1 The CCLS covered in the lesson are given.

2 This section gives a student-friendly overview of the skills, concepts, strategies, and vocabulary of the covered standard(s).

3 Key vocabulary appears in boldface.

4 Visual aids, such as tables and charts, engage struggling readers and visual learners.

Guided Practice

The Guided Practice activity allows students to apply what they have learned in the Introduction. Students may work with partners in this part of the lesson.

5 The direction lines clearly identify how to complete the activity.

6 The Hint provides guidance to help students complete the activity.

7 Students apply the targeted language concept as they respond to a variety of activities, such as fill in the blanks, circling, and sentence completion.

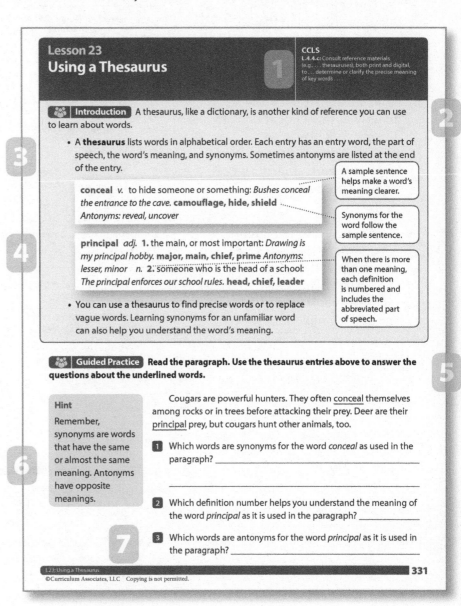

Common Core Practice

In the Common Core Practice section the scaffolding is removed. Students work independently.

8 Students answer multiple-choice questions related to the targeted standard. One lesson has short-response items.

9 Students mark their answers directly in the Student Book by filling in bubbles in an Answer Form. For short-response items, students write on writing lines.

10 Students record the number of questions they answered correctly in the scoring box. The lesson with short-response items has no scoring box.

Student Book

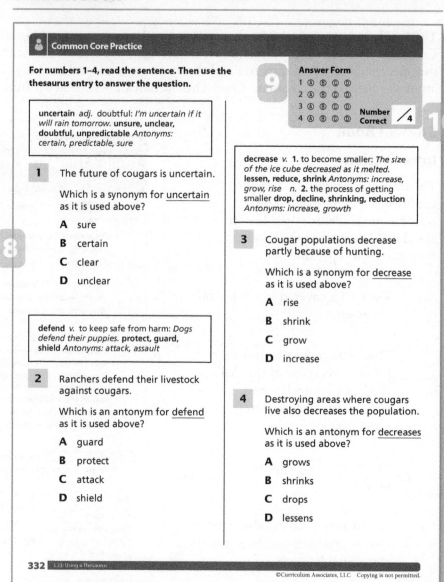

Common Core Practice

For numbers 1–4, read the sentence. Then use the thesaurus entry to answer the question.

uncertain *adj.* doubtful: *I'm uncertain if it will rain tomorrow.* **unsure, unclear, doubtful, unpredictable** *Antonyms: certain, predictable, sure*

1 The future of cougars is uncertain.

Which is a synonym for <u>uncertain</u> as it is used above?

A   sure

B   certain

C   clear

D   unclear

defend *v.* to keep safe from harm: *Dogs defend their puppies.* **protect, guard, shield** *Antonyms: attack, assault*

2 Ranchers defend their livestock against cougars.

Which is an antonym for <u>defend</u> as it is used above?

A   guard

B   protect

C   attack

D   shield

Answer Form
1 Ⓐ Ⓑ Ⓒ Ⓓ
2 Ⓐ Ⓑ Ⓒ Ⓓ
3 Ⓐ Ⓑ Ⓒ Ⓓ
4 Ⓐ Ⓑ Ⓒ Ⓓ   **Number Correct** /4

decrease *v.* **1.** to become smaller: *The size of the ice cube decreased as it melted.* **lessen, reduce, shrink** *Antonyms: increase, grow, rise* *n.* **2.** the process of getting smaller **drop, decline, shrinking, reduction** *Antonyms: increase, growth*

3 Cougar populations decrease partly because of hunting.

Which is a synonym for <u>decrease</u> as it is used above?

A   rise

B   shrink

C   grow

D   increase

4 Destroying areas where cougars live also decreases the population.

Which is an antonym for <u>decreases</u> as it is used above?

A   grows

B   shrinks

C   drops

D   lessens

332 L23: Using a Thesaurus

©Curriculum Associates, LLC   Copying is not permitted.

Supporting Research

Overview

Ready® New York CCLS Instruction is founded on research from a variety of federal initiatives, national literacy organizations, and literacy experts. As a result, this program may be used in support of several instructional models.

Ready® Uses . . .	Examples	Research Says . . .
Instructional Strategies		
Close Reading Close reading refers to the slow, deliberate reading of short pieces of text, focusing solely on the text itself, to achieve a deep understanding.	**SB:** Study Buddy and Close Reading features help students focus on the most important elements of the text.	"The Common Core State Standards place a high priority on the close, sustained reading of complex text. . . . Such reading focuses on what lies within the four corners of the text." (Coleman & Pimentel, Revised Publishers' Criteria, 2012, p. 4)
Multiple Readings Through reading a text more than once, students are able to access different levels of its meaning.	**TRB:** In Guided Practice, students read the text first, with follow-up discussion to confirm literal understanding before delving into more complex questions.	"[Close reading] often requires compact, short, self-contained texts that students can read and re-read deliberately and slowly to probe and ponder the meanings of individual words, the order in which sentences unfold, and the development of ideas over the course of the text." (Coleman & Pimentel, Revised Publishers' Criteria, 2012, p. 4)
Text-Dependent Questions Questions that are text-dependent can be answered only by information contained in the text itself, not personal opinion or background knowledge.	**SB:** Questions in each section of the *Ready* lesson are text-dependent. Students are required to support answers with evidence from the text.	"When examining a complex text in depth, tasks should require careful scrutiny of the text and specific references to evidence from the text itself to support responses." (Coleman & Pimentel, Revised Publishers' Criteria, 2012, p. 6)
Citing Textual Evidence The Common Core Learning Standards require students to provide evidence directly from the text to support their inferences about a text.	**SB:** Questions in the *Ready* lessons and Interim Assessments specifically require students to cite evidence from the text to support their answers.	"Students cite specific evidence when offering an oral or written interpretation of a text. They use relevant evidence when supporting their own points in writing and speaking..." (Common Core State Standards, 2010, p. 7)
Building Content Knowledge Reading multiple texts on a single topic builds knowledge and an increasingly deeper understanding of the topic.	**SB:** Passages in each lesson focus on a single topic or theme. Informational topics align with grade-level science and social studies curricula as well as high-interest grade level topics. **TRB:** The Theme Connection feature helps students make connections among lesson passages. Additional Activities allow students to expand their understanding of the lesson topic.	"Students establish a base of knowledge across a wide range of subject matter by engaging with works of quality and substance." (Common Core State Standards, 2012, p. 7)

Ready® Uses . . .	Examples	Research Says . . .
Instructional Strategies (continued)		
Direct Instruction Scripted lesson plans include explicit step-by-step instruction of reading and learning strategies and lesson objectives.	**SB:** The Introduction gives an overview of the lesson content. Step-by-step directions for answering questions are provided in Modeled Instruction. **TRB:** In the Step-by-Step section, explicit instructions are provided for the teacher.	"The research demonstrates that the types of questions, the detailed step-by-step breakdowns, and the extensive practice with a range of examples . . . will significantly benefit students' comprehension." (Gersten & Carnine, 1986, p. 72)
Scaffolded Instruction Scaffolded instruction is the gradual withdrawal of support through modeled, guided, and independent instruction.	**SB:** Graphic organizers, Study Buddy, and Close Reading provide support in earlier parts of the lesson, allowing students to achieve independence by the Common Core Practice section. **TRB:** The gradual-release model of Modeled/Guided Instruction and Guided Practice provides appropriate support that is gradually withdrawn as students gain mastery of the standard.	"Scaffolded instruction optimizes student learning by providing a supportive environment while facilitating student independence." (Larkin, 2002)
Prior Knowledge Prior knowledge activities activate knowledge from previous experiences.	**TRB:** Tap Prior Knowledge at the beginning of each lesson engages students in a discussion to connect the new skill to what they already know.	"Research clearly emphasizes that for learning to occur, new information must be integrated with what the learner already knows." (Rumelhart, 1980)
An Integrated Model of Literacy The processes of communication (reading, writing, listening, and speaking) are closely connected, a fact which should be reflected in literacy instruction.	**TRB:** Integrating Standards provides opportunities to apply Common Core Learning Standards beyond the target one. Additional Activities expand the lesson to include activities in the areas of Writing, Language, Listening & Speaking, Research, and Media.	"While the Standards delineate specific expectations in reading, writing, speaking, listening, and language, each standard need not be a separate focus for instruction. Often, several standards can be addressed by a single, rich task." (Common Core State Standards, 2010, p. 5)
Instructional Features		
Complex Text A major emphasis of the Common Core Learning Standards is for students to encounter appropriately complex texts at each grade level in order to develop the skills and conceptual knowledge they need for success in school and life.	**SB:** All passages in **Ready** conform to the leveling criteria outlined by the CCLS. (See page A11 of this document for more information on these criteria.)	"To grow, our students must read lots, and more specifically, they must read lots of 'complex' texts—texts that offer them new language, new knowledge, and new modes of thought." (Adams, 2009, p. 182)

Ready® Uses . . .	Examples	Research Says . . .
Instructional Features (continued)		
Balance of Informational and Literary Text; Emphasis on Literary Nonfiction at Grades 6–8 The Common Core Learning Standards align with the requirements of the National Assessment of Educational Progress (NAEP) in calling for a greater emphasis on informational text.	**SB:** Six units in each grade alternate Literary and Informational text. Nonfiction units at grades 6–8 include essays, speeches, opinion pieces, biographies, journalism, and other examples of literary nonfiction. **TRB:** The Genre Focus feature introduces the characteristics of each genre.	"Most of the required reading in college and workforce training programs is informational in structure and challenging in content . . . . the Standards follow NAEP's lead in balancing the reading of literature with the reading of informational texts. . . ." (Common Core State Standards, 2010, pp. 4–5. See also National Assessment Governing Board, 2008)
Answer Explanations for Students As a part of scaffolded instruction, students receive immediate feedback on their answer choices and the reasoning behind correct and incorrect answers.	**TRB:** In the Guided Instruction, Guided Practice, and Common Core Practice sections of each lesson, as well as in the Interim Assessments, answer explanations are given for each question.	Research (Pashler et al. 2007) has shown that when students receive direct instruction about the reasons why an answer choice is correct or incorrect, they demonstrate long-term retention and understanding of newly learned content.
ELL Support Some teaching strategies that have been proven to be effective for English learners include scaffolded instruction, use of graphic organizers, and modeling of language by teachers and peers.	**SB:** Features such as graphic organizers, Close Reading, Study Buddy, Hints, and Pair/Share partner discussions support English learners throughout the lesson. **TRB:** ELL Support boxes provide linguistic instruction at appropriate points.	"Graphic organizers facilitate ELLs' comprehension through visual illustrations of key terms, vocabulary, ideas, and the relationship among them." (Sigueza, 2005) Researchers state that one of the best practices for teaching ELL students is to model standard pronunciation and grammar. (Mohr & Mohr, 2007)
General Academic Vocabulary (Tier Two) General academic, or Tier Two, words are words a reader encounters in rich, complex texts of all types.	**TRB:** Tier Two Vocabulary boxes at point of use support the teacher in helping students use text-based strategies to figure out the meanings of challenging words.	"Tier Two words are frequently encountered in complex written texts and are particularly powerful because of their wide applicability to many sorts of reading. Teachers thus need to be alert to the presence of Tier Two words and determine which ones need careful attention." (Common Core State Standards, Appendix A, 2010, p. 33. The three-tier model of vocabulary is based on the work of Beck, McKeown, & Kucan, 2002, 2008)
Graphic Organizers Graphic organizers are visual representations of a text's organization of ideas and concepts.	**SB:** In the introduction, a graphic organizer is presented to represent the concepts and ideas of the lesson.	"Graphic organizers can provide students with tools they can use to examine and show relationships in a text." (Adler, 2004)

References

Adams, M. J. (2009). The challenge of advanced texts: The interdependence of reading and learning. In Hiebert, E. H. (ed.), *Reading more, reading better: Are American students reading enough of the right stuff?* (pp. 183–189). New York, NY: Guilford.

Adler, C. R. (2004). Seven strategies to teach students text comprehension. Accessed at: *http://www.readingrockets. org/article/3479.*

Beck, I. L., McKeown, M. G., & Kucan, L. (2002). *Bringing words to life: Robust vocabulary instruction.* New York, NY: Guilford.

Beck, I. L., McKeown, M. G., & Kucan, L. (2008). *Creating robust vocabulary: Frequently asked questions and extended examples.* New York, NY: Guilford.

Boyles, N. (2012/2013). Closing in on close reading. *Educational Leadership, 70*(4), 36–41.

Coleman, D., & Pimentel, S. (2012). *Revised Publishers' Criteria for the Common Core State Standards in English Language Arts and Literacy, Grades 3–12.* Accessed at: *http://www.corestandards.org/resources.*

Fisher, D., Frey, N., & Lapp, D. (2012). *Text complexity: Raising rigor in reading.* Washington, DC: International Reading Association.

Gersten, R., & Carnine, D. (1986). Direct instruction in reading comprehension. *Educational Leadership, 43*(7), 70–79.

Hess, K. K., Carlock, D., Jones, B., & Walkup, J. R. (2009). *What exactly do "fewer, clearer, and higher standards" really look like in the classroom? Using a cognitive rigor matrix to analyze curriculum, plan lessons, and implement assessments.* Accessed at: *http://www.nciea.org/cgi-bin/pubspage.cgi?sortby=pub_date.*

Larkin, M. (2002). *Using scaffolded instruction to optimize learning.* ERIC Digest ED474301 2002-12-00. Retrieved from *www.eric.ed.gov.*

Mohr, K., & Mohr, E. (2007). *Extending English language learners' classroom interactions using the response protocol.* Accessed at: *http://www.readingrockets.org/article/26871.*

National Assessment Governing Board. (2008). *Reading framework for the 2009 National Assessment of Educational Progress.* Washington, D.C.: U.S. Government Printing Office.

National Governors Association Center for Best Practices and Council of Chief State School Officers. (2010). *Common Core State Standards for English Language Arts and Literacy in History/Social Studies, Science, and Technical Subjects.* Accessed at: *http://www.corestandards.org/the-standards.*

————. *English Language Arts Appendix A.* Accessed at: *http://www.corestandards.org/the-standards.*

Partnership for Assessment of Readiness for College and Careers. (2011). *PARCC model content frameworks: English language arts/literacy grades 3–11.* Accessed at: *http://www.parcconline.org/parcc-model-content-frameworks.*

Pashler, H., Bain, P., Bottge, B., Graesser, A., Koedinger, K., McDaniel, M., & Metcalfe, J. (2007). *Organizing instruction and study to improve student learning* (NCER 2007–2004). Washington, D.C.: National Center for Education Research, Institute of Education Sciences, U.S. Department of Education. Retrieved from *http://ncer.ed.gov.*

Rumelhart, D. E. (1980). Schemata: the building blocks of cognition. In Spiro, R. J., Bruce, B. C., & Brewer Erlbaum, W. F. (eds.), *Theoretical issues in reading comprehension* (pp. 33–58).

Sigueza, T. (2005). Graphic organizers. *Colorín Colorado!* Accessed at: *http://www.colorincolorado.org/article/13354.*

Smarter Balanced Assessment Consortium. (2012). *General Item Specifications.* Accessed at: *http://www. smarterbalanced.org/wordpress/wp-content/uploads/2012/05/TaskItemSpecifications/ItemSpecifications/ GeneralItemSpecifications.pdf.*

Correlation Charts

Common Core Learning Standards Coverage by *Ready® Instruction*

The chart below correlates each Common Core Learning Standard to each **Ready® New York CCLS Instruction** lesson that offers comprehensive instruction on that standard. Use this chart to determine which lessons your students should complete based on their mastery of each standard.

Common Core Learning Standards for Grade 6—English Language Arts Standards		*Ready New York CCLS* Student Lesson(s)	Additional Coverage in Teacher Resource Book Lesson(s)
Reading Standards for Literature			
Key Ideas and Details			
RL.6.1	Cite textual evidence to support analysis of what the text says explicitly as well as inferences drawn from the text.	5	6–9, 13–17, 20
RL.6.2	Determine a theme or central idea of a text and how it is conveyed through particular details; provide a summary of the text distinct from personal opinions or judgments.	8, 9	5–7, 13, 15–17, 20
RL.6.3	Describe how a particular story's or drama's plot unfolds in a series of episodes as well as how the characters respond or change as the plot moves toward a resolution.	6, 7	5, 8, 9, 16, 17, 20
Craft and Structure			
RL.6.4	Determine the meaning of words and phrases as they are used in a text, including figurative and connotative meanings; analyze the impact of a specific word choice on meaning and tone.	13, 14	5–9, 11, 15–17, 20
RL.6.5	Analyze how a particular sentence, chapter, scene, or stanza fits into the overall structure of a text and contributes to the development of the theme, setting, or plot.	15, 16	5, 13, 14, 20
RL.6.6	Explain how an author develops the point of view of the narrator or speaker in a text.	17	6, 20
RL.6.6.a	Explain how an author's geographic location or culture affects his or her perspective.	17	17
Integration of Knowledge and Ideas			
RL.6.7	Compare and contrast the experience of reading a story, drama, or poem to listening to or viewing an audio, video, or live version of the text, including contrasting what they "see" and "hear" when reading the text to what they perceive when they listen or watch.	Media Feature 2	5, 7, 8, 13–15, 20
RL.6.8	(Not applicable to literature)	N/A	N/A
RL.6.9	Compare and contrast texts in different forms or genres (e.g., stories and poems; historical novels and fantasy stories) in terms of their approaches to similar themes and topics.	20	5
Range of Reading and Level of Text Complexity			
RL.6.10	By the end of the year, read and comprehend literature, including stories, dramas, and poems, in the grades 6–8 text complexity band proficiently, with scaffolding as needed at the high end of the range.	All Lessons	
Reading Standards for Informational Text			
Key Ideas and Details			
RI.6.1	Cite textual evidence to support analysis of what the text says explicitly as well as inferences drawn from the text.	3	1, 2, 4, 10–12, 19
RI.6.2	Determine a central idea of a text and how it is conveyed through particular details; provide a summary of the text distinct from personal opinions or judgments.	1, 2	3, 4, 10–12, 18, 19

New York State P-12 Common Core Learning Standards for ELA and Literacy ©2011.
New York State Department of Education. All rights reserved.

Common Core State Standards © 2010. National Governors Association Center for Best Practices and Council of Chief State School Officers. All rights reserved.

Common Core Learning Standards for Grade 6—English Language Arts Standards		Ready New York CCLS Student Lesson(s)	Additional Coverage in Teacher Resource Book Lesson(s)
Reading Standards for Informational Text *(continued)*			
Key Ideas and Details *(continued)*			
RI.6.3	Analyze in detail how a key individual, event, or idea is introduced, illustrated, and elaborated in a text (e.g., through examples or anecdotes).	4	1–3, 10, 11, 19
Craft and Structure			
RI.6.4	Determine the meaning of words and phrases as they are used in a text, including figurative, connotative, and technical meanings.	10	1, 3, 4, 11, 12, 18, 19
RI.6.5	Analyze how a particular sentence, paragraph, chapter, or section fits into the overall structure of a text and contributes to the development of the ideas.	11	12, 18
RI.6.6	Determine an author's point of view or purpose in a text and explain how it is conveyed in the text.	12	3, 4, 10, 18, 19
Integration of Knowledge and Ideas			
RI.6.7	Integrate information presented in different media or formats (e.g., visually, quantitatively) as well as in words to develop a coherent understanding of a topic or issue.	Media Feature 1	1–3, 10, 11, 18, 19
RI.6.8	Trace and evaluate the argument and specific claims in a text, distinguishing claims that are supported by reasons and evidence from claims that are not.	18	2, 19
RI.6.9	Compare and contrast one author's presentation of events with that of another (e.g., a memoir written by and a biography on the same person).	19	3
Range of Reading and Level of Text Complexity			
RI.6.10	By the end of the year, read and comprehend literary nonfiction in the grades 6–8 text complexity band proficiently, with scaffolding as needed at the high end of the range.	All Lessons	
Writing Standards			
Text Types and Purposes			
W.6.2	Write informative/explanatory texts to examine a topic and convey ideas, concepts, and information through the selection, organization, and analysis of relevant content.	19W	1, 5, 9–12, 19, 20
Research to Build and Present Knowledge			
W.6.9	Draw evidence from literary or informational texts to support analysis, reflection, and research.	19W	2, 7, 18
Language Standards			
Conventions of Standard English			
L.6.1	Demonstrate command of the conventions of standard English grammar and usage when writing or speaking.	—	7–11, 14, 17–20
L.6.1.a	Ensure that pronouns are in the proper case (subjective, objective, possessive).	L1–L3	7, 16
L.6.1.b	Use intensive pronouns (e.g., *myself, ourselves*).	L4	4, 6
L.6.1.c	Recognize and correct inappropriate shifts in pronoun number and person.	L5	3
L.6.1.d	Recognize and correct vague pronouns (i.e., ones with unclear or ambiguous antecedents).	L6	5
L.6.1.e	Recognize variations from standard English in their own and others' writing and speaking, and identifiy and use strategies to improve expression in conventional language.	L7	—

*Lesson numbers such as L12 refer to the Language Handbook.

A40

Common Core Learning Standards for Grade 6—English Language Arts Standards		*Ready New York CCLS* Student Lesson(s)	Additional Coverage in Teacher Resource Book Lesson(s)
Language Standards (*continued*)			
Conventions of Standard English (*continued*)			
L.6.2	Demonstrate command of the conventions of standard English capitalization, punctuation, and spelling when writing.	—	10
L.6.2.a	Use punctuation (commas, parentheses, dashes) to set off nonrestrictive/parenthetical elements.	L8	2, 9, 14, 16, 19
L.6.2.b	Spell correctly.	—	11, 20
Knowledge of Language			
L.6.3.a	Vary sentence patterns for meaning, reader/listener interest, and style.	L9	1, 18
L.6.3.b	Maintain consistency in style and tone.	L10	—
Vocabulary Acquisition and Use			
L.6.4.a	Use context (e.g., the overall meaning of a sentence or paragraph; a word's position or function in a sentence) as a clue to the meaning of a word or phrase.	L11	1, 3–20
L.6.4.b	Use common, grade-appropriate Greek or Latin affixes and roots as clues to the meaning of a word (e.g., *audience, auditory, audible*).	L12	1, 3–5, 8, 12–14, 19
L.6.4.c	Consult reference materials (e.g., dictionaries, glossaries, thesauruses), both print and digital, to find the pronunciation of a word or determine or clarify its precise meaning or its part of speech.	L13, L14	5, 6, 15–17, 19, 20
L.6.4.d	Verify the preliminary determination of the meaning of a word or phrase (e.g., by checking the inferred meaning in context or in a dictionary).	—	7, 8, 10, 11, 15, 16, 18, 19
L.6.5.a	Interpret figures of speech (e.g., personification) in context.	L15	2, 5, 7, 12, 13, 15, 17, 19, 20
L.6.5.b	Use the relationship between particular words (e.g., *cause/effect, part/whole, item/category*) to better understand each of the words.	L16	—
L.6.5.c	Distinguish among the connotations (associations) of words with similar denotations (definitions) (e.g., *stingy, scrimping, economical, unwasteful, thrifty*).	L17	12

Additional Coverage of Common Core ELA Standards, Grade 6	*Ready* *New York CCLS* Teacher Resource Book Lesson(s)

Reading Standards for Literature

Responding to Literature

RL.6.11.a	Self-select text based on personal preferences.	19, 20
RL.6.11.b	Use established criteria to classify, select, and evaluate texts to make informed judgments about the quality of the pieces.	16

Reading Standards for Informational Text

Integration of Knowledge and Ideas

RI.6.9.a	Use their experience and their knowledge of language and logic, as well as culture, to think analytically, address problems creatively, and advocate persuasively.	18

Writing Standards

Text Types and Purposes

W.6.1	Write arguments to support claims with clear reasons and relevant evidence.	1, 3, 5, 9, 16, 18, 19
W.6.2.a	Introduce a topic; organize ideas, concepts, and information, using strategies such as definition, classification, comparison/contrast, and cause/effect; include formatting (e.g., headings), graphics (e.g., charts, tables), and multimedia when useful to aiding comprehension.	4
W.6.3	Write narratives to develop real or imagined experiences or events using effective technique, relevant descriptive details, and well-structured event sequences.	3, 4, 6, 13–15, 17
W.6.3.b	Use narrative techniques, such as dialogue, pacing, and description, to develop experiences, events, and/or characters.	7, 8

Production and Distribution of Writing

W.6.4	Produce clear and coherent writing in which the development, organization, and style are appropriate to task, purpose, and audience.	4–7, 10–13, 15, 18, 19
W.6.4a	Produce text (print or nonprint) that explores a variety of cultures and perspectives.	11
W.6.6	Use technology, including the Internet, to produce and publish writing as well as to interact and collaborate with others; demonstrate sufficient command of keyboarding skills to type a minimum of three pages in a single sitting.	15

Research to Build and Present Knowledge

W.6.7	Conduct short research projects to answer a question, drawing on several sources and refocusing the inquiry when appropriate.	2, 3, 6, 8, 10–12, 14–17
W.6.8	Gather relevant information from multiple print and digital sources; assess the credibility of each source; and quote or paraphrase the data and conclusions of others while avoiding plagiarism and providing basic bibliographic information for sources.	1, 4, 5, 19
W.6.9.a	Apply grade 6 Reading standards to literature (e.g., "Compare and contrast texts in different forms or genres [e.g., stories and poems; historical novels and fantasy stories] in terms of their approaches to similar themes and topics").	8, 16, 17
W.6.9.b	Apply grade 6 Reading standards to literary nonfiction (e.g., "Trace and evaluate the argument and specific claims in a text, distinguishing claims that are supported by reasons and evidence from claims that are not").	11

Responding to Literature

W.6.11	Create and present a text or art work in response to literary work.	7–9, 13, 15
W.6.11.a	Develop a perspective or theme supported by relevant details.	5, 16
W.6.11.b	Recognize and illustrate social, historical, and cultural features in the presentation of literary texts.	9, 15, 17
W.6.11.c	Create poetry, stories, plays, and other literary forms (e.g. videos, art work).	3, 4, 6, 9–12, 14–18, 20

Additional Coverage of Reading Standards for Literacy in History/Social Studies and Science and Technical Subjects, Grade 7	*Ready New York CCLS* Teacher Resource Book Lesson(s)

Speaking and Listening Standards

Comprehension and Collaboration

SL.6.1	Engage effectively in a range of collaborative discussions (one-on-one, in groups, and teacher-led) with diverse partners on *grade 6 topics, texts, and issues,* building on others' ideas and expressing their own clearly.	1–20
SL.6.1.c	Pose and respond to specific questions with elaboration and detail by making comments that contribute to the topic, text, or issue under discussion.	4, 16
SL.6.2	Interpret information presented in diverse media and formats (e.g., visually, quantitatively, orally) and explain how it contributes to a topic, text, or issue under study.	1, 3, 5, 6, 8, 13
SL.6.2.a	Use their experience and their knowledge of language and logic, as well as culture, to think analytically, address problems creatively, and advocate persuasively.	2, 7, 9–11, 17–19
SL.6.3	Delineate a speaker's argument and specific claims, distinguishing claims that are supported by reasons and evidence from claims that are not.	18

Presentation of Knowledge and Ideas

SL.6.4	Present claims and findings, sequencing ideas logically and using pertinent descriptions, facts, and details to accentuate main ideas or themes; use appropriate eye contact, adequate volume, and clear pronunciation.	1, 3–6, 8–17, 19
SL.6.5	Include multimedia components (e.g., graphics, images, music, sound) and visual displays in presentations to clarify information.	2, 4, 7–10, 12, 18
SL.6.6	Adapt speech to a variety of contexts and tasks, demonstrating command of formal English when indicated or appropriate.	1, 3, 9, 14

Reading Standards for Literacy in History/Social Studies

Key Ideas and Details

RH.6-8.1	Cite specific textual evidence to support analysis of primary and secondary sources.	4, 19

Craft and Structure

RH.6-8.4	Determine the meaning of words and phrases as they are used in a text, including vocabulary specific to domains related to history/social studies.	10
RH.6-8.5	Describe how a text presents information (e.g., sequentially, comparatively, causally).	11
RH.6-8.6	Identify aspects of a text that reveal an author's point of view or purpose (e.g., loaded language, inclusion or avoidance of particular facts).	12

Integration of Knowledge and Ideas

RH.6-8.8	Distinguish among fact, opinion, and reasoned judgment in a text.	18
RH.6-8.9	Analyze the relationship between a primary and secondary source on the same topic.	19

Reading Standards for Literacy in Science and Technical Subjects

Key Ideas and Details

RST.6-8.1	Cite specific textual evidence to support analysis of science and technical texts.	1, 2, 3
RST.6-8.2	Determine the central ideas or conclusions of a text; provide an accurate summary of the text distinct from prior knowledge or opinions.	1, 2

Integration of Knowledge and Ideas

RST.6-8.7	Integrate quantitative or technical information expressed in words in a text with a version of that information expressed visually (e.g., in a flowchart, diagram, model, graph, or table).	Media Feature 1
RST.6-8.8	Distinguish among facts, reasoned judgment based on research findings, and speculation in a text.	18
RST.6-8.9	Compare and contrast the information gained from experiments, simulations, video, or multimedia sources with that gained from reading a text on the same topic.	Media Feature 1

Interim Assessment Answer Keys, Correlations, and Rubrics

The charts below show the answers to multiple-choice items in each unit's Interim Assessment along with the page numbers for sample responses to constructed-response items. The charts also display the depth-of-knowledge (DOK) index, standard(s) addressed, and corresponding *Ready® New York CCLS Instruction* lesson(s) for every item. Use this information to adjust lesson plans and focus remediation.

Ready New York CCLS Interim Assessment Answer Keys and Correlations

Unit 1: Key Ideas and Details in Informational Text

Question	Key	DOK[1]	Standard(s)	Ready New York CCLS Student Lesson(s)
1	D	2	RI.6.1	3
2A	B	3	RI.6.1	3
2B	See page 37.	3	RI.6.1	3
3	B	2	RI.6.1, RI.6.3	3, 4
4	C	3	RI.6.2	1
5	A	2	RI.6.3	4
6	B	2	RI.6.2	2
7	See page 38.	3	RI.6.3	4
8	See page 38.	3	RI.6.2	1
9	See page 38.	3	RI.6.3, W.6.2, W.6.9	4, 19W

Unit 2: Key Ideas and Details in Literature

Question	Key	DOK	Standard(s)	Ready New York CCLS Student Lesson(s)
1	D	2	RL.6.1	5
2	A	2	RL.6.1	5
3	C	3	RL.6.2	8
4	C	3	RL.6.3	7
5A	B	2	RL.6.3	7
5B	D	2	RL.6.1	5
6	See page 85.	3	RL.6.1	5
7	See page 85.	2	RL.6.2, RL.6.3	6, 9
8	See page 85.	3	RL.6.3	7
9	See page 85.	3	RL.6.1, W.6.2, W.6.9	5, 19W

Unit 3: Craft and Structure in Informational Text

Question	Key	DOK	Standard(s)	Ready New York CCLS Student Lesson(s)
1A	D	2	RI.6.4	10
1B	C	2	RI.6.4	10
2	C	2	RI.6.6	12
3	A	2	RI.6.4	10
4	A	3	RI.6.6	12
5	C	3	RI.6.5	11
6	D	2	RI.6.5	11
7	See page 114.	3	RI.6.5	11
8	See page 114.	3	RI.6.5	11
9	See page 114.	3	RI.6.6	12
10	See page 114.	3	RI.6.6, W.6.2, W.6.9	12, 19W

[1]Depth of Knowledge measures:
1. The item requires superficial knowledge of the standard.
2. The item requires processing beyond recall and observation.
3. The item requires explanation, generalization, and connection to other ideas.
4. The item requires analysis, synthesis, or evaluation of multiple sources or texts.

Unit 4: Craft and Structure in Literature

Question	Key	DOK	Standard(s)	*Ready New York CCLS* Student Lesson(s)
1A	A	2	RL.6.4	13
1B	D	2	RL.6.4	13
2	See page 161.	3	RL.6.5	15
3	D	2	RL.6.5	16
4	C	3	RL.6.6	17
5	C	2	RL.6.5	16
6	B	3	RL.6.4	14
7	A	3	RL.6.4	13
8	See page 161.	3	RL.6.6	17
9	See page 161.	3	RL.6.5, W.6.2, W.6.9	16, 19W

Unit 5: Integration of Knowledge and Ideas in Informational Text

Question	Key	DOK	Standard(s)	*Ready New York CCLS* Student Lesson(s)
1	D	2	RI.6.8	18
2	B	3	RI.6.8	18
3	B	2	RI.6.8	18
4	D	3	RI.6.8	18
5A	See page 190.	3	RI.6.9	19
5B	See page 190.	3	RI.6.9	19
6	See page 190.	3	RI.6.9	19
7	See page 190.	3	RI.6.9	19
8	See page 190.	3	RI.6.9, W.6.2, W.6.9	19, 19W

Unit 6: Integration of Knowledge and Ideas in Literature

Question	Key	DOK	Standard(s)	*Ready New York CCLS* Student Lesson(s)
1	B	3	RL.6.9	20
2	A	3	RL.6.9	20
3	B	3	RL.6.9	20
4	C	3	RL.6.9	20
5A	See page 207.	3	RL.6.9	20
5B	See page 207.	3	RL.6.9	20
5C	See page 207.	3	RL.6.9	20
6	See page 207.	3	RL.6.9	20
7	See page 207.	3	RL.6.9	20
8	See page 207.	3	RL.6.9	20
9	See page 207.	3	RL.6.9, W.6.2, W.6.9	20, 19W

English Language Arts Rubrics for Scoring*

2-Point Rubric—Short Response

Score	Response Features
2 Point	The features of a 2-point response are • Valid inferences and/or claims from the text where required by the prompt • Evidence of analysis of the text where required by the prompt • Relevant facts, definitions, concrete details, and/or other information from the text to develop response according to the requirements of the prompt • Sufficient number of facts, definitions, concrete details, and/or other information from the text as required by the prompt • Complete sentences where errors do not impact readability
1 Point	The features of a 1-point response are • A mostly literal recounting of events or details from the text as required by the prompt • Some relevant facts, definitions, concrete details, and/or other information from the text to develop response according to the requirements of the prompt • Incomplete sentences or bullets
0 Point	The features of a 0-point response are • A response that does not address any of the requirements of the prompt or is totally inaccurate • No response (blank answer) • A response that is not written in English • A response that is unintelligible or indecipherable

*Reprinted courtesy of New York State Education Department.

New York State Grade 6–8 Expository Writing Evaluation Rubric*

Use the following rubric (beginning below and ending on page A48) to score students' extended responses.

Criteria	Score 4 — Essays at this level:	Score 3 — Essays at this level:
Content and Analysis—the extent to which the essay conveys complex ideas and information clearly and accurately in order to support claims in an analysis of topics or texts	• clearly introduce a topic in a manner that is compelling and follows logically from the task and purpose • demonstrate insightful analysis of the text(s)	• clearly introduce a topic in a manner that follows from the task and purpose • demonstrate grade-appropriate analysis of the text(s)
Command of Evidence—the extent to which the essay presents evidence from the provided texts to support analysis and reflection	• develop the topic with relevant, well-chosen facts, definitions, concrete details, quotations, or other information and examples from the text(s) • sustain the use of varied, relevant evidence	• develop the topic with relevant facts, definitions, details, quotations, or other information and examples from the text(s) • sustain the use of relevant evidence, with some lack of variety
Coherence, Organization, and Style—the extent to which the essay logically organizes complex ideas, concepts, and information using formal style and precise language	• exhibit clear organization, with the skillful use of appropriate and varied transitions to create a unified whole and enhance meaning • establish and maintain a formal style, using grade-appropriate, stylistically sophisticated language and domain-specific vocabulary with a notable sense of voice • provide a concluding statement or section that is compelling and follows clearly from the topic and information presented	• exhibit clear organization, with the use of appropriate transitions to create a unified whole • establish and maintain a formal style using precise language and domain-specific vocabulary • provide a concluding statement or section that follows from the topic and information presented
Control of Conventions—the extent to which the essay demonstrates command of the conventions of standard English grammar, usage, capitalization, punctuation, and spelling	• demonstrate grade-appropriate command of conventions, with few errors	• demonstrate grade-appropriate command of conventions, with occasional errors that do not hinder comprehension

*Reprinted courtesy of New York State Education Department.

New York State Grade 6–8 Expository Writing Evaluation Rubric (*continued*)*

Criteria	Score		
	2 **Essays at this level:**	1 **Essays at this level:**	0 **Essays at this level:**
Content and Analysis—the extent to which the essay conveys complex ideas and information clearly and accurately in order to support claims in an analysis of topics or texts	• introduce a topic in a manner that follows generally from the task and purpose • demonstrate a literal comprehension of the text(s)	• introduce a topic in a manner that does not logically follow from the task and purpose • demonstrate little understanding of the text(s)	• demonstrate a lack of comprehension of the text(s) or task
Command of Evidence—the extent to which the essay presents evidence from the provided texts to support analysis and reflection	• partially develop the topic of the essay with the use of some textual evidence, some of which may be irrelevant • use relevant evidence inconsistently	• demonstrate an attempt to use evidence, but only develop ideas with minimal, occasional evidence which is generally invalid or irrelevant	• provide no evidence or provide evidence that is completely irrelevant
Coherence, Organization, and Style—the extent to which the essay logically organizes complex ideas, concepts, and information using formal style and precise language	• exhibit some attempt at organization, with inconsistent use of transitions • establish but fail to maintain a formal style, with inconsistent use of language and domain-specific vocabulary • provide a concluding statement or section that follows generally from the topic and information presented	• exhibit little attempt at organization, or attempts to organize are irrelevant to the task • lack a formal style, using language that is imprecise or inappropriate for the text(s) and task • provide a concluding statement or section that is illogical or unrelated to the topic and information presented	• exhibit no evidence of organization • use language that is predominantly incoherent or copied directly from the text(s) • do not provide a concluding statement or section
Control of Conventions—the extent to which the essay demonstrates command of the conventions of standard English grammar, usage, capitalization, punctuation, and spelling	• demonstrate emerging command of conventions, with some errors that may hinder comprehension	• demonstrate a lack of command of conventions, with frequent errors that hinder comprehension	• are minimal, making assessment of conventions unreliable

- If the prompt requires two texts and the student only references one text, the response can be scored no higher than a 2.

- If the student writes only a personal response and makes no reference to the text(s), the response can be scored no higher than a 1.

- Responses totally unrelated to the topic, illegible, incoherent, or blank should be given a 0.

- A response totally copied from the text(s) with no original student writing should be scored a 0.

*Reprinted courtesy of New York State Education Department.

Determining Central Idea and Details

LESSON OBJECTIVES

- Determine the central idea of a text.
- Identify how a central idea is conveyed through particular details.

THE LEARNING PROGRESSION

- **Grade 5:** CCLS RI.5.2 requires students to identify two or more central ideas in a text.

- **Grade 6: CCLS RI.6.2 builds on the Grade 5 standard by requiring students to put together the most important details in a text in order to find the central idea.**

- **Grade 7:** CCLS RI.7.2 requires students to analyze how the central ideas develop over the course of the text.

PREREQUISITE SKILLS

- Identify two or more central ideas of a text.
- Explain how the central ideas of a text are supported by key details.

TAP STUDENTS' PRIOR KNOWLEDGE

- Tell students that they will learn about identifying a text's central idea and its important details. Review that a central idea is what a text or section of text is mostly about. Ask students what details are. (*facts, examples, and other information that tell about a topic*)

- Point out that sometimes central ideas aren't stated. Readers must put details together to understand the central idea. Write the following sentences on the board: *On our trip to the aquarium, we found out that dolphins can talk to each other. We also discovered that manatees are related to elephants.* Ask students what the two details have in common. (*They are both about what students learned at the aquarium.*)

- Explain that similar to individual paragraphs, entire passages also have a central idea. Emphasize that although each paragraph has a central idea, the passage as a whole has one overall central idea that the author wants readers to understand.

- Explain to students that understanding the central idea of a text and being able to find supporting details will help them gain a better understanding of not just what the author is saying but why the author is saying it.

Ready *Teacher Toolbox*

teacher-toolbox.com

	Prerequisite Skills	RI.6.2
Ready Lessons	✓	✓
Tools for Instruction		✓
Interactive Tutorials		✓

CCLS Focus

RI.6.2 Determine a central idea of a text and how it is conveyed through particular details. . . .

ADDITIONAL STANDARDS: **RI.6.1, RI.6.3, RI.6.4, RI.6.7; W.6.1, W.6.2, W.6.8; SL.6.1, SL.6.2, SL.6.4, SL.6.6; L.6.3.a, L.6.4.a, L.6.4.b**
(*See page A39 for full text.*)

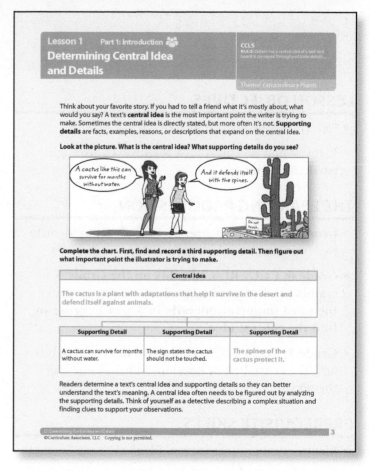

AT A GLANCE

Through an illustration, students begin looking for a central idea and supporting details.

STEP BY STEP

- Read the definitions of *central idea* and *supporting details*. Direct students to the illustration. Have them think about the central idea and the supporting details they see.

- Explain that the graphic organizer shows how supporting details are connected to a central idea.

- Read the supporting details given in the graphic organizer. Have students compare them to the details they saw. Ask them to add a third supporting detail based on what the girl in the illustration says about cactus spines.

- Work with students to complete the central idea bubble of the graphic organizer. If necessary, ask: What do all the supporting details have in common? What is the most important point the illustrator is trying to make?

- Guide students to understand that the central idea is that a cactus is a plant with adaptations that help it survive in the desert and defend itself against animals.

- Ask students to share real-life situations when they have needed to determine the central idea of an article or other type of writing.

- Share a brief example of how you have used details when reading in order to determine the central idea. Explain how using this skill helped you to better understand the purpose of what you were reading.

Genre Focus

Informational Texts: Scientific Accounts

Tell students that in this lesson they will read informational texts. One type of informational text is a scientific account, or a piece of writing that provides information about scientific research or another science-related topic.

- Its purpose is to explain scientific findings or any event or discovery with ties to science.

- It can be written by professional scientists to relate findings to the scientific community or to contribute to knowledge in a particular field of study. It may also be written by someone with scientific expertise for the general public.

- It often opens with an explanation about the thesis or theory behind the scientific topic and then gives examples or further details to elaborate on it.

- Some may include charts, graphics, or photos. Others may have sidebars with additional facts or subheadings to show how the ideas are organized.

Explain that the three passages in this lesson are all about plants. "The Unusual Venus Flytrap" tells about this unique plant. "The Corpse Flower" tells about the worst-smelling flower in the world. Lastly, "Against All Odds: Earth's Fragile Pioneers" is a lengthy article about how plants colonized Hawaii.

AT A GLANCE

Students determine the central idea of a scientific account and identify the supporting details.

STEP BY STEP

- Invite volunteers to tell what they learned on the previous page about determining the central idea of a passage and identifying supporting details.

- Read aloud the passage about Venus flytraps.

- Then read the questions: "What is the central idea of the paragraph? What details support this idea?"

- Now tell students you will perform a Think Aloud to demonstrate a way of answering the questions.

Think Aloud: I know a central idea is the most important point an author wants to make. Sometimes it is not directly stated. I can use the title and the first and last sentence of the paragraph to help me. I see the words *unusual, unique,* and *fascinating.* I'll use these clues to determine the central idea.

- Direct students to the graphic organizer and ask where they've seen a similar one before. Review that it shows a passage's central idea and the details that support it. Have students write the central idea in the graphic organizer.

Think Aloud: Now that I have identified that the central idea is that Venus flytraps are unusual plants that many people think are incredible, I'll skim the account for supporting details that give examples or tell more about this central idea. When I skim a text, I reread it quickly, looking for key words that relate to the information I'm looking for.

- Point out the two supporting details listed in the graphic organizer. Discuss how they support the central idea.

- Then have students locate an additional detail in the account about Venus flytraps that supports the central idea they wrote down in the graphic organizer.

- Review that students can check the central idea they wrote by thinking about what all the supporting details have in common.

- Invite volunteers to share their answers with the class.

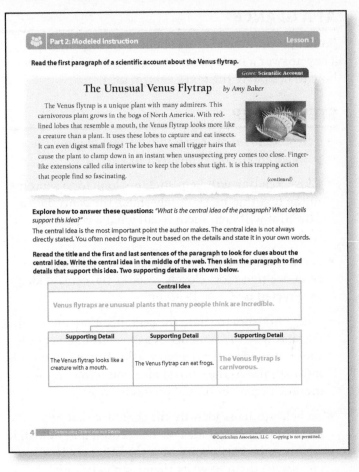

Tier Two
Vocabulary: *Unsuspecting*

- Point out the word *unsuspecting.* Have students tell what is described as unsuspecting. *(prey)* What does the unsuspecting prey do? *(comes too close to the Venus flytrap).* Ask students to use these context clues to help them determine the meaning of *unsuspecting* ("without being aware that something is going to happen"). **(RI.6.4; L.6.4.a)**

- As needed, ask students to identify the base word *(suspect)* and tell its meaning (*"to think something might happen"*). Point out the inflected ending *-ing* and the prefix *un-*. Have students describe how these word parts affect the meaning of the base word (*-ing changes* suspect *to an adjective;* un- *means "not," so it changes the meaning of the word to "not suspecting").* **(L.6.4.b)**

AT A GLANCE

Students continue reading about the Venus flytrap. They answer a multiple-choice question and analyze how to best state the text's central idea.

STEP BY STEP

- Tell students that they will continue reading the passage about the Venus flytrap.

- Close Reading will help students look for a sentence in the text that most closely states the central idea. The Hint will help them recall what a central idea is in order to select the best central idea of the account.

- Have students read the passage and underline the sentence that most closely restates the central idea, as directed by Close Reading.

- Ask volunteers to share the sentence they underlined. Discuss why the sentence is a close restatement of the central idea. If necessary, ask: Which sentence is most similar to the central idea you wrote in the graphic organizer on the previous page?

- To help students identify the sentence that best restates the central idea of the account and talk about why it is the best choice over the other choices, encourage them to write their own definition of *central idea*, including what it is and what it is not.

ANSWER ANALYSIS

Choice A is incorrect. It provides a detail about a mysterious feature of the Venus flytrap.

Choice B is incorrect. It provides a detail that describes the mystery of the plant's movement.

Choice C is incorrect. It hypothesizes about how the plant's "trap" might close.

Choice D is correct. This sentence uses the word *unusual* to describe the plant and mentions people's fascination. Both aspects relate to the central idea of the whole account.

ERROR ALERT: Students who did not choose D may have misunderstood the difference between a central idea and supporting details. Tell students that a text is a "whole" made up of "parts." The central idea is the whole, and the details are the specific parts.

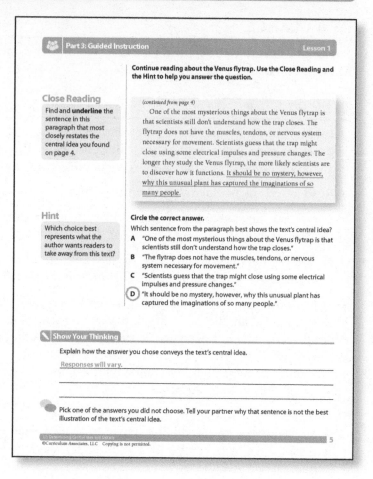

ELL Support: Compound Words

- Explain to students that a compound word is made up of two smaller words. You can look at the two smaller words to figure out the meaning of the compound word.

- Guide them to identify the two smaller words in *flytrap*. Together, talk about the meaning of the word *fly* ("an insect"). Then discuss the meaning of the word *trap* ("a thing that catches something"). Now ask students what they think the word *flytrap* means. ("a thing that catches flies")

- Point out that some compound words mean something different from the two smaller words. *Understand*, for example, does not mean "to stand under something." Talk about the importance of checking the meaning of a compound word by looking at clues in the surrounding text.

AT A GLANCE

Students read a passage about the corpse flower twice. After the first reading, you will ask three questions to check your students' comprehension of the passage.

STEP BY STEP

- Have students read the passage silently without referring to the Study Buddy or Close Reading text.

- Ask the following questions to ensure student comprehension of the text:

  Why is the *Titan arum*'s nickname "the corpse flower"? (*The* Titan arum's *nickname is "the corpse flower" because when it blooms it has a smell like a decomposing body.*)

  What is unusual about how the corpse flower grows? (*It can grow as tall as nine feet high and as quickly as six inches a day.*)

  What is unusual about the bloom of the corpse flower? (*The way it smells and that it blooms for one or two days at a time.*)

- Then ask students to reread paragraph 1 and look at the Study Buddy think aloud. What does the Study Buddy help them think about?

Tip: The Study Buddy reminds students to pay attention to the opening of an account. Point out that many authors state or imply their central idea in the opening paragraph so readers know what to expect. Students may be familiar with doing this in their own writing.

- Have students read the rest of the account. Tell them to follow the directions in the Close Reading.

Tip: Discuss with students that just as most authors state the central idea in the opening, they also restate the central idea at the end to be sure readers know what the author wants them to learn about the topic.

- Finally, have students answer the questions on page 7. When students have finished, use the Answer Analysis to discuss correct and incorrect responses.

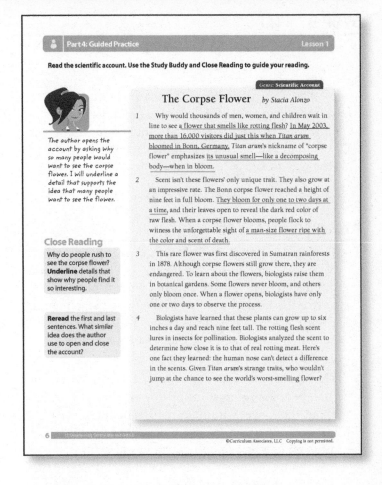

ELL Support: Possessives

- Point out the singular possessive *world's* in paragraph 4 and the plural possessive *flowers'* in paragraph 2. Explain to students that possessives are words that show who or what owns something.

- Discuss that to make a singular noun a possessive noun, add an apostrophe and *s* (*world's*). To make a plural noun a possessive, add only an apostrophe (*flowers'*).

- Work with students to make other possessive nouns. Write the words *boy*, *girl*, and *puppies* on the board. Identify each noun as either singular or plural and make each noun possessive, explaining how it is done.

STEP BY STEP

- Have students read questions 1–3, using the Hints to help them answer the questions.

Tip: If students have trouble answering question 2, have them consider each answer choice and ask themselves whether this detail about the corpse flower might be a reason that they would want to fly all the way to Germany to see the flower in bloom.

- Discuss with students the Answer Analysis below.

ANSWER ANALYSIS

1 The correct answer is B. It tells that a great number of people came to see the flower, so clearly they are interested in it. Choice A is not correct because it only tells the details of what the flower smells like. Choice C only explains the flower's name. Choice D describes what the flower looks like, not how people respond to the flower.

2 The correct answer is D. It describes insects' rather than people's interest in the flower. Choice A tells about the flower's unique smell, which may be of interest to people. Choice B describes the plant's unusual height, which people may also find interesting. Choice C tells about the short time the flower is in bloom, which may also interest people.

3 Sample response: The central idea is that the corpse flower is a unique plant that fascinates people. The text says, "When a corpse flower blooms, people flock to witness the unforgettable sight of a man-size flower ripe with the color and scent of death."

RETEACHING

Use a graphic organizer to verify the correct answer to question 3. Draw the graphic organizer below, leaving the boxes blank. Work with students to fill in the boxes, using information from the passage. Sample responses are provided.

Central Idea: The corpse flower is a unique plant that fascinates people.		
Supporting Detail: "smells like rotting flesh"	**Supporting Detail:** "can grow up to six inches a day and reach nine feet tall"	**Supporting Detail:** "bloom for only one to two days at a time"

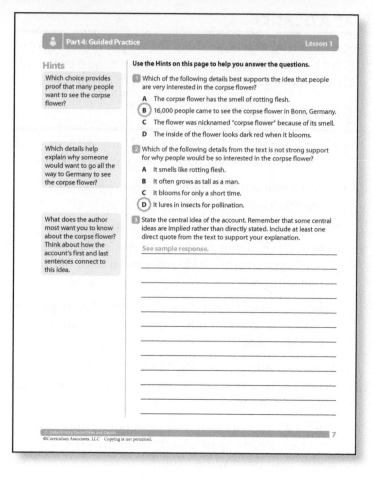

 Part 4: Guided Practice   Lesson 1

Hints

Which choice provides proof that many people want to see the corpse flower?

Which details help explain why someone would want to go all the way to Germany to see the corpse flower?

What does the author most want you to know about the corpse flower? Think about how the account's first and last sentences connect to this idea.

Use the Hints on this page to help you answer the questions.

1 Which of the following details best supports the idea that people are very interested in the corpse flower?

A The corpse flower has the smell of rotting flesh.
B 16,000 people came to see the corpse flower in Bonn, Germany.
C The flower was nicknamed "corpse flower" because of its smell.
D The inside of the flower looks dark red when it blooms.

2 Which of the following details from the text is not strong support for why people would be so interested in the corpse flower?

A It smells like rotting flesh.
B It often grows as tall as a man.
C It blooms for only a short time.
D It lures in insects for pollination.

3 State the central idea of the account. Remember that some central ideas are implied rather than directly stated. Include at least one direct quote from the text to support your explanation.

See sample response.

©Curriculum Associates, LLC Copying is not permitted.   7

Integrating Standards

Use these questions to further students' understanding of "The Corpse Flower."

1 What information about the corpse flower do you learn in paragraph 3? *(RI.6.1)*

Sample response: This paragraph tells about where the plant is found and how rare it is.

2 What example does the author include in the text that helps you understand how unique the bloom of the corpse flower is? *(RI.6.3)*

The author includes the example that in May 2003, more than 16,000 visitors waited in line to see the bloom of the corpse flower. This helps me understand how unique the bloom is, since so many people waited to see it.

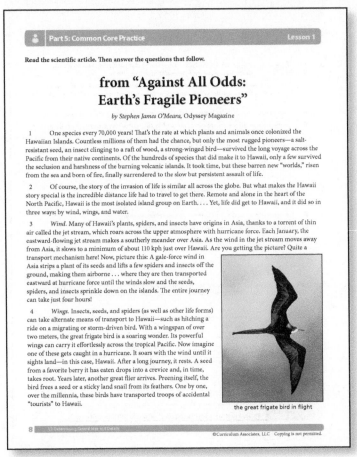

Part 5: Common Core Practice   Lesson 1

Read the scientific article. Then answer the questions that follow.

from "Against All Odds: Earth's Fragile Pioneers"

by Stephen James O'Meara, Odyssey Magazine

1   One species every 70,000 years! That's the rate at which plants and animals once colonized the Hawaiian Islands. Countless millions of them had the chance, but only the most rugged pioneers—a salt-resistant seed, an insect clinging to a raft of wood, a strong-winged bird—survived the long voyage across the Pacific from their native continents. Of the hundreds of species that did make it to Hawaii, only a few survived the seclusion and harshness of the burning volcanic islands. It took time, but these barren new "worlds," risen from the sea and born of fire, finally surrendered to the slow but persistent assault of life.

2   Of course, the story of the invasion of life is similar all across the globe. But what makes the Hawaii story special is the incredible distance life had to travel to get there. Remote and alone in the heart of the North Pacific, Hawaii is the most isolated island group on Earth. . . . Yet, life did get to Hawaii, and it did so in three ways: by wind, wings, and water.

3   *Wind.* Many of Hawaii's plants, spiders, and insects have origins in Asia, thanks to a torrent of thin air called the jet stream, which roars across the upper atmosphere with hurricane force. Each January, the eastward-flowing jet stream makes a southerly meander over Asia. As the wind in the jet stream moves away from Asia, it slows to a minimum of about 110 kph just over Hawaii. Are you getting the picture? Quite a transport mechanism here! Now, picture this: A gale-force wind in Asia strips a plant of its seeds and lifts a few spiders and insects off the ground, making them airborne . . . where they are then transported eastward at hurricane force until the winds slow and the seeds, spiders, and insects sprinkle down on the islands. The entire journey can take just four hours!

4   *Wings.* Insects, seeds, and spiders (as well as other life forms) can take alternate means of transport to Hawaii—such as hitching a ride on a migrating or storm-driven bird. With a wingspan of over two meters, the great frigate bird is a soaring wonder. Its powerful wings can carry it effortlessly across the tropical Pacific. Now imagine one of these gets caught in a hurricane. It soars with the wind until it sights land—in this case, Hawaii. After a long journey, it rests. A seed from a favorite berry it has eaten drops into a crevice and, in time, takes root. Years later, another great flier arrives. Preening itself, the bird frees a seed or a sticky land snail from its feathers. One by one, over the millennia, these birds have transported troops of accidental "tourists" to Hawaii.

the great frigate bird in flight

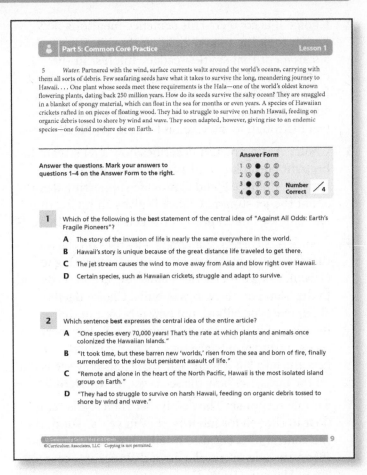 **Part 5: Common Core Practice**   Lesson 1

5   *Water.* Partnered with the wind, surface currents waltz around the world's oceans, carrying with them all sorts of debris. Few seafaring seeds have what it takes to survive the long, meandering journey to Hawaii. . . . One plant whose seeds meet these requirements is the Hala—one of the world's oldest known flowering plants, dating back 250 million years. How do its seeds survive the salty ocean? They are snuggled in a blanket of spongy material, which can float in the sea for months or even years. A species of Hawaiian crickets rafted in on pieces of floating wood. They had to struggle to survive on harsh Hawaii, feeding on organic debris tossed to shore by wind and wave. They soon adapted, however, giving rise to an endemic species—one found nowhere else on Earth.

Answer the questions. Mark your answers to questions 1–4 on the Answer Form to the right.

Answer Form
1 Ⓐ ● Ⓒ Ⓓ
2 ● Ⓑ Ⓒ Ⓓ
3 Ⓐ Ⓑ Ⓒ Ⓓ   **Number Correct** ___/4
4 ● Ⓑ Ⓒ Ⓓ

1   Which of the following is the **best** statement of the central idea of "Against All Odds: Earth's Fragile Pioneers"?

A   The story of the invasion of life is nearly the same everywhere in the world.

B   Hawaii's story is unique because of the great distance life traveled to get there.

C   The jet stream causes the wind to move away from Asia and blow right over Hawaii.

D   Certain species, such as Hawaiian crickets, struggle and adapt to survive.

2   Which sentence **best** expresses the central idea of the entire article?

A   "One species every 70,000 years! That's the rate at which plants and animals once colonized the Hawaiian Islands."

B   "It took time, but these barren new 'worlds,' risen from the sea and born of fire, finally surrendered to the slow but persistent assault of life."

C   "Remote and alone in the heart of the North Pacific, Hawaii is the most isolated island group on Earth."

D   "They had to struggle to survive on harsh Hawaii, feeding on organic debris tossed to shore by wind and wave."

AT A GLANCE

Students independently read a longer article and answer questions in a format that provides test practice.

STEP BY STEP

- Tell students to use what they have learned about determining central ideas and supporting details to read the passage on pages 8 and 9.

- Remind students to underline or circle important points in the text.

- Tell students to answer the questions on pages 9 and 10. For questions 1–4, they should fill in the correct circle on the Answer Form.

- When students have finished, use the Answer Analysis to discuss correct responses and the reasons for them. Have students fill in the Number Correct on the Answer Form.

ANSWER ANALYSIS

1   Choice B is correct. It states the central idea that Hawaii's story of the invasion of life is unique because of the great distance life had to travel in order to get there. Choice A is about how the invasion of life is similar everywhere in the world, while the article is mostly about the invasion of life in Hawaii. Choice C is a supporting detail about the jet stream causing winds to blow right over Hawaii. Choice D is a supporting detail about how Hawaiian crickets have adapted and survived. **(DOK 2)**

Theme Connection

- In what ways do all three passages relate to the theme of extraordinary plants?

- Based on what you have read, what is one conclusion you can draw about scientists' interactions with unique plant life?

2   Choice B is correct. This sentence mentions how long it took life to take hold on Hawaii. Choice A is a statement that sparks readers' interest in the central idea. Choice C is a supporting detail about how isolated and remote Hawaii is. Choice D is a supporting detail about the struggle living things went through to survive on Hawaii. **(DOK 2)**

3   Choice A is correct. It describes how a jet stream has brought both plant and animal life from Asia to Hawaii. Choices B and C provide supporting details about the jet stream. Choice D gives an interesting fact but does not represent the central idea. **(DOK 2)**

4   Choice A is correct. Paragraph 4 focuses on the role that flying has played in living things migrating to Hawaii. Choice A describes how insects and seeds got to the island on the wings of birds. Choice B tells about one type of bird, not how it helped in the invasion of life on Hawaii. Choice C tells how berry seeds start to grow once they get to the island, not how the bird got it there. Choice D tells how seeds fall off the birds, not how the seeds got there. **(DOK 2)**

5   Sample response: The detail that Hala seeds "can float in the sea for months or even years" supports the central idea because it tells about one way that seeds are able to travel a great distance in order to get to Hawaii. **(DOK 3)**

Integrating Standards

Use these questions and tasks as opportunities to interact with "Against All Odds: Earth's Fragile Pioneers."

1   How does the author introduce the idea that the invasion of life on Hawaii is amazing? **(RI.6.3)**

The statement "One species every 70,000 years!" introduces this idea. It is an exclamation about how incredibly long it has taken for life to invade Hawaii.

2   What evidence supports the claim that the story of Hawaii's invasion of life is "special"? **(RI.6.1)**

Sample response: The text states, "Hawaii is the most isolated island group on Earth."

3   The author uses the word *pioneers* to describe species that survived the trip to Hawaii. Why do you think the author chose this word? **(L.6.4)**

Sample response: Pioneers are usually defined as people who bravely settle isolated land. Early species

that arrived on Hawaii were also isolated from others and had to survive harsh conditions to get there.

4   Write an informative paragraph about one of the ways that life got to Hawaii (wind, wings, or water). Include relevant facts and quotations from the article. **(W.6.2)**

Students' paragraphs will vary. Sample response: Much life made its way to Hawaii by traveling with the help of birds. For example, a bird might fly from one place to Hawaii and then "preening itself, the bird frees a seed or a sticky land snail from its feathers."

5   Discuss in small groups: What inferences can you draw about the invasion of life from this article? Use text evidence to support your answers. **(RI.6.1; SL.6.1)**

Discussions will vary. Remind students that when they make an inference, they combine what they already know with evidence from the text.

©Curriculum Associates, LLC   Copying is not permitted.

Writing Activities

Argumentative Essay *(W.6.1)*

- Have students review "The Unusual Venus Flytrap," "The Corpse Flower," and "Against All Odds: Earth's Fragile Pioneers." Ask them to think about which plant they consider to be the most extraordinary. What does it mean to be extraordinary? Which plant was most remarkable and why?

- Challenge students to write an argument to support their opinion. Remind them to include relevant evidence from the passages and to organize the reasons clearly.

- Allow students to share their writing with the class.

Sentence Patterns *(L.6.3.a)*

- Have students reread the paragraph on page 4. Work with students to identify the different sentence patterns the writer uses to vary the sentence structure. Discuss how this varied structure helps keep readers interested in the text.

- Ask students to write their own paragraphs that use varied sentence structures. Have them exchange paragraphs with a partner and talk about what they did to keep the writing interesting.

LISTENING ACTIVITY *(SL.6.1; SL.6.2)*

Listen Closely/Connecting Topics

- After reading "Against All Odds: Earth's Fragile Pioneers," have students form small groups.

- Have each student write down one or two questions about the topic that can be answered using information from the text.

- Then ask students to take turns answering each others' questions. Students must listen closely to the question before answering it with evidence from the text.

DISCUSSION ACTIVITY *(SL.6.6)*

Talk in a Group/Discuss the Effects of Weather

- Ask students to discuss in small groups how weather has played a role in bringing some species of plants and animals to the Hawaiian Islands.

- Have students create a mock climate report detailing the effect weather has had on pioneering plants and animals in the Hawaiian Islands.

- Have students present their reports to the class, utilizing a "reporter" or "newscaster" style.

MEDIA ACTIVITY *(RI.6.1; RI.6.7)*

Be Creative/Photo Details

- Have students look at the picture on page 4 that accompanies "The Unusual Venus Flytrap."

- Ask students to find quotes in the account that accurately describe the photograph.

- Allow time for students to share with the class why and how they think the quotes relate to the photograph.

RESEARCH ACTIVITY *(W.6.8; SL.6.4)*

Research and Present/Write a Report

- Ask students to use the information in "Against All Odds: Earth's Fragile Pioneers" to write a report on the development of various species on the Hawaiian islands.

- Ask students to use print and digital sources to research additional information to include, such as more specific examples about the scientific history of a plant or animal's colonization in Hawaii.

- Have students take notes and write their reports. Then allow time for students to read aloud their reports to the class.

Summarizing Informational Texts

LESSON OBJECTIVES

- Use central idea and key details to summarize a text.

- Summarize a text without introducing opinions or judgments.

THE LEARNING PROGRESSION

- **Grade 5:** CCLS RI.5.2 requires students to identify main ideas and key details; students then use main ideas and key details to summarize a text.

- **Grade 6: CCLS RI.6.2 builds on the Grade 5 standard by requiring students to use central ideas and key details to summarize a text and also to omit personal opinions or judgments from the summary.**

- **Grade 7:** CCLS RI.7.2 requires students to determine two or more central ideas in a text and provide an objective summary of the text without the inclusion of personal opinions or judgments.

PREREQUISITE SKILLS

- Identify the central idea of a text.

- Identify key details that support the central idea.

- Use central ideas and key details to summarize a text.

TAP STUDENTS' PRIOR KNOWLEDGE

- Tell students that they will be working on a lesson about summarizing informational texts. Ask students what a summary is. (*A summary briefly retells a passage's central points or events.*)

- Ask students to think about a movie they have recently seen. Invite them to summarize the movie. Who is the main character? What big problem does this character face? What are the main events in the movie? How is the problem solved? Encourage students to imagine that they are explaining what happens in the movie to a friend who has not seen it.

- Discuss with students which parts of a passage they include when they summarize an informational text. (*The passage's central idea and most important supporting details.*)

- Ask students to share how they figure out which details in the passage are most important. Guide students to understand that supporting details answer the questions *who, what, where, when, how,* and *why* about the central idea.

- Point out that when students summarized a movie they have seen recently, they did not include what they thought about the movie, such as whether they liked it or not. Similarly, a summary of an informational text only includes information that is presented in a text, not what the writer of the summary thinks about that information.

📖 Ready *Teacher Toolbox*　　　*teacher-toolbox.com*

	Prerequisite Skills	*RI.6.2*
Ready Lessons	✓	✓
Tools for Instruction	✓	✓
Interactive Tutorials	✓	✓

CCLS Focus

RI.6.2 … provide a summary of the text distinct from personal opinions or judgments.

ADDITIONAL STANDARDS: **RI.6.1, RI.6.3, RI.6.7, RI.6.8; W.6.7, W.6.9; SL.6.1, SL.6.2.a, SL.6.5; L.6.2.a, L.6.5.a** (*See page A39 for full text.*)

AT A GLANCE

By analyzing a sample summary, students build an understanding of how to write summaries that are free of personal opinions or judgments.

STEP BY STEP

- Read the definition of *summary*. Then have students read the passage.

- Tell students that the chart illustrates how identifying a text's important details can help to create an effective summary of the text. Invite students to complete the chart.

- Read aloud the details in the chart. Point out how each detail in the box ends up in the summary at the bottom of the chart, albeit in abbreviated form.

- Next, have a volunteer read the draft summary of that passage. Ask students to cross out phrases in that summary that are opinions.

- Invite volunteers to share the phrases they crossed out and explain why each reflects an opinion. Point out that personal pronouns such as *I* and *me* often signal personal opinions. Words such as *think*, *feel*, and *believe* also signal opinions.

- Discuss with students that being able to summarize the central idea and key details of a text in their own words will help them make sure they understood the text and help them remember the information.

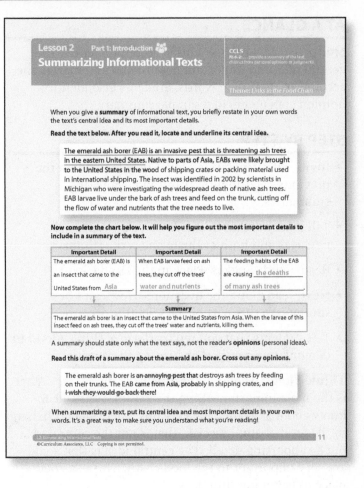

Genre Focus

Informational Texts: Scientific Accounts

Tell students that in this lesson they will read informational texts. One type of informational text is a scientific account, or a piece of writing that provides information about scientific research or another science-related topic.

- Its purpose is to explain scientific findings or any event or discovery with ties to science.

- It can be written by professional scientists to relate findings to the scientific community or to contribute to knowledge in a particular field of study. It may also be written by someone with scientific expertise for the general public.

- It often opens with an explanation about the thesis or theory behind the scientific topic and then gives examples or further details to elaborate on it.

- Some may include charts, graphics, or photos. Others may have sidebars with additional facts or subheadings to show how the ideas are organized.

"Snakes' Place in the Food Chain" is a scientific account of how energy from the sun moves up a chain of plants and animals. "Food Web," a scientific article from National Geographic magazine, discusses how food chains are connected to each other. Finally, "Spiders: In Pursuit of Prey," is a scientific account which tells about special ways in which spiders catch their prey.

AT A GLANCE

Students read a brief scientific account, identify the central idea and important details, and summarize the account in their own words. Students also identify opinion statements in a sample summary.

STEP BY STEP

- Invite volunteers to tell what they learned on the previous page about writing and evaluating summaries.

- Tell students that in this lesson they will read passages and both evaluate and write summaries.

- Read aloud "Snakes' Place in the Food Chain."

- Next, read aloud the question: "How can I best summarize this part of the scientific account?"

- Tell students that you will perform a Think Aloud to demonstrate a way of answering the question.

Think Aloud: The first question I ask myself is, "What is the most important thing the author wants me to know about snakes?" She explains where snakes belong in the food chain; however, that is not the central idea but a supporting detail. The central idea is that snakes are very important to the food chain. This is a good place to begin my summary.

- Have students underline the central idea and important details.

- Tell students that you will read aloud the sample summary. After reading, share another Think Aloud.

Think Aloud: There are some words and phrases that signal opinions, such as the pronouns *I* and *my*. If you are using these words to summarize informational text, you are probably expressing an opinion. I notice the word *I* near the end of the first sentence. This clue leads me to the opinion statement. "I think they are pests" is an expression of the writer's opinion. It does not belong in a summary.

- Tell students other words that might signal opinions include strong emotional words such as *annoying* or *fantastic* and comparing words such as *best* or *most disappointing*.

- Allow students time to complete their summaries of "Snakes' Place in the Food Chain" and to discuss their ideas with partners.

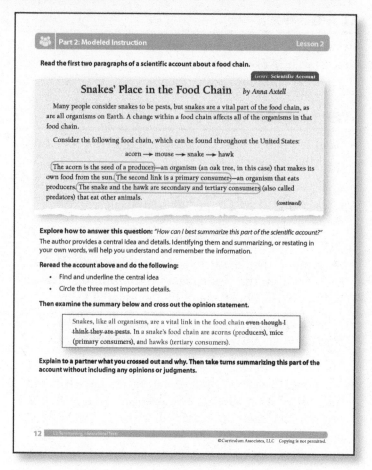

Tier Two Vocabulary: *Consumer*

- Have students find the word *consumer* in the last paragraph. Guide them to identify the base word *consume*. Ask them to name a few other things they consume (eat or drink) regularly. (*vegetables, fruit juice*)

- Tell students that adding *-er* to the end of a verb changes it to a noun, as in *dance* and *dancer*. Work with them to determine that *consumer* means "a living thing that eats other living things" in this context. (***RI.6.4; L.6.4.a***)

- Ask students to use *consumer* and the related word *consume* in their own sentences.

AT A GLANCE

Students continue reading about snakes' role in the food chain. They answer a multiple-choice question and analyze the incorrect choices.

STEP BY STEP

- Tell students that they will continue reading about the role of snakes in a typical food chain.

- Remind students that Close Reading will help them identify the central idea and important details. The Hint will help them recall what information to include and exclude from a summary.

- Have students read the account. Then ask them to circle the central idea and underline supporting details, as directed by Close Reading.

- Ask students to share which sentence they circled. Discuss why this sentence best represents the central idea. Then have students explain why the sentence "Fewer mice are left to eat acorns." doesn't better represent the paragraph's central idea. *(It does not discuss snakes, the topic.)*

- Encourage students to describe what a good summary both should and should not include.

ANSWER ANALYSIS

Choice A is incorrect. It focuses on opinions rather than on facts. It does not identify the central idea.

Choice B is incorrect. It includes an opinion, and it does not correctly identify the central idea of the paragraph.

Choice C is incorrect. It presents one of the text's supporting details instead of the central idea.

Choice D is correct. This summary is focused on the central idea of the passage, and it does not contain any opinions.

ERROR ALERT: Students who did not choose D may have confused central ideas and supporting details. Encourage students to summarize the passage in their own words and then select the choice that is most similar to their summary.

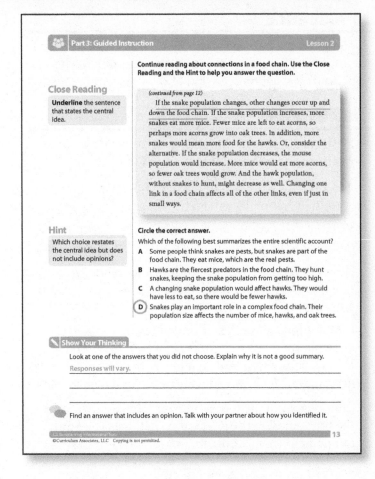

👥 Part 3: Guided Instruction   Lesson 2

Close Reading

Underline the sentence that states the central idea.

Continue reading about connections in a food chain. Use the Close Reading and the Hint to help you answer the question.

(continued from page 12)

    If the snake population changes, other changes occur up and down the food chain. If the snake population increases, more snakes eat more mice. Fewer mice are left to eat acorns, so perhaps more acorns grow into oak trees. In addition, more snakes would mean more food for the hawks. Or, consider the alternative. If the snake population decreases, the mouse population would increase. More mice would eat more acorns, so fewer oak trees would grow. And the hawk population, without snakes to hunt, might decrease as well. Changing one link in a food chain affects all of the other links, even if just in small ways.

Hint

Which choice restates the central idea but does not include opinions?

Circle the correct answer.

Which of the following best summarizes the entire scientific account?

A Some people think snakes are pests, but snakes are part of the food chain. They eat mice, which are the real pests.

B Hawks are the fiercest predators in the food chain. They hunt snakes, keeping the snake population from getting too high.

C A changing snake population would affect hawks. They would have less to eat, so there would be fewer hawks.

D Snakes play an important role in a complex food chain. Their population size affects the number of mice, hawks, and oak trees.

✏ **Show Your Thinking**

Look at one of the answers that you did not choose. Explain why it is not a good summary.

Responses will vary.

Find an answer that includes an opinion. Talk with your partner about how you identified it.

L2: Summarizing Informational Texts
©Curriculum Associates, LLC   Copying is not permitted.   13

ELL Support: Plural Forms of Regular Nouns

- Explain to students that nouns name people, places, or things. Students can look at the endings of nouns to know *how many*. Explain that to form the plural of a regular noun, you add either *s* or *es*.

- Point out the regular plural nouns *snakes*, *hawks*, and *trees* on student book page 13. Work with students to identify how each plural was formed (*snakes*: add *s*; *hawks*: add *s*; *trees*: add *s*) and to tell how many (*more than one*).

- For additional support, work with students to form the plural of *book* (*books*) and tell *how many* (*more than one*). Then write the words *marsh* and *bee* on the board. Work together to form the plurals. Pronounce the words as you explain how each plural is formed (*marsh*: add *es*; *bee*: add *s*).

AT A GLANCE

Students read a passage about food webs twice. After the first reading, you will ask three questions to check your students' comprehension of the passage.

STEP BY STEP

- Have students read the passage silently without referring to the Study Buddy or Close Reading text.

- Ask the following questions to ensure student comprehension of the text:

  What is this article mostly about? (*The central idea is that food webs are made up of a variety of food chains.*)

  How is a food web different from a food chain? (*Specific food chains make up the larger food web of an ecosystem.*)

  Explain how a food chain might begin and end with an apple tree. (*Worms eat the apples; birds eat the worms; a fox eats a bird; and finally the fox's decomposing body provides nutrients for an apple tree.*)

- Then ask students to reread paragraph 1 and look at the Study Buddy think aloud. What does the Study Buddy help them think about?

Tip: The Study Buddy guides students to look for "big ideas" about the topic. Explain that each section or paragraph often has its own "big idea" that relates to the article's central idea. Identifying the big idea of each section helps students summarize the text.

- Have students read the rest of the article. Tell them to follow the directions in the Close Reading.

Tip: Point out to students that the information they are identifying using the Close Reading are supporting details about the central idea. These details answer questions such as *what* and *how*. This will help them write a good summary of the article.

- Finally have students answer the questions on page 15. When students have finished, use the Answer Analysis to discuss correct and incorrect responses.

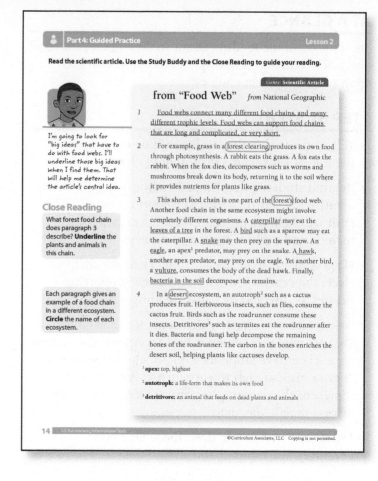

Tier Two Vocabulary: *Support*

- Direct students to the word *support* in paragraph 1. Ask them what *support* means in this context (*"provide what is needed"*). Have them describe which context clues helped them determine this meaning. (***RI.6.4; L.6.4.a***)

- Have students give examples of items at school that support their learning, using the word *support* in each of their answers.

STEP BY STEP

- Have students read questions 1–3, using the Hints to help them answer the questions.

Tip: If students have trouble answering question 1, remind them of the "big idea" that the Study Buddy underlined on the previous page. Have them compare the idea stated in these sentences to each answer choice to select the correct answer.

- Discuss with students the Answer Analysis below.

ANSWER ANALYSIS

1   The correct answer is B. The central idea is that food webs connect different food chains and trophic levels. Choice A is a supporting detail. Choice C focuses on one example of a food chain. Choice D includes a statement of opinion.

2   The correct answer is D. This summary includes the paragraph's central idea and important details without including an opinion. Choice A is not supported by information in the passage. Choice B gives an example but does not state the central idea. Choice C includes a statement of opinion, which is not a part of a good summary.

3   Sample response: Within an ecosystem's food web, there are a number of different food chains. These chains can involve different organisms from different trophic levels. Examples include food chains from a grass ecosystem, a forest ecosystem, and a desert ecosystem.

RETEACHING

Use a chart to verify the correct answer to question 2. Draw the chart below, leaving the boxes blank. Work with students to fill in the boxes, using information from the passage. Sample responses are provided.

Important Detail:	**Important Detail:**	**Important Detail:**
Another food chain might involve different organisms.	Caterpillar eats leaves; sparrow eats caterpillar; eagle eats sparrow.	Hawk eats eagle; vulture eats hawk; bacteria decompose remains.

Summary: One ecosystem may have many different food chains. One example of a food chain in a forest involves leaves, caterpillars, sparrows, snakes, eagles, hawks, vultures, and bacteria.

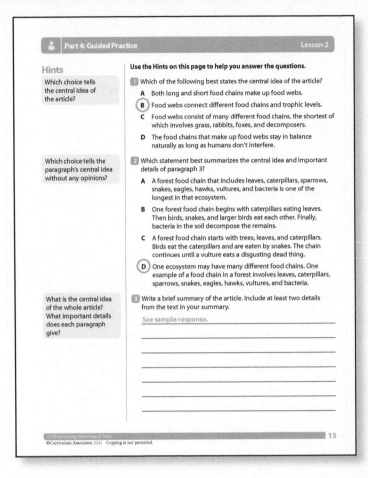

Hints

Which choice tells the central idea of the article?

Which choice tells the paragraph's central idea without any opinions?

What is the central idea of the whole article? What important details does each paragraph give?

Use the Hints on this page to help you answer the questions.

1   Which of the following best states the central idea of the article?

   A   Both long and short food chains make up food webs.

   B   Food webs connect different food chains and trophic levels.

   C   Food webs consist of many different food chains, the shortest of which involves grass, rabbits, foxes, and decomposers.

   D   The food chains that make up food webs stay in balance naturally as long as humans don't interfere.

2   Which statement best summarizes the central idea and important details of paragraph 3?

   A   A forest food chain that includes leaves, caterpillars, sparrows, snakes, eagles, hawks, vultures, and bacteria is one of the longest in that ecosystem.

   B   One forest food chain begins with caterpillars eating leaves. Then birds, snakes, and larger birds eat each other. Finally, bacteria in the soil decompose the remains.

   C   A forest food chain starts with trees, leaves, and caterpillars. Birds eat the caterpillars and are eaten by snakes. The chain continues until a vulture eats a disgusting dead thing.

   D   One ecosystem may have many different food chains. One example of a food chain in a forest involves leaves, caterpillars, sparrows, snakes, eagles, hawks, vultures, and bacteria.

3   Write a brief summary of the article. Include at least two details from the text in your summary.

   See sample response.

15
©Curriculum Associates, LLC   Copying is not permitted.

Integrating Standards

Use these questions to further students' understanding of "Food Web."

1   Fungi play an important role in a food chain. Cite evidence in the article that supports this claim. **(RI.6.1)**

   The following sentences support the statement about fungi: "When a fox dies, decomposers such as worms and mushrooms break down its body, returning it to the soil where it provides nutrients for plants like grass." "Bacteria and fungi help decompose the remaining bones of the roadrunner."

2   Explain how a food chain in a grass ecosystem might be circular; that is, the food chain begins and ends with grass. **(RI.6.3)**

   Sample response: First, the grass makes its own food through photosynthesis. Then it is eaten by a rabbit, which is then eaten by a fox. When the fox dies, it decomposes, providing nutrients for the growing grass.

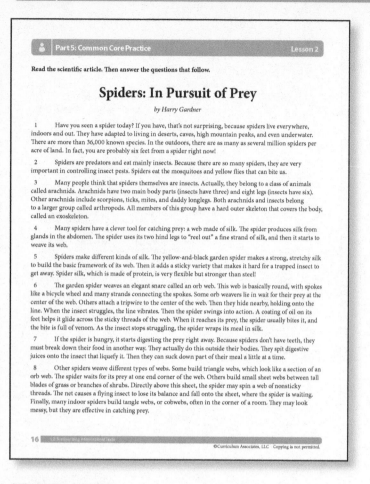

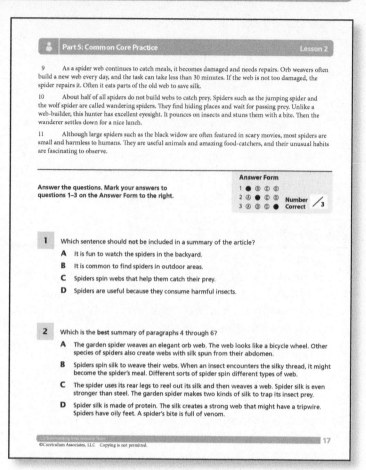

AT A GLANCE

Students independently read a longer article and answer questions in a format that provides test practice.

STEP BY STEP

- Tell students to use what they have learned about reading closely and summarizing informational text to read the passage on pages 16 and 17.

- Remind students to underline central ideas and circle important details.

- Tell students to answer the questions on pages 17 and 18. For questions 1–3, they should fill in the correct circle on the Answer Form.

- When students have finished, use the Answer Analysis to discuss correct responses and the reasons for them. Have students fill in the Number Correct on the Answer Form.

ANSWER ANALYSIS

1   The correct answer is A. This sentence expresses an opinion, which does not belong in a summary. Choice B mentions an important supporting detail from the passage and would be included in a summary. Choice C focuses on another important detail, and it would also be included in a summary. Choice D shares another important detail without stating an opinion or judgment, so it would be included in a summary. **(DOK 2)**

Theme Connection

- How do all the articles in this lesson relate to the theme of links in the food chain?

- What is one fact or idea you learned about food chains from each article in this lesson?

2 The correct answer is B. This summary includes the section's central idea and important details without including an opinion. Choice A is focused on the garden spider, but it leaves out important details from these paragraphs about the passage's central idea, spider webs. Choices C and D list details but they do not state a central idea related to the topic of spider webs. **(DOK 2)**

3 Choice D is correct. It describes the nature of spiders, their unusual web-building ability, and their value as insect-eating predators. Choice A gives some interesting details, but these in themselves do not constitute a summary. Choice B is incorrect because it is a summary of one paragraph. Choice C gets off to a good start but then it gives a broad generalization followed by a rather specific detail about spiders, neither of which contribute much to an overall summary. **(DOK 2)**

4 Sample response: More than half of all spiders catch their prey using webs. These webs are made from silk that the spider produces itself. The webs trap insects that come into contact with them. Spiders that do not make webs catch their prey mainly by hiding and then pouncing on passing insects. These spiders stun prey with a bite and then eat them. **(DOK 2)**

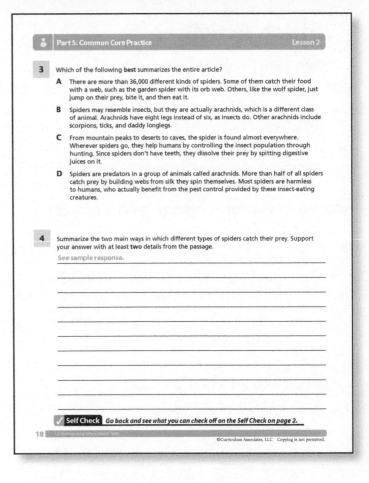

Integrating Standards

Use these questions and tasks as opportunities to interact with "Spiders: In Pursuit of Prey."

1 How are arachnids and insects similar? How are they different? **(RI.6.1)**

Both arachnids and insects are arthropods, which are animals with an exoskeleton. Arachnids have two main body parts and eight legs, while insects have three main body parts and six legs.

2 What facts in the text develop the idea that spiders are a well-adapted animal? **(RI.6.3)**

Facts about where spiders can be found all over the world in many different climates develop the idea that spiders are well adapted. Spiders "have adapted to living in deserts, caves, high mountain peaks, and even underwater." The author adds that "you are probably six feet from a spider right now!"

3 Write a paragraph identifying one claim by the author that is not well supported with reasons or evidence. **(W.6.9)**

Sample response: The author claims "most spiders are small and harmless to humans." The author does not give any examples, facts, or other information to support this claim. Therefore, this claim is not as well supported as other claims the author makes.

4 The author uses the figure of speech "reel out." What does this phrase mean? How does it help you understand what the spider does? **(L.6.5.a)**

"Reel out" means "to unwind," as in a fishing line. This helps me picture how the spider unwinds a thin piece of silk, similar to a fishing line.

5 Discuss in small groups: How might this article be different if the author had a strong fear of spiders? **(SL.6.1)**

Discussions will vary. Students might mention that such words as important, clever, elegant, amazing, fascinating, *and other words with positive connotations might not be used as frequently.*

Writing Activities

Spiders in a Food Chain (W.6.2)

- Challenge students to synthesize the information they read in "Snakes' Place in the Food Chain," "Food Web," and "Spiders: In Pursuit of Prey" to write an informative essay about the spider's place in a food chain. What are some prey of spiders? What might some predators of spiders be? How might a spider's place in a food chain be similar to and different from the snake's place in its food chain?

- Remind students to introduce the topic, develop it with relevant information using precise language, and provide a concluding statement. Allow students time to share their dialogue with the class.

Commas and Nonrestrictive Phrases (L.6.2.a)

- Direct students to this sentence on page 14: "An eagle, an apex predator, may prey on the snake."

- Write the sentence on the board and underline the nonrestrictive element *an apex predator*. Explain that this phrase tells more about the noun before it, *eagle*. Because this phrase provides extra information not necessary to understand the meaning of the main sentence, it is set off with commas.

- Have students write a sentence that includes a nonrestrictive phrase and uses appropriate punctuation.

LISTENING ACTIVITY (SL.6.1)

Listen Closely/Connect Ideas

- Have small groups review the central idea and important details in "Spiders: In Pursuit of Prey."

- Have one student tell the first step involved in a spider building a web. Then ask students to take turns describing how a web is built and how the spider captures prey.

- Each student listens closely, repeating the steps that were already said before adding a new step.

DISCUSSION ACTIVITY (SL.6.1)

Talk in a Group/Extending Scientific Concepts

- Write on the board the five key terms in understanding a food web: *producer, consumer, decomposer, predator, prey.*

- Have students form small groups to discuss these roles and to create a list of examples of each. Have one group member act as recorder, creating five individual lists to track the discussion.

- Allow 10 to 15 minutes for the discussion. Then have each group share their lists with the class.

MEDIA ACTIVITY (RI.6.7)

Be Creative/Illustrate a Food Chain

- Have students review the food chain shown on page 12. Discuss the links in the food chain.

- Invite students to create an illustrated food chain that includes spiders as one link. Students may illustrate the food chain they described in the informative writing piece they completed.

- Have students display their food chains.

RESEARCH ACTIVITY (W.6.7; SL.6.5)

Research and Present/Give a Presentation

- Ask students to use the information in "Spiders: In Pursuit of Prey" as a starting point to create a presentation about spider webs.

- In addition to describing the different types of spiders and their webs, students should also provide a labeled illustration or photograph of each type of web.

- As students give their presentations, have the audience take notes and then discuss the similarities and differences in how each student approached the same assignment.

Citing Evidence to Make Inferences

Theme: *Mysterious Creatures*

LESSON OBJECTIVES

- Use supporting details and examples to make inferences about the text.

- Cite textual evidence to support inferences drawn from the text.

- Provide an analysis of the text.

THE LEARNING PROGRESSION

- **Grade 5:** CCLS RI.5.1 requires students to provide textual evidence to explain information and inferences drawn from the text. They are not required to analyze the text.

- **Grade 6: CCLS RI.6.1 builds on the Grade 5 standard by emphasizing analysis and requiring students to use details and quotations from the text to consider how explicit and inferential information relate to the text as a whole.**

- **Grade 7:** CCLS RI.7.1 requires students to provide greater depth in their analyses by citing several pieces of textual evidence to support their analyses.

PREREQUISITE SKILLS

- Identify central idea.

- Identify supporting details.

- Understand that some information in a text is not directly stated.

- Use supporting details and examples to make inferences.

- Quote details and examples accurately from a text when making inferences.

TAP STUDENTS' PRIOR KNOWLEDGE

- Tell students they will be working on a lesson about citing text evidence to make inferences. Ask students what an inference is. (*an informed guess*)

- Ask students what they would think if they walked by a house decorated with colorful streamers and balloons. (*Someone is having a party.*) Point out that no one directly told them that someone was having a party. They used clues and their own experience to figure it out.

- Next, ask what students can do when they need to figure something out in a text when the author does not tell them directly. (*Use clues in the text and think about what you already know.*) Discuss how students can use what they already know to help them understand what they read. For example, if students are reading about skateboarding, they might use their experiences with skateboarding to help them understand the terms used in the text. Encourage students to give other examples.

- Then ask students what text evidence is (*facts, examples, and other information from the text*). Review that quoting from a text means copying a part of a text exactly and putting quotation marks around it. Model how to quote a text by writing a sentence from an account students have read recently and then placing quotation marks around it. Point out that quoting from a text is a powerful way to offer evidence, or proof, to support an inference.

Ready Teacher Toolbox

teacher-toolbox.com

	Prerequisite Skills	RI.6.1
Ready Lessons	✓	✓
Tools for Instruction		✓ ✓
Interactive Tutorials		✓ ✓

CCLS Focus

RI.6.1 Cite textual evidence to support analysis of what the text says explicitly as well as inferences drawn from the text.

ADDITIONAL STANDARDS: **RI.6.2, RI.6.3, RI.6.4, RI.6.6, RI.6.7, RI.6.9; W.6.1, W.6.3, W.6.7, W.6.11.c; SL.6.1, SL.6.2, SL.6.4, SL.6.6; L.6.1.c, L.6.4.a, L.6.4.b** (*See page A39 for full text.*)

AT A GLANCE

Through a short passage about giant squids, students are introduced to the idea of making inferences about texts. They learn that they must cite textual evidence to support any inferences they make about a passage.

STEP BY STEP

- Read the first paragraph, which defines *inference*.

- Read the passage. Explain that the writer does not openly state whether she wants the research to continue, but she drops plenty of hints. Tell students to underline words suggesting what she thinks.

- Tell students that they can use a chart like the one shown to organize and analyze their prior knowledge and textual evidence to support a logical inference.

- Have students read the first column, which makes a general statement about human behavior that students can apply to their reading of the text.

- Now read the quotes in the second column, which come directly from the passage. Point out the words *significant*, *fascinating*, and *important*. These words tell how the writer feels about the research, but they do not openly declare whether she feels the work should continue.

- Read the third column aloud. Discuss whether the inference in the last column is logical and why. Ask students whether they could make and support this inference if words such as *significant*, *fascinating*, and *important* were absent from the text.

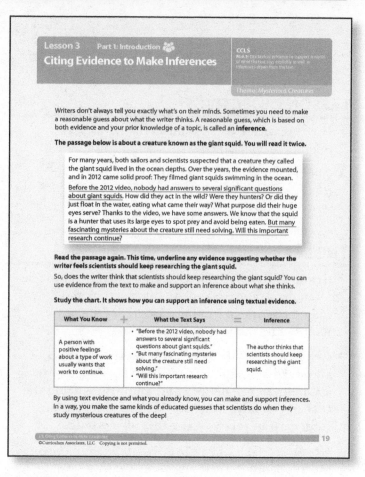

- Reinforce how making inferences is a valuable strategy by sharing an inference you made about an author's intentions in an account or book you are reading. Explain how you supported your inference with textual evidence and personal knowledge.

Genre Focus

Informational Text: Scientific Accounts

Tell students that in this lesson they will read scientific accounts. Explain that scientific accounts provide facts and details about a topic, and they include the following characteristics:

- Inform or explain, rather than entertain or give an opinion about something.

- Provide facts and details about a topic.

- Answer the questions *who*, *what*, *when*, *where*, *why*, and *how* about the topic.

- Often include photos, captions, and subheadings, which signal what is coming next.

Based on these characteristics, ask students to name some places where they have read scientific accounts, such as websites, science magazines, or their textbooks. What did they read about and what did they learn? How did the photos or other text features help them better understand the information in the account?

Explain that "A Scientist's Search for Bigfoot" and "Tales of Chupacabras" are scientific accounts about mythical animals. "Looking for the Loch Ness Monster" is a longer account about people's search for the Loch Ness monster.

AT A GLANCE

Students use text evidence to support an inference about a scientific account.

STEP BY STEP

• Invite volunteers to tell what they learned on the previous page about making an inference.

• Tell students they will continue practicing how to make and support inferences when they read.

• Read aloud "A Scientist's Search for Bigfoot." Then read the question: "Dr. Meldrum thinks that some samples are hoaxes, but others interest him. Why is he most likely interested in those other samples?"

• Now tell students you will perform a Think Aloud to demonstrate a way of answering the question.

Think Aloud: The account doesn't directly say why Meldrum is interested in some of the Bigfoot samples, but I can make an inference about what he thinks.

• Direct students to the chart. Point out the column for prior knowledge, titled "What You Know."

Think Aloud: What do I know about people and scientists? I know that people collect things they are interested in; that a scientist might collect things with scientific value; and that a scientist might keep samples that could lead to a discovery. This is knowledge a reader might have before even starting to read.

• Now direct students to the second column in the chart, titled "What the Text Says."

Think Aloud: Even though I have some prior knowledge about people and scientists, I need textual evidence if I'm going to make and support an inference about why Meldrum is interested in some of the Bigfoot samples. The second paragraph states that Meldrum has more than 200 casts and artifacts. That statement is in the chart. The second paragraph also states that Meldrum thinks only some samples are hoaxes.

• Tell students to add the second piece of evidence to the chart.

Think Aloud: Based on my prior knowledge and evidence from the text, I can now make and support an inference about what Meldrum most likely thinks.

• Ask students to complete the sentence in the third column and share their answers with the class.

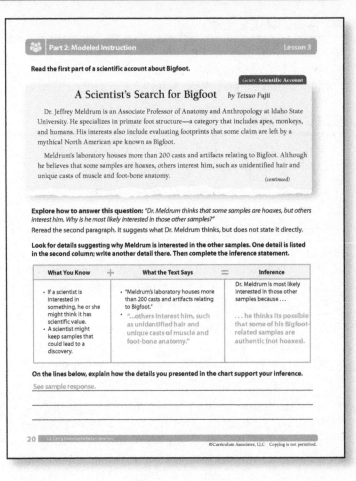

Tier Two Vocabulary: *Specializes*

• Direct students to the word *specializes* in the second sentence. Does Dr. Meldrum study all the body parts of primates? (*no*) Ask students what *specializes* means. ("*to focus on one type of work*") Have them tell which context clues helped them determine this meaning. (**RI.6.4; L.6.4.a**)

• Ask students to think of other words that mean about the same as *specializes*. (*concentrates, focuses*)

• On the board, write the related words *specialty* and *specialist*. Discuss with students some contexts in which these words might appear. (*The restaurant's specialty is seafood. My doctor sent me to see a specialist.*)

AT A GLANCE

Students continue reading about Dr. Meldrum. They answer a multiple-choice question and analyze the evidence that helped them select the correct answer.

STEP BY STEP

- Tell students that they will continue reading about Dr. Meldrum's research on Bigfoot.

- Close Reading will help students identify and remember important evidence. The Hint will help them look for specific evidence in each answer choice in order to select the best answer.

- Have students read the account and underline the evidence of other scientists' feelings about Meldrum's work, as directed by Close Reading.

- Ask volunteers to share the sentence they underlined. Discuss why that sentence shows evidence of scientists' feelings. If necessary, ask: What do other scientists feel Meldrum is trying to find?

- Have students circle the answer to the question, using the Hint to help. Then have them respond to the question in Show Your Thinking. Encourage students to distinguish evidence of what Meldrum thinks from evidence of what other scientists think.

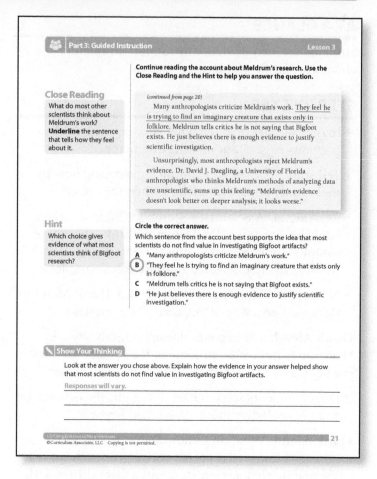

ANSWER ANALYSIS

Choice A is incorrect. It tells that anthropologists are critical of Meldrum's work but not why they don't find value in it.

Choice B is correct. It explains why scientists find little value in investigating Bigfoot artifacts.

Choice C is incorrect. It gives Meldrum's response to other scientists. It does not explain why scientists find little value in investigating Bigfoot artifacts.

Choice D is incorrect. It tells what Meldrum thinks or believes, not what other scientists think or believe.

ERROR ALERT: Students who did not choose B may have misunderstood the question. Explain that the question asks about why other scientists do not find value in Meldrum's work. Have students eliminate answer choices that tell Meldrum's beliefs.

ELL Support: Comparatives

- Explain that comparatives are words that compare two things. Superlatives compare three or more things. Regular comparative and superlative adjectives are formed by adding -er and -est or *more* and *most*. Irregular comparatives and superlatives have special forms.

- Point out the comparative *worse* in the last sentence on page 21. Tell students that *worse* is the comparative form of *bad*. *Worst* is the superlative form. Have students use each form in a sentence.

- Work with students to identify other irregular comparatives and superlatives. On the board, write: *I like spaghetti better than chicken. I think pizza is the best food of all.* Work together to identify the irregular comparative or superlative in each sentence. *(better, best)* Point out that *better* compares two things, spaghetti and chicken. *Best* compares pizza to all other foods.

AT A GLANCE

Students read a passage about chupacabras twice. After the first reading, you will ask three questions to check your students' comprehension of the passage.

STEP BY STEP

- Have students read the passage silently without referring to the Study Buddy or Close Reading text.

- Ask the following questions to ensure student comprehension of the text:

  What is the chupacabra? (*The chupacabra is a monster that sucks the blood of livestock.*)

  Do people agree about what the chupacabra looks like? How do you know? (*No; some people think chupacabras are two-legged, lizard-like creatures. Others insist they are hairless, four-legged creatures that are part kangaroo, part dog, and part rat.*)

  What have most animals that were thought to be chupacabras turned out to be? (*Most have been coyotes with mange.*)

- Then ask students to reread the title and look at the Study Buddy think aloud. What does the Study Buddy help them think about?

> **Tip:** Point out to students that authors do not always state their point of view about the topic. Students need to infer the author's feelings based on text evidence. This will help them better understand the text's overall message and recognize an author's bias.

- Have students read the rest of the passage. Tell them to follow the directions in the Close Reading.

> **Tip:** Close Reading helps students identify explanations and examples that can be used as text evidence. Learning to identify and analyze text evidence will help students infer the author's opinions and beliefs in any texts they read.

- Finally, have students answer the questions on page 23. When they have finished, use the Answer Analysis to discuss correct and incorrect responses.

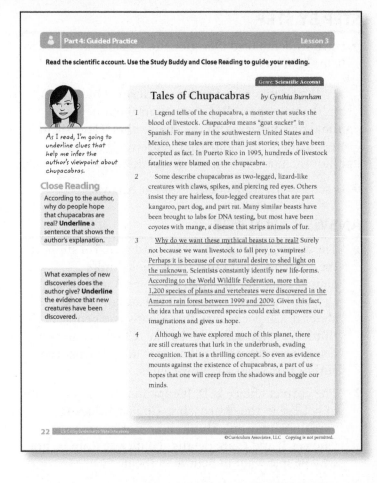

Tier Two Vocabulary: *Empowers*

- Have students find the word *empowers* in paragraph 3 on page 22. Work with them to determine that it means "to put strength into" in this context. **(RI.6.4; L.6.4.b)**

- As needed, point out the base word *power*. Say, "Teachers have the power to assign homework." Explain that when you have power, you have the strength or ability to do something. Ask students to share powers they would like to have.

- Then ask students what the prefix -*em* means ("*put into*"). Relate this discussion back to the meaning of *empowers* in the context of the account.

STEP BY STEP

- Have students read Questions 1–3, using the Hints to help them answer those questions.

Tip: If students have trouble answering Question 3, help them connect the information about new animal discoveries with the chupacabra. Have them reread paragraph 3 and ask themselves why the author includes facts about actual discoveries.

- Discuss with students the Answer Analysis below.

ANSWER ANALYSIS

1   The correct choice is C. The word *mythical* supports the students' claim that the author thinks chupacabras are imaginary. Choice A tells what *chupacabra* means, not what the author thinks about it. Choice B describes what some people think the chupacabra looks like. Choice D gives a detail from the passage but does not tell what the author thinks about chupacabras.

2   The correct choice is D. It explains why people want to believe in the chupacabra. Choice A doesn't explain why people think these stories are fact. Choices B and C are details about chupacabras, not why people want to believe in them.

3   Sample response: Actual scientific discoveries support the idea that chupacabras may be found because if scientists are finding new species, it is possible they will still find proof of chupacabras. The text says, "The idea that undiscovered species could exist empowers our imaginations."

RETEACHING

Use a graphic organizer to verify the correct answer to Question 1. Draw the graphic organizer below, leaving the boxes blank. Work with students to fill in the boxes, using information from the passage. Sample responses are provided.

Text Evidence	What I Know	Inference
"Why do we want these mythical beasts to be real?"	The word *mythical* means something doesn't exist.	The author believes chupacabras aren't real.

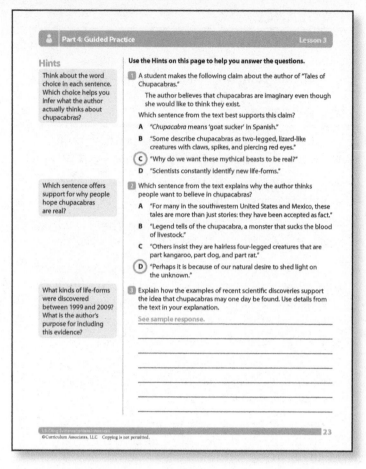

Integrating Standards

Use these questions to further students' understanding of "Tales of Chupacabras."

1   What is one fact from the text that develops the idea that no reliable evidence has been found to show that chupacabras are real? **(RI.6.3)**

The fact that many "beasts have been brought to labs for DNA testing, but most have been coyotes with mange" shows that there is still no evidence that chupacabras are real.

2   Write a one- or two-sentence summary of "Tales of Chupacabras." **(RI.6.2)**

Sample response: Chupacabras are thought to be vampire-like creatures that suck blood from livestock. Though there is no proof that they are real, many people would like to believe in them.

Read the scientific account. Then answer the questions that follow.

Looking for the Loch Ness Monster

by Stuart Clyburn

1   The word *loch* is a Scottish Gaelic word for *lake*. And there are a whole lot of lochs in Scotland—more than 500 of them! But one loch, Loch Ness in the Scottish Highlands, is known around the world. The reason for its fame is not its great size or beauty. People know the name *Loch Ness* because it is said to be the home of a mysterious, giant creature known as "the Loch Ness monster." Whether the creature really exists or not has been a matter of great debate for decades.

2   What does "Nessie," the popular nickname for the monster, supposedly look like? By most accounts, she has a small head on a very long neck. Her body is broad and rounded, with four flippers and a long tail. If you know your prehistoric creatures, you might be thinking: Nessie sounds like a *plesiosaur*, a giant sea reptile that lived hundreds of millions of years ago. One common theory about Nessie is that she actually *is* a plesiosaur. Other explanations for Nessie are far less dramatic. Some people think that the "mysterious" creature people have mistaken for a monster may have been nothing more than a walrus, seal, or eel.

an artist's depiction of a plesiosaur

3   How could a creature as big as a plesiosaur hide in a lake? Well, Loch Ness is a huge body of water. It's the second largest loch in Scotland, based on the surface area of its water. Loch Ness covers more than 21 square miles, and only Loch Lomond is bigger. But if you look at the volume of water, Loch Ness is the biggest. And that's because it's deep—about 755 feet at its deepest point. This single loch contains more water than all the freshwater lakes in England. In other words, it's one big place to hide.

4   Some people who believe in Nessie say that she's made her home in the region for more than a thousand years. A book written in the seventh century tells about an Irish monk who saw a giant "water beast" in the River Ness in 565 C.E. No one thought much about that story until 1933. A couple was driving home along the loch late one night. They said they were forced to stop when a giant, dragon-like creature crossed the road and slid into the water. Their story appeared in newspapers. Soon, many more people claimed to have seen the monster. The following year, in 1934, a doctor from England took a photo that became famous worldwide. The poorly lit, grainy photo shows what looks like the head and long neck of a plesiosaur-like creature rising from the water. The photo served as "proof" of the monster until 60 years later—when it was revealed to be a fake.

5   Since the 1930s, dozens of serious, scientific searches have been undertaken to find the Loch Ness monster. One early effort involved placing scouts with cameras and binoculars around the loch for five weeks. Later searches relied on the use of sonar. This method involves bouncing sound waves through the deep

waters of the loch to detect moving objects. In 2003, the famous British Broadcasting Corporation (BBC) sponsored one of the most thorough searches ever. Scientists used 600 sonar beams and satellite tracking. What did they find? Nothing of note, really. They concluded that Nessie was a myth.

6   After so many attempts, you have to wonder why people keep looking for the Loch Ness monster. It may just be that there's something exciting about the idea of mysterious creatures living so close to us, always just out of view. There's a word for such creatures: *cryptids*. It comes from a Greek word meaning "to hide." The Loch Ness monster is one of many cryptids that have captured the public imagination. Others include Bigfoot in North America, the Yeti in the Himalaya Mountains, and the chupacabra in the southwestern United States and Mexico.

7   Many animals whose existence we take for granted today might once have been considered cryptids. Komodo dragons and giant squids were once thought to be tall tales. Until 1902, people regarded stories of "giant ape-men" living in Africa as just a myth. Today, we know them as mountain gorillas. The odds of "Nessie" turning out to be real may not be quite as good. But if it were true, we'd all love it, wouldn't we? It's exciting to think that a real live monster lives deep in a loch in Scotland.

1   According to the account, what is one reason many people believe the Loch Ness monster does not exist?

A   The earliest sighting of the Loch Ness monster occurred in 565 C.E.

B   The photo taken in 1934 has been proven to be a fake.

C   Plesiosaurs, like the dinosaurs, lived hundreds of millions of years ago.

D   Sonar beams and satellite tracking found no evidence in the loch.

Answer Form
1 Ⓐ Ⓑ Ⓒ ●
2 ● Ⓑ Ⓒ Ⓓ
3 Ⓐ Ⓑ Ⓒ Ⓓ
4 Ⓐ Ⓑ ● Ⓓ

Number Correct /4

2   Which detail provides evidence that a creature as huge as a plesiosaur could really hide in Loch Ness?

A   Loch Ness has a surface area of 21 square miles and is 755 feet deep.

B   The Loch Ness monster might actually be an ordinary walrus, seal, or eel.

C   Dozens of scientific searches of Loch Ness have been conducted.

D   The Loch Ness monster is known as a cryptid, a word whose root word means "to hide."

AT A GLANCE

Students independently read a longer informational account and answer questions in a format that provides test practice.

STEP BY STEP

- Tell students to use what they have learned about reading closely, and about making inferences that are supported by text evidence to read the passage on pages 24 and 25.

- Remind students to underline or circle important text evidence.

- Tell students to answer the questions on pages 25 and 26. For questions 1–4, they should fill in the correct circle on the Answer Form.

- When students have finished, use the Answer Analysis to discuss correct responses and the reasons for them. Have students fill in the Number Correct on the Answer Form.

ANSWER ANALYSIS

1   Choice D is correct. It explains why many people believe the Loch Ness monster does not exist. Choice A does not explain why people don't believe in the Loch Ness monster. Choice B shows that the picture was not real, but it does not show why people think the Loch Ness monster isn't real. Choice C tells about a kind of creature the Loch Ness monster might be, not why people don't believe in it. **(DOK 2)**

Theme Connection

- How do all the passages in this lesson relate to the theme of mysterious creatures?

- Which of the mysterious creatures that you read about seems the most unbelievable to you? Tell why.

2 Choice A is correct. It shows that Loch Ness is wide enough and deep enough to hide a huge creature. Choices B and D give details about the Loch Ness monster, not the size of the lake. Choice C tells about the searches of Loch Ness, not its size. *(DOK 2)*

3 Choice D is correct. The author states that cryptids have captured the public's imagination. Choice A is incorrect because the author gives evidence that Loch Ness is big enough to hide a plesiosaur. Choice B is incorrect because the author doesn't say that scientists are still trying to prove the monster doesn't exist. Choice C is not correct. The text does not state whether people ignore scientific evidence. *(DOK 2)*

4 Choice C is correct. This statement supports the conclusion that it is unlikely that the Loch Ness monster exists. Choice A states a central idea of the account but does not support either side of the argument. Choices B and D are incorrect because both support the possible existence of the monster. *(DOK 2)*

5 Sample response: Some people think that the Loch Ness monster is a plesiosaur because it is said to have a small head, a long neck, four flippers, and a broad, round body. This description matches the physical characteristics of the plesiosaur, a giant sea reptile that lived hundreds of millions of years ago. *(DOK 3)*

Part 5: Common Core Practice Lesson 3

3 Which statement is **best** supported by the account?

A It is illogical to think that a plesiosaur could still be living in Loch Ness today.

B Someday, scientists will prove that no giant creatures live in Loch Ness.

C Some people want to believe in the Loch Ness monster and ignore scientific evidence showing it does not exist.

D People have always been fascinated by the idea of strange creatures such as Bigfoot and the Loch Ness monster.

4 Despite the great interest in the Loch Ness monster, it is highly unlikely that such an animal actually exists. Which sentence from the passage **best** supports this conclusion?

A "Whether the creature really exists or not has been a matter of great debate for decades."

B "Some people who believe in Nessie say that she's made her home in the region for more than a thousand years."

C "Since the 1930s, dozens of serious, scientific searches have been undertaken to find the Loch Ness monster."

D "Many animals whose existence we take for granted today might once have been considered cryptids."

5 Some people firmly believe that the Loch Ness monster is actually a plesiosaur. Use at least **three** details from the account to explain why some people believe this.

See sample response.

☑ **Self Check** Go back and see what you can check off on the Self Check on page 2.

26 L3: Citing Evidence to Make Inferences

©Curriculum Associates, LLC Copying is not permitted.

Integrating Standards

Use these questions and tasks as opportunities to interact with "Looking for the Loch Ness Monster."

1 How is the Loch Ness monster introduced in this account? What examples are included to develop the topic? *(RI.6.3)*

The first paragraph introduces readers to the Loch Ness monster. The second paragraph develops the readers' understanding of the monster by describing it in detail. Then the text gives examples of possible sightings and the efforts to find the monster.

2 Write a brief summary of "Looking for the Loch Ness Monster." *(RI.6.2)*

Sample response: Loch Ness in Scotland is said to be home to a creature called the Loch Ness monster. Many people have claimed to have seen the monster over the years, but no scientific proof that it exists has been found.

3 What is a cryptid? How does the Greek word meaning "to hide" relate to the meaning? *(RI.6.4; L.6.4.b)*

Cryptid means "a creature that may or may not be real." The Greek word relates to this meaning because these mysterious animals supposedly hide in lakes and forests and are very rarely seen.

4 What do you think is the author's point of view about the Loch Ness monster? How is it conveyed in the text? Write a paragraph to explain your opinion. *(W.6.1)*

Sample response: The author would love for the Loch Ness monster to be real. He says, "But if it were true, we'd all love it, wouldn't we? It's exciting to think that a real live monster lives deep in a loch in Scotland."

5 Discuss in small groups: Do you think that scientists might one day find the Loch Ness monster? Why or why not? Cite evidence from the account to support your opinion. *(SL.6.1)*

Discussions will vary. Students who believe that the Loch Ness monster might one day be found might point out that Loch Ness is 755 feet deep, so it is possible scientists missed it in their earlier searches.

Writing Activities

Write a Story (W.6.3)

- Have students review the different mysterious creatures described in this lesson.

- Challenge them to choose one creature they read about and write a narrative about an imaginary encounter with this creature.

- Tell them to include relevant descriptive details and sensory language to convey the experience.

- Allow time for students to share their stories with the class.

Pronoun Shifts in Number and Person (L.6.1.c)

- Have students read the first paragraph on student book page 20 and identify the pronouns. (He, His)

- Share the following sentence: *Meldrum believes that some samples are hoaxes. Others interest them.* Explain that this sentence has a pronoun shift in number. Have students correct the pronoun. (*change* them *to* him)

- Have students write sentences using pronouns incorrectly. Have them switch papers with a partner and correct each other's sentences for pronoun shifts in number or person.

LISTENING ACTIVITY (SL.6.4; SL.6.6)

Listen Closely/Conduct a News Interview

- Have pairs of students use the information from "Tales of Chupacabras" to create a news interview announcing a sighting of the chupacabra.

- One student is the interviewer from a news station while the other student is the person who sighted this mysterious creature.

- Students must listen carefully to each other as they ask and answer questions. Encourage them to be creative while basing their discussion on information from the account.

DISCUSSION ACTIVITY (RI.6.9; SL.6.1)

Talk in a Group/Compare and Contrast Creatures

- Have students form small groups to compare and contrast two of the creatures they read about.

- Provide the following prompts: How are the creatures alike? How are they different? What points of view about the creatures do the authors of the accounts share?

- Appoint one member of each group to take notes. Allow 10 to 15 minutes for discussion. Then have each group share its results with the class.

MEDIA ACTIVITY (RI.6.7; SL.6.2)

Be Creative/Draw a Creature

- Remind students that the lesson is about creatures—some real, some imagined.

- Invite students to create an image of an imaginary creature. Encourage them to mix and match characteristics from all sorts of creatures—fish and reptiles and birds and mammals and insects.

- Have students exchange images of creatures and describe to each other how and where they live.

RESEARCH ACTIVITY (W.6.7; SL.6.4)

Research and Present/Give a Presentation

- Have students use "Looking for the Loch Ness Monster" to plan an oral presentation on the search for the Loch Ness monster.

- Students should produce a visual display, such as a time line of important dates in the search for the Loch Ness monster, including sightings and major searches.

- Ask students to research additional information to include, such as more information about the BBC's investigation. Students should take notes and write a brief report for their oral presentations.

Analyzing Key Ideas in a Text

LESSON OBJECTIVES

- Analyze how an author develops a key individual, event, or idea in informational text through facts, examples, and anecdotes.

- Identify the differences between facts, examples, and anecdotes in informational text.

THE LEARNING PROGRESSION

- **Grade 5:** CCLS RI.5.3 focuses on the relationship between two ideas, events, or individuals within a text.

- **Grade 6: CCLS RI.6.3 requires students to analyze the development of a major idea (event, individual, concept, etc.) in a text.**

- **Grade 7:** CCLS RI.7.3 asks students to combine what they've learned in Grades 5 and 6 to analyze *and* explore the relationship between two major ideas within a text.

PREREQUISITE SKILLS

- Identify main ideas and supporting details presented in an informational text.

- Understand how two or more individuals, events, or ideas are related.

- Support understanding with specific information from the text.

TAP STUDENTS' PRIOR KNOWLEDGE

- Tell students that they will work on a lesson about analyzing key ideas in a text. Ask students to describe what facts and supporting details are. (*Facts are statements that can be proven. Supporting details give more information about a central idea.*) Explain that authors expand and elaborate on their ideas using examples and anecdotes. Tell them that an anecdote is a brief story about a real event and is often amusing or entertaining.

- Present students with two statements: "Athletes from many different countries compete in the Olympics." "The U.S. swimmer Michael Phelps won Olympic medals in 2012." Ask students which is a key idea (*former*) and which is a detail (*latter*).

- Finally, ask students to identify the following as a fact, example, or anecdote: "I was cheering our team as I watched the 2012 Olympic swimming events on television. I cheered so loudly that my throat was sore the next day and I could barely speak." (*anecdote*) Invite students to tell their own Olympics anecdote.

- Tell students that identifying examples and anecdotes that expand on key ideas helps them better understand the key ideas and stay interested in the text.

Ready Teacher Toolbox

teacher-toolbox.com

	Prerequisite Skills	RI.6.3
Ready Lessons	✓	✓
Tools for Instruction	✓	
Interactive Tutorials		✓

CCLS Focus

RI.6.3 Analyze in detail how a key individual, event, or idea is introduced, illustrated, and elaborated in a text (eg., through examples or anecdotes).

ADDITIONAL STANDARDS: *RI.6.1, RI.6.2, RI.6.4, RI.6.6; W.6.2.a, W.6.3, W.6.4, W.6.8, W.6.11.c; SL.6.1, SL.6.1.c, SL.6.4, SL.6.5; L.6.1.b, L.6.4.a, L.6.4.b* (See page A39 for full text.)

AT A GLANCE

Students read a historical account. They learn to recognize that facts, examples, and anecdotes expand on and provide more information about the account's important idea.

STEP BY STEP

- Read the paragraph and instruction about anecdotes. Then have students read the text about lost cities. Tell students to circle the person mentioned in the text and underline the anecdote about a lost city.

- Explain that the chart's first column shows a fact about lost cities. Ask students to find this fact in the text.

- Read the chart's second column, and ask students to find where the lost city of El Dorado is mentioned in the text.

- Read the third column, and have students compare it to the text they circled and underlined. Discuss how the fact, example, and anecdote support the key idea of the search for lost cities.

- Ask students to share other articles they have read that included facts, examples, and anecdotes. Students may mention a chapter in a history textbook or a newspaper article.

- Tell students that authors include facts, examples, and anecdotes that elaborate on key ideas in order to keep readers interested in the text and to help readers better understand the key ideas.

Lesson 4   Part 1: Introduction

Analyzing Key Ideas in a Text

CCLS
RI.6.3: Analyze in detail how a key individual, event, or idea is introduced, illustrated, and elaborated in a text (e.g., through examples or anecdotes).

Theme: Legendary Places

How do you keep your friends interested when you're talking to them? You might tell them a story. An **anecdote** is a brief story about an interesting, funny, or strange event, told to entertain or to make a point. An author might use examples and anecdotes to introduce unfamiliar ideas or events in a way that helps readers better understand them.

Read the passage below. Consider the types of information it provides about lost cities.

> ### Lost Cities
>
> Lost cities are places that were once well populated but whose locations were later forgotten. In a few cases, there is physical proof that a city once existed. Other lost cities live only in stories.
>
> Did the lost city of El Dorado, ruled by a king covered in gold, really exist? In 1594, the Englishman Sir Walter Raleigh led an expedition to South America to find the mythical golden kingdom. He did not find the city, but upon his return he claimed to have done so. Stories such as Raleigh's help keep the idea of finding lost cities alive.

Now read the passage again. This time, circle the name of the person mentioned in the text, and underline the anecdote about that person.

Who was the person? What anecdote did the passage tell about them? Read the table below to see one fact, one example, and one anecdote from the passage above.

Fact	Example	Anecdote
Lost cities are places that were once well populated, but whose locations were later forgotten.	El Dorado is one example of a lost city.	Sir Walter Raleigh led an expedition to South America to find El Dorado and told people he succeeded even though he failed.

In a text, the purpose of anecdotes and examples is to help readers better understand individuals, events, or ideas. Anecdotes and examples introduce, illustrate, and elaborate on important information. They turn dry facts into lively discussions of the real world around us.

Genre Focus

Informational Texts: Historical Account

Tell students that in this lesson they will read a type of informational text called a historical account. A historical account provides information about a topic in history. A historical account often has an engaging opening and a body text that contains facts, examples, anecdotes, reasons, and descriptions. The author's purpose is to inform or explain.

Based on these characteristics, ask students to name historical textbooks or other books they have read. What were the books' topics? What facts, examples, or anecdotes were included? Students may mention books about the American Revolution.

Discuss that students should identify the account's topic when they read a historical account. Then they look for names, dates, places, and other factual details that tell more about the topic. Finally, they should distinguish anecdotes and recognize how the anecdotes add additional information and elaborate on the topic.

Explain that "Atlantis: Lost City?" tells about a legendary city that may have existed in the Atlantic Ocean. "Seven Cities of Gold" and "The Search for El Dorado" tell about the possible long-ago existence of wealthy cities in North and South America. The account "Secrets of the Lost City of Z" tells about the adventures of explorers who searched for a lost city in South America.

AT A GLANCE

Students read a historical account about the lost city of Atlantis. They identify facts and examples that elaborate on the key idea.

STEP BY STEP

- Invite volunteers to tell what they learned on the previous page about identifying a fact, an example, and an anecdote in a passage. Now they will learn how to identify facts and examples that elaborate on a key idea.

- Read aloud "Atlantis: Lost City?"

- Read the question: "What information does the author include to elaborate on the history of Atlantis?"

- Tell students you will use a Think Aloud to help answer the question.

Think Aloud: As I reread, I can look for facts about what may have happened to Atlantis. The article states that there were two theories about Atlantis. I read that one theory is that Atlantis was located off Europe in the Atlantic Ocean. An example related to this fact is that a massive earthquake devastated the island.

- Direct students to the chart. Review that it shows facts and examples from the article.

- Point out the first row of the chart and the fact given about the first theory. Read the example and discuss how it helps readers understand the first theory that an earthquake may have caused Atlantis to sink. Have students find and underline this example in the first paragraph.

Think Aloud: Now I'll reread about the second theory. The second theory is that Atlantis may have existed on the island of Thera in the Aegean Sea. The example in the text is that the island sank into the sea after a major volcanic eruption.

- Tell students to underline the sentence in the article that shows an example of what may have happened to Atlantis on the island of Thera. Have students write the example in the chart.

- Finally, have students answer the question at the bottom of the page. Invite volunteers to share their answers with the class.

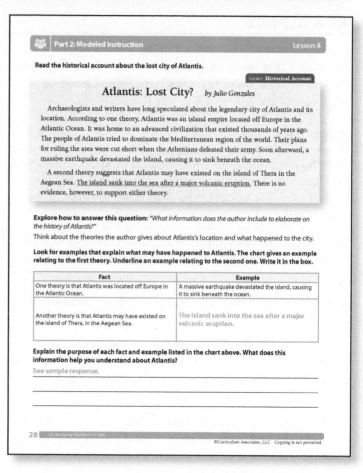

Tier Two Vocabulary: *Speculated*

- Guide students to the word *speculated* in the first sentence. Ask students to tell what *speculated* means in this sentence. Guide them to point out context clues that help them understand this meaning. (*"to make a guess"; the clues "legendary" and "according to one theory" help me know*) **(RI.6.4; L.6.4.a)**

- As needed, explain that the Latin root *spec* means "look." Discuss other words with the root: *spectator, inspect, spectacle.* **(L.6.4.b)**

AT A GLANCE

Students read about the Seven Cities of Gold. They answer a multiple-choice question and analyze how an anecdote helped them select the correct answer.

STEP BY STEP

- Tell students that they will read an article about a place said to have cities of gold.

- Remind students that good readers look for details that tell more about the key idea. Close Reading will help students identify Coronado's reaction upon reaching Cibola. The Hint will help them understand Coronado's feelings when he reaches the place Niza told him about.

- Have students read the article and underline the sentence that tells Coronado's feelings, as directed by Close Reading.

- Ask volunteers to share the sentence they underlined. Discuss how the sentence shows Coronado's feelings. If necessary, ask: How do people's expectations relate to their feelings? Why do you think Coronado was disappointed?

- Emphasize the importance of considering each answer choice to a multiple-choice question and eliminating those that are obviously incorrect.

ANSWER ANALYSIS

Choice A is incorrect. The sentence tells about Niza's stories, not how Coronado is affected by them.

Choice B is correct. It correctly tells Coronado's feelings upon reaching the place told in Niza's stories.

Choice C is incorrect. The sentence describes what Niza told about in his stories, not how the stories affected Coronado.

Choice D is incorrect. Although the sentence describes how Coronado sets out for Cibola based on information in Niza's stories, it does not describe Coronado's feelings.

ERROR ALERT: Students who did not choose B may have thought the question asked about Niza's stories or Coronado's actions. Point out the phrase in the question *how Coronado is affected* and explain that only B gives an example of Coronado's feelings.

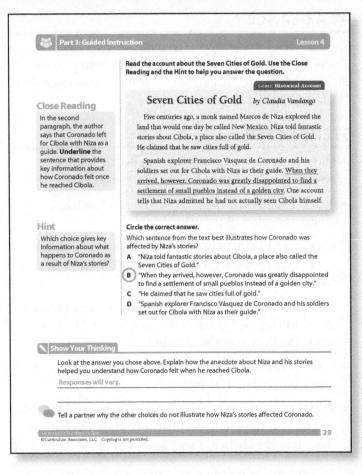

Read the account about the Seven Cities of Gold. Use the Close Reading and the Hint to help you answer the question.

Genre: Historical Account

Seven Cities of Gold *by Claudia Vandango*

Five centuries ago, a monk named Marcos de Niza explored the land that would one day be called New Mexico. Niza told fantastic stories about Cibola, a place also called the Seven Cities of Gold. He claimed that he saw cities full of gold.

Spanish explorer Francisco Vásquez de Coronado and his soldiers set out for Cibola with Niza as a guide. When they arrived, however, Coronado was greatly disappointed to find a settlement of small pueblos instead of a golden city. One account tells that Niza admitted he had not actually seen Cibola himself.

Close Reading

In the second paragraph, the author says that Coronado left for Cibola with Niza as a guide. **Underline** the sentence that provides key information about how Coronado felt once he reached Cibola.

Hint

Which choice gives key information about what happens to Coronado as a result of Niza's stories?

Circle the correct answer.

Which sentence from the text best illustrates how Coronado was affected by Niza's stories?

A "Niza told fantastic stories about Cibola, a place also called the Seven Cities of Gold."

B "When they arrived, however, Coronado was greatly disappointed to find a settlement of small pueblos instead of a golden city."

C "He claimed that he saw cities full of gold."

D "Spanish explorer Francisco Vásquez de Coronado and his soldiers set out for Cibola with Niza as their guide."

✎ **Show Your Thinking**

Look at the answer you chose above. Explain how the anecdote about Niza and his stories helped you understand how Coronado felt when he reached Cibola.

Responses will vary.

💬 Tell a partner why the other choices do not illustrate how Niza's stories affected Coronado.

L4: Analyzing Key Ideas in a Text
©Curriculum Associates, LLC Copying is not permitted. **29**

Tier Two Vocabulary: *Account*

- Direct students to the word *account* in the last sentence of the passage. Review that some words have more than one meaning. Remind them to use context clues in nearby words and phrases to figure out which meaning is intended. Ask them what *account* means in this context (*"a story about an event"*). **(RI.6.4; L.6.4.a)**

- Explain that the noun *account* can also mean "a financial or business record." Have students use the word *account* in a sentence using this meaning.

AT A GLANCE

Students read a passage twice about searches for the city of El Dorado. After the first reading, you will ask three questions to check your students' comprehension of the passage.

STEP BY STEP

- Have students read the passage silently without referring to the Study Buddy or Close Reading text.

- Ask the following questions to ensure student comprehension of the text:

  How did El Dorado get its name? (*The place was said to be ruled by a chief "covered in gold," which is El Dorado in Spanish.*)

  What did Gonzalo Pizarro do when he heard stories about El Dorado? (*He led an expedition to find this place, but he was not successful.*)

  What real place might El Dorado be based on? (*an area near Bogota, Colombia*)

- Then ask students to reread the first three paragraphs and look at the Study Buddy think aloud. What does the Study Buddy help them think about?

Tip: The Study Buddy helps students identify an important sentence in the anecdote. This helps them better understand the key idea that several explorers searched for the fabled city. Ask students to whose *disappointment*, *wasted years*, and *death* the sentence refers.

- Have students read the rest of the historical article. Tell them to follow the directions in the Close Reading.

Tip: Reinforce how thinking about facts and examples helps students better understand key ideas in a text. In Close Reading, students look for a fact about a Muisca ritual. Identifying the fact helps them relate it to the key idea of how the stories about El Dorado began. They also look for examples of actual riches in mythical El Dorado and the real Muisca region. These examples help students to compare and contrast these places.

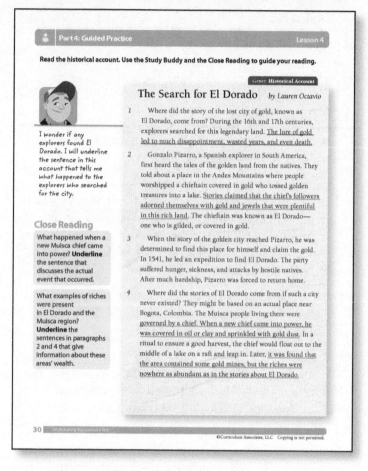

Part 4: Guided Practice Lesson 4

Read the historical account. Use the Study Buddy and the Close Reading to guide your reading.

Genre: Historical Account

The Search for El Dorado by Lauren Octavio

1   Where did the story of the lost city of gold, known as El Dorado, come from? During the 16th and 17th centuries, explorers searched for this legendary land. The lure of gold led to much disappointment, wasted years, and even death.

2   Gonzalo Pizarro, a Spanish explorer in South America, first heard the tales of the golden land from the natives. They told about a place in the Andes Mountains where people worshipped a chieftain covered in gold who tossed golden treasures into a lake. Stories claimed that the chief's followers adorned themselves with gold and jewels that were plentiful in this rich land. The chieftain was known as El Dorado— one who is gilded, or covered in gold.

3   When the story of the golden city reached Pizarro, he was determined to find this place for himself and claim the gold. In 1541, he led an expedition to find El Dorado. The party suffered hunger, sickness, and attacks by hostile natives. After much hardship, Pizarro was forced to return home.

4   Where did the stories of El Dorado come from if such a city never existed? They might be based on an actual place near Bogota, Colombia. The Muisca people living there were governed by a chief. When a new chief came into power, he was covered in oil or clay and sprinkled with gold dust. In a ritual to ensure a good harvest, the chief would float out to the middle of a lake on a raft and leap in. Later, it was found that the area contained some gold mines, but the riches were nowhere as abundant as in the stories about El Dorado.

I wonder if any explorers found El Dorado. I will underline the sentence in this account that tells me what happened to the explorers who searched for the city.

Close Reading

What happened when a new Muisca chief came into power? **Underline** the sentence that discusses the actual event that occurred.

What examples of riches were present in El Dorado and the Muisca region? **Underline** the sentences in paragraphs 2 and 4 that give information about these areas' wealth.

30   L4: Analyzing Key Ideas in a Text   ©Curriculum Associates, LLC   Copying is not permitted.

- Finally, have students answer the questions on page 31. Use the Answer Analysis to discuss correct and incorrect responses.

ELL Support: Homophones

- Explain that homophones are words that sound alike but have different spellings and meanings. Point out the homophone *tales* in paragraph 2. Write the word *tails* on the board.

- Pronounce the two words and discuss their meanings. (*"stories" and "animals' body part"*)

- To reinforce understanding of homophones, say the word *knew*. Some students may hear *new*. Work with students to define the word they heard. Write students' definitions on the board; then write the words next to them. For example, if students say "understood," write *knew* next to it. Repeat for the other word (*new:* "latest"). Explain that the words sound alike but have different meanings.

STEP BY STEP

- Have students read questions 1–3, using the Hints to help them answer the questions.

Tip: If students have trouble answering question 1, have them refer to the underlined text in the account. Ask students what the author means by *the lure of gold*.

- Discuss with students the Answer Analysis below.

ANSWER ANALYSIS

1   The correct choice is C. It tells what happened to explorers who tried to find El Dorado. Choice A tells how Pizarro felt at the beginning of his search. Choice B describes only the stories about El Dorado. Choice D does not relate to the idea of many explorers searching for El Dorado.

2   Choice B is correct. A chief sprinkled with gold dust may have led people to think El Dorado had a golden chief. Choice A describes people telling a story about El Dorado. It does not elaborate on how those hearing the story may have come to believe in a golden chief. Choice C tells a fact about Pizarro. Choice D tells the origin of the name El Dorado but not why some thought it had a golden chief.

3   Sample response: Stories about El Dorado said, "The chieftain's followers adorned themselves with gold and jewels that were plentiful in this rich land." No evidence in the text suggests that the Muisca people were richly clad. The gold dust covering the Muisca chief may have floated in the water during the harvest ritual, but the chief did not toss golden treasures into a lake, as claimed in the stories about El Dorado. The area where the Muisca people lived "contained some gold mines, but the riches were nowhere as abundant as in the stories about El Dorado."

RETEACHING

Use a chart to verify the answer to question 1. Draw the chart below, leaving the boxes blank. Fill in the boxes with students. Sample responses are provided.

Fact	Example	Anecdote
Many explorers have searched for the legendary land of El Dorado.	Some explorers did not survive their long, unsuccessful searches for El Dorado.	"Even Pizarro's expedition had to give up their search for El Dorado."

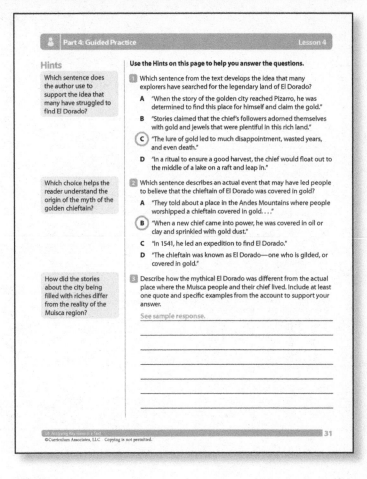

Part 4: Guided Practice   Lesson 4

Hints

Use the Hints on this page to help you answer the questions.

Which sentence does the author use to support the idea that many have struggled to find El Dorado?

1   Which sentence from the text develops the idea that many explorers have searched for the legendary land of El Dorado?

A   "When the story of the golden city reached Pizarro, he was determined to find this place for himself and claim the gold."

B   "Stories claimed that the chief's followers adorned themselves with gold and jewels that were plentiful in this rich land."

C   "The lure of gold led to much disappointment, wasted years, and even death."

D   "In a ritual to ensure a good harvest, the chief would float out to the middle of a lake on a raft and leap in."

Which choice helps the reader understand the origin of the myth of the golden chieftain?

2   Which sentence describes an actual event that may have led people to believe that the chieftain of El Dorado was covered in gold?

A   "They told about a place in the Andes Mountains where people worshipped a chieftain covered in gold. . . ."

B   "When a new chief came into power, he was covered in oil or clay and sprinkled with gold dust."

C   "In 1541, he led an expedition to find El Dorado."

D   "The chieftain was known as El Dorado—one who is gilded, or covered in gold."

How did the stories about the city being filled with riches differ from the reality of the Muisca region?

3   Describe how the mythical El Dorado was different from the actual place where the Muisca people and their chief lived. Include at least one quote and specific examples from the account to support your answer.

See sample response.

_____

_____

_____

_____

_____

_____

_____

L4: Analyzing Key Ideas in a Text   31
©Curriculum Associates, LLC   Copying is not permitted.

Integrating Standards

Use these questions to further students' understanding of "The Search for El Dorado."

1   When did explorers search for the lost city of El Dorado? Cite evidence from the text in your response. **(RI.6.1)**

"During the 16th and 17th centuries, explorers searched for this legendary land."

2   What is the central idea of this text? How is it explained through specific details? **(RI.6.2)**

This text is about the search and possible explanations of the legend of the golden city of El Dorado that had a chieftain covered in gold. Pizarro was an explorer who led an expedition to find this place, but he failed. The legend of El Dorado may have been based on the Muisca people who sprinkled their chief with gold dust.

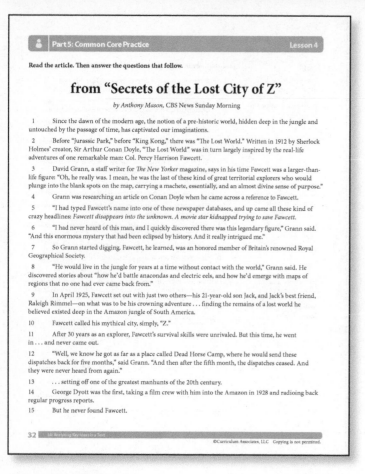

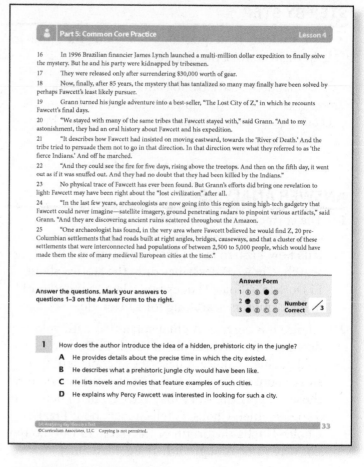

AT A GLANCE

Students independently read a longer article and answer questions in a format that provides test practice.

STEP BY STEP

- Tell students to use what they have learned about reading closely and analyzing how key ideas are elaborated on to read the passage on pages 32–33.

- Remind students to underline or circle important points.

- Tell students to answer the questions on pages 33–34. For questions 1–3, they should fill in the correct circle on the Answer Form.

- When students have finished, use the Answer Analysis to discuss correct responses and the reasons for them. Have students fill in the Number Correct on the Answer Form.

ANSWER ANALYSIS

1   Choice C is correct. The second paragraph gives examples of movies and books about lost cities. Choice A is not supported by the text. Choice B is incorrect. It describes how the author sums up the article, not introduces it. Choice D is incorrect. The author does not explain why Fawcett is fascinated with prehistoric lost cities. **(DOK 2)**

Theme Connection

- How do all the accounts in this lesson relate to the theme of legendary places?

- Based on what you have read in the accounts, what similarities and differences are there between these legendary places?

2 Choice A is correct. Describing the time, money, and effort spent in looking for Fawcett supports the claim that the search for him was a great manhunt. Although the text does discuss Choices B and C, neither choice directly supports the idea that the search for Fawcett was a great manhunt. Choice D is untrue; archaeologists are using the high-tech gadgetry to map the area, not to find Fawcett. **(DOK 2)**

3 Choice A is correct. Lynch's search shows that he was one of several people who searched for Fawcett. Choice B is incorrect. The author's purpose is not to compare and contrast the explorers' abilities. Choice C is incorrect. There is no evidence that the tribesmen who kidnapped Lynch killed Fawcett. Choice D is incorrect. Lynch's search is not connected to Fawcett's theories. **(DOK 3)**

4 Sample response: The author describes important accomplishments of Fawcett, such as how he came back from journeys with maps of regions no one had ever been to before. He also describes many stories of Fawcett's daring and courage, such as how he battled anacondas or electric eels. These details strongly support the author's statement that Fawcett was "a remarkable man." **(DOK 3)**

---

2 How does the author support the claim that the search for Fawcett was "one of the greatest manhunts of the 20th century"?

  A by discussing the time, money, and effort put into finding Fawcett

  B by describing the mystery surrounding Fawcett's disappearance

  C by telling how researcher David Grann went looking for Fawcett

  D by describing the high-tech gadgetry used to find Fawcett

3 Why does the author include the anecdote about James Lynch's search for Fawcett?

  A It illustrates the idea that many people tried unsuccessfully to find Fawcett.

  B It proves that David Grann is a more capable explorer than James Lynch.

  C It shows that the tribesmen who kidnapped Lynch also killed Fawcett.

  D It suggests that Fawcett's theories about a "lost civilization" were correct.

4 The author of the passage thinks that Percy Fawcett was "a remarkable man." Write a short paragraph explaining how the text supports the idea that Fawcett was a remarkable man. Use at least **two** details from the text in your response.

See sample response.

✓ Self Check Go back and see what you can check off on the Self Check on page 2.

34 | L4: Analyzing Key Ideas in a Text ©Curriculum Associates, LLC Copying is not permitted.

Integrating Standards

Use these questions and tasks as opportunities to interact with "Secrets of the Lost City of Z."

1 What experience does Grann use as the basis for his book *The Lost City of Z*? Cite evidence from the text. **(RI.6.1)**

Grann uses his own experience of traveling to the same jungle as Fawcett traveled to. Grann writes, "We stayed with many of the same tribes that Fawcett stayed with."

2 Cite two details from the text that support the idea that Grann did not initially intend to write about Fawcett. **(RI.6.2)**

"Grann was researching an article on Conan Doyle when he came across a reference to Fawcett." "I had never heard of this man …"

3 The last paragraph describes "a cluster of these settlements that were interconnected." What does *interconnected* mean? **(RI.6.4; L.6.4.b)**

The prefix inter *means "between," so interconnected means "having connections between things."*

4 Explain who the author is referring to when he mentions Fawcett's "least likely pursuer." **(RI.6.1)**

The author is referring to Grann because Grann may have solved the mystery of Fawcett's disappearance despite the fact that the author mentioned previously that Grann did not set out to write about Fawcett.

5 Discuss as a class: Have students take turns reading sections of the article and summarizing each section's key points. **(RI.6.2, SL.6.1)**

Discussions will vary. Encourage students to use their own words in their summaries.

Writing Activities

Reader's Theater (W.6.3)

- Have students consider what they learned about Colonel Percy Fawcett's life and adventures in "Secrets of the Lost City of Z."

- Challenge students to write a reader's theater script based on one or more events in Fawcett's life. Explain that a reader's theater is like a play. Tell students to use specific details from events described in the article "Secrets of the Lost City of Z" in their scripts and include what they think Fawcett might have said.

- Allow time for students to share their scripts with the class.

Intensive Pronouns (L.6.1.b)

- Have students reread the last sentence in "Seven Cities of Gold." Ask students to identify the pronouns in the sentence (*he, himself*). Point out the intensive pronoun *himself*. Explain that intensive pronouns are used to place extra emphasis on the subject of a sentence.

- Have students identify the subject of the sentence that *himself* refers to (*Niza*). Ask students to list other intensive pronouns (*myself, yourself, itself, ourselves, yourselves, themselves*). Have students write three sentences using three different intensive pronouns.

LISTENING ACTIVITY (SL.6.1.c)

Listen Closely/Pose a Question

- Have one student read aloud "Atlantis: Lost City?" while the other students listen closely.

- Then have each student pose a question they have about the information in the account.

- Encourage students to pose basic questions, as well as more complex questions, such as "What similarities are there between the two theories about Atlantis?" Have students listen carefully to one another's questions and take turns responding.

DISCUSSION ACTIVITY (SL.6.1)

What's Your Perspective?

- After rereading "The Search for El Dorado," have students discuss in small groups how Pizarro's quest was influenced by the tales he heard.

- Students can paraphrase sections of text to support their point of view.

- Have students picture themselves in Pizarro's place and describe how they would feel and act.

- Have students appoint a group leader, choose one student's perspective from the group, and report to the class.

MEDIA ACTIVITY (RI.6.2; W.6.2.a; W.6.4)

Be Creative/Make a Book Cover and Flap

- Invite students to create a book cover and flap for "Secrets of the Lost City of Z." Have them create their own drawings or collages for the cover. Tell them to incorporate details that illustrate the main idea of the book.

- Tell students to write copy for the cover flap that includes a brief summary of the book.

RESEARCH ACTIVITY (W.6.8; SL.6.4; SL.6.5)

Write a Report/Create a Display

- Have students use the information in "Secrets of the Lost City of Z" to write a report on the lost city of Z.

- Have students create a visual display, such as a map, to accompany the report.

- Students should research additional information to include, such as more details about Grann or Fawcett, as well as create a bibliography containing valid sources that they used to write their report.

- Students should read their report for the class.

SCORING GUIDE AND ANSWER ANALYSIS

Informational Passage Answer Analysis

1 Ⓐ Ⓑ Ⓒ ●   4 Ⓐ Ⓑ ● Ⓓ

2A Ⓐ ● Ⓒ Ⓓ   5 ● Ⓑ Ⓒ Ⓓ

3 Ⓐ ● Ⓒ Ⓓ   6 Ⓐ ● Ⓒ Ⓓ

1 Choice D is correct. It supports the idea that the discovery of X-rays improved people's health. If doctors use X-rays to examine broken bones, they are better able to treat injuries.

Choice A is incorrect. It supports the idea that the new discovery was surprising and unfamiliar to Röntgen, not that X-rays may improve health. Choice B gives more general details about X-rays and Röntgen's findings but doesn't show how X-rays have improved health. Choice C does not support the idea that X-rays improved health. It gives a detail about Röntgen and his discovery. *(RI.6.1; DOK 2)*

2 **Part A:** Choice B is correct. Fleming was surprised to discover the penicillin had killed the bacteria. Choices A and C are incorrect because, although Fleming was working on medical treatments, the penicillin mold was not part of his work. Choice D is incorrect because if he had known this, he would not have been surprised. *(RI.6.1; DOK 3)*

Part B: The first and fourth quotations are the best evidence that Alexander Fleming did not intend or expect penicillin to be an effective antibiotic. None of the other choices support the correct answer to Part A. *(RI.6.1; DOK 3)*

3 Choice B is correct. This sentence supports the idea that Goodyear was a dedicated scientist who kept improving his work. It shows that he was not satisfied until he got it right.

Choice A is incorrect. It introduces Goodyear and explains why he is included in this passage. Choice C gives a detail about how Goodyear accidentally discovered rubber vulcanization. Choice D gives a historical detail about how Goodyear handled his discovery, not support for the idea that he was a dedicated scientist. *(RI.6.1, RI.6.3; DOK 2)*

4 Choice C is correct. It shows a match between a central idea and a supporting detail. The idea that accidental discoveries help people is an important idea in the passage. A detail such as the uses of penicillin demonstrates that accidental discoveries can be helpful to people.

Choice A is incorrect. The detail given is not related to these experiments. Choice B is incorrect. It is true that some discoveries are not understood at first. However, the detail about artificial sweetener and coal tar does not illustrate this idea. Choice D does not demonstrate a central idea matched with a supporting detail. The idea that dedicated scientists may make great accidental discoveries is important, but the detail about petri dishes does not help prove it. *(RI.6.2; DOK 3)*

5 Choice A is correct. This sentence explains how the author illustrates the idea that vulcanized rubber is still in use today. In paragraph 8, the author lists examples of modern uses for vulcanized rubber.

Choice B is incorrect. The author tells many stories in this passage, but does not use a story to illustrate the idea that vulcanized rubber is still in use today. Choice C is incorrect. The author does compare the two forms of rubber, but she does not do so to show how vulcanized rubber continues to be used. Choice D is incorrect. This sentence does not explain how the author illustrates the idea that vulcanized rubber is still in use today. The author notes that vulcanized rubber was patented in the year 1844, but this fact does not show the material's continued importance. *(RI.6.3; DOK 2)*

6 Choice B is correct. It is the only one that touches on all the major ideas: the role of accident in scientific discovery, the stories of three famous "accidental" discoveries, and the importance of experience in making these discoveries.

Choice A gives too much emphasis to the items mentioned in the article's lead, downplaying the discoveries that make up most of the article. Choice C is incorrect because it summarizes only one section of the article. Choice D gets off to a good start, but it fails to mention all three of the discoveries prominently featured in the article. *(RI.6.2; DOK 2)*

SAMPLE RESPONSES

Short Response (See 2-Point Rubric—Short Response on page A46 for scoring.)

7   The author illustrates key ideas of the passage by giving short histories of important accidental discoveries. For example, when telling about the discovery of X-rays, the author tells the story of Wilhelm Röntgen's experiments and his first pictures using X-rays. To illustrate the discovery of penicillin, the author tells the story of Alexander Fleming's studies of bacteria and how he found a mold that could help people. The author gives more stories to explain the discoveries of other items, such as microwaves and vulcanized rubber. *(RI.6.3; DOK 3)*

8

Central idea	X-rays were another accidental discovery.
Supporting detail	Röntgen was performing experiments by passing an electric current through gas.
Supporting detail	Every time the gas sparked, a plate treated with a special chemical lit up.
Example used to make a point	Röngten's image of his wife's hand showed that X-rays do not pass through bone.

(RI.6.2; DOK 3)

Performance Task (See New York State Grade 6–8 Expository Writing Evaluation Rubric on pages A47 and A48 for scoring.)

9   In this passage, the author demonstrates that many great discoveries came about by accident. Some of these discoveries were complete accidents. The author lists a few stories about discoveries that were made while people were doing other things. For example, a scientist discovered microwaves when the chocolate bar in his pocket melted. Another scientist who was working with coal tar discovered that it could be used to make an artificial sweetener.

However, the author points out that for the most part, "accidental discoveries" are the result of a dedicated scientist working hard to learn and make new things. The author gives several examples of how this happens. For example, the author tells about Charles Goodyear, who accidentally discovered vulcanized rubber. She points out that Goodyear actually made this discovery while he was trying to figure out the best way to prepare and use rubber. Another example used by the author is Alexander Fleming. While he discovered penicillin accidentally, he did so while he was studying bacteria to find new kinds of medicine.

The author seems to feel that both types of discoveries are important. She tells some of the reasons the different discoveries are helpful to people. For example, some uses of vulcanized rubber include tires, bowling balls, and the soles of shoes. However, the author also makes it clear that she believes that important "accidental discoveries" are more likely to happen to hard-working scientists than to just anyone. She points out that they are already working with the materials so they can understand and apply what they learn from results they did not expect. *(RI.6.3; DOK 3)*

Citing Evidence to Make Inferences

LESSON OBJECTIVES

- Use explicitly stated details in a literary text about a character (e.g., appearance, actions, inner thoughts, spoken words) along with background knowledge to make inferences about that character, such as his/her feelings, attitude, personality, relationships, and inner conflicts.

THE LEARNING PROGRESSION

- **Grade 5:** CCLS RL.5.1 requires students to quote accurately from a text when explaining what the text says explicitly and when drawing inferences.

- **Grade 6: CCLS RL.6.1 builds on the Grade 5 standard by having students cite textual evidence to support analysis of what the text says explicitly as well as inferences drawn from the text.**

- **Grade 7:** CCLS RL.7.1 requires students to cite several pieces of textual evidence to support an inference. Inferences can be about characters, setting, and plot events.

PREREQUISITE SKILLS

- Quote accurately from a text.

- Identify and describe characters, setting, plot, and sequence of events in a story.

- Use context clues and supporting details to draw conclusions and make inferences.

TAP STUDENTS' PRIOR KNOWLEDGE

- Tell students they will be working on a lesson about citing evidence to make inferences. Remind students that an inference is an educated guess. Ask students what evidence is. (*pieces of information from the text*)

- Ask students what they would think if they smelled something sweet coming from the kitchen. (*Someone is baking cookies or a cake.*) Point out that no one directly told them that someone was baking. They used clues and their own experience to figure it out.

- Then have students describe what they do when they need to figure something out in a story that the author does not tell them directly. (*Use story clues and think about what you already know.*)

- Offer students the following scenario: suppose they read a story in which the character is frowning as she rushes around, opening drawers and looking under the bed. Ask them to tell what they can infer about the character based on her actions. (*She probably feels worried and frantic about trying to find something that is missing.*) Point out that story details provide evidence for the character's feelings.

- Ask volunteers to explain why it is important to make inferences while reading. Guide students to understand that sometimes authors don't give all the information in a story directly. It is up to readers to use information from the story and their own knowledge to make inferences.

Ready *Teacher Toolbox* · *teacher-toolbox.com*

	Prerequisite Skills	RL.6.1
Ready Lessons	✓	✓
Tools for Instruction		✓ ✓
Interactive Tutorials		✓

CCLS Focus

RL.6.1 Cite textual evidence to support analysis of what the text says explicitly as well as inferences drawn from the text.

ADDITIONAL STANDARDS: **RL.6.2, RL.6.3, RL.6.4, RL.6.5, RL.6.7, RL.6.9; W.6.1, W.6.2, W.6.4, W.6.8, W.6.11.a; SL.6.1, SL.6.2, SL.6.4; L.6.1.d, L.6.4.a, L.6.4.b, L.6.4.c, L.6.5.a** (*See page A39 for full text.*)

AT A GLANCE

By studying a fictional passage, students practice making an inference based on text details and their prior knowledge.

STEP BY STEP

- Remind students that an *inference* is a reasonable guess based on details in a picture or text about something that is not shown or stated explicitly. Clues and facts in the text provide evidence to help them make and support that inference.

- Read the passage. Ask students to think of themselves as detectives. Explain that the narrator does not directly say that he has just had a bad recital experience, but he gives plenty of clues.

- Explain to students that the chart will help them organize and analyze textual details and their prior knowledge to support a logical inference.

- Have students read the first column. It makes a statement about human behavior that students can apply to their reading of the story.

- Read the second column. Have students add details that show how the narrator feels and what he has just experienced, comparing these with what they underlined in the passage.

- Read the third column. Discuss how students' knowledge of how people typically feel in certain situations helped them double-check the inference about what has happened to the narrator.

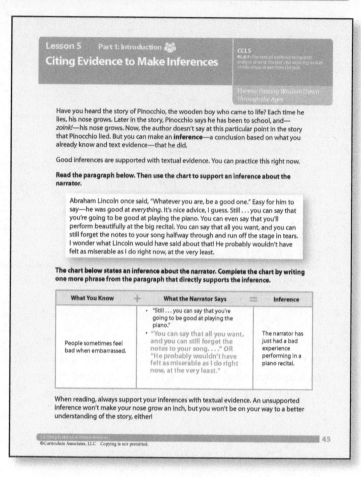

- Finally, review the entire strategy of making and supporting an inference, and discuss why the inference in the last column is logical.

Genre Focus

Literary Texts: Myth

Explain to students that, in this lesson, they will read two myths. A myth is a fictional story, the purpose of which is often to explain something about human behavior or the natural world.

Common characteristics of myths include the following:

- They teach a lesson or explain the natural world.

- The characters are gods, goddesses, or godlike beings with extraordinary powers.

- The characters can make impossible things happen.

- Gods and goddesses often appear in disguises.

- Good is rewarded and evil is punished.

Myths are closely tied to the beliefs and ideals of the particular culture from which they came. The hero of a myth often possesses the exemplary traits that are most valued by that culture.

Have students describe myths they have read or heard. Students might already be familiar with characters from Greek mythology, such as Athena, Poseidon, and Zeus. Familiar characters from Roman mythology include Cupid and Hercules. Point out that many of the planets in our solar system are named after Roman mythological characters.

AT A GLANCE

Students read a myth about Athena and Arachne. They then make and support an inference about Athena.

STEP BY STEP

- Invite volunteers to tell what they learned on the previous page about making inferences.

- Tell students that in this lesson they will make other inferences based on details they read in texts.

- Read aloud the myth "Athena, Arachne, and the Weaving Contest."

- Then read the question: "How does Athena feel about Arachne's bragging? Make an inference about how Athena feels. Support your inference with two details from the text."

- Tell students you will perform a Think Aloud to demonstrate a way of answering the question.

Think Aloud: The author doesn't state how Athena feels, so I'll need to find details in the story and use my own knowledge about why people act as they do.

- Direct students to the chart. Remind them that it represents the process of making an inference.

Think Aloud: In my experience, I know that people who expect gratitude are upset if they do not receive it.

- Show students the quote in the second column. Have them review the story to add a second quote.

Think Aloud: How can I tell that Athena is upset? In paragraph 1, I read that she expects gratitude from those she teaches to weave. How does Athena react when she hears Arachne's bragging?

- Show students the third column in the chart. Remind them to use their personal knowledge and evidence from the text to make an inference.

- Have students fill in the third column of the chart based on their own knowledge and on text evidence.

- Finally, read the final prompt: "Use details from the chart to support the inference that Athena is upset about Arachne's bragging."

Have students write down their answers. Then have them pair off to discuss these answers with one another, using text evidence and personal knowledge as support.

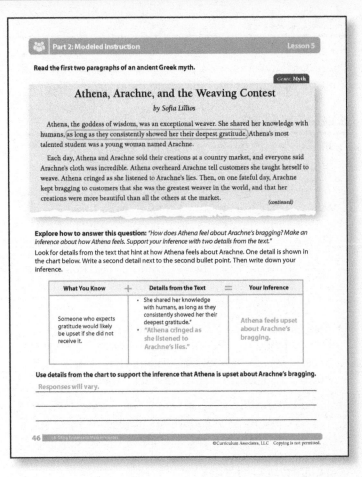

Tier Two Vocabulary: *Cringed*

- Direct students to the word *cringed* in the second paragraph. Work with students to identify context clues that help them determine the meaning of the word.

- Ask students to identify the word's ending and tell what it means. (-ed; *past tense*) Then have students look up the word in a dictionary to compare the actual meaning with the one they determined from context clues.

- Encourage students to demonstrate the action of cringing and think of situations in which they might cringe. What sounds or scenarios do they find cringe-worthy?

- Refer back to the word *cringed* in the story. Ask, "Why did Athena cringe? What did she hear?" (*She heard Arachne lie.*) **(RL.6.4; L.6.4.a, L.6.4.c)**

AT A GLANCE

Students continue reading the myth about Athena and Arachne. They answer a multiple-choice question and analyze the clues that help them make an inference.

STEP BY STEP

- Tell students they will continue reading the myth about Athena and Arachne.

- Close Reading will help students identify a detail from earlier in the story that will help them understand the events on this page. The Hint will help students recognize the order of specific events.

- Have students read the story and circle the phrase that explains Athena's one condition, as directed by Close Reading.

- Ask volunteers to share the phrases they circled. Discuss why this detail is important to the story. If necessary, ask, "Why did Athena share her knowledge? Did Arachne respect Athena's rule?"

- Then have students respond to the prompt in Show Your Thinking. Place students into pairs and encourage them to share the clues they identified.

ANSWER ANALYSIS

Choice A is incorrect. It is true that the old woman had special powers, but this is not the reason *why* she turned Arachne into a spider. It is *how* she did it.

Choice B is correct. The old woman was Athena in disguise. Because Arachne did not show thanks for Athena's help and instead took all the credit herself, she was turned into a spider as punishment.

Choice C is incorrect. The old woman was Athena in disguise. However, this was part of the plot, and it is not a reason *why* she turned Arachne into a spider.

Choice D is incorrect. This explains why the spider was an appropriate animal for Arachne, but it is not a reason why she was turned into one.

ERROR ALERT: Students who did not choose *B* might have been confused by the other answer choices, all of which are factually correct. Remind students that even though the choices are true, they don't necessarily answer the question *why*.

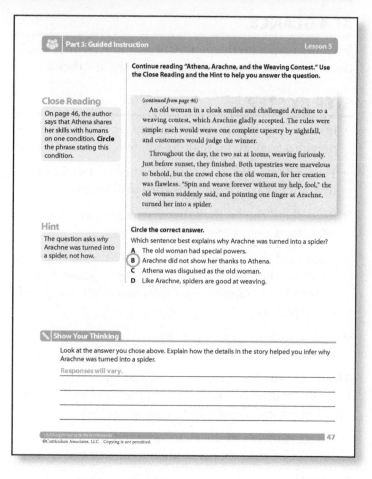

ELL Support: Suffixes

- Explain to students that many English words have suffixes. A suffix is a group of letters that is added to the end of a word to change the word's meaning.

- Direct students to the word *furiously* in paragraph 2. Help students identify the suffix (*-ly*) and the base word (*furious*). Tell students that *-ly* means "in a certain way," and it changes adjectives to adverbs. Ask students what *furiously* means. (*'in a furious way'*)

- Repeat the activity with *suddenly* in paragraph 2. (*"in a sudden way"*) **(RL.6.4; L.6.4.b)**

AT A GLANCE

Students read a Native American legend twice. After the first reading, you will ask three questions to check your students' comprehension of the passage.

STEP BY STEP

- Have students read the story silently without referring to the Study Buddy or Close Reading text.

- Ask the following questions to ensure students' comprehension of the text:

  Why does Young Man crawl to the willow tree? *(He is hot, thirsty, and desperate for shade after a long hike.)*

  Does the willow tree actually speak to Young Man? *(No, Young Man has a dream in which the tree speaks to him and helps him.)*

  What lesson does Young Man learn by the end of the story? *(He learns that he must grow older like the tree and help younger people when they feel lost and defeated. Only then can he become Wise Man.)*

- Ask students to reread the story and look at the Study Buddy think aloud. What does the Study Buddy help them think about?

Tip: The Study Buddy tells students to underline a clue that helps describe the main character. Recognizing and using context clues helps students draw conclusions, make inferences, understand new vocabulary, and fully comprehend a text.

- Have students answer the questions and follow the directions in the Close Reading.

Tip: Understanding the reasons Young Man takes a journey in the first place, and why he learns from the kindness of the willow tree, provides textual evidence that helps students understand the change in Young Man's feelings.

- Finally, have students answer the questions on page 48. Use the Answer Analysis to discuss correct and incorrect responses.

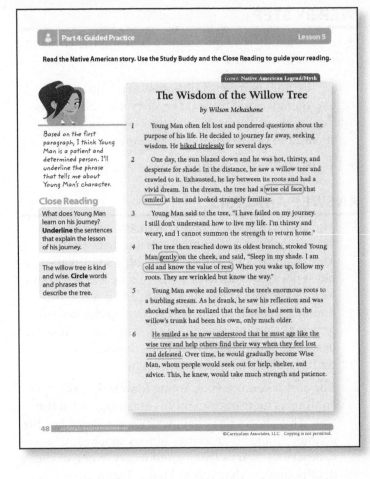

Read the Native American story. Use the Study Buddy and the Close Reading to guide your reading.

Genre: Native American Legend/Myth

The Wisdom of the Willow Tree

by Wilson Mekashone

Based on the first paragraph, I think Young Man is a patient and determined person. I'll underline the phrase that tells me about Young Man's character.

Close Reading

What does Young Man learn on his journey? **Underline** the sentences that explain the lesson of his journey.

The willow tree is kind and wise. **Circle** words and phrases that describe the tree.

1 Young Man often felt lost and pondered questions about the purpose of his life. He decided to journey far away, seeking wisdom. He <u>hiked tirelessly</u> for several days.

2 One day, the sun blazed down and he was hot, thirsty, and desperate for shade. In the distance, he saw a willow tree and crawled to it. Exhausted, he lay between its roots and had a vivid dream. In the dream, the tree had a wise old face that smiled at him and looked strangely familiar.

3 Young Man said to the tree, "I have failed on my journey. I still don't understand how to live my life. I'm thirsty and weary, and I cannot summon the strength to return home."

4 The tree then reached down its oldest branch, stroked Young Man gently on the cheek, and said, "Sleep in my shade. I am old and know the value of rest. When you wake up, follow my roots. They are wrinkled but know the way."

5 Young Man awoke and followed the tree's enormous roots to a burbling stream. As he drank, he saw his reflection and was shocked when he realized that the face he had seen in the willow's trunk had been his own, only much older.

6 He smiled as he now understood that he must age like the wise tree and help others find their way when they feel lost and defeated. Over time, he would gradually become Wise Man, whom people would seek out for help, shelter, and advice. This, he knew, would take much strength and patience.

Tier Two Vocabulary: *Pondered*

- Direct students to the word *pondered* in paragraph 1. Have students identify context clues that help them determine the meaning of the word (*"questions about the purpose of his life," "seeking wisdom"*). Then ask them what they think the word means. (*"thought about seriously"*)

- Ask students to describe times they have pondered something. What kinds of questions did they ponder?

- Then have students suggest synonyms that have nearly the same meaning as *pondered*. *(asked, examined)* **(RL.6.4; L.6.4.a)**

STEP BY STEP

- Have students read questions 1–3, using the Hints to help them answer those questions.

Tip: If students have trouble answering question 3, guide them to look back at the story and tell what is different about Young Man at the end of the story compared to the beginning of the story.

- Discuss with students the Answer Analysis below.

ANSWER ANALYSIS

1 The correct choice is B. Strength and patience are two skills Young Man must learn to become Wise Man. Choice A describes Young Man's motivation, but it does not address the lessons he learned about how to become Wise Man. Choice C is a line of dialogue spoken by the willow tree, and it doesn't help make an inference about Young Man. Choice D describes the character's actions. It doesn't deal with the skills he needs to develop.

2 The correct choice is D. Young Man is described as smiling as he thinks about his encounter with the tree. This shows he is happy. Choice A describes his actions. Choice B describes him as shocked. Choice C describes him as thirsty and weary. None of these details suggest that Young Man is happy.

3 Sample response: When Young Man approaches the willow tree, he is "hot, thirsty, and desperate for shade." He is described as "exhausted," and he says, "I have failed on my journey." The willow tree's kindness and wisdom make Young Man happy and help him understand what he must do.

RETEACHING

Use a chart to organize details from the story to answer question 1. Draw the chart below, and have students fill in the boxes. Sample responses are provided.

Clues or Facts	What You Already Know	Inference
"This, he knew, would take much strength and patience."	Strength and patience are two skills necessary to become wise.	Young Man has to develop skills if he wants to become Wise Man.

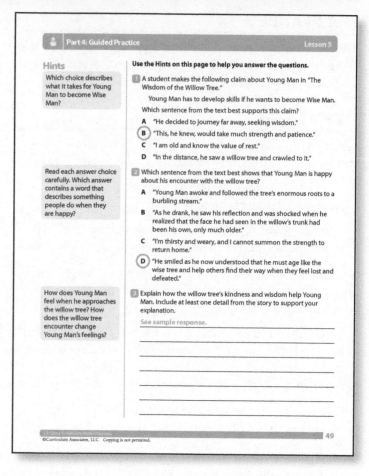

Hints

Which choice describes what it takes for Young Man to become Wise Man?

Use the Hints on this page to help you answer the questions.

1 A student makes the following claim about Young Man in "The Wisdom of the Willow Tree."

> Young Man has to develop skills if he wants to become Wise Man.

Which sentence from the text best supports this claim?

- A "He decided to journey far away, seeking wisdom."
- B "This, he knew, would take much strength and patience."
- C "I am old and know the value of rest."
- D "In the distance, he saw a willow tree and crawled to it."

Read each answer choice carefully. Which answer contains a word that describes something people do when they are happy?

2 Which sentence from the text best shows that Young Man is happy about his encounter with the willow tree?

- A "Young Man awoke and followed the tree's enormous roots to a burbling stream."
- B "As he drank, he saw his reflection and was shocked when he realized that the face he had seen in the willow's trunk had been his own, only much older."
- C "I'm thirsty and weary, and I cannot summon the strength to return home."
- D "He smiled as he now understood that he must age like the wise tree and help others find their way when they feel lost and defeated."

How does Young Man feel when he approaches the willow tree? How does the willow tree encounter change Young Man's feelings?

3 Explain how the willow tree's kindness and wisdom help Young Man. Include at least one detail from the story to support your explanation.

See sample response.

_____
_____
_____
_____
_____
_____
_____

49

Integrating Standards

Use these questions to further students' understanding of "The Wisdom of the Willow Tree."

1 What is a theme of this story? Which details support this theme? *(RL.6.2)*

The theme of this story is that true wisdom requires time, strength, and patience. Young Man realized this after he understood that the face in the tree was his own, but much older. "Over time, he would gradually become Wise Man, whom people could come to for help, shelter, and advice."

2 How does Young Man change as the plot develops and moves toward a resolution? *(RL.6.3)*

At the beginning of the story, Young Man is exhausted and feels that his life is a failure. After his dream about the willow tree, he is happy and sees hope. By the end of the story, he understands what he must do with his life to make it meaningful and help others.

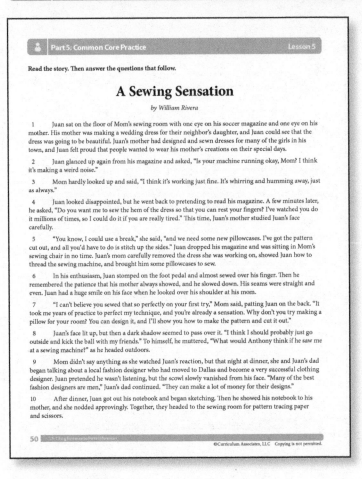

Read the story. Then answer the questions that follow.

A Sewing Sensation

by William Rivera

1   Juan sat on the floor of Mom's sewing room with one eye on his soccer magazine and one eye on his mother. His mother was making a wedding dress for their neighbor's daughter, and Juan could see that the dress was going to be beautiful. Juan's mother had designed and sewn dresses for many of the girls in his town, and Juan felt proud that people wanted to wear his mother's creations on their special days.

2   Juan glanced up again from his magazine and asked, "Is your machine running okay, Mom? I think it's making a weird noise."

3   Mom hardly looked up and said, "I think it's working just fine. It's whirring and humming away, just as always."

4   Juan looked disappointed, but he went back to pretending to read his magazine. A few minutes later, he asked, "Do you want me to sew the hem of the dress so that you can rest your fingers? I've watched you do it millions of times, so I could do it if you are really tired." This time, Juan's mother studied Juan's face carefully.

5   "You know, I could use a break," she said, "and we need some new pillowcases. I've got the pattern cut out, and all you'd have to do is stitch up the sides." Juan dropped his magazine and was sitting in Mom's sewing chair in no time. Juan's mom carefully removed the dress she was working on, showed Juan how to thread the sewing machine, and brought him some pillowcases to sew.

6   In his enthusiasm, Juan stomped on the foot pedal and almost sewed over his finger. Then he remembered the patience that his mother always showed, and he slowed down. His seams were straight and even. Juan had a huge smile on his face when he looked over his shoulder at his mom.

7   "I can't believe you sewed that so perfectly on your first try," Mom said, patting Juan on the back. "It took me years of practice to perfect my technique, and you're already a sensation. Why don't you try making a pillow for your room? You can design it, and I'll show you how to make the pattern and cut it out."

8   Juan's face lit up, but then a dark shadow seemed to pass over it. "I think I should probably just go outside and kick the ball with my friends." To himself, he muttered, "What would Anthony think if he saw me at a sewing machine?" as he headed outdoors.

9   Mom didn't say anything as she watched Juan's reaction, but that night at dinner, she and Juan's dad began talking about a local fashion designer who had moved to Dallas and become a very successful clothing designer. Juan pretended he wasn't listening, but the scowl slowly vanished from his face. "Many of the best fashion designers are men," Juan's dad continued. "They can make a lot of money for their designs."

10   After dinner, Juan got out his notebook and began sketching. Then he showed his notebook to his mother, and she nodded approvingly. Together, they headed to the sewing room for pattern tracing paper and scissors.

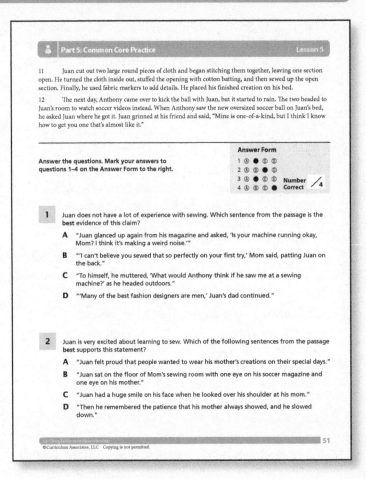

11   Juan cut out two large round pieces of cloth and began stitching them together, leaving one section open. He turned the cloth inside out, stuffed the opening with cotton batting, and then sewed up the open section. Finally, he used fabric markers to add details. He placed his finished creation on his bed.

12   The next day, Anthony came over to kick the ball with Juan, but it started to rain. The two headed to Juan's room to watch soccer videos instead. When Anthony saw the new oversized soccer ball on Juan's bed, he asked Juan where he got it. Juan grinned at his friend and said, "Mine is one-of-a-kind, but I think I know how to get you one that's almost like it."

Answer the questions. Mark your answers to questions 1–4 on the Answer Form to the right.

Answer Form

1   Ⓐ ● Ⓒ Ⓓ
2   Ⓐ Ⓑ ● Ⓓ
3   Ⓐ ● Ⓒ Ⓓ
4   Ⓐ Ⓑ Ⓒ Ⓓ   Number Correct /4

1   Juan does not have a lot of experience with sewing. Which sentence from the passage is the **best** evidence of this claim?

A   "Juan glanced up again from his magazine and asked, 'Is your machine running okay, Mom? I think it's making a weird noise.'"

B   "'I can't believe you sewed that so perfectly on your first try,' Mom said, patting Juan on the back."

C   "To himself, he muttered, 'What would Anthony think if he saw me at a sewing machine?' as he headed outdoors."

D   "'Many of the best fashion designers are men,' Juan's dad continued."

2   Juan is very excited about learning to sew. Which of the following sentences from the passage **best** supports this statement?

A   "Juan felt proud that people wanted to wear his mother's creations on their special days."

B   "Juan sat on the floor of Mom's sewing room with one eye on his soccer magazine and one eye on his mother."

C   "Juan had a huge smile on his face when he looked over his shoulder at his mom."

D   "Then he remembered the patience that his mother always showed, and he slowed down."

AT A GLANCE

Students independently read a longer story and answer questions in a format that provides test practice.

STEP BY STEP

- Tell students to use what they have learned about reading carefully and citing evidence to make inferences to read the story on pages 50 and 51.

- Remind students to underline or circle important points.

- Tell students to answer the questions on pages 51 and 52. For questions 1–4, they should fill in the correct circle on the Answer Form.

- When students have finished, use the Answer Analysis to discuss correct responses and the reasons for them. Have students fill in the Number Correct on the Answer Form.

ANSWER ANALYSIS

1   Choice B is correct. This is Juan's first time at sewing, which indicates he does not have a lot of experience at it. Choices A, C, and D do not support the inference stated in the question. **(DOK 2)**

2   Choice C is correct. Juan's smile shows his excitement about learning to sew. Choice A tells that Juan felt proud of his mother's sewing, not being excited about doing his own work. Choice B describes Juan making an effort not to show his interest in his mother's work. Choice D describes Juan getting control of his feelings, but it does not support the idea that he's excited about sewing. **(DOK 2)**

Theme Connection

- How do all the stories in this lesson relate to the theme of passing wisdom down through the ages?

- What is one fact or idea you learned about wisdom from each story in this lesson?

3 Choice B is correct. By giving Juan supplies, his mother shows her support of his interest. Choice A is Juan's mom's response to Juan's first question about the sewing machine. Her response does not encourage his interests. Choice C is incorrect because Juan chooses to go outside. Choice D is incorrect because Juan gets the notebook himself. **(DOK 2)**

4 Choice D is correct. Juan thinks, "What would Anthony think if he saw me at a sewing machine?" From this, readers can infer that Juan thinks his friends might tease him. Choice A is incorrect because the details do not suggest that Juan wants to improve his soccer skills. Choice B is incorrect because Juan is motivated by a fear that his friends would find him sewing. Choice C is incorrect because Juan thinks of his friend, not his father. **(DOK 2)**

5 Sample response: I agree that Juan seems embarrassed by his interest in sewing. Early in the story, he seems interested in his mother's sewing, but he doesn't want her to know that, so he pretends to read his soccer magazine. Later, when his mom suggests he design his own pillow, he says that maybe he should go outside and play soccer. He then wonders, "What would Anthony think if he saw me at a sewing machine?" These examples show Juan is embarrassed about his desire to sew. **(DOK 3)**

Reproduced student page:

Integrating Standards

Use these questions and tasks as opportunities to interact with "A Sewing Sensation."

1 What is a theme of this story? What details from the story support this idea? **(RL.6.2)**

The theme can be summed up as "Follow your heart." Juan enjoys sewing and is good at it, but he is afraid his friends will make fun of him. After his parents encourage him, Juan "got out his notebook and began sketching." When his friend comments on the soccer ball pillow Juan made, he is proud and happy.

2 How does the scene described in Paragraphs 10 and 11 contribute to the development of the theme? **(RL.6.5)**

This scene occurs after Juan lost his enthusiasm for sewing because of his fear about what his friends would think. His mother and father tell him that many fashion designers are men, and they encourage him to follow his heart. This scene shows Juan following his heart and making his own design.

3 What does the phrase "in no time" mean in Paragraph 5? **(RL.6.4; L.6.5.a)**

Once Juan's mother tells him he can sew, he is sitting in the sewing chair in no time. This means he moved fast and got in the chair quickly. It does not literally mean that it took no time.

4 Write a summary of this story. **(RL.6.2; W.6.2)**

Summaries will vary. Juan secretly is interested in sewing, but he thinks his friends would make fun of him. When Juan's mother lets him try sewing, he sews a pillowcase perfectly. His parents encourage his interest. Juan is proud and happy at the end.

5 Discuss in small groups: Think about what might happen next. How might Anthony react if Juan tells him that he made the soccer ball? **(SL.6.1)**

Discussions will vary. Remind students to use details from the text to support their ideas. They should also demonstrate understanding of other students' perspectives through paraphrasing their ideas.

Writing Activities

Argument (W.6.1, W.6.4)

• Have students think about "Athena, Arachne, and the Weaving Contest" and "The Wisdom of the Willow Tree." What purpose do myths and legends have in the modern world? Do they still have a use? Are they still relevant? Can people in the 21st century learn anything from ancient myths and legends?

• Ask students to write an argument that supports a claim about the role and purpose of myths and legends in the 21st century. Students can take either side of the issue, but they should support their claims with clear reasons and relevant evidence from the two selections they read in this lesson.

Vague Pronouns (L.6.1.d)

• Remind students that pronouns are words that refer to other nouns. *She*, *he*, *they*, and *it* are pronouns. Point out that pronouns should have clear antecedents, which are who or what the pronoun is naming.

• Direct students to the pronoun *she* in the second sentence of "Athena, Arachne, and the Weaving Contest." Explain that this is a clear pronoun because the previous sentence is about Athena. *She* refers to Athena.

• Have students find pronouns in this lesson's stories and identify whom or what they name. Then have students write a paragraph with two or three pronouns. Remind them to include clear antecedents.

LISTENING ACTIVITY (SL.6.2)

Listen Closely/Interpret Information

• Have small groups of students study and describe the illustration on page 45 and "The Wisdom of the Willow Tree" read aloud.

• Students must listen closely to the descriptions and group discussion. They should be able to interpret information and explain how it contributes to their understanding of the selections.

DISCUSSION ACTIVITY (RL.6.9; SL.6.1)

Talk in a Group/Compare Stories

• Ask students to compare and contrast one of this lesson's myths with "A Sewing Sensation."

• Have students form small groups to compare and contrast the characters and events. What are the similarities between the myth and story? How do the characters in each story learn something important about themselves? How is the myth different from the story?

• Appoint one member of each group to take notes. Allow 10–15 minutes for discussion, and then have each group share its results with the class.

MEDIA ACTIVITY (RL.6.7)

Be Creative/Watch or Listen to a Myth

• Direct students to audio or video presentations of "Arachne, Athena, and the Weaving Contest." Have them choose one to listen to or watch.

• Students should compare and contrast the experience of reading a myth with listening to or viewing a myth. How does what they see and hear contribute to their understanding? How does it differ from what they "see" and "hear" in their minds' eye as they read?

RESEARCH ACTIVITY (W.6.8; SL.6.4)

Research and Present/Give a Presentation

• Ask students to research how myths contribute to and influence modern literature. Encourage them to gather relevant information from multiple print and digital sources.

• Remind students to assess the credibility of each source they choose and quote or paraphrase the information they find.

• Students should present their findings orally to the class. Have them create a references list that includes all of their sources.

Describing Plot

LESSON OBJECTIVES

- Identify and analyze the elements of a story's or drama's plot structure, including the beginning (exposition), rising action, climax, falling action, and resolution.

THE LEARNING PROGRESSION

- **Grade 5:** CCLS RL.5.3 requires students to focus on comparing two or more characters, settings, or events in a story.

- **Grade 6: CCLS RL.6.3 builds on the Grade 5 standard by requiring students to focus on how the plot unfolds and how the characters respond or change.**

- **Grade 7:** CCLS RL.7.3 builds on the Grade 6 standard by focusing on how story elements interact and affect the plot.

PREREQUISITE SKILLS

- Identify a story's plot by distinguishing major events.

- Understand character traits and motivations.

- Identify how characters change throughout a story.

TAP STUDENTS' PRIOR KNOWLEDGE

- Tell students that they will work on a lesson about story plot. Ask what a plot is. (*It's what happens in a story. It's the series of events that make up a story. It includes what problems the characters face and how they try to solve them.*)

- Ask students to think about a story they have read in class. Where does the story take place? Who are the characters? What problem does the main character face or solve? Talk about what happens in the story. What is the sequence of events that moves the story forward?

- Write several story events on the board in sequential order with arrows showing the progress of one event to the next. Discuss how the plot relates to the story's characters and/or problem.

- Ask why the plot is important in a story. Elicit that without a plot, there is no story—there is just a series of random events. Recognizing the key events in a story's plot, and how the events affect the characters, will help students to better understand the text.

Ready *Teacher Toolbox*		teacher-toolbox.com
	Prerequisite Skills	RL.6.3
Ready Lessons	✓	✓
Tools for Instruction		✓
Interactive Tutorials		✓ ✓

CCLS Focus

RL.6.3 Describe how a particular story's or drama's plot unfolds in a series of episodes as well as how the characters respond or change as the plot moves toward a resolution.

ADDITIONAL STANDARDS: RL.6.1, RL.6.2, RL.6.4, RL.6.6; W.6.3, W.6.4, W.6.7, W.6.11.c; SL.6.1, SL.6.2, SL.6.4; L.6.1.b, L.6.4.a, L.6.4.c (*See page A39 for full text.*)

AT A GLANCE

Through a comic strip, students explore the idea that the plot is a series of events that make up the story. They learn how the plot unfolds with one event leading to another, building to a climax, and ultimately being resolved as the story ends.

STEP BY STEP

- Read the first paragraph, which contains definitions of *plot*, *conflict*, and *resolution*.

- Next, have students study the images and describe the episodes. Discuss how each episode contributes to the development of the next. (*When a storm at sea causes a boat to crash, the survivors are faced with the problem of how to get home, so they write a message to signal for help.*)

- Then, read the diagram with students and discuss each box. Explain the following:

  Exposition introduces the characters and setting, and sets the stage for what will happen.

  Rising action is the events in which a conflict is introduced and problems increase, leading to the *climax*, or turning point.

  Falling action is the events that lead to solving the conflict.

  Resolution is the final outcome. It tells what happens to the characters after the conflict is solved.

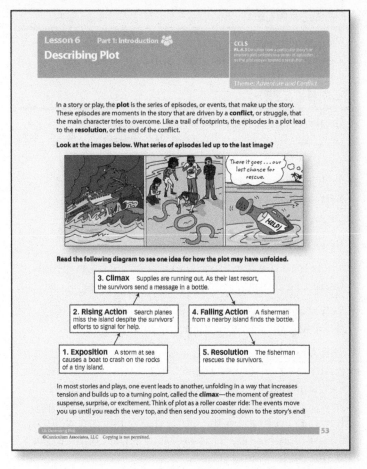

- Ask students to share the plot of a story they've read, identifying the exposition, rising action, climax, falling action, and resolution.

- Share details about the plot of a book you've read to reinforce how understanding the plot is a valuable reading strategy.

Genre Focus

Literary Texts: Historical Fiction

Tell students that in this lesson they will read literature that is historical fiction. Explain that historical fiction is a story set in the past and includes the following characteristics:

- The story may be about real people who lived in the past, real events that happened in the past, or both.

- The details are always realistic for the time period.

- Parts of the story, such as dialogue and some characters, are usually made up.

Based on these characteristics, ask students to share historical fiction they have read. During what time in history did the story take place? Who were the characters? Were they real people who lived during that time? Did the events really happen? What details reflected the time period? Students may be familiar with *Little Women* by Louisa May Alcott or *Bud, Not Buddy* by Christopher Paul Curtis.

Tell students that they will read three pieces of historical fiction in this lesson. "Alma's First Cattle Drive" tells about a girl who participates in a cattle drive more than 100 years ago, *Black Beauty* is a story set in 19th-century England, and "Lost in Time" is a play about two boys lost in a history museum.

AT A GLANCE

Students read the first part of a short story and recognize how the story's plot builds to a climax.

STEP BY STEP

- Invite volunteers to tell what they learned on the previous page about using a plot diagram to map out the plot of a story.

- Tell students that in this lesson they will read the first part of a story and complete a plot diagram to show the rising action and climax.

- Read aloud "Alma's First Cattle Drive."

- Then read the question: "How does the story's plot build to a climax?"

- Tell students you will use a Think Aloud to demonstrate a way of mapping out the plot.

Think Aloud: The first paragraph relates to the exposition. It describes the setting, a trail in a terrible storm, and introduces the characters, Alma and her father. The story says that Alma wants to prove to her father she can help on the cattle drive, but bad weather makes it challenging. This problem is the conflict that introduces the rising action.

- Direct students to the diagram and ask where they've seen this diagram before. Review that it shows the sequence of events that make up the plot.

- Have students read the text in the first two boxes.

Think Aloud: As the story continues to unfold, the cattle begin to cross the river, and Alma notices a calf getting swept up in the current. This builds on the conflict toward the climax.

- Ask students to complete the Rising Action box to describe how Alma's problem increases.

Think Aloud: Now the story is getting exciting as the rising action builds to a climax. The story says that when Alma noticed the calf, she "charged into the water and stopped her horse downstream to keep the horse from losing its footing." I think this moment of suspense is the climax.

- Have students fill in the Climax box to finish mapping out the plot. Ask volunteers to share their answers with the class.

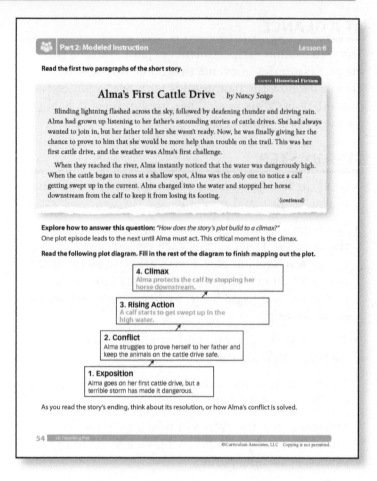

ELL Support: Multiple-Meaning Words

- Explain to students that some words have more than one meaning and are called multiple-meaning words. Tell students that they can use other words or phrases in a sentence to help them know which meaning of a multiple-meaning word is being used.

- Point out the word *driving* in the first sentence. In this sentence, does *driving* mean "operating a motor vehicle" or "falling fast and hard?" (*falling fast and hard*)

- What context clues help you figure out which meaning is intended? Guide students to see that *blinding lightning* and *deafening thunder* describe a storm and are clues that *driving* describes how the rain is falling. Explain that in this sentence *driving* is an adjective that describes the rain. The verb *driving* can mean "operating a motor vehicle." (**RL.6.4; L.6.4.a**)

AT A GLANCE

Students continue reading about Alma and the cattle drive. They answer a multiple-choice question and evaluate the story's resolution.

STEP BY STEP

- Tell students they will continue reading about Alma and the cattle drive.

- Close Reading will help students focus on the story's conflict and the falling action, or what happens that leads to solving the conflict. The Hint reminds students that the resolution tells what happens after the conflict is solved.

- Have students read the text and underline the sentence that tells the result of Alma's action, as directed by Close Reading.

- Ask volunteers to share the sentence they underlined (*the second sentence in paragraph 1*) and tell what part of the plot it describes (*falling action*).

- To help students respond to Show Your Thinking, remind them that the resolution tells what happens after the conflict is solved. Review the conflict of the story, Alma's quest to prove herself, and the events that happen after it is solved: Alma's father tips his hat to her in recognition of her good work, and she knows she has proven herself.

ANSWER ANALYSIS

Choices A and B are incorrect. They describe the falling action, not the resolution.

Choice C is incorrect. Alma's father waves to get her attention so he can acknowledge the good job she did. This is part of the resolution, but it doesn't best describe the resolution.

Choice D is correct. The story's conflict involves Alma's quest to prove herself to her father. This text tells that Alma knew she had proven herself to him.

> **ERROR ALERT:** Students who did not choose D might have confused *resolution* and *falling action*. Review that the resolution tells how the conflict is solved. The conflict was Alma's quest to prove she could be a valuable member of the team. This conflict was solved when she knew she had proven herself to her father.

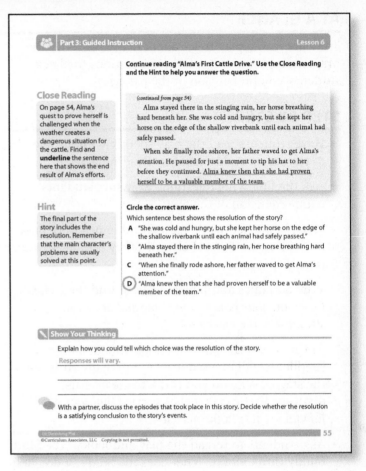

ELL Support: Homophones

- Explain that homophones are two words that sound alike but have different meanings and spellings. Call attention to the homophone *rode* in paragraph 2. Have students look at context clues to figure out the meaning (*"carried on an animal's back"*) and tell what clues helped them. (*From previous paragraphs, readers know Alma is riding on a horse.*)

- Write *road* on the board, and help students to come up with a definition (*"a path"*). Explain that *road* is a homophone of *rode*.

- Tell students they can use context clues to figure out the correct meanings of homophones. (***RL.6.4; L.6.4.a***)

AT A GLANCE

Students read a play twice about two boys. After the first reading, you will ask three questions to check students' comprehension of the passage.

STEP BY STEP

- Have students read the play silently without referring to the Study Buddy or Close Reading text.

- Ask the following questions to ensure students' comprehension of the text:

  What happened while Jamaal and James were busy looking at the T-rex skeleton? (*They became separated from their class.*)

  Why do James and Jamaal want to find their class? (*They are four hours from home and don't want to be stranded at the museum.*)

  At the end of the play, the stage directions say, "Suddenly a distressed teacher hurriedly runs onto the stage." Why do you think the teacher is distressed? (*He is probably worried that James and Jamaal are lost in the museum.*)

- Ask students to reread the play and look at the Study Buddy think aloud. What does the Study Buddy help them think about?

- Have students answer the questions and follow the directions in Close Reading.

> **Tip:** Remind students of the terms *exposition, rising action, climax, falling action,* and *resolution,* and review their definitions, if necessary. Suggest that as students reread the play, they draw brackets around sections of the text and number them 1 to 5 to correspond with these elements of plot development. Point out that being able to recognize elements of plot when reading stories or plays will add to the enjoyment and understanding of the text and also help students when they write stories or plays.

- Finally, have students answer the questions on page 57. Use the Answer Analysis to discuss correct and incorrect responses.

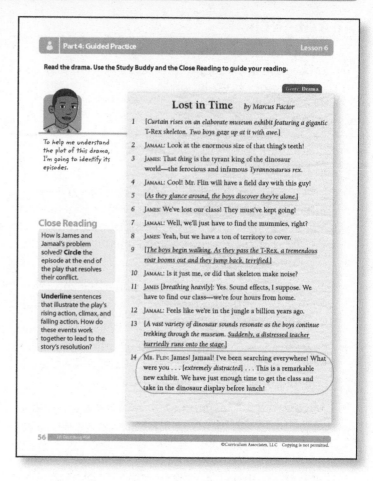

Tier Two Vocabulary: *Tremendous*

- Point out the word *tremendous* in line 9. Ask students to look at the surrounding words and concepts, and tell what *tremendous* means (*"very loud, very intense"*). Work with students to help them understand which other words in the stage directions helped them figure out the definition. (*"roar booms out"*).

- Suggest that students look up *tremendous* in a dictionary or thesaurus to find synonyms. Ask: What are some words that could be used in place of tremendous? (*Sample response: huge, enormous, colossal, gigantic*) **(RL.6.4; L.6.4.c)**

STEP BY STEP

- Have students read Questions 1–3, using the Hints to help them answer those questions.

> **Tip:** If students have trouble answering question 2, have them consider each answer choice and ask themselves what element of the plot it describes.

- Discuss with students the Answer Analysis below.

ANSWER ANALYSIS

1 The correct choice is B. The conflict is the major problem the characters face. In this play, the conflict is that Jamaal and James have lost their class. Choice A is incorrect. It relates to the exposition. Choice C is incorrect because the text never says the museum is in a city. Choice D is incorrect. The teacher's arrival is part of the resolution, and he does not express anger at the boys.

2 The correct choice is D. The resolution tells what happens after the conflict is solved. The conflict is that James and Jamaal have lost their class. This is solved when their teacher finds them. Choices A, B, and C are supported by the text, but none relate to the resolution.

3 Sample response: The author could have had the boys find their class by pretending they're in the jungle, rather than having Mr. Flin find them. This would be a good resolution because the boys would solve their own conflict and would no longer be lost.

RETEACHING

Use a plot diagram to verify the answer to question 2. Draw the diagram below, and have students fill in the boxes. Sample responses are provided.

1. Exposition	Jamaal and James get distracted by a dinosaur exhibit at the museum.
2. Rising Action	The boys get separated from their class. They plan to search.
3. Climax	The boys hear the *T-Rex* roar.
4. Falling Action	The boys are scared.
5. Resolution	Their teacher finds them.

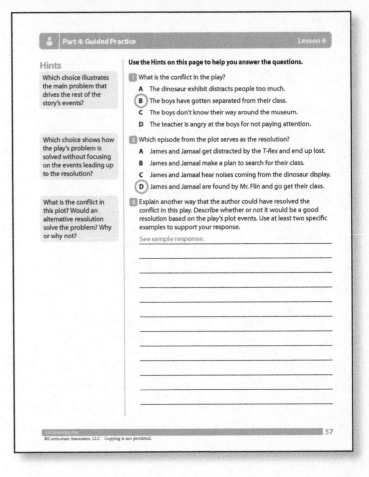

Integrating Standards

Use these questions to further students' understanding of "Lost in Time."

1 How do you know from the text that Jamaal and James are frightened and worried after they hear the T-rex roar? *(RL.6.1)*

The stage directions say that when they hear the roar, "they jump back, terrified." Also, they say James is "breathing heavily" when he says "we're four hours from home." He's probably worried about how they'll get home if they don't find their class.

2 Summarize this play in your own words. *(RL.6.3)*

Sample response: On a class trip to the museum, Jamaal and James get distracted by a T-rex exhibit and lose their class. They are frightened when they hear noises coming from the dinosaur display. Finally, their teacher finds them.

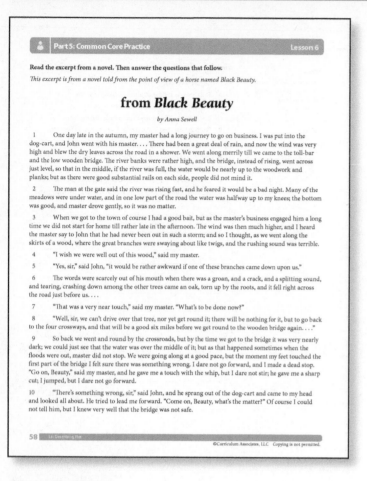

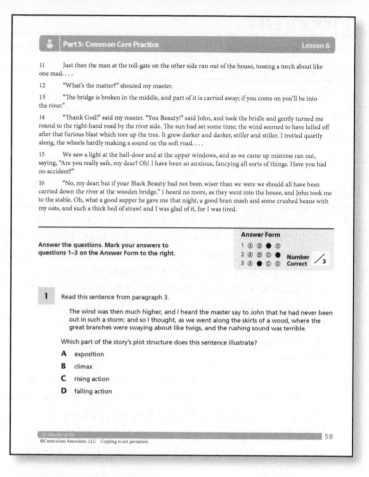

AT A GLANCE

Students independently read a longer historical fiction story and answer questions in a format that provides test practice.

STEP BY STEP

- Tell students to use what they have learned about reading carefully and recognizing plot elements to read the story on pages 58 and 59.

- Remind students to underline or circle important points.

- Tell students to answer the questions on pages 59 and 60. For questions 1–3, they should fill in the correct circle on the Answer Form.

- When students have finished, use the Answer Analysis to discuss correct responses and the reasons for them. Have students fill in the Number Correct on the Answer Form.

ANSWER ANALYSIS

1   Choice C is correct because paragraphs 2–8 make up the rising action. A problem is introduced (the river rising) and increases as the storm gets worse. Choice A is incorrect because the exposition is in paragraph 1, where the setting and characters are introduced. Choice B is incorrect. The climax, or moment of greatest tension, is illustrated in paragraphs 9 and 10, when Beauty recognizes that the bridge is not safe to cross and refuses to move forward. Choice D is incorrect because the falling action happens in paragraphs 11–14, when the man at the toll-gate warns the travelers that the bridge is broken and unsafe to cross. **(DOK 2)**

Theme Connection

- How do all the stories in this lesson relate to the theme of adventure and conflict?

- Which story did you like the best? Why?

2 Choice D is correct. The resolution tells what happens after the conflict is solved. This sentence tells what happens at the end of the story, when the group arrives home safely and the master is grateful to Black Beauty for being wise. Choices A and B are incorrect. They describe events in the climax. Choice C is incorrect. It is the falling action. **(DOK 2)**

3 Choice B is correct. The conflict has to do with travelers getting home safely in a storm. Although all of the answer choices relate to episodes in the story, only B describes the main conflict. Choices A and C describe events that contribute to the main conflict, but neither is the main conflict. Choice D is part of the exposition. It helps set the scene by explaining why the master is traveling in the storm. **(DOK 2)**

4 Sample response: Because Black Beauty refused to cross the bridge, the man at the toll-gate was able to warn the travelers that the bridge was out. They took a different route and got home safely. If Black Beauty had not stopped, the travelers would have been swept into the river. They would have been hurt or possibly killed instead of arriving home safely. **(DOK 3)**

Part 5: Common Core Practice Lesson 6

2 Which of these sentences shows how the plot is resolved?

A "We were going along at a good pace, but the moment my feet touched the first part of the bridge I felt sure there was something wrong."

B "Of course I could not tell him, but I knew very well that the bridge was not safe."

C "'The bridge is broken in the middle, and part of it is carried away; if you come on you'll be into the river.'"

D "'No, my dear; but if your Black Beauty had not been wiser than we were we should all have been carried down the river at the wooden bridge.'"

3 What is the main conflict in the story?

A The storm causes a large branch to fall and nearly hit Black Beauty and the men.

B The men want Black Beauty to cross the bridge, but he knows it is out.

C The bridge breaks and is washed away by the rising water.

D The master must go into town for business during a terrible storm.

4 Explain how Black Beauty's decision not to cross the bridge changes the story. Use at least **two** details from the story in your answer.

See sample response.

✓ **Self Check** *Go back and see what you can check off on the Self Check on page 44.*

60 L6: Describing Plot

©Curriculum Associates, LLC Copying is not permitted.

Integrating Standards

Use these questions and tasks as opportunities to interact with "Black Beauty."

1 How might the story be different if it were told from the point of view of the master? **(RL.6.6)**

Sample response: The story would not include Black Beauty's thoughts. Readers would not know why Black Beauty refused to cross the bridge.

2 Why did the man at the toll-gate run out of the house tossing a torch like a mad man? **(RL.6.1)**

He wanted to get the travelers' attention to warn them that the bridge was broken. He had to toss a torch because it was dark outside.

3 At the end of the story, why did John give Black Beauty a good supper and a thick bed of straw? **(RL.6.1)**

It was John's way of rewarding Black Beauty for saving his life during the storm. He probably knew that Black Beauty would enjoy a good supper and a thick bed of straw after the long, hard trip.

4 Summarize: Write a brief summary of the passage. Use transition words to convey the sequence of episodes in the plot. **(RL.6.2; W.6.4)**

Sample response: Black Beauty, John, and the master go into town during a bad storm. During their return trip, they reach a bridge, and Black Beauty senses it is not safe to cross. Despite being prodded, Beauty will not move forward. Because they are stopped, a man has time to warn the group that the bridge is out. As a result, they take a different route and finally arrive home safely.

5 Discuss as a class: How is this story similar to "Alma's First Cattle Drive"? How is it different? Use evidence from both stories to support your answers. **(RL.6.9, SL.6.1)**

Discussions will vary. Students should recognize similar settings and events that involve horses crossing water in stormy weather. They should also recognize the difference in the points of view from which the stories are told.

Writing Activities

Write a Narrative (W.6.3)

- Challenge students to think about how "Lost in Time" could be written as a story instead of a play. Encourage students to think about the characters, setting, and plot as well as the sequence and dialogue. Who would tell the story? A narrator? Jamaal? James? How would the characters' lines and the stage directions be incorporated into the story?

- Have students write "Lost in Time" as a story. Allow time for students to share their stories with the class.

Intensive Pronouns (L.6.1.b)

- Have students read the last sentence in "Alma's First Cattle Drive." Ask them to identify the pronouns in the sentence (*she, herself*). Point out the intensive pronoun *herself*. Explain that intensive pronouns are used to place extra emphasis on the subject of a sentence.

- Have students identify the subject of the sentence that *herself* refers to (*Alma*). Ask students to name other intensive pronouns (*myself, ourselves, yourself, yourselves, himself, itself, themselves*). List them on the board.

- Then have students write two sentences using two different intensive pronouns.

LISTENING ACTIVITY (SL.6.1; SL.6.2)

Listen Closely/Summarize

- Have student pairs assign roles as speaker and listener.

- First, have the speaker read aloud from "Alma's First Cattle Drive," pausing after each paragraph. Then have the listener summarize the paragraph by paraphrasing.

- Have pairs reverse roles and repeat the activity until they have paraphrased the entire passage.

DISCUSSION ACTIVITY (SL.6.1)

Talk in a Group/Discuss Producing a Play

- Point out to students that "Lost in Time" is a play: a story written to be acted out on stage.

- Have students form small groups to discuss how they would produce the play on stage. If necessary, share these prompts: What would the scenery look like? What costumes would the characters wear? How would the characters behave?

- Allow 10 to 15 minutes for discussion. Then have students present their ideas to the class.

MEDIA ACTIVITY (RL.6.2)

Be Creative/Create a Comic Strip

- Use the images on page 53 as a springboard to point out that a comic strip tells the basic plot of a story in words and pictures.

- Review the five key elements of a plot and have students create a five-frame comic strip to tell the plot of one of the passages in this lesson.

- Remind students to sequence the frames to show how one event leads to another.

RESEARCH ACTIVITY (W.6.7; SL.6.4)

Research and Present/Give a Presentation

- Have students use "Black Beauty" as a starting point for research on horses and the jobs they do.

- Ask students to use print and digital sources to research information about other ways horses were used in the past as well as how horses are used today.

- Students should take notes and write a brief report for an oral presentation. Suggest that they produce a visual display, such as photographs downloaded from the Internet, to accompany the presentation.

Analyzing Character Development

LESSON OBJECTIVES

- Analyze literary characters, including their traits, motivations, attitudes, and relationships.

- Describe the main conflict a character faces in a story or drama and determine how the character develops or changes in response to that conflict.

THE LEARNING PROGRESSION

- **Grade 5:** CCLS RL.5.3 requires students to focus on comparing two or more characters, settings, or events in a story.

- **Grade 6: CCLS RL.6.3 builds on the Grade 5 standard by requiring students to focus on how the plot unfolds and how the characters respond or change.**

- **Grade 7:** CCLS RL.7.3 builds on the Grade 6 standard by focusing on how story elements interact and affect the plot.

PREREQUISITE SKILLS

- Recognize that writers describe characters through physical appearance, words and thoughts, and actions.

- Identify and describe a setting.

- Identify and describe an event in a story or drama.

- Understand how to compare and contrast two elements in a text.

TAP STUDENTS' PRIOR KNOWLEDGE

- Tell students that they will work on a lesson about analyzing how characters develop in a story. Explain that characters have traits, attitudes, and motivations. Ask students what traits are. (*physical features*) Explain that attitude is the way a character acts, thinks, and feels, and motivations are the reasons a character acts in certain ways.

- Ask students how they might act if they were happy (*smile or laugh*) or tired (*yawn or put their head down*). Discuss how you can tell how people feel by their expressions or actions.

- Next, display these sentences: "Did you hear that Mark won the journalism contest?" Mia squealed. "I knew he would." Ask students what they tell you about Mark. (*He is talented.*) Discuss how someone's statements about a person can give clues about the person's character.

- Explain to students that recognizing character traits will help them understand a character's behavior and enable them to predict how a character may act or react as a story's plot unfolds.

Ready *Teacher Toolbox*   teacher-toolbox.com

	Prerequisite Skills	*RL.6.3*
Ready Lessons	✓	✓
Tools for Instruction		✓
Interactive Tutorials		✓

CCLS Focus

RL.6.3 Describe how a particular story's or drama's plot unfolds in a series of episodes as well as how the characters respond or change as the plot moves toward a resolution.

ADDITIONAL STANDARDS: **RL.6.1, RL.6.2, RL.6.4, RL.6.7; W.6.3.b, W.6.4, W.6.9; SL.6.1, SL.6.5; L.6.1, L.6.1.a, L.6.4.a, L.6.4.d, L.6.5.a** (*See page A39 for full text.*)

AT A GLANCE

Through a cartoon, students learn about a character and how the character changes in response to events.

STEP BY STEP

- Read the definitions of a character's *attitude* and *motivation*, and how a character may change as a story unfolds.

- Now have students look at each panel of the cartoon to find details telling what the boy is like. Have students make notes about those details, such as the boy's facial expressions and his actions.

- Explain that the chart shows the main events in the cartoon's story and what these events reveal about the boy's attitude and motivation.

- Read the first event in the chart, pointing out that this occurs in the first panel.

- Then have students complete the "Why He Does It" column, connecting the boy's actions with a possible purpose based on his facial expressions.

- Direct students' attention to the "What This Shows About Him" column. Have them write notes about what each action reveals about who the boy is as a person. Do the same for the second and third events. Discuss how the boy's feelings change over time.

- Ask students to share an experience when they have changed their feelings or attitude in response to another person's actions. Students may mention changing their attitude while playing on a sports

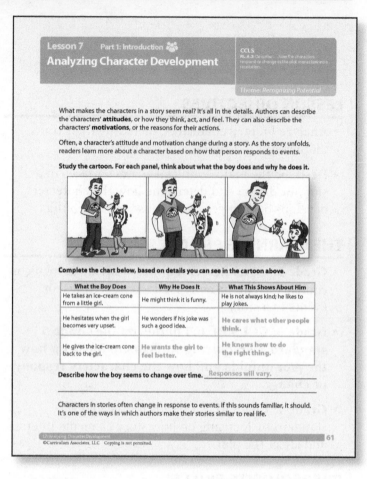

team after receiving encouragement from a team member.

- Review that characters, just like real people, change as they react to events around them.

Genre Focus

Literary Texts: Drama

Tell students that they will read a type of literature called drama. Drama is a story meant to be performed by actors, such as a play. It is written in script form, which contains dialogue and stage directions.

A script tells each character, or actor, what to say. The dialogue is presented with the character's name followed by a colon and the words the character speaks. Stage directions are often shown in parentheses. They describe the setting and tell the actors how to speak, move, or behave.

Ask students to name plays they have read or seen.

What stage directions were given? How were settings and characters described?

Explain that "Reaching the Top" is a play with two characters. The script shows the dialogue between the characters. The stage directions tell each character how to speak. They also describe the setting.

Discuss how when reading a play, readers think about the characters and their interactions. They may have to make inferences to understand a character. The stage directions can help them do this. Paying attention to the characters' actions and words allows readers to see how characters react and change as events in the story unfold.

AT A GLANCE

Students read a realistic fiction story about a girl who loses her grandmother's dog. Students make inferences about the character and recognize how her character changes by analyzing how she reacts to events.

STEP BY STEP

- Invite volunteers to tell what they learned on the previous page about analyzing how a character changes during a story.

- Read aloud "Lost!" Then read the question: "Based on her responses to events, what kind of person is Rosalyn? Support your response with details from the story."

- Tell students you will perform a Think Aloud to demonstrate a way of answering the question.

Think Aloud: What Rosalyn does and how she reacts to events can help me understand what kind of person she is. The first event is that Peanut gets lost. I know Rosalyn is upset by this because the text says that "panic surged through her veins." I also know that Gram loves Peanut because the text says that Gram would be lost without Rosalyn and Peanut.

- Direct students to the first row of the chart. Review that the chart shows story events and responses to the events.

Think Aloud: The next event is that Rosalyn worries about getting lost, too. I'll reread the text to see what Rosalyn does. I read that she makes a map.

- Ask students what making a map reveals about Rosalyn. Have them complete the second row.

Think Aloud: The next event is that Rosalyn sees Peanut. I'll understand how Rosalyn feels by reading how she reacts when she sees Peanut.

- Have students complete the third row of the chart.

- Finally, have students use the information in the chart to write a description of Rosalyn's character. Invite volunteers to share their descriptions with the class. (*Sample response: Rosalyn is old enough to be left home alone. She loves and respects Gram. She is clever to think of using a map to find Peanut and to keep from getting lost.*)

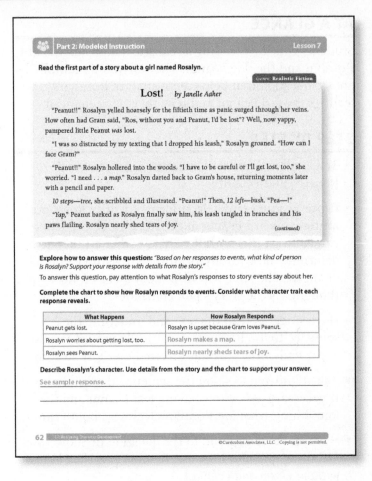

Tier Two Vocabulary: *Hoarsely*

- Read the first sentence. Tell students that context clues in nearby words and phrases can help them figure out the meaning of *hoarsely*.

- Point out the word *yelled* and the phrase *for the fiftieth time*. Ask what they tell you about Rosalyn's actions. (*Rosalyn has been calling out loudly over and over again.*)

- Discuss what happens to your voice if you shout for a long time. (*It gets rough, raspy, and faint.*)

- Point out that *hoarsely* is an adverb because it has the suffix *-ly*. Ask students what they think *hoarsely* means. ("*in a raspy, faint-sounding way*") **(RL.6.4; L.6.4.a)**

AT A GLANCE

Students continue reading a realistic fiction story about Rosalyn and the dog Peanut. They answer a multiple-choice question that helps them analyze Rosalyn's feelings toward Peanut and how they have changed.

STEP BY STEP

- Tell students they will continue reading about Rosalyn and Peanut.

- Close Reading will help students identify Rosalyn's attitude toward Peanut at the story's end. Students can contrast this with Rosalyn's earlier attitude to determine how Rosalyn's attitude toward Peanut has changed. The Hint will help them focus on Rosalyn's thoughts as the story's plot concludes.

- Have students read the text and underline the sentence that tells Rosalyn's attitude toward Peanut at the end of the story, as directed by Close Reading.

- Ask volunteers to share the sentence they underlined. If necessary, ask: After having lost Peanut and then found him, what are Rosalyn's feelings about Peanut?

- Have students respond to the question in Show Your Thinking. (*Sample response: Rosalyn says she'd be lost without Gram and Peanut.*)

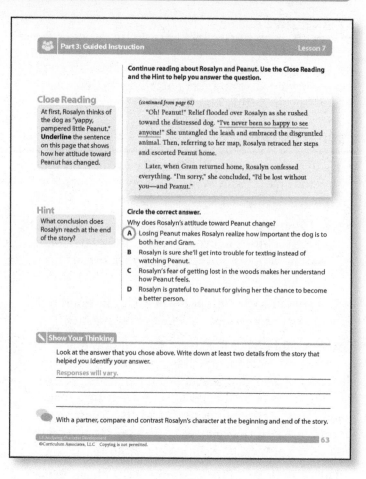

ANSWER ANALYSIS

Choice A is correct. Before Rosalyn loses Peanut, she thinks the dog is pampered. At the end, Rosalyn realizes she'd be lost without Gram and Peanut.

Choice B is incorrect. Although Rosalyn thinks she'll get into trouble with Gram for texting, this is not why Rosalyn's attitude toward Peanut changes.

Choice C is incorrect. Rosalyn's fear of getting lost may make her sympathize with Peanut, but that doesn't influence the way her attitude toward Peanut changes.

Choice D is incorrect. Rosalyn's attitude changes because she realizes how important Peanut is to her, not because this experience has made her a better person.

ERROR ALERT: Students who did not choose A might not have understood that the question asks for the reason why Rosalyn's attitude changes. Each choice is based on story events, but only A explains why Rosalyn's feelings about Peanut change.

Tier Two Vocabulary: *Disgruntled*

- Read this sentence from the story: "She untangled the leash and embraced the disgruntled animal." Tell students that context clues can help them figure out the meaning of *disgruntled*.

- Explain that synonyms can be context clues. Ask students to find a phrase in a previous sentence that has nearly the same meaning as *disgruntled animal*. (*distressed dog*)

- Tell students to use the meaning of the synonym *distressed* to figure out the meaning of *disgruntled*. Ask what *disgruntled* means. (*"irritated, annoyed, unhappy"*) **(RL.6.4; L.6.4.a)**

- Have students confirm the meaning of *disgruntled* by consulting a dictionary. **(L.6.4.d)**

AT A GLANCE

Students read a play twice about two boys hiking. After the first reading, you will ask three questions to check your students' comprehension of the passage.

STEP BY STEP

- Have students read the play silently without referring to the Study Buddy or Close Reading text.

- Ask the following questions to ensure students' comprehension of the text:

  What activity are Yu and Lian doing? (*They are hiking up a mountain trail to the top of Cannon Mountain.*)

  How do you know that Lian is an experienced hiker? (*Lian says that he and his dad hiked the same trail three times last month.*)

  What is Yu's reaction when he reaches the mountain's summit and sees the view from there? (*Yu is awestruck by the view and wants to climb another nearby mountain that he sees.*)

- Ask students to reread the play and look at the Study Buddy think aloud. What does the Study Buddy help them think about?

Tip: Analyzing character development by describing how characters respond or change as the plot moves toward a resolution will help students be able to improve the use of narrative techniques in their own writing, such as using dialogue, pacing, and description to develop experiences, events, and characters.

- Have students answer the questions and follow the directions in the Close Reading.

Tip: Students can ask themselves questions to help them identify a character's thoughts. For example, "Does a character use words of praise or ridicule?" "Is the character's tone of speech friendly or unpleasant?"

- Finally, have students answer the questions on page 65. Use the Answer Analysis to discuss correct and incorrect responses.

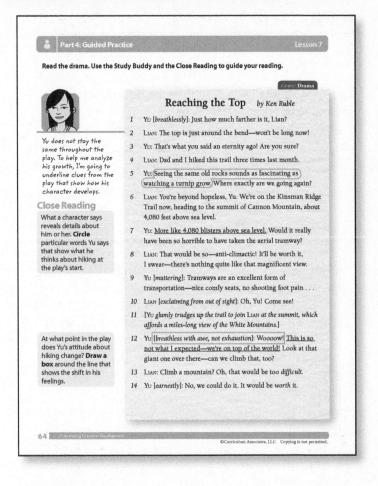

ELL Support: Contractions

- Explain that a contraction is two words that have been joined together and shortened. Letters are dropped, and an apostrophe is put in place of the dropped letters.

- Point out the contraction *that's* in line 3. Identify the two words in the contraction, *that* and *is*. Tell students the letter *i* in *is* has been dropped and an apostrophe inserted. Substitute *that is* in the sentence from the play: *That's what you said an eternity ago!* Explain that the meaning remains the same.

- Repeat with other contractions that appear in the text: *you're, it'll, there's, we're, won't.* **(L.6.1)**

STEP BY STEP

• Have students read questions 1–3, using the Hints to help them answer those questions.

Tip: If students have trouble answering question 3, remind them that they can see how Yu's attitude changes by referring to the words and phrases they circled in the play's beginning as well as the text they boxed near the end of the play.

• Discuss with students the Answer Analysis below.

ANSWER ANALYSIS

1 The correct choice is C. As Yu and Lian climb the mountain, Yu complains. For example, he asks how far they have to go; wishes they had taken the tram; he talks about getting blisters on his feet, and so on. Choice A misrepresents what Yu says: He is bored by the rocks. Choice B is incorrect because Lian, not Yu, has hiked the trail before. Choice D is wrong because Yu is breathless; he's having trouble keeping up with Lian.

2 The correct choice is A. When Yu asks how much farther they have to go, it is because he wants the climb to be over. He is not enjoying it, and he finds it difficult. Choice B doesn't really express any strong feelings on Yu's part. Choice C is a statement made after the climb is completed, as is Choice D. As such, neither choice shows Yu's negative feelings about the climb itself.

3 Sample response: At first, Yu does not like the hike. He complains and asks a lot of questions. When they reach the summit, however, his attitude changes. The incredible view makes him want to go and climb another mountain, and he realizes his own potential.

RETEACHING

Use a chart to organize details from the story to answer question 3. Draw the chart below, and have students fill in the boxes. Sample responses are provided.

Event	Response
Lian describes the 4,080-foot mountain they are hiking.	Yu complains that it's more like 4,080 blisters.
Yu arrives at the summit.	Yu is awestruck.

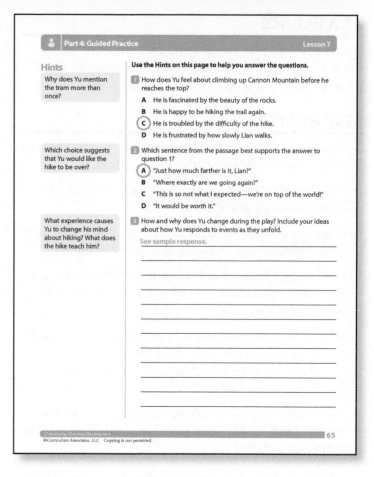

Integrating Standards

Use these questions to further students' understanding of "Reaching the Top."

1 Which statement by Lian summarizes his attitude about hiking a mountain trail? **(RL.6.1)**

"It'll be worth it, I swear—there's nothing quite like that magnificent view."

2 At the beginning of the play, Yu makes the following comparison: "Seeing the same old rocks sounds as fascinating as watching a turnip grow." What does this comparison reveal about Yu's attitude toward hiking? **(RL.6.4)**

It tells that Yu is disinterested in hiking and looking at the scenery, because Yu sarcastically compares the view on a hike to watching a vegetable grow, which is not an interesting activity for most people. A vegetable grows slowly.

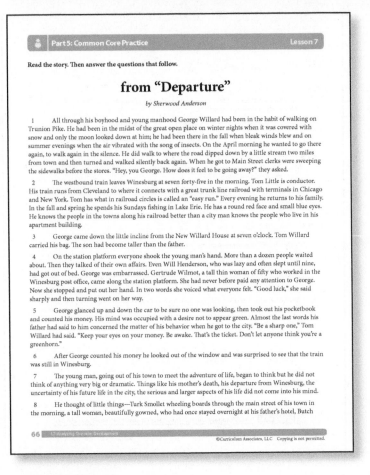

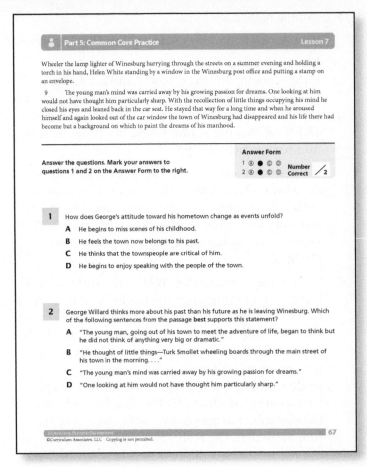

AT A GLANCE

Students independently read a longer realistic fiction story and answer questions in a format that provides test practice.

STEP BY STEP

- Tell students to use what they have learned about reading carefully and analyzing character development to read the story on pages 66 and 67.

- Remind students to underline or circle important points.

- Tell students to answer the questions on pages 67 and 68. For questions 1 and 2, they should fill in the correct circle on the Answer Form.

- When students have finished, use the Answer Analysis to discuss correct responses and the reasons for them. Have students fill in the Number Correct on the Answer Form.

ANSWER ANALYSIS

1 The correct answer is B. As George leaves, he realizes that his past life is now background. Choice A is incorrect. George puts his childhood behind him by the end of the story. Choice C is incorrect. The townspeople wish George well. Choice D is incorrect. George was embarrassed by the townspeople and did not enjoy speaking with them. **(DOK 2)**

2 The correct answer is B. This is an excerpt in which George thinks back on the "little things." Choice A doesn't say whether George thinks about the past or future. Choice C mentions George's "growing passion for dreams," a phrase which suggests the future. Choice D comments on George's distracted demeanor, but it doesn't support the assertion. **(DOK 2)**

Theme Connection

- How do all the stories in this lesson relate to the theme of people recognizing their potential?

- Cite examples from the stories that show how a character changes or grows in a positive way.

3 Sample responses:

Part A: Student circles "dreamy" or "inexperienced"

Parts B and C:

If the student circled "dreamy" in Part A, then possible sentences are: "The young man's mind was carried away by his growing passion for dreams" and "One looking at him would not have thought him particularly sharp."

If the student circled "inexperienced" in Part A, possible sentences are: "His mind was occupied with a desire not to appear green" and "Almost the last words his father had said to him concerned the matter of his behavior when he got to the city." **(DOK 3)**

4 Sample response: George is having a difficult time leaving Winesburg even though he is ready to move to the big city. Early on, George walks the Trunion Pike one more time. This is relevant because he has walked there many times before and is realizing how much he will miss it. When he gets to the station, George is surprised at how many people have come to see him off. This is relevant because George sees that people care about him and like him more than the realized. These things show that George is having a difficult time leaving. **(DOK 3)**

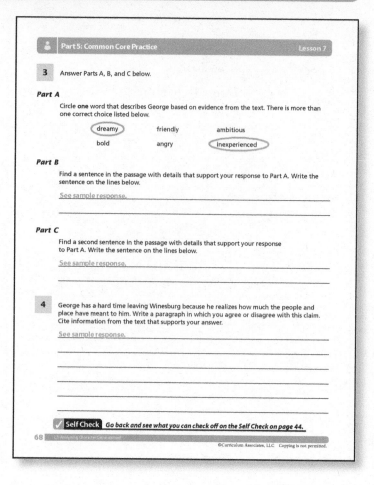

Integrating Standards

Use these questions and tasks as opportunities to interact with "Departure."

1 What evidence shows George enjoys solitude? **(RL.6.1)**

George took walks by himself. He "had been in the midst of the great open place when...only the moon looked down at him...."

2 Give a brief summary of the story's plot in your own words. **(RL.6.2)**

George revisits places from his youth. He leaves to take the train from his town to a new life in the city. Townspeople see him off. He boards and checks that his money is in order. He thinks about the town and his past, but as the train moves along, he dreams about his future.

3 What does the author mean by referring to Winesburg as "a background on which to paint the dreams of his manhood"? **(RL.6.4; L.6.5.a)**

The author means that Winesburg forms the basis for George's life experiences because it is where George grew up.

4 Write a sentence describing what George might say about his hometown to someone he meets in the city. **(W.6.3.b)**

Sample response: Winesburg is a small country town where everyone knows and cares about everyone else.

5 Discuss in small groups: How do you think George will act when he arrives in the city? Use evidence from the text to support your thinking. **(SL.6.1)**

Discussions will vary. Students might mention that George will act confident because he doesn't want to appear a greenhorn.

Writing Activities

Compare-and-Contrast Essay *(W.6.4, W.6.9)*

- Have students consider the character development of Yu in "Reaching the Top" and George in "Departure."

- Challenge students to write an essay that compares and contrasts the ways the authors show how Yu and George change and grow. Remind students to use evidence from the text in each story to support their ideas.

- Students can use an outline to organize their ideas. Tell students to be sure to write clearly and coherently.

- Have volunteers share their essays with the class.

Objective Pronouns *(L.6.1.a)*

- Display this sentence: *"Yap," Peanut barked frantically as Rosalyn finally caught a glimpse of him, his leash tangled in branches and his paws flailing.* Have students identify the pronouns. *(him, his)*

- Point out the objective pronoun *him* and the possessive pronoun *his. Him* is used as the object following the preposition *of.* Identify other objective pronouns. *(me, you, her, it, us, them)*

- Have students rewrite the sentence by changing the gender of the pronouns to female. Then have students write two sentences using objective pronouns.

LISTENING ACTIVITY *(SL.6.1)*

Listen Closely/Interpret Point of View

- Have students work in small groups and study the cartoon on page 61.

- One student describes what happens in each image from the boy's point of view. The rest of the group listens closely.

- Another student then clearly describes the events and character's feelings in each image from the girl's point of view as the group listens.

- A third student sums up the similarities and differences in the characters' points of view.

DISCUSSION ACTIVITY *(SL.6.1)*

Talk in a Group/Discuss a Character's Motivation

- After reading "Departure," have students discuss the motivation behind George's actions.

- Provide these prompts: Why do you think George revisited the places he had walked when he was young? Why did George count his money so secretly? After the train leaves, do you think George still wants to go to the city?

- Allow 15 minutes for discussion. Have students take turns speaking and listening.

MEDIA ACTIVITY *(RL.6.7)*

Be Creative/Make an Audio Recording

- Have students work in pairs to make a digital audio recording of the drama "Reaching the Top." Partners each take the role of a character. Students follow stage directions and supply additional sound effects as desired.

- Play selected recordings for the class and discuss how the experience of listening to the drama compares to the reading experience.

RESEARCH ACTIVITY *(W.6.9; SL.6.5)*

Write/Present a Multimedia Journal

- Have students analyze Rosalyn's character in "Lost!" by writing a character journal.

- Students reread the story and write several journal entries from Rosalyn's point of view. Each entry should relate to a different event in the story.

- Encourage students to include images and music in their journals. Students might use a dog's photo for Peanut or a song that illustrates a particular emotion that Rosalyn was feeling.

- Have students present their journals to the class.

Determining Theme or Central Idea

Theme: *A Time to Change*

LESSON OBJECTIVES

- Determine the theme of a literary text.
- Determine the central idea of a literary text.
- Make inferences.
- Identify relevant details.

THE LEARNING PROGRESSION

- **Grade 5:** CCLS RL.5.2 requires students to find the theme of the text only, not the central idea.

- **Grade 6: CCLS RL.6.2 builds on the Grade 5 standard by requiring students not only to find the theme but also to identify supporting details in the text that help to develop the theme or central idea.**

- **Grade 7:** CCLS RL.7.2 requires students to analyze how the theme and central idea develop over the course of the text.

PREREQUISITE SKILLS

- Determine the theme of a story.
- Identify details in a text.
- Recognize how characters in a story respond to challenges that they face.

TAP STUDENTS' PRIOR KNOWLEDGE

- Tell students that they will be working on a lesson about theme. Ask students to review what a theme is. (*The main message or lesson in a text*)

- Point out to students that a theme is different from the topic or central idea of a text. A topic or central idea is what the text is mostly about. A theme is a message that an author wants readers to learn by reading the text.

- Encourage students to think about their favorite movie. Invite a volunteer to share the name of a movie that most students in the class have seen.

- Ask students to explain what the movie is mostly about, including who the main characters are and what happens to them.

- Write on the board some of the important details about the movie. Then guide students in using these words to identify the theme of the movie. Ask, What is the main lesson about life that the movie teaches? How does knowing the movie's central idea help you understand its theme? Have students use the key details recorded on the board to state the theme of the movie.

- Point out to students that just like movies, fictional stories have a theme. Explain that understanding the theme of a text will help them better understand the author's purpose, and it will also help them to connect the text to their own lives and experiences.

Ready Teacher Toolbox

teacher-toolbox.com

	Prerequisite Skills	RL.6.2
Ready Lessons	✓ ✓	✓
Tools for Instruction	✓	✓
Interactive Tutorials	✓	✓

CCLS Focus

RL.6.2 Determine a theme or central idea of a text and how it is conveyed through particular details.

ADDITIONAL STANDARDS: RL.6.1, RL.6.3, RL.6.4, RL.6.7; W.6.3.b, W.6.7, W.6.9.a; SL.6.1, SL.6.2, SL.6.4, SL.6.5; L.6.1, L.6.4.a, L.6.4.b, L.6.4.d (*See page A39 for full text.*)

AT A GLANCE

Through a picture, students use particular details to determine a text's central idea and general theme.

STEP BY STEP

- Tell students that a *central idea* tells what a specific text is about, whereas a *theme* provides a generalized statement on life that many texts might share.

- Direct students' attention to the picture. Ask a volunteer to describe the first thing they learn when looking at it. (*The picture is about a soccer award.*) Help students identify details and words that seem to be the most important information in the picture.

- Explain that the chart shows how important details produce the central idea. Have a volunteer read the central idea at the top of the chart. (*The boy practiced soccer every day and became Most Improved Player.*)

- Have a volunteer read the first detail. Ask students to compare these words to what they previously identified in the picture. Guide students to identify two additional details that support this idea, e.g., "Holding a plaque," "Most Improved Player."

- Discuss with students what theme, or general lesson, this central idea might convey. (*Hard work and determination pay off.*)

- Discuss the differences between the central idea, which tells what a specific picture or text is about, and the theme, which tells a broader lesson or message that many pictures or texts might share.

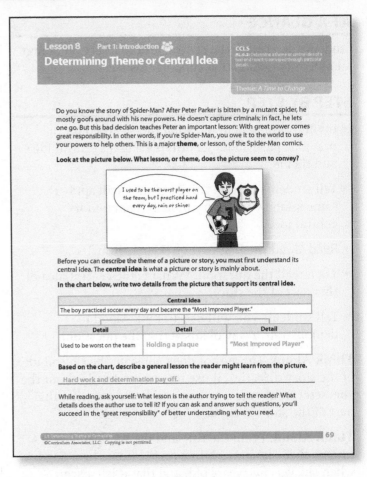

- Close out your introduction by telling students that the first step to understanding the theme of a text is to figure out its central idea.

- Share with them an anecdote about a story you read in which figuring out its central idea led you to understanding its theme.

Genre Focus

Literary Texts: Realistic Fiction

Tell students that in this lesson they will read realistic fiction stories. Explain that realistic fiction stories share the following characteristics:

- They have characters who take part in activities that could really happen.

- They include characters, settings, and situations that are believable and could really happen.

- Some aspects of the story are made up.

Based on these characteristics, ask students to recall examples of realistic fiction that they have read. Invite students to give a brief description of each story. Who were the characters? What was the setting? What are some events that happened? Did the events really happen, or were they made up? Why was the story believable? Some examples students may be familiar with include *Hatchet* by Gary Paulsen and *Holes* by Louis Sachar.

Tell students that they will read three pieces of realistic fiction in this lesson. "Tiana's Scar" is about a girl who is afraid of dogs. "Rushmore" is a story about a boy who is not excited about visiting Mount Rushmore with his family. "Vivian's Move" is a play about a girl who is sad to move from her beloved hometown of Boston to San Francisco.

AT A GLANCE

Students determine the central idea in a section of text and identify details that support this idea.

STEP BY STEP

- Invite volunteers to tell what they learned on the previous page about identifying a text's central idea and theme.

- Tell students that on this page they will apply the same strategy to a story to help them find its central idea.

- Read aloud the first part of "Tiana's Scar."

- Then read the question: "What is the central idea of this part of the story?"

- Tell students you will use a Think Aloud to demonstrate a way of answering the question.

Think Aloud: The author does not state the central idea of the story directly. I'll use important details about the characters and events to help me figure out what this part of the story is about.

Think Aloud: From the title and the first paragraph, I know that Tiana was bitten on her finger by a dog when she was five years old, and that it left a scar.

- Direct students to the chart. Ask where they've seen a similar chart before. Review that it shows how important details from the story help to produce a central idea. Point out the first important detail in the first column.

Think Aloud: What else does the author want me to know about Tiana's scar? I read in paragraph 2 that Tiana is now 11 years old, and she still avoids dogs wherever she goes. In paragraph 3, she calls them "ferocious beast[s]."

- Have students look for and write down two additional details in the "Detail" boxes.

Think Aloud: Now that I have identified important details from the story, I can think about the central idea that they produce. The details all suggest that Tiana's dog bite is a big deal to her, even many years after she was bitten.

- Have students fill in the top box of the chart by suggesting a central idea. (*This part of the story is about a girl named Tiana who has a deep fear of dogs.*)

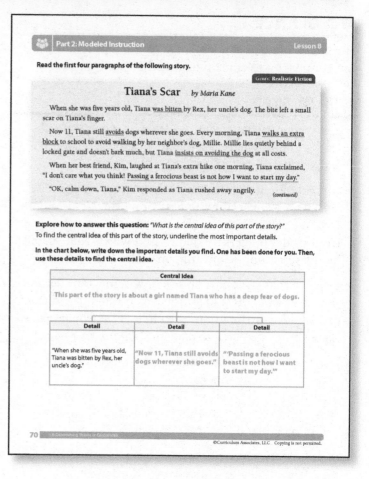

ELL Support: Regular Past Tense

- Explain to students that the past tense of a verb tells that the action has already happened. The past tense of a regular verb ends with -*ed*.

- Point out the regular past-tense verbs *exclaimed* and *responded* in "Tiana's Scar" on page 70. Explain to students that the present-tense verbs *exclaim* and *respond* were changed to the past tense by adding -*ed*.

- Challenge students to identify two more regular past-tense verbs in "Tiana's Scar" (*laughed, rushed*) and identify how they were formed (*add* -ed).

- Write on the board: *I strum a guitar.* Point out the verb *strum*. Work with students to form the past tense (*strummed*) and tell how it is formed (*by adding* -med). **(L.6.1)**

AT A GLANCE

Students continue reading about Tiana's fear of dogs. They answer a multiple-choice question and explain which details helped them figure out the story's theme.

STEP BY STEP

- Tell students that they will continue reading about Tiana's fear of dogs.

- Close Reading will help students identify the important details that reveal the story's theme. The Hint will remind students what a theme is in order to select the best theme statement for this story.

- Have students read the story and underline important details, as directed by Close Reading.

- Invite volunteers to share the sentence that shows Tiana is changing. Have students explain why the sentence shows this idea best. If necessary, ask: What does Tiana do that she has not done before?

- Have students respond to Show Your Thinking, and place students into pairs to discuss the Pair Share prompt. Guide them to use their answer to the Close Reading to help them complete these activities.

ANSWER ANALYSIS

Choice A is correct. Once Tiana learned how to behave around a dog, she was able to overcome her fear.

Choice B is incorrect. Tiana's friend Kim did not understand Tiana's fear of dogs, and Kim was not with Tiana when she pushed herself to overcome that fear.

Choice C is incorrect. The passage suggests that dogs are less likely to bark at confident people, but this detail is not the theme of the story.

Choice D is correct. This statement is not supported by the story. Tiana's newfound confidence did help her solve her problem of being afraid of dogs.

ERROR ALERT: Students who did not choose A may have difficulty distinguishing details, which are stated in a text, from the central idea and theme, which are usually inferred from the details in a text. Guide students to consider each answer choice carefully to determine which choice is supported by all of the important details in the story, rather than by just some of them.

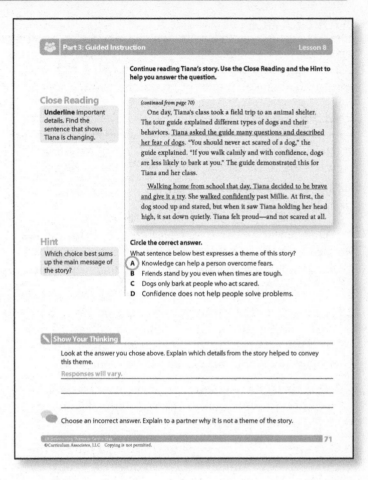

Tier Two
Vocabulary: *Demonstrated*

- Direct students to the word *demonstrated* in paragraph 1. Remind students that they can use clues in the surrounding text to help them figure out the meaning of an unfamiliar word. Point out the word *this* that follows *demonstrated*. Suggest that understanding what *this* is referring to will help them understand the meaning of *demonstrated*.

- Ask volunteers to identify in the surrounding text what *this* refers to (*"walk calmly and with confidence"*). Then have students suggest the meaning of *demonstrated* (*"showed how to do something"*). *(RL.6.4; L.6.4.a)*

AT A GLANCE

Students read a story twice about a trip to Mount Rushmore. After the first reading, you will ask three questions to check students' comprehension.

STEP BY STEP

- Have students read the passage silently without referring to the Study Buddy or Close Reading text.

- Ask the following questions to ensure students' comprehension of the text:

  What reason does the narrator give for thinking his vacation will be boring? (*He says that he learned about Mount Rushmore in school and that he did not find the monument interesting.*)

  What part of the vacation makes the narrator begin to think that the vacation might be interesting after all? (*When the narrator and his family take a drive through a wildlife park, he begins to feel hopeful.*)

  What does the narrator think was most interesting about Mount Rushmore? (*He was amazed by the size of the statue carvings.*)

- Ask students to reread paragraph 1 and look at the Study Buddy think aloud. What does the Study Buddy help them think about?

Tip: The Study Buddy reminds students to look for clues that show how the main character changes. This is a way to start looking for the message that the author wants readers to learn because authors often show how a character learns a lesson to teach a message about life to the audience.

- Have students reread the rest of the story. Tell them to follow the directions in the Close Reading.

Tip: Close Reading helps students identify important details at the beginning and end of the story. By comparing these details, students can better understand the central idea. Reinforce that identifying important details in a text helps students determine the central idea, which is an important step in uncovering the theme.

- Finally, have students answer the questions on page 73. Use the Answer Analysis to discuss correct and incorrect responses.

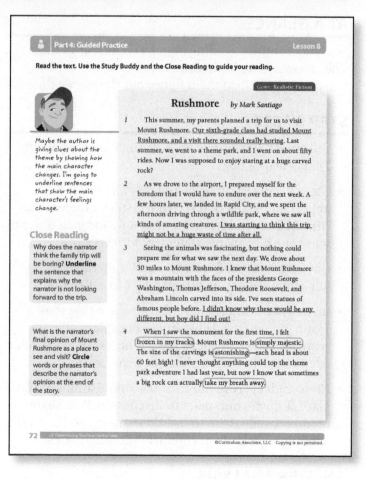

Tier Two Vocabulary: *Majestic*

- Point out the word *majestic* in paragraph 4. Guide students to look for context clues that help them understand the meaning of *majestic* ("*felt frozen in my tracks,*" "*astonishing,*" "*take my breath away*").

- Explain to students that they can use a dictionary to check the definition of a word. Point out that the way a word is used in a sentence can help show which dictionary definition best fits the word. Have students suggest the meaning of *majestic* ("*having astonishing beauty*"). **(RL.6.4; L.6.4.a, L.6.4.d)**

STEP BY STEP

- Have students read questions 1 and 2, using the Hints to help them answer those questions.

Tip: If students have trouble answering question 2, remind them to think about how the main character changes. Encourage students to ask themselves, "What lesson does the main character learn about life?" when they are trying to uncover a text's theme.

- Discuss with students the Answer Analysis below.

ANSWER ANALYSIS

1   The correct choice is B. It shares an important detail about the narrator's feelings. Choice A is a detail about the narrator's vacation the year before, not his feelings. Choice C is a detail about the narrator's vacation this year, not his feelings. Choice D states the fact that the narrator has seen statues before, but it does not tell his feelings about the statues.

2   Choice A is correct. The narrator dreads his trip, but the reality turns out to be the opposite of what he expects. Choices B, C, and D are not illustrated by the story.

3   The correct choices are 2 ("and a visit there sounded really boring") and 4 ("the size of the carvings is astonishing"). These excerpts most clearly support the theme stated in Part A, which has to do with unfounded fears about the future. Choice 1, 3, and 5 are incorrect. While all mention events that occur before the actual visit, none of them convey the negative attitudes and emotions of the narrator. Choices 6 and 7 both touch on the narrator's expectations about the visit, but again, neither provides direct support to the theme from question 2.

RETEACHING

Use a chart to answer question 2. Draw the chart below, leaving the boxes blank. Work with students to fill in the boxes. Sample responses are provided.

Important Details	Theme
• family goes to Mount Rushmore • narrator thinks it will be boring because he studied it in school • actual visit astonishes narrator	People can learn and grow by experiencing new things.

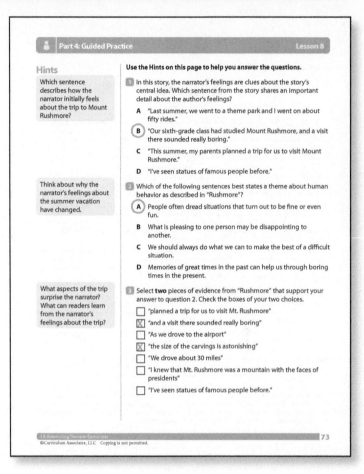

Integrating Standards

Use these questions to further students' understanding of "Rushmore."

1   Summarize the story in your own words. **(RL.6.2)**

The narrator is disappointed to visit Mount Rushmore for vacation because he studied the monument in school and thought it would be boring to visit. The vacation begins well with an interesting visit to a wildlife park. The story ends with the narrator being pleasantly surprised and awestruck by the majesty of Mount Rushmore.

2   Identify evidence from the story that supports the idea that the narrator was surprised when he saw Mount Rushmore. **(RL.6.1)**

Sample response: The narrator says he was "frozen in his tracks" when he first saw the monument. This means the view made him stop moving and suggests that he was surprised by seeing something he didn't expect.

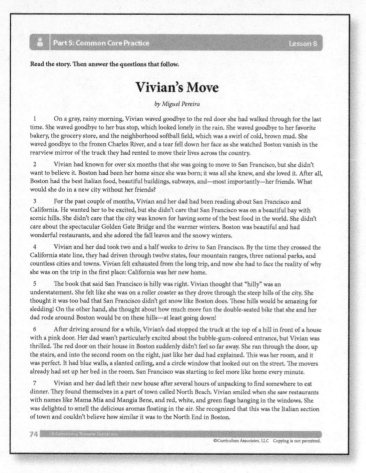

Read the story. Then answer the questions that follow.

Vivian's Move
by Miguel Pereira

1   On a gray, rainy morning, Vivian waved goodbye to the red door she had walked through for the last time. She waved goodbye to her bus stop, which looked lonely in the rain. She waved goodbye to her favorite bakery, the grocery store, and the neighborhood softball field, which was a swirl of cold, brown mud. She waved goodbye to the frozen Charles River, and a tear fell down her face as she watched Boston vanish in the rearview mirror of the truck they had rented to move their lives across the country.

2   Vivian had known for over six months that she was going to move to San Francisco, but she didn't want to believe it. Boston had been her home since she was born; it was all she knew, and she loved it. After all, Boston had the best Italian food, beautiful buildings, subways, and—most importantly—her friends. What would she do in a new city without her friends?

3   For the past couple of months, Vivian and her dad had been reading about San Francisco and California. He wanted her to be excited, but she didn't care that San Francisco was on a beautiful bay with scenic hills. She didn't care that the city was known for having some of the best food in the world. She didn't care about the spectacular Golden Gate Bridge and the warmer winters. Boston was beautiful and had wonderful restaurants, and she adored the fall leaves and the snowy winters.

4   Vivian and her dad took two and a half weeks to drive to San Francisco. By the time they crossed the California state line, they had driven through twelve states, four mountain ranges, three national parks, and countless cities and towns. Vivian felt exhausted from the long trip, and now she had to face the reality of why she was on the trip in the first place: California was her new home.

5   The book that said San Francisco is hilly was right. Vivian thought that "hilly" was an understatement. She felt like she was on a roller coaster as they drove through the steep hills of the city. She thought it was too bad that San Francisco doesn't get snow like Boston does. These hills would be amazing for sledding! On the other hand, she thought about how much more fun the double-seated bike that she and her dad rode around Boston would be on these hills—at least going down!

6   After driving around for a while, Vivian's dad stopped the truck at the top of a hill in front of a house with a pink door. Her dad wasn't particularly excited about the bubble-gum-colored entrance, but Vivian was thrilled. The red door on their house in Boston suddenly didn't feel so far away. She ran through the door, up the stairs, and into the second room on the right, just like her dad had explained. This was her room, and it was perfect. It had blue walls, a slanted ceiling, and a circle window that looked out on the street. The movers already had set up her bed in the room. San Francisco was starting to feel more like home every minute.

7   Vivian and her dad left their new house after several hours of unpacking to find somewhere to eat dinner. They found themselves in a part of town called North Beach. Vivian smiled when she saw restaurants with names like Mama Mia and Mangia Bene, and red, white, and green flags hanging in the windows. She was delighted to smell the delicious aromas floating in the air. She recognized that this was the Italian section of town and couldn't believe how similar it was to the North End in Boston.

74   L8 Determining Theme or Central Idea   ©Curriculum Associates, LLC   Copying is not permitted.

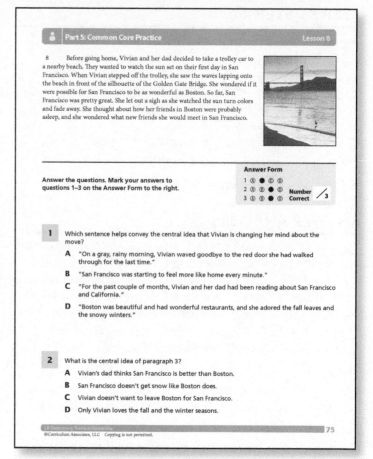

8   Before going home, Vivian and her dad decided to take a trolley car to a nearby beach. They wanted to watch the sun set on their first day in San Francisco. When Vivian stepped off the trolley, she saw the waves lapping onto the beach in front of the silhouette of the Golden Gate Bridge. She wondered if it were possible for San Francisco to be as wonderful as Boston. So far, San Francisco was pretty great. She let out a sigh as she watched the sun turn colors and fade away. She thought about how her friends in Boston were probably asleep, and she wondered what new friends she would meet in San Francisco.

Answer the questions. Mark your answers to questions 1–3 on the Answer Form to the right.

Answer Form
1 Ⓐ ● Ⓒ Ⓓ
2 Ⓐ Ⓑ ● Ⓓ   Number Correct ___/3
3 Ⓐ Ⓑ ● Ⓓ

1   Which sentence helps convey the central idea that Vivian is changing her mind about the move?

A   "On a gray, rainy morning, Vivian waved goodbye to the red door she had walked through for the last time."

B   "San Francisco was starting to feel more like home every minute."

C   "For the past couple of months, Vivian and her dad had been reading about San Francisco and California."

D   "Boston was beautiful and had wonderful restaurants, and she adored the fall leaves and the snowy winters."

2   What is the central idea of paragraph 3?

A   Vivian's dad thinks San Francisco is better than Boston.

B   San Francisco doesn't get snow like Boston does.

C   Vivian doesn't want to leave Boston for San Francisco.

D   Only Vivian loves the fall and the winter seasons.

©Curriculum Associates, LLC   Copying is not permitted.   L8 Determining Theme or Central Idea   75

AT A GLANCE

Students independently read a longer story and answer questions in a format that provides test practice.

STEP BY STEP

- Tell students to use what they have learned about reading carefully and determining theme to read the story on pages 74 and 75.

- Remind students to underline or circle important points.

- Tell students to answer the questions on pages 75 and 76. For questions 1–3, they should fill in the correct circle on the Answer Form.

- When students have finished, use the Answer Analysis to discuss correct responses and the reasons for them. Have students fill in the Number Correct on the Answer Form.

ANSWER ANALYSIS

1   Choice B is correct. At the beginning, Vivian did not want to believe she was moving to San Francisco because Boston was her home. This sentence indicates that she is now thinking of San Francisco as home. Choices A and D show how Vivian felt about Boston at the beginning of the story, not how she is changing her mind about San Francisco. Choice C is incorrect. Reading about San Francisco didn't help Vivian change her mind. **(DOK 2)**

Theme Connection

- How do all the stories in this lesson relate to the theme, a time to change?

- Which character in this lesson's stories went through the greatest change from the beginning to the end of the story? Why?

©Curriculum Associates, LLC   Copying is not permitted.

2 Choice C is correct. It sums up the important details in paragraph 3. Choice A is incorrect because Vivian's dad never suggests that San Francisco is better than Boston. Choice B is incorrect because it is a detail, not a central idea. Choice D is incorrect because the story does not compare Vivian's feelings to anyone else's. **(DOK 2)**

3 Choice C is correct. When Vivian sees all the Italian restaurants, it makes her like San Francisco more. Choice A is incorrect. It describes a difference between the two cities, not a similarity. Choice B describes a way in which San Francisco is different from Boston. Choice D shows Vivian's positive attitude toward San Francisco, but it doesn't describe a way in which the city is like Boston. **(DOK 2)**

4 Sample response: By the end of the story, Vivian may be feeling sad about her change, but I think she is mostly feeling excitement. Before she moved, she did not want to leave Boston because "it was all she knew, and she loved it." That starts to change when she arrives in San Francisco. She is "thrilled" by the pink door on her new house. By the time she sees her new room, she thinks San Francisco is "starting to feel more like home every minute." When she and her dad go out to dinner, she is excited to see all the Italian restaurants in the area. By day's end she thinks, "So far, San Francisco was pretty great." **(DOK 3)**

Part 5: Common Core Practice Lesson 8

3 Vivian starts to like San Francisco better when she sees ways in which it is like Boston. A reader could agree or disagree with this statement. Choose the sentence from the story that could be used to support **agreement** with the statement.

A "She thought it was too bad that San Francisco didn't get snow like Boston does."

B "On the other hand, she thought about how much more fun the double-seated bike that she and her dad rode around Boston would be on these hills—at least going down!"

C "Vivian smiled when she saw restaurants with names like Mama Mia and Mangia Bene, and red, white, and green flags hanging in the windows."

D "She wondered if it were possible for San Francisco to be as wonderful as Boston."

4 The story "Vivian's Move" explores the theme that change can be both sad and exciting. Write a short paragraph in which you describe how Vivian is feeling about her move by the end of the story. Use details from the text to support your answer.

See sample response.

✓ **Self Check** Go back and see what you can check off on the Self Check on page 44.

76 L8: Determining Theme or Central Idea ©Curriculum Associates, LLC Copying is not permitted.

Integrating Standards

Use these questions and tasks as opportunities to interact with "Vivian's Move."

1 How would you describe Vivian's dad? Use details from the story to support your answer. **(RL.6.1)**

Vivian's dad is a caring father. While still in Boston, he tries to comfort Vivian by trying to get her excited about some of the best things about San Francisco. Once they move, he takes time to show Vivian some of the things he thinks she'll like best about San Francisco.

2 What evidence in the story shows how Vivian's attitude about San Francisco started changing once she arrived there? **(RL.6.3)**

When Vivian thinks about how much fun the hills will be for bike riding, it shows her attitude about San Francisco is changing. Being thrilled by the pink door and smiling when she sees the Italian section of the city also show her attitude is changing.

3 Write a summary of "Vivian's Move," leaving out personal opinions. **(RL.6.2; W.6.9.a)**

Sample response: Vivian is sad about moving from Boston to San Francisco with her dad. She loves Boston and will miss her friends. Vivian is not interested in San Francisco until she begins to experience it. As she explores, she realizes that San Francisco is a great city, too.

4 Discuss in small groups: What prediction can you make about Vivian's new life in San Francisco? Use text evidence to support your prediction. **(RL.6.1; SL.6.1)**

Discussions will vary. Remind students that predictions are like inferences about future events. They should use what they already know, along with details from the text, to make their predictions. Students may cite evidence such as Vivian being thrilled by her new home and thinking about what new friends she will meet.

Writing Activities

Write a Dialogue *(W.6.3.b)*

- Have students review "Vivian's Move" to look for events in the story that may have included a discussion between Vivian and her father. Ask them to think about what Vivian and her father might have said to each other during these events.

- Challenge students to enhance "Vivian's Move" with dialogue between Vivian and her father. They might choose to replace an existing paragraph with dialogue, or add dialogue to the existing story.

- Allow time for students to share their dialogue with the class.

Latin Roots *(L.6.4.b)*

- Point out the words *confidence* and *confidently* on page 71, and write the words on the board.

- Discuss how words are made up of word parts, including prefixes, word roots, and suffixes. Underline the root *fid* in each word, and explain that this is a Latin root that means "faith" or "trust." Discuss how knowing the meaning of this root helps to understand the meaning of the words.

- Have students write three sentences using different words that contain the root *fid*.

LISTENING ACTIVITY *(SL.6.1)*

Listen Closely/Pose a Question

- Have a student read aloud "Tiana's Scar" while the rest of the class listens closely and takes notes on important details they hear.

- After reading, ask students to write two questions based on the notes they took, such as "What is the name of the dog that bit Tiana?" *(Rex)*

- Have pairs of students pose their questions to each other and answer using evidence from the story.

DISCUSSION ACTIVITY *(SL.6.4)*

Talk in a Group/Discuss Abstract Concepts

- Have small groups of students discuss the concept of change.

- Ask them to begin by discussing how each main character in the lesson's stories changes. Can students identify with any of these changes?

- Have students share their personal opinions about change, answering such questions as "How do you feel about change?" or "Do you think change is good for a person? Why or why not?"

- Have groups share their responses with the class.

MEDIA ACTIVITY *(RL.6.7; SL.6.2)*

Be Creative/Compare Text and Video Descriptions

- Have students perform an Internet search for video footage of Mount Rushmore.

- Have students write a comparison of the experience of Mount Rushmore as described in "Rushmore" and as presented in the videos.

- Allow time for students to share their work.

RESEARCH AND SPEAKING ACTIVITY *(W.6.7; SL.6.4; SL.6.5)*

Research and Present/Give a Presentation

- Have students use "Vivian's Move" to plan a virtual tour of either Boston or San Francisco, focusing on the places mentioned in the story.

- Tell them to not only identify specific places, such as the Golden Gate Bridge, but also more general places, such as Boston's "beautiful buildings."

- Have students research descriptions and pictures of the places they identify, and put together a virtual tour of the city. They should write brief descriptions of each picture they choose, organize the information logically, and present it to the class as a tour guide might.

Summarizing Literary Texts

LESSON OBJECTIVES

- Summarize a literary text by restating, in one's own words, the main characters, setting, and key events in sequence.

- Produce a summary free of personal opinions or judgments.

THE LEARNING PROGRESSION

- **Grade 5:** CCLS RL.5.2 requires students to summarize a literary text.

- **Grade 6: CCLS RL.6.2 builds on the Grade 5 standard by emphasizing the need to exclude personal opinions and judgments from summaries.**

- **Grade 7:** CCLS RL.7.2 requires students to provide an objective summary of a literary text.

PREREQUISITE SKILLS

- Identify the main characters, setting, conflict, and plot events in a literary text.

- Differentiate between important and unimportant details in a text.

- Understand that a summary is a brief retelling of a story that includes the story elements and the most important plot details of a text.

- Create summaries of literary texts.

TAP STUDENTS' PRIOR KNOWLEDGE

- Tell students they will be working on a lesson about how to summarize a story without including personal opinions. Remind them that a summary is a brief retelling of the important parts of a story.

- Ask students what kinds of information they would include in a story summary. (*main characters, setting, problem or conflict, important plot events*)

- Read or display these two plot summaries:

1 In the ancient city of Pompeii, in the year 79 C.E., a young shepherd tries to figure out why his father's sheep are dying. Could it be related to the strange odor seeping from the ground near Mount Vesuvius? The boy sets out to investigate as events lead to a grim conclusion.

2 In this fantastic and realistic story, a clever young boy tries to figure out why his father's sheep are dying. You will not believe what he discovers. This is one of the best stories you will ever read!

- Ask students which is the better summary and why. (*The first because it includes the main character, setting, and problem.*)

- Ask what is wrong with the second summary. (*It doesn't give the setting or enough information about the plot, and it includes several opinions.*)

- Explain to students that readers summarize a story to help them better remember and understand it.

⬛ Ready *Teacher Toolbox*

teacher-toolbox.com

	Prerequisite Skills	RL.6.2
Ready Lessons	✓	✓
Tools for Instruction		✓
Interactive Tutorials		✓

CCLS Focus

RL.6.2 … provide a summary of the text distinct from personal opinions or judgments.

ADDITIONAL STANDARDS: **RL.6.1, RL.6.3, RL.6.4; W.6.1, W.6.2, W.6.11.b, W.6.11.c; SL.6.1, SL.6.2.a, SL.6.4, SL.6.5, SL.6.6; L.6.1, L.6.2.a, L.6.4.a** (*See page A39 for full text.*)

AT A GLANCE

Through a cartoon, students consider what information to include in a summary of a text. They learn to focus on only the most important details and to leave personal opinions and judgments out of a summary.

STEP BY STEP

- Read the first two paragraphs, focusing on the definitions of *summary*, *personal opinions*, and *judgments*.

- Tell students to examine the pictures and identify the characters, settings, and events. Encourage students to think about how they would describe the events to another person without revealing their personal opinions. Have them write margin notes to help them focus on the important details.

- Explain that the summary following the pictures includes irrelevant information that reveals the writer's opinions and judgments. Read the summary. Have students cross out statements that are irrelevant to an objective summary of the events.

- Discuss how summaries must briefly and accurately capture the most important information of a picture or text. Share a completed summary (with opinions and judgments removed) with the class, pointing out how it incorporates details into a succinct statement.

- Ask students to suggest real-life situations, such as certain jobs, when it would be important to be able to briefly summarize events.

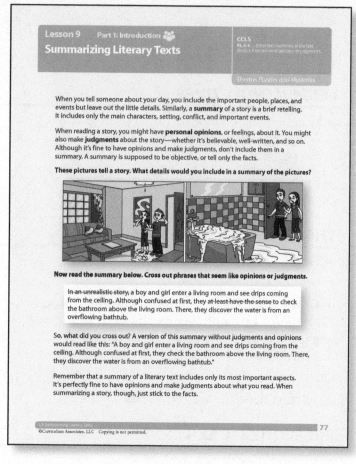

- Read the last paragraph. Reinforce how being able to summarize a text without introducing feelings and opinions will help them understand what they read.

Genre Focus

Literary Texts: Mystery

Tell students that in this lesson they will read literary texts. One type of literary text is a mystery. A mystery is a story with characters who try to solve a crime or explain unusual events. Common features include:

- The main character may be a detective or an investigative reporter but could also be an ordinary person who works to figure out puzzling events.

- The main character uses clues to make logical conclusions. Clues may be obvious or may require the characters—and readers—to make inferences.

- Mysteries often include the element of suspense, a feeling of anticipation, anxiety, or excitement.

- They can include foreshadowing, or hints about what will happen later in the story.

Explain that becoming familiar with these genre characteristics will help students better understand and appreciate mystery stories. Discuss how good mysteries engage the reader with enticing clues that stimulate the reader to make predictions along with the main characters.

Tell students that "Where Is Lady Fish Pants" is a mystery that is set in motion by a very young child. "Mystery on 'The Blue Ghost'" tells the story of a missing camera. Finally, *The Magician's Elephant* is an intriguing snippet of a story that presents, but does not solve, a mystery.

AT A GLANCE

Students evaluate a summary of the first part of a story, which introduces a mysterious lady. Then they explain why some statements are inappropriate for a summary.

STEP BY STEP

- Invite volunteers to tell what they learned on the previous page about summarizing a picture or text.

- Read aloud "Where Is Lady Fish Pants?" Then read the questions: "What would be a good summary of this story? What would it include and not include?"

- Tell students you will perform a Think Aloud to demonstrate a way of answering the question.

Think Aloud: I know a summary has to include the main characters and the setting, which are a boy and his little brother at an aquarium on a very hot day. I will go back and read the story again to find the important events.

- Direct students to the student's draft of a summary. Have a volunteer read it aloud.

- Then, direct students to the chart below the summary. Point out that the left column lists statements that do not belong in the summary because they introduce personal opinions and judgments. The right column explains why each statement does not belong.

Think Aloud: As I read the summary, I see that it does tell me what the important events are, where these events happened, and who they happened to.

Think Aloud: But some parts of the summary give me more information than what's in the story. They tell me what the writer of the summary thinks about the characters and the story as a whole.

Think Aloud: For a summary to be objective, I need to remove these details.

- Work with students to fill in the "Statements That Don't Belong" and "Why They Don't Belong" columns.

- Finally, have partners take turns summarizing the story in their own words. Invite volunteers to share their summaries with the class.

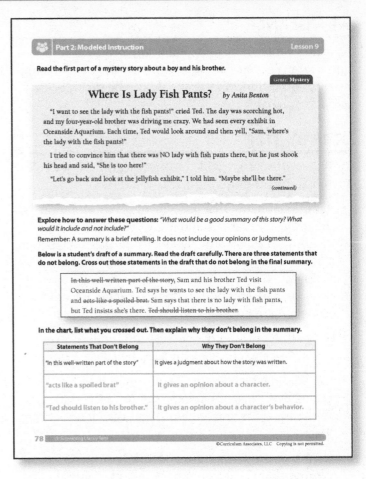

Tier Two Vocabulary: *Exhibit*

- Direct students' attention to the word *exhibit* in paragraph 1. Ask what context clues can help students figure out its meaning. (*"Oceanside Aquarium," "seen," "look around"*) Remind students that the boys are at an aquarium. Ask them to name other places an aquarium is similar to. (*a museum, an animal park, a planetarium*)

- Ask what these places have in common. (*special displays of art, animals, and celestial bodies that are meant for visitors to see*)

- Based on the context clues, ask students what *exhibit* means as it is used in the story. (*"something meant to be shown or displayed to the public"*). **(RL.6.4; L.6.4.a)**

- On the board, write the related words *exhibited* and *exhibition*. Discuss with students some contexts in which these words might appear.

AT A GLANCE

Students continue reading about the brothers at the aquarium. They answer a multiple-choice question and analyze what information should not be included in a good summary.

STEP BY STEP

- Tell students they will continue reading about Ted and Sam at the aquarium.

- Remind students that good readers pay attention to the important details and events in a story. Close Reading will help students focus on these important details. Underlining the characters and plot clues will make the summarizing process quick and efficient. The Hint will remind students what does not belong in a summary.

- Have students read the passage and underline the characters and clues, as directed by Close Reading.

- Ask volunteers to share the information they underlined. Have them explain how each clue built on the previous one to help reveal the identity of the "Lady."

- Then have students respond to Show Your Thinking. Remind them that a summary includes only the important events. Ask, "What is the most important thing that happens in this part of the story?"

ANSWER ANALYSIS

Choice A is incorrect. The words *should have* are a hint that this choice might express a judgment not a fact.

Choice B is correct. It includes the characters, setting, and most important event—the revelation of the identity of the Lady with Fish Pants.

Choice C is incorrect. It accurately states a story detail, but it is not an important detail that advances the plot.

Choice D is incorrect. The story says that Sam takes Ted to the gift shop to wait for their mother, not because he is tired of Ted's whining.

ERROR ALERT: Students who did not choose B may have lost sight of the fact that the question asks for a summary. Remind students that a summary includes the characters, setting, and most important events. Choice B is the only choice that includes all three.

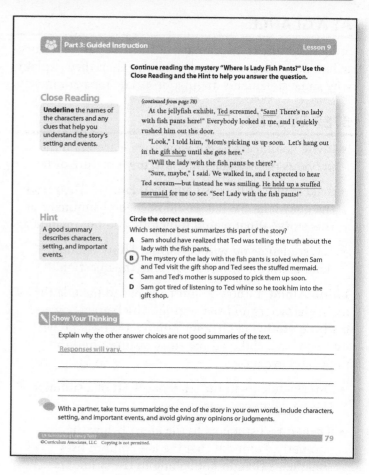

ELL Support: Irregular Past-Tense Verbs

- Remind students that the past tense of most verbs is formed by adding *-d* or *-ed* to the present-tense form of the verb, as in *solve, solved.* However, some verbs, called irregular verbs, have special forms.

- Point out the past-tense verb *told* in paragraph 2 on page 79. Ask, "What is the present-tense form of this verb?" *(tell)*

- Then guide students to find another irregular past-tense verb in paragraph 4 *(held)* and have them name the present-tense form *(holds).*

- Tell students that some irregular verbs have the same form for the present and past tense, as in *My feet hurt right now in these new shoes. I hurt my feet yesterday playing soccer.*

- Explain that students must learn and remember the past tense of irregular verbs. **(L.6.1)**

AT A GLANCE

Students read a passage twice about a mystery aboard an aircraft carrier. After the first reading, you will ask three questions to check your students' comprehension of the passage.

STEP BY STEP

- Have students read the story silently without referring to the Study Buddy or Close Reading text.

- Ask the following questions to ensure student comprehension of the text:

  What is the setting of the story? (*an aircraft carrier, the U.S.S.* Lexington, *during a school field trip*)

  Explain what "The Blue Ghost" refers to. (*It is a nickname for the* Lexington, *which was thought to have been sunk during World War II. Blue connects to the sea; ghost to something that lives on after supposedly being destroyed.*)

  What is the "silver rectangle" referred to at the end of Paragraph 8? (*Harrison's camera*)

- Ask students to reread paragraph 1 and look at the Study Buddy think aloud. What does the Study Buddy help them think about?

> **Tip:** The Study Buddy reminds students that the story is a mystery and they should recall the characteristics of the genre. When summarizing a mystery, the setting is usually significant and the clues signal the most important events.

- Have students read the rest of the mystery. Tell them to follow the directions in the Close Reading.

> **Tip:** Tell students that the reader of a mystery often has to make an inference based on the story clues. As students look for clues, remind them that one clue usually leads to another. Recognizing these connections will help them interpret the clues.

- Finally, have students answer the questions on page 81. Use the Answer Analysis to discuss correct and incorrect responses.

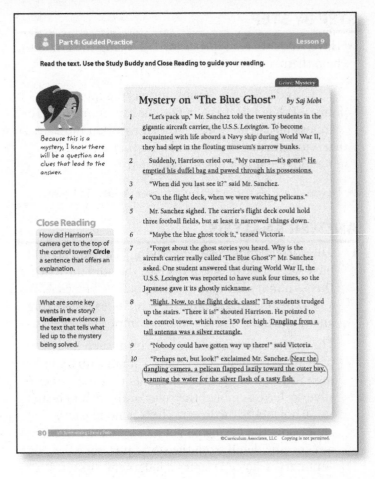

Tier Two Vocabulary: *Acquainted*

- Point out the word *acquainted* in paragraph 1. Ask: What are the students becoming acquainted with? What words in the surrounding text give clues about the meaning of *acquainted*? (*"life aboard a Navy ship during World War II," "slept in the floating museum's narrow bunks"*) (**RL.6.4; L.6.4.a**)

- Tell students that when you become acquainted with someone or something, you learn about that person or thing. Ask students to name persons or things they have become acquainted with. (*classmates, neighbors, specific sports, historical events, current events*)

- Have students describe how they became acquainted with them. (*talking, spending time together, playing on teams together, visiting museums, reading*)

- Ask what other words would make sense in the text in place of *acquainted*: *familiar, informed about, to learn about.*

STEP BY STEP

- Have students read questions 1–3, using the Hints to help them answer those questions.

Tip: If students have trouble answering question 3, point out that adjectives may signal an opinion, as in "careless boy." The words *should have* often indicate that a judgment is being made. Neither an opinion nor a judgment belongs in a summary.

- Discuss with students the Answer Analysis below.

ANSWER ANALYSIS

1 The correct choice is C. By saying Harrison should have kept his camera in his bag, the student writing this summary is making a judgment. Choices A, B, and D belong in a summary: A includes the setting and characters, and B and D are important events.

2 The correct choice is B. A large bird, such as a pelican, is capable of carrying a small camera to a high tower, and the story suggests that the camera's silver color resembled the color of the fish pelicans eat. Choice A is incorrect. There is no mystery about how the *Lexington* got its nickname. Choice C is a specific detail from the story. It is not a summary. Choice D states a judgment. It says nothing about how the mystery was solved.

3 Sample response: Mr. Sanchez's class spends the night on a World War II aircraft carrier. When Harrison can't find his camera, the class must solve the mystery of what happened to it. They discover that a pelican took it because the camera looked like a fish.

RETEACHING

Use a chart to help students answer question 3. Draw the chart below. Work with students to fill in the boxes. Sample responses are provided.

Setting	Characters	Events
aircraft carrier	Mr. Sanchez and his class, including Harrison.	Harrison can't find his camera. The class searches the ship's flight deck. They find it on an antenna. They decide a pelican took the silver camera, mistaking it for a fish.

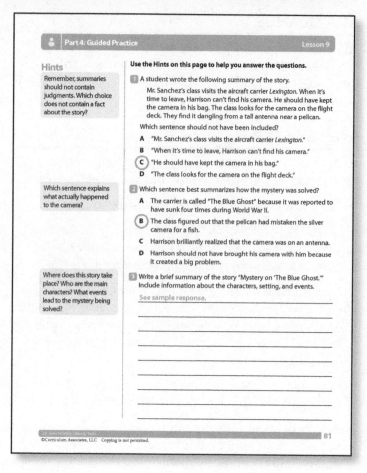

Use the Hints on this page to help you answer the questions.

Hints

Remember, summaries should not contain judgments. Which choice does not contain a fact about the story?

1 A student wrote the following summary of the story.

Mr. Sanchez's class visits the aircraft carrier *Lexington*. When it's time to leave, Harrison can't find his camera. He should have kept the camera in his bag. The class looks for the camera on the flight deck. They find it dangling from a tall antenna near a pelican.

Which sentence should not have been included?

A "Mr. Sanchez's class visits the aircraft carrier *Lexington*."

B "When it's time to leave, Harrison can't find his camera."

C "He should have kept the camera in his bag."

D "The class looks for the camera on the flight deck."

Which sentence explains what actually happened to the camera?

2 Which sentence best summarizes how the mystery was solved?

A The carrier is called "The Blue Ghost" because it was reported to have sunk four times during World War II.

B The class figured out that the pelican had mistaken the silver camera for a fish.

C Harrison brilliantly realized that the camera was on an antenna.

D Harrison should not have brought his camera with him because it created a big problem.

Where does this story take place? Who are the main characters? What events lead to the mystery being solved?

3 Write a brief summary of the story "Mystery on 'The Blue Ghost.'" Include information about the characters, setting, and events.

See sample response.

_____

_____

_____

_____

_____

_____

_____

_____

_____

Integrating Standards

Use these questions to further students' understanding of "Mystery on 'The Blue Ghost.'"

1 Why does the author call the U.S.S. *Lexington* a "floating museum"? **(RL.6.1)**

The ship is an aircraft carrier from World War II that people can visit to experience life aboard a ship that was part of an important event in U.S. history.

2 Describe the sequence of events that leads the class to solve the mystery of the missing camera. **(RL.6.3)**

First, the class sees the camera dangling from an antenna high up on the flight deck. One student says that no person could have gotten up so high. Then Mr. Sanchez points out a pelican flying near the camera and scanning the sea for fish. The students conclude that the pelican took the camera, mistaking its silver color for the skin of a fish. They think that when the bird realized its error, it dropped the camera on the antenna.

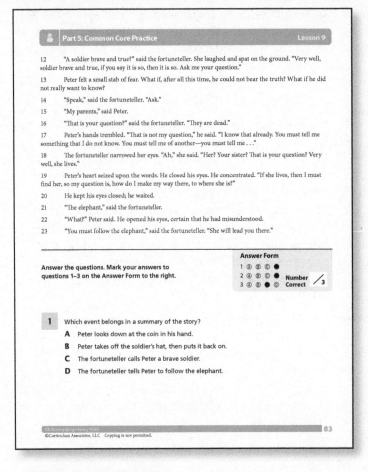

AT A GLANCE

Students independently read a longer story and answer questions in a format that provides test practice.

STEP BY STEP

- Tell students to use what they have learned about reading carefully and summarizing literary texts to read the story on pages 82 and 83.

- Remind students to underline or circle the setting, characters, and important events.

- Tell students to answer the questions on pages 83 and 84. For questions 1–3, they should fill in the correct circle on the Answer Form.

- When students have finished, use the Answer Analysis to discuss correct responses and the reasons for them. Have students fill in the Number Correct on the Answer Form.

ANSWER ANALYSIS

1 Choice D is correct. Telling Peter to follow the elephant is the climax of this part of the story. The other choices contain less important story details that are not needed in a summary. Choice A says that Peter looks at the coin in his hand. This is true, but this detail alone does not really convey Peter's indecision. Choice B also hints at Peter's indecision, but it is only one of several details that, taken all together, show the boy's hesitation. Choice C says the fortuneteller calls Peter a brave soldier. This statement does not fully capture the event. This detail is not important to the main problem of the story. *(DOK 2)*

Theme Connection

- How do all the stories in this lesson relate to the theme of puzzles and mysteries?

- What did you learn about solving mysteries from each story?

2 Choice D is correct. Describing Peter's decision as "good," indicates that this is an opinion, not a fact. It may be a good decision, but it cannot be proven to be good, at least not in this part of the story. Choices A, B, and C each state a fact from the story, not an opinion. **(DOK 3)**

3 Choice C is correct. It sums up several details from this part of the story that, together, show Peter's indecision about visiting the fortuneteller. Choice A cites one event, and according to the story, Peter never even walks around the tent. Choice B is accurate, but it does not summarize details from several paragraphs, it just states one detail from paragraph 4. Choice D, too, is accurate, but it only provides a detail about what Peter thinks. It does not provide a summary of these paragraphs. **(DOK 2)**

4 Sample response: Peter visits the market to buy bread and sees a fortuneteller's tent. He decides that he must learn the truth, and pays the fortuneteller with his bread money even though it makes him feel guilty. He learns that his sister is still alive and that he must follow the elephant to find her. **(DOK 2)**

Part 5: Common Core Practice   Lesson 9

2 Which sentence expresses an opinion?
A   Peter has a coin that belongs to his guardian.
B   Peter sees a fortuneteller's sign pinned to a tent.
C   Peter learns that his sister is still alive.
D   Peter makes a good decision in giving up his coin.

3 Which sentence **best** summarizes paragraphs 4 through 6?
A   Peter walks around the fortuneteller's red tent.
B   Peter worries about telling a lie to his guardian, Vilna Lutz.
C   Peter has trouble deciding whether to visit the fortuneteller.
D   Peter tells himself that the truth is definitely worth knowing.

4 Write a brief summary of the excerpt. Include at least **three** details from the story.
See sample response.

Self Check   *Go back and see what you can check off on the Self Check on page 44.*

84   L9: Summarizing Literary Texts   ©Curriculum Associates, LLC   Copying is not permitted.

Integrating Standards

Use these questions and tasks as opportunities to interact with "The Magician's Elephant."

1 According to the story, the sign on the fortuneteller's tent is written in a "cramped but unapologetic hand." What inferences can you make about the fortuneteller from this description? **(RL.6.1)**

The word cramped *indicates that the fortuneteller is old. Writing that is cramped is jammed together and hard to read. I know that the fingers of elderly people often curl up, making writing difficult. Unapologetic tells me that the fortuneteller is proud and not afraid to make an outrageous claim, such as being able to answer difficult questions of the human heart.*

2 The fortuneteller's sign specifies that she can answer "the most profound and difficult questions." What does *profound* mean? What kinds of questions are profound and what kind are not? **(RL.6.4; L.6.4.a)**

Profound means deep and complicated. Profound questions may be about things that affect many

people's lives, such as questions related to family. Profound questions are not questions such as "How hot is the sun?" or "What should my science fair project be?" Questions about facts or everyday matters may be difficult, but they are not profound.

3 Write about the story's theme. **(RL.6.2; W.6.2)**

Sample response: One theme is that matters of the human heart are hard to ignore, are all-consuming, and can compel people to do things they might not ordinarily do. This is shown through Peter's decision to talk to the fortuneteller.

4 Discuss in small groups: How can you describe the character of Peter? What do you learn about him through what he thinks, says, and does? **(RL.6.1; SL.6.1)**

Discussions will vary. Students should cite specific evidence from the text to support their understanding. They may mention that Peter is an honest person who has lost his parents and is desperate to find his sister.

Writing Activities

Should He or Shouldn't He? *(W.6.1)*

- Challenge students to think about how Peter will describe his experience in the marketplace to his guardian, Vilna Lutz. Will he tell the truth about the coin? Will he describe his encounter with the fortuneteller? What thoughts will go through his mind as he decides on a course of action?

- Have students use what they have learned about Peter from the excerpt to write an argument for or against Peter's telling the truth about his experience to Vilna Lutz. Tell them to consider how Peter might weigh his desire to do the honorable thing against his need to find his sister.

Appositives *(L.6.2.a)*

- Read aloud the phrase "an old soldier named Vilna Lutz" in paragraph 1. Tell students that this is an appositive, a word or phrase that adds information about the noun that directly precedes it. Ask students what noun the appositive tells about. *(guardian)* Explain that if the appositive is not necessary to identify the noun, it is a nonrestrictive element. A comma separates this element from the rest of the sentence.

- Have students find another appositive in Paragraph 3. *("the single florint")*

- Have students write a paragraph about a friend and include at least one appositive.

LISTENING ACTIVITY *(SL.6.6)*

Listen Closely/Listen to a Dramatic Reading

- Paragraphs 3–6 of "The Magician's Elephant" describe Peter's dialogue with himself over whether to spend the florint on the fortuneteller.

- Have volunteers take the roles of Peter and the narrator and do a dramatic reading of these paragraphs, using appropriate rate and expression.

- Remind students to listen respectfully and comment constructively on the readings.

DISCUSSION ACTIVITY *(SL.6.1)*

Talk in a Group/Talk About Mysteries

- Ask students to recall the characteristics of mysteries and think about how the three stories in this lesson conform to or digress from the genre.

- Have students form small groups to discuss the stories in the lesson as well as other examples of the genre. Have each group make a list of qualities for mysteries: "What Makes a Great Mystery."

- Appoint one member of each group to take notes. Allow 10 to 15 minutes for discussion, and then have each group share its results with the class.

MEDIA ACTIVITY *(RL.6.1, RL.6.2)*

Be Creative/Illustrate a Mystery

- Have students review the illustrations on page 77. Remind them that these pictures clearly show characters, settings, and events.

- Invite students to illustrate their own short mystery. Have students exchange illustrations and summarize the mystery.

RESEARCH ACTIVITY *(W.6.2; SL.6.4, SL.6.5)*

Research/Write a Report

- Have students use the information in "Mystery on 'The Blue Ghost'" to plan a written report on aircraft carriers in World War II.

- Ask students to research additional information to include, such as the role carriers played, the jobs performed on the ships, the difficulty of landing planes on the decks, or famous battles involving aircraft carriers. Students should take notes and write a brief report.

- Encourage students to include photographs or videos of the U.S.S. *Lexington* or other aircraft carrier in their reports.

SCORING GUIDE AND ANSWER ANALYSIS

Literature Passage Answer Analysis

1 Ⓐ Ⓑ Ⓒ ●
2 ● Ⓑ Ⓒ Ⓓ
3 Ⓐ Ⓑ ● Ⓓ
4 Ⓐ Ⓑ ● Ⓓ
5A Ⓐ ● Ⓒ Ⓓ
5B Ⓐ Ⓑ Ⓒ ●

1 Choice D is correct. It explains that Edwin sold his cow, Nelly, at the Baileys' farm. Although he cares about his cow, he feels he needs to do something to help his family get some much-needed money.

Choice A is incorrect. It says that Edwin overhead his parents having a serious discussion. However, this does not show that Edwin wants to help his family during this difficult time. Choice B is incorrect. It explains that Pa asked Edwin to ride into town to purchase some provisions. While doing chores helps a little, this does not support the idea that Edwin wants to help his family during this difficult time. Choice C is also incorrect. It says that Edwin put the picture of the orange grove near his bed. Although Edwin finds the picture inspiring, tacking it up next to his bed does not really help his family. *(RL.6.1; DOK 2)*

2 Choice A is correct. It says that Ma had to skim the dust from the milk. This shows that even basic necessities, like milk, were affected by the Dust Bowl, making it difficult for families to survive.

Choice B is incorrect. It explains that the dust storm outside made the house dark and dismal. While this most likely made life a little more depressing, it is not the best choice to show how the Dust Bowl made survival difficult for families. Choice C is incorrect. It shows Edwin's feelings about the dust, but it does not support the idea that the Dust Bowl made it difficult for families to survive. Choice D is also incorrect. It shows how the Dust Bowl affected life, but it does not support the idea that the Dust Bowl made it difficult for families to survive. *(RL.6.1; DOK 2)*

3 Choice C is correct. It explains that one should try to find the good in every situation. Edwin's family struggles to find the good in their difficult situation. This is an important theme in the story.

Choice A is incorrect. It explains that one should not rely on others for help. The characters in the story do not rely on others outside their family, but this is not the theme of the story. Choice B is incorrect. It says that you can't make a person change. While this may be true, this theme does not apply to the story. In fact, Edwin's parents end up changing their lives for the benefit of their family. Choice D is also incorrect. It says that you shouldn't want more than you have. However, Pa, Ma, and Edwin do want a better life, and they take action to try to improve their situation. Therefore, this theme does not apply to the story. *(RL.6.2; DOK 3)*

4 Choice C is correct. By selling off their livelihood, the family (and other farmers of the time) demonstrate the lengths they will go to provide for themselves.

Choice A is incorrect. The girl's wheezing may represent a different behavior based on changing circumstances, but it does not demonstrate human adaptability. Choice B is incorrect. It shows how Dust Bowl storms impact the atmosphere at the farmhouse, but it does not reveal anything about the family's behavior. Choice D is also incorrect. This sentence demonstrates how Edwin will attempt to solve his family's problems, but it is not the best example of the family's overall adaptability in the face of adversity. *(RL.6.3; DOK 3)*

5 **Part A:** Choice B is correct. The text shows that Ma grows more comfortable with the idea of moving. The text does not have any evidence supporting the other claims about Ma's feelings. *(RL.6.3; DOK 2)*

Part B: Choice D is correct. Ma smiling about the orange grove shows that she is looking forward to moving, i.e., becoming more comfortable with it. Choice A is a sentence from before Ma learns about moving. Choices B and C show Ma's immediate resistance to moving and represent the emotional condition from which she changes. *(RL.6.1; DOK 2)*

SAMPLE RESPONSES

Short Response (See 2-Point Rubric—Short Response on page A46 for scoring.)

6 Several events help the reader know that the family will move to California. The first event is when Edwin tacks up the picture of the orange grove next to his bed and sees his mother looking at it and smiling. After that, Edwin's parents decide to sell their livestock, which makes Edwin think that a change is coming. These events help the reader know that the family will move to California. *(RL.6.1; DOK 3)*

7 The conflict in the story is that the family cannot grow food on their farm because of the Dust Bowl. The ground is hard and barren, so nothing will grow. To provide for his family, Pa must leave them behind to live and work in other places. To solve this problem, Pa proposes that the family should move to California, where there is work on commercial farms. Eventually, he convinces his wife that this is the best way to keep the family together and make enough money to support their family. Edwin does his part by selling his cow to help earn money for the move. *(RL.6.2, RL.6.3; DOK 2)*

8 Sample responses:
Part A: Student circles "resourceful," "observant," or "optimistic." *(RL.6.3; DOK 3)*

Parts B and C:
If a student circles "resourceful," possible sentences include: "Without hesitation, Edwin grabbed two pieces of heavy twine, tied one around each girl's waist, and then tied the two girls together" and "He returned home with 16 dollars in his pocket and a little relief knowing that Nelly would be cared for."

If a student circles "observant," possible sentences include: "After Pa had been home a few days, Edwin overheard his parents having a serious discussion" and "One day, Edwin even caught his mother examining the photograph of the orange grove, smiling for the first time in a long time."

If a student circles "optimistic," possible sentences include: "He was weary of the dust, too, but he was smiling inside because tomorrow his father was coming home" and "He returned home with 16 dollars in his pocket and a little relief knowing that Nelly would be cared for." *(RL.6.3; DOK 3)*

Performance Task (See New York State Grade 6–8 Expository Writing Evaluation Rubric on pages A47 and A48 for scoring.)

9 The reader can make several inferences about Edwin based on the text. First, the reader can tell that Edwin is very responsible. This is shown when he finds a way to get his sisters to safety during a dust storm. The way he helps with chores, such as milking the cow and sweeping the house, is also evidence that he is responsible.

The reader can also infer that Edwin cares about his family very much. We see this first when Edwin thinks about his father coming home from a long trip. The story says that Edwin "raced outside" when he heard his father arrive. It also explains that Edwin does not like it when his father is away from home for so long, which shows that he wants his family to be together.

Finally, the reader can infer that Edwin is a positive person. He tries to look on the bright side. In the beginning of the story it says, "He was weary of the dust, too, but he was smiling inside because tomorrow his father was coming home." His positive nature is also seen when he takes the picture of the orange grove home and tacks it up by his bed. This gives Edwin something hopeful to focus on. *(RL.6.1; DOK 3)*

Determining Word Meanings: Figurative, Connotative & Technical

Theme: *The Power of Music*

LESSON OBJECTIVES

- Understand that words may have more layers of meaning beyond their literal meaning.

- Analyze context to determine a word's figurative, connotative, or technical meaning.

THE LEARNING PROGRESSION

- **Grade 5:** CCLS RI.5.4 focuses on students determining the meaning of words or phrases in a text; students are not yet asked to identify a word's connotative or figurative meaning.

- **Grade 6: CCLS RI.6.4 emphasizes that students need to understand not only the denotative definitions of individual words in context, but also the figurative, connotative, and technical meanings.**

- **Grade 7:** CCLS RI.7.4 continues to emphasize connotation and technical and figurative language.

PREREQUISITE SKILLS

- Understand and use different strategies to determine the meaning of vocabulary.

- Use context clues to figure out the meaning of grade-level appropriate academic and domain-specific words and phrases.

TAP STUDENTS' PRIOR KNOWLEDGE

- Tell students that they will work on a lesson about analyzing word meanings in context to determine a word's figurative, connotative, or technical meaning. Remind students that context in surrounding text provides clues to a word's meaning and that they can use context clues to figure out the intended meaning of multiple-meaning words.

- Explain that the technical meaning of a word is the meaning the word has in a specific subject area.

- Explain that a word's connotative meaning reveals a person's feelings. Display: *My nosy neighbor watches me walk my dog each morning.* Ask students whether the neighbor is portrayed positively or negatively. *(negatively)* Discuss the connotative meaning of *nosy* versus the neutral meaning of *curious*.

- Discuss the way figurative meaning goes beyond a word's dictionary meaning to create a special effect or feeling. Display: *My legs turned to jelly when I climbed the ladder.* Ask students how the narrator felt. *(scared)* Discuss the figurative meaning of *legs turned to jelly* to indicate fear.

- Explain that analyzing context to determine figurative, connotative, and technical meanings of words will help students better understand authors' intended meanings.

Ready *Teacher Toolbox*

teacher-toolbox.com

	Prerequisite Skills	RI.6.4
Ready Lessons	✓	✓
Tools for Instruction	✓ ✓	✓ ✓
Interactive Tutorials		✓

CCLS Focus

RI.6.4 Determine the meaning of words and phrases as they are used in a text, including figurative, connotative, and technical meanings ….

ADDITIONAL STANDARDS: **RI.6.1, RI.6.2, RI.6.3, RI.6.6, RI.6.7; W.6.2, W.6.4, W.6.7, W.6.11.c; SL.6.1, SL.6.4, SL.6.5; L.6.1, L.6.2, L.6.4.a, L.6.4.d** (*See page A39 for full text.*)

AT A GLANCE

Through a cartoon, students learn about figurative and connotative meanings of words.

STEP BY STEP

- Read the description of figurative, connotative, and technical word meanings and discuss how context surrounding an unfamiliar word provides clues to meaning. Have students look at the picture and circle words and images that tell how the boy and the girl feel about the music.

- Discuss how *intense* and *earsplitting* have a similar meaning, "loud."

- Have students answer the questions to analyze the context of *earsplitting*.

- Lead students to the conclusion that the girl does not enjoy the music: her ears are not literally splitting; she means the music is loud; she is covering her ears; she doesn't like the music.

- Discuss how *earsplitting* is used figuratively to exaggerate how unpleasant the girl finds the music.

- Explain that paying attention to the surrounding words and phrases helps students determine whether a word is meant literally, technically, connotatively, or figuratively.

- Share an example of when you have used figurative or connotative language. For example, you may have "turned white as a sheet" at a time when you were frightened.

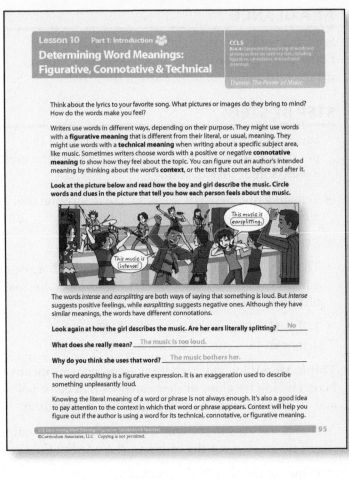

Genre Focus

Informational Texts: Technical Account

Tell students that in this lesson, they will read informational texts that are technical accounts. Explain that a technical account is written to inform or explain how scientific knowledge has been used for practical purposes in everyday life. It may explain a process or structure or describe features of a specific device. Often, a technical account uses precise language and content-specific terms. These words might be unfamiliar if readers are reading about a topic new to them. For example, the words *pitch, roll,* and *yaw* might be used in a technical account that explains how airplanes work.

Based on these characteristics, ask students to share examples of technical accounts they have read. What was the nature of the text? What technical terms do they recall? Did the text successfully explain how to operate something, such as an electronic device? Was the information easy or difficult to follow? Why?

Explain that "The Evolution of the Guitar" gives a brief history of the guitar and explains technical details about how guitars produce sound. *The Power of Music* is a section of a book that describes the scientific aspects of sound, especially musical sounds, and their interaction with the human body.

AT A GLANCE

Students read an article about the musician Chuck Berry. They use context to understand the technical meaning of a musical term used in the article.

STEP BY STEP

- Invite volunteers to tell what they learned on the previous page about using context clues to determine a word's figurative meaning.

- Tell students they will learn how to determine the technical meaning of a term used in music.

- Read aloud "The Father of Rock and Roll."

- Then read the question: "What does the author mean when she says that Chuck Berry 'was known for his phrasing'?"

- Tell students you will use a Think Aloud to demonstrate a way of answering the question.

Think Aloud: I wonder what the term *phrasing* means here. I'll look for clues in the sentences that come before and after the term to help me figure out its meaning.

- Direct students to the chart. Point out that they can use it to figure out the meaning of a word in the text.

- Point out the text in the Example column.

Think Aloud: I'll reread and look for context clues. I read that Berry "grouped notes into quick bursts." This probably has something to do with phrasing because it tells how Berry played his music. I'll write this context clue in the chart.

- Have students write this context clue in the Context Clues column.

Think Aloud: Now I'll look for more clues. I read that another guitarist described "that double-note stop, where you get the two notes bending against each other." This also tells how Berry played music.

- Have students write this context clue in the chart.

- Finally, have students respond to the prompt at the bottom of the page. Invite volunteers to share their explanations with the class. (*Sample response: The context shows that Berry grouped his notes together. This context helps me understand that phrasing means "grouping together notes into a single unit."*)

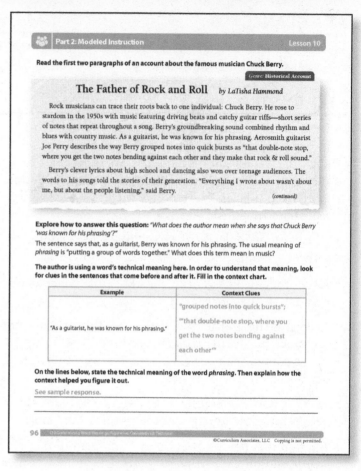

ELL Support: Pronouns

- Display the pronouns *their, he, they, me.* Explain that a pronoun is a word that is used in place of a noun. A pronoun refers to a person, place, or thing that was mentioned earlier.

- Display the sentence *Rock musicians can trace their roots back to one individual: Chuck Berry.* Underline *their* and draw an arrow from *their* to *musicians.* Point out that *their* takes the place of the noun *musicians.* Underline *musicians.*

- Repeat for the sentences in the article that contain the pronouns *he, they,* and *me,* and have students identify the noun that each pronoun refers to. **(L.6.1)**

AT A GLANCE

Students continue reading an article about Chuck Berry. They answer a multiple-choice question and explain how context helps them select the correct answer.

STEP BY STEP

- Tell students they will continue reading about Chuck Berry.

- Close Reading alerts students that the phrase "shined a light on many rock stars' paths" is not meant to be taken literally, but figuratively. The Hint suggests that by substituting each answer choice in place of the phrase, students can identify the choice that gives the correct meaning of the phrase.

- Have students read the text and identify context clues that explain the meaning of the figurative phrase, as directed by the Close Reading. Ask volunteers to share the context clues they identified. If necessary, ask: "What musician thought Chuck Berry was most closely identified with rock and roll?"

- Have students respond to the Show Your Thinking. (*Sample response: The context shows that many musicians were influenced by Berry's music. This helps me understand that "shined a light on many rock stars' paths" means that Berry inspired many musicians and helped show them the way.*)

ANSWER ANALYSIS

Choice A is incorrect. There are no context clues that refer to playing rock and roll for a living.

Choice B is incorrect. Only part of the phrase, *shining a light*, could mean "drawing attention to."

Choice C is correct. Chuck Berry's songwriting and performing inspired other musicians, as indicated by John Lennon's remark.

Choice D is incorrect. There are no context clues that suggest Berry exposed secrets.

ERROR ALERT: Students who did not choose C might not have understood how to relate the phrase to the other sentences. Help students see that this example shows how another famous musician admired Chuck Berry's music.

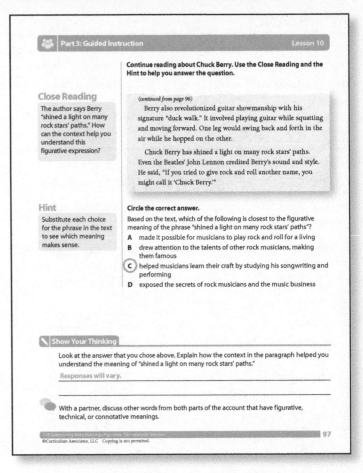

Tier Two Vocabulary: *Credited*

- Point out the word *credited* in paragraph 2. Tell students that context clues can help them figure out the meaning of *credited*. Explain that one way to find context clues is to read on and look for examples. Have students read the next sentence and ask what John Lennon did. (*He said something in praise of Berry.*)

- Tell students to use the example of what Lennon did to figure out the meaning of *credited*. Ask what *credited* means. ("*attributed an achievement to someone*")

- Have students confirm the meaning of *credited* by consulting a dictionary. (***RI.6.4; L.6.4.a; L.6.4.d***)

AT A GLANCE

Students read an article twice about the development of the guitar. After the first reading, you will ask three questions to check your students' comprehension of the text.

STEP BY STEP

- Have students read the article silently without referring to the Study Buddy or Close Reading text.

- Ask the following questions to ensure students' comprehension of the text:

  How does a guitarist make a guitar string change its tone? (*A guitarist presses the string down onto a fret cut into the guitar's neck, changing the string's length and thus its tone.*)

  How did 15th-century guitars differ from today's guitars? (*Some early guitars had only four strings as opposed to today's six-string guitars. They were also much smaller than today's guitars. They were all acoustic, while today there are electric guitars, too.*)

  Why was Lloyd Loar's invention of the magnetic pickup important? (*The magnetic pickup amplified the sound of guitar strings' vibrations and sent it through a speaker, making the sound louder.*)

- Then ask students to reread the article and look at the Study Buddy think aloud. What does the Study Buddy help them think about?

- Tell them to follow the directions in the Close Reading.

Tip: Students can ask themselves as they read whether the words the author chose to use have any positive or negative connotations. Understanding the words' connotations provides clues about the author's feelings. Learning this skill will help prepare students for the successive skill at the next level: analyzing the impact of specific word choice on meaning and tone.

- Finally, have students answer the questions on page 99. Use the Answer Analysis to discuss correct and incorrect responses.

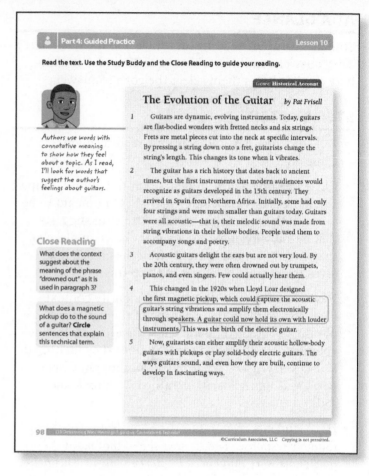

Tier Two Vocabulary: *Dynamic*

- Direct students to the word *dynamic* in paragraph 1. Tell students that context clues can help them figure out the meaning of *dynamic*. Explain that synonyms can be context clues. Ask students to find a word in the sentence that may be a synonym for *dynamic*. (*evolving*)

- Tell students to use the meaning of the synonym *evolving* to figure out the meaning of *dynamic*. Ask what *dynamic* means. (*"changing"*)

- Have students find other synonyms for *dynamic* by consulting a thesaurus. (**RI.6.4; L.6.4.a; L.6.4.d**)

STEP BY STEP

- Have students read questions 1–3, using the Hints to help them answer those questions.

> **Tip:** If students have trouble answering question 1, they can ask themselves whether they can substitute a more neutral word for each word in a given set. This strategy will help them determine whether the given words have positive connotations.

- Discuss with students the Answer Analysis below.

ANSWER ANALYSIS

1   The correct choice is C. The words *wonders*, *rich*, *delight*, and *fascinating* reveal that the author finds the subject of guitars pleasurable and entertaining. Choice A is incorrect. It lists technical words. Choice B is incorrect. It lists neutral words. Choice D is incorrect. It lists descriptive and comparative words that have a neutral connotation.

2   The correct choice is C. Acoustic guitars were not loud enough to be heard. Choice A is incorrect. The context does not suggest *drowned out* means guitars would be replaced. Choice B is incorrect. No context clues suggest that moisture in a guitar is related to its loudness. Choice D is incorrect. The text states that few people could hear guitars when played with other instruments, which does not imply that the guitar was becoming less popular.

3   Sample response: The word *amplify* means "to make louder or increase a sound's volume." The context clues "capture the acoustic guitar's string vibrations," "speakers," and "hold its own with louder instruments" help me understand that amplifying something involves making a sound louder so it can be heard more easily.

RETEACHING

Use a chart to answer question 3. Draw the chart below, and work with students to fill in the boxes. Sample responses are provided.

Example	Context Clues
"By the 20th century, they were often drowned out by trumpets, pianos, and even singers."	"Acoustic guitars … are not very loud." "Few could actually hear them."

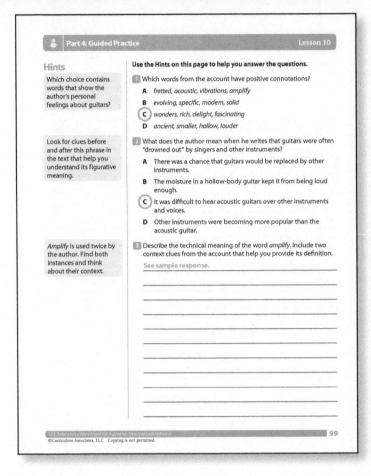

Part 4: Guided Practice   Lesson 10

Hints

Which choice contains words that show the author's personal feelings about guitars?

Look for clues before and after this phrase in the text that help you understand its figurative meaning.

Amplify is used twice by the author. Find both instances and think about their context.

Use the Hints on this page to help you answer the questions.

1   Which words from the account have positive connotations?

   A   *fretted, acoustic, vibrations, amplify*
   B   *evolving, specific, modern, solid*
   C   *wonders, rich, delight, fascinating*
   D   *ancient, smaller, hollow, louder*

2   What does the author mean when he writes that guitars were often "drowned out" by singers and other instruments?

   A   There was a chance that guitars would be replaced by other instruments.
   B   The moisture in a hollow-body guitar kept it from being loud enough.
   C   It was difficult to hear acoustic guitars over other instruments and voices.
   D   Other instruments were becoming more popular than the acoustic guitar.

3   Describe the technical meaning of the word *amplify*. Include two context clues from the account that help you provide its definition.

See sample response.

L10: Determining Word Meanings: Figurative, Connotative & Technical   99
©Curriculum Associates, LLC   Copying is not permitted.

Integrating Standards

Use these questions to further students' understanding of "The Evolution of the Guitar."

1   Which sentence from the article supports the inference that the magnetic pickup led to the invention of the electric guitar? **(RI.6.1)**

"This was the birth of the electric guitar."

2   Does the author of the article illustrate the key idea that a guitar is a dynamic, evolving instrument through the use of examples or the use of anecdotes? Cite evidence in the text in your response. **(RI.6.3)**

The author uses examples to illustrate that a guitar is a dynamic, evolving instrument. The author describes how 15th-century guitars had four strings, were small in size, and were all acoustic. Then the author describes modern guitars with six strings, as well as some guitars with magnetic pickups. The author finally provides the example of today's modern instrument, the solid-body electric guitar.

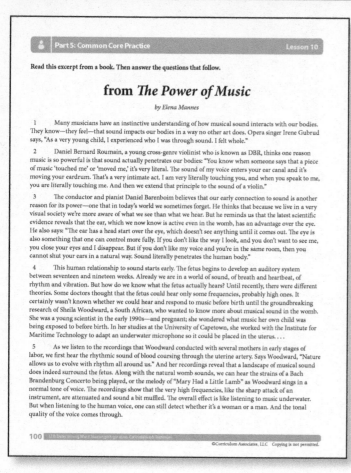

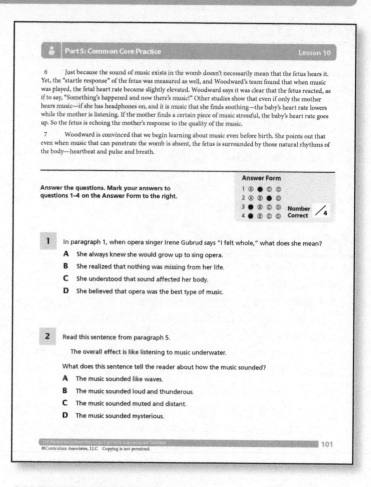

AT A GLANCE

Students independently read an excerpt from a book and answer questions in a format that provides test practice.

STEP BY STEP

- Tell students to use what they have learned about determining the figurative, connotative, and technical meaning of words and phrases to read the article on pages 100 and 101.

- Remind students to underline or circle important points.

- Tell students to answer the questions on pages 101 and 102. For questions 1–4, they should fill in the correct circle on the Answer Form.

- When students have finished, use the Answer Analysis to discuss correct responses and the reasons for them. Have students fill in the Number Correct on the Answer Form.

ANSWER ANALYSIS

1   The correct answer is B. Something that is whole isn't missing anything. Choice A is incorrect. Gubrud was not talking about singing opera. Choice C is incorrect. The context does not suggest this language means Gubrud understood her body. Choice D is incorrect because Gubrud's statement "I felt whole" was in the context of experiencing sound as a child, not in reference to her beliefs. **(DOK 3)**

2   The correct answer is C. It uses a simile to compare hearing musical sounds in the womb to listening to music underwater. Choices A, B, and D are incorrect. The text does not state that the sound is like waves, loud and thunderous, or mysterious. **(DOK 3)**

Theme Connection

- How do all the articles in this lesson relate to the theme of the power of music?

- What is one fact or idea you learned about the power of music from each article?

3 The correct answer is A. The author emphasizes the importance of sound's effect on the human body. This shows the author's belief that the art of music can have a powerful influence. Choice B is incorrect. It supports the idea that vision is a more powerful sense than hearing. Choices C and D are incorrect. They are facts about how people interact with music early in their lives, and facts do not have any positive or negative connotations. *(DOK 2)*

4 The correct answer is A. The term "startle response" refers to a physical change signaled by an elevated heart rate. Choice B describes a response that is the opposite of a "startle response." Choice C is incorrect. While music that the mother finds "stressful" could possibly cause a startle response, the phrase in itself does not explain the term. Choice D is also incorrect because the fetus "echoing" the mother's response does not necessarily involve a "startle response." *(DOK 2)*

5 Sample response: Tonal quality describes whether a sound is loud or soft. The sound might also be harsh or soothing like the voice of a mother. *(DOK 2)*

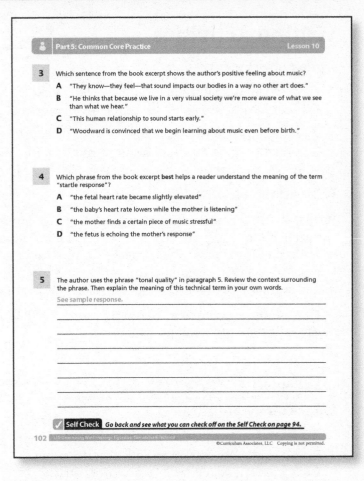

Integrating Standards

Use these questions and tasks as opportunities to interact with *The Power of Music.*

1 Which musicians does the author cite as examples to support the statement that many musicians have an instinctive understanding of how sound interacts with our bodies? *(RI.6.3)*

The author uses the examples of opera singer Irene Gubrud, violinist Daniel Bernard Roumain, and conductor and pianist Daniel Barenboim.

2 What world is the author referring to when he writes that "Already we are in a world of sound, of breath and heartbeat, of rhythm and vibration"? *(RI.6.1)*

He is referring to the fetus's world inside the womb.

3 How does the author illustrate the key idea that scientific evidence is now available that the ear is active even in the womb? *(RI.6.3)*

The author introduces the researcher Sheila Woodward and tells how she was inspired by her own pregnancy to investigate sounds that fetuses can hear. The author also explains technical details of the recordings used to do the research and the biological measurements used to gauge the fetus's reactions to sound.

4 What is the author's purpose in writing this article? Write your answer. *(RI.6.6; W.6.4)*

The author's purpose is to show how music and sound affect the human body and have an important influence on people, even before they are born.

5 Discuss as a class: Take turns reading each paragraph of the article and summarizing the paragraph's key ideas. *(RI.6.2; SL.6.1)*

Discussions will vary. Remind students that summaries include the most important ideas and leave out unimportant details.

Writing Activities

Explanatory Essay (W.6.2)

- Have students analyze in detail how Chuck Berry's musical style (as described by LaTisha Hammond in "The Father of Rock and Roll") led to the development of rock and roll music.

- Ask students to write essays to explain this development. They should include specific examples from the text that describe how the author introduces, illustrates, and elaborates upon Berry's techniques. Have students use precise language and specific terms in their explanations, as well as appropriate transitions.

Capitalization (L.6.2)

- Display this sentence from paragraph 5 of *The Power of Music*: ". . . we can hear the strains of a Bach Brandenburg Concerto being played, or the melody of 'Mary Had a Little Lamb' as Woodward sings in a normal tone of voice." Point out the capital letters in *Bach Brandenburg Concerto*. Explain that names of musical pieces are capitalized, as are names of songs and people's surnames. Have students identify the song and surname capitalized in the sentence. (*"Mary Had a Little Lamb," Woodward*)

- Have students write two descriptive sentences that include the names of a song and a person, using proper capitalization of the proper nouns.

LISTENING ACTIVITY (SL.6.1)

Listen Closely/Visualize

- Ask a student speaker to read aloud the paragraph in "The Father of Rock and Roll" that describes Chuck Berry's "duck walk" while others listen.

- Have students use the strategy of visualization to determine the meaning of the term *duck walk*.

- Listeners create pictures in their minds to visualize the "duck walk" as the speaker describes it. Volunteers give their interpretations of the "duck walk." As a class, discuss differences in interpretations.

DISCUSSION ACTIVITY (SL.6.1)

Talk in a Group/Questions and Answers

- Have partners write four questions based on information in "The Evolution of the Guitar."

- Encourage students to ask specific and open-ended questions, such as "How might people's use of guitars have changed over the centuries?"

- Have pairs exchange and answer questions with another pair. Both pairs reconvene in a small group, taking turns asking and answering their questions. Allow 20 minutes for group discussion.

MEDIA ACTIVITY (RI.6.4; RI.6.7)

Be Creative/Create a Music Video

- Have students form small groups to make a video recording based on the illustration on page 95.

- Students select a piece of music and write two lines of dialogue, using connotative words to express two different opinions of the music.

- Groups film their videos, acting out the dialogue with the chosen music playing in the background.

- Play selected videos for the class and discuss the connotations of words used in the dialogue.

RESEARCH ACTIVITY (W.6.7; SL.6.4; SL.6.5)

Research and Present/Write a Report

- Have students use *The Power of Music* as a starting point to research how music affects people's physical and emotional states. Have small groups plan an oral presentation based on a report they write.

- Students determine and use reliable research sources based on a given set of criteria. Encourage students to include excerpted musical clips in their presentations.

Analyzing Text Structures

LESSON OBJECTIVES

- Analyze how a particular sentence, paragraph, chapter, or section fits into the overall structure of a text (e.g., description, sequence, compare and contrast, cause and effect, or problem and solution) and contributes to the development of the text's central idea.

THE LEARNING PROGRESSION

- **Grade 5:** CCLS RI.5.5 requires students to identify and compare the text structures of two or more texts.

- **Grade 6: CCLS RI.6.5 builds on the Grade 5 standard by requiring students to analyze specific sections of text and place these sections in the context of the text's overall structure and ideas.**

- **Grade 7:** CCLS RI.7.5 requires students to recognize text structures and identify the connections between major sections of text and the central ideas.

PREREQUISITE SKILLS

- Identify main ideas and supporting details.

- Identify text structures and organizational patterns.

- Recognize how individual sections of a text help shape and develop ideas.

TAP STUDENTS' PRIOR KNOWLEDGE

- Tell students that this lesson focuses on text structures. Explain that text structure refers to how an author organizes the ideas and details he or she wants a reader to understand. Explain that authors sometimes use different text structures within a text to present different types of information.

- First, ask students how they might organize material if they were writing a report about an event in history. (*in sequence, in the order in which the events occurred*)

- Next, ask how they might organize information if they were writing about a problem. (*by describing the problem and then explaining how to solve it*)

- Then ask how they might organize information if they were going to write about how rainbows form. (*by describing cause and effect, or by sequence*) How might they organize their text if they wanted to compare their school to a friend's school? (*by telling how the schools are alike and how they are different*)

- Point out that understanding the text structure(s) within an article can help readers better understand the main ideas that the author is sharing.

Ready *Teacher Toolbox*   teacher-toolbox.com

	Prerequisite Skills	RI.6.5
Ready Lessons	✓ ✓	✓
Tools for Instruction		✓
Interactive Tutorials		✓ ✓

CCLS Focus

RI.6.5: Analyze how a particular sentence, paragraph, chapter, or section fits into the overall structure of a text and contributes to the development of the ideas.

ADDITIONAL STANDARDS: **RI.6.1, RI.6.2, RI.6.3, RI.6.4, RI.6.7, RL.6.4; W.6.2, W.6.4, W.6.4.a, W.6.7, W.6.9.b, W.6.11.c; SL.6.1, SL.6.2.a, SL.6.4; L.6.1, L.6.2.b, L.6.3.a, L.6.4.a, L.6.4.d** (See page A39 for full text.)

AT A GLANCE

Students explore the idea of writers choosing specific text structures for specific purposes. They look at segments of a text that are pieced together like a puzzle and determine how each piece is structured to develop the main idea.

STEP BY STEP

- Read the first two paragraphs and the descriptions of *text structure, problem and solution, chronology, compare and contrast,* and *causes and effects.* Discuss the jigsaw puzzle analogy.

- Then have students study the image, circle each reference to Greece, and underline each reference to Rome. Encourage them to think about how the parts fit together to form a whole.

- Explain that the chart describes the structure of each "puzzle piece" and how each piece functions to develop the main idea.

- Read each row of the chart, and discuss the function of each sentence with students. Then ask students to complete the chart for sentence 4. If necessary, guide them to understand that sentence 4 adds information about Rome that contrasts with the information in sentence 3.

- Reinforce the idea that parts of a text work together. Explain that authors craft their texts carefully, building text structures that work together to develop the main idea.

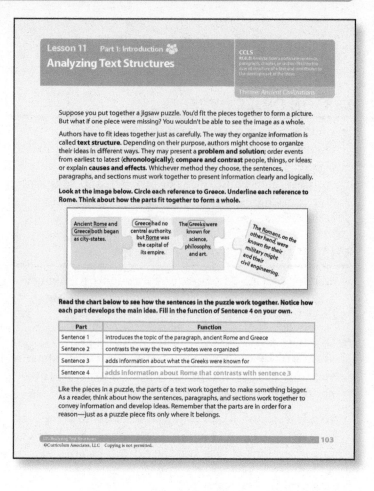

Genre Focus

Informational Texts: Historical Accounts

Tell students that in this lesson they will read informational accounts that tell about historical events. Accounts about historical events are usually written to inform the reader about the events and to explain why they happened. These accounts often include facts and details about the historical events. They also provide information that answers the questions *who, what, where, when, why,* and *how.*

Explain that the accounts in this lesson describe important historical discoveries. The first account, "Terra-Cotta Army Protects First Emperor's Tomb," tells about the discovery of a collection of clay soldiers that were built to protect the tomb of the first emperor of China. "Secrets in the Stones" tells about Stonehenge and provides theories about how and why these monuments were built. Finally, "The Dead Sea Scrolls" provides information about the discovery of the Dead Sea Scrolls.

Explain that these accounts provide historical facts and details intended to inform the reader about these discoveries. In this lesson, students will analyze each account to understand the text structures that the authors use to present their information in a cohesive, meaningful way.

AT A GLANCE

Students read an article about a discovery. They explain how the text's structure adds to their understanding.

STEP BY STEP

- Invite volunteers to tell what they learned on the previous page about text structures.

- Tell students that in this lesson they will analyze the text structure in an article.

- Read "Terra-Cotta Army Protects First Emperor's Tomb." Then read the question: "How does paragraph 3 build on the information presented in paragraphs 1 and 2?"

- Tell students you will use a Think Aloud to demonstrate a way of answering the question.

Think Aloud: I see that this text has a chronological structure because the events are told in sequence. The first event is that workers dig a well and find a life-size clay soldier. I'll write a 1 next to this sentence. Then the workers tell Chinese authorities of their discovery and archaeologists come to the site. Next, thousands of clay soldiers are uncovered. I'll number these events, too.

- Have students number the events in the text. Point out that one of the sentences should not be numbered because it is a description, not an event.

Think Aloud: Now I will look back at paragraph 1 to determine its function. How does this paragraph add to my understanding of the discovery? I see that it tells how workers found the first clay solder. So, this paragraph introduces what the article will be about.

- Have students fill in the chart.

Think Aloud: In paragraph 2, I learn more about the discovery by finding out how archaeologists became involved in the process.

- Point out the function of paragraph 2 in the chart.

- Next, have students respond to the prompt at the bottom of the page. Invite volunteers to share their responses with the class. (*Sample response: The paragraph gives visual descriptions of the clay army. These details help readers understand what a terra-cotta army is and why it is a significant historical find.*)

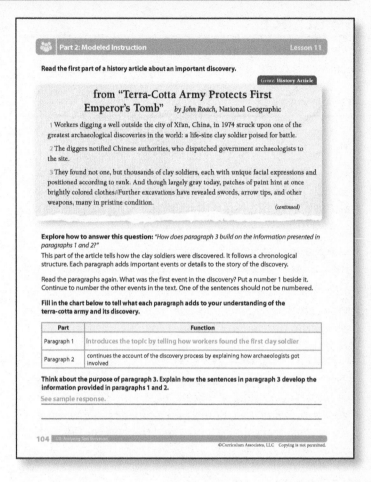

ELL Support: Regular Plural Nouns

- Explain to students that nouns name people, places, or things. Students can look at the endings of nouns to know *how many*.

- Work with students to identify regular plural nouns in the article. Point out the word *workers* in the first sentence. Have students tell how many (*more than one*) and identify how the plural was formed (*add* s). Then point out the word *patches* in paragraph 3 and discuss how the plural was formed (*add* es).

- Direct attention to the word *discoveries*. Have students identify the singular form. (*discovery*) Point out to students that to form the plural of a noun that ends in *y*, they first change the *y* to *i* and then add *es*. Have students identify another example in the article of a plural noun that has this spelling change. (*authorities*) (**L.6.1; L.6.2.b**)

AT A GLANCE

Students continue reading about the clay soldiers and answer questions about the text structure of the article.

STEP BY STEP

- Tell students that they will continue reading about the clay soldier discovery.

- Close Reading helps students identify how the sentences and paragraphs develop the key ideas of the article. The Hint will help them find information that will help them answer the question.

- Have students read the article. Discuss what information is presented in each paragraph and how this new information develops the main idea.

- Have students answer the multiple-choice question, using the information in the Close Reading and the Hint to guide them. Then have them respond to the question in Show Your Thinking. (*Sample response: The final sentence builds on the idea that the discovery of the first clay soldier was the beginning of one of the greatest archaeological discoveries by describing the vast number of soldiers found and the idea that there is still more to learn.*)

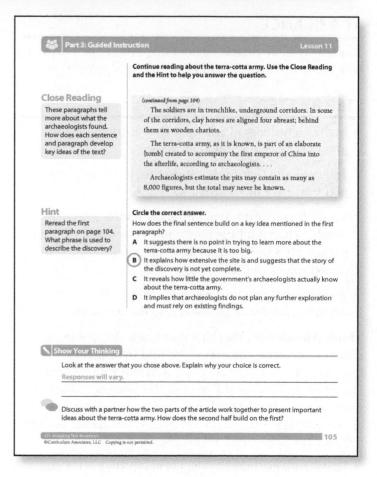

ANSWER ANALYSIS

Choice A is incorrect. The last sentence does not indicate that there is no point in further research.

Choice B is correct. The last sentence tells the reader that the discovery is not yet complete.

Choice C is incorrect. The last sentence does not point out how little the scientists know about other details.

Choice D is incorrect. The last sentence does not indicate whether further exploration is planned.

ERROR ALERT: Students who did not choose B may have neglected to use the Hint. Guide students to see that the first paragraph describes the discovery as "one of the greatest archaeological discoveries in the world." The last sentence builds on this idea by describing the vast number of soldiers found, which adds to the idea that this discovery was an amazing archaeological find.

Tier Two Vocabulary: *Elaborate*

- Point out the word *elaborate* in paragraph 2. Explain that the word *elaborate* can have two meanings, one as an adjective and one as a verb. Have students identify the part of speech in this context. (*adjective*) Ask students to tell what *elaborate* describes. (*tomb*) Then have students look for context clues to determine the meaning of *elaborate*. Ask volunteers to share their answers. (*elaborate: "detailed and complicated"*)

- Have students use a dictionary to check this meaning and find other meanings of this term. (**RL.6.4; L.6.4.a; L.6.4.d**)

AT A GLANCE

Students read an account twice about Stonehenge. After the first reading, you will ask three questions to check your students' comprehension of the account.

STEP BY STEP

- Have students read the account silently without referring to the Study Buddy or Close Reading text.

- Ask the following questions to ensure students' comprehension of the text:

  When and where was Stonehenge built? (*more than 5,000 years ago in southern England*)

  What are two theories about why Stonehenge was built? (*as a burial ground; as a tool to track seasons*)

  Why do archaeologists continue to study Stonehenge? (*because they are still trying to determine how and why Stonehenge was built*)

- Then ask students to look at the subheadings and the Study Buddy think aloud. What does the Study Buddy help them think about?

Tip: The Study Buddy points out the subheads of the account. Explain to students that these subheads help readers identify the text's structure. Point out to students that paying attention to subheads and other text features, such as diagrams and captions, can provide them with clues about how the text is organized and how the main ideas are developed. Being able to recognize a text's structure will help them to better understand the author's purpose and what the author wants readers to understand.

- Have students reread the account. Tell them to follow the directions in the Close Reading.

- Finally, have students answer the questions on page 107. Use the Answer Analysis to discuss correct and incorrect responses.

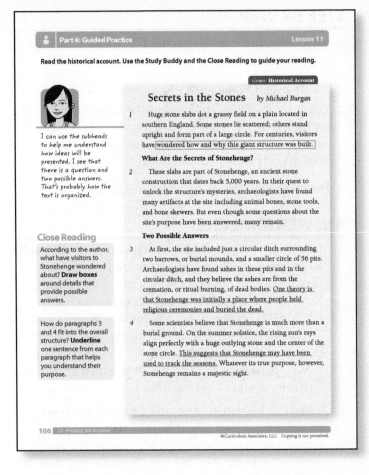

Read the historical account. Use the Study Buddy and the Close Reading to guide your reading.

Genre: Historical Account

Secrets in the Stones　*by Michael Burgan*

I can use the subheads to help me understand how ideas will be presented. I see that there is a question and two possible answers. That's probably how the text is organized.

1　Huge stone slabs dot a grassy field on a plain located in southern England. Some stones lie scattered; others stand upright and form part of a large circle. For centuries, visitors have wondered how and why this giant structure was built.

What Are the Secrets of Stonehenge?

2　These slabs are part of Stonehenge, an ancient stone construction that dates back 5,000 years. In their quest to unlock the structure's mysteries, archaeologists have found many artifacts at the site including animal bones, stone tools, and bone skewers. But even though some questions about the site's purpose have been answered, many remain.

Close Reading

According to the author, what have visitors to Stonehenge wondered about? **Draw boxes** around details that provide possible answers.

How do paragraphs 3 and 4 fit into the overall structure? **Underline** one sentence from each paragraph that helps you understand their purpose.

Two Possible Answers

3　At first, the site included just a circular ditch surrounding two barrows, or burial mounds, and a smaller circle of 56 pits. Archaeologists have found ashes in these pits and in the circular ditch, and they believe the ashes are from the cremation, or ritual burning, of dead bodies. One theory is that Stonehenge was initially a place where people held religious ceremonies and buried the dead.

4　Some scientists believe that Stonehenge is much more than a burial ground. On the summer solstice, the rising sun's rays align perfectly with a huge outlying stone and the center of the stone circle. This suggests that Stonehenge may have been used to track the seasons. Whatever its true purpose, however, Stonehenge remains a majestic sight.

106　L11: Analyzing Text Structures　　　　©Curriculum Associates, LLC　Copying is not permitted.

Tier Two Vocabulary: *Upright*

- Point out the word *upright* in paragraph 1. Remind students that context clues can include synonyms and antonyms of an unfamiliar word. Ask students which words and phrases in this paragraph give them clues about the meaning of *upright*. (*It's the opposite of "lie scattered."*) Then have students suggest the meaning of *upright*. (*"vertical"*) **(RI.6.4; L.6.4.a)**

- Have students identify related words that would make sense in place of *upright* in this context. (*straight up, standing on one end*)

STEP BY STEP

- Have students read questions 1–3, using the Hints to help them answer the questions.

Tip: If students have trouble answering question 3, encourage them to think about the author's purpose. Then have them think about how the first two paragraphs help to develop the main idea. Remind them to review their marked text to help them.

- Discuss with students the Answer Analysis below.

ANSWER ANALYSIS

1 Choice D is correct. This statement leads the reader to the next two paragraphs, which provide some theories about Stonehenge. Choice A is incorrect because some questions have been answered. Choice B is incorrect because archaeologists have answered many questions about the past. Choice C is incorrect because the account states that people have visited the site for centuries, which shows that curiosity about the site persists.

2 Choice A is correct. The subhead tells the reader that there are two possible answers, and each paragraph that follows provides one of the two answers. Choice B is incorrect because it states only one of the possible secrets. Choice C is incorrect because the final paragraph does not raise new questions. Choice D is incorrect because the account does not state that scientists disagree.

3 Sample response: The first two paragraphs describe what is known about Stonehenge, such as its location, its shape, and its age. They also introduce the problem that the account later tries to answer, which is that Stonehenge's purpose is still unknown.

RETEACHING

Use a chart to answer question 3. Draw the chart below, and work with students to fill in the boxes. Sample responses are provided.

Part	Function
Paragraph 1	describes what is known about Stonehenge
Paragraph 2	introduces the problem that Stonehenge's purpose is still unknown

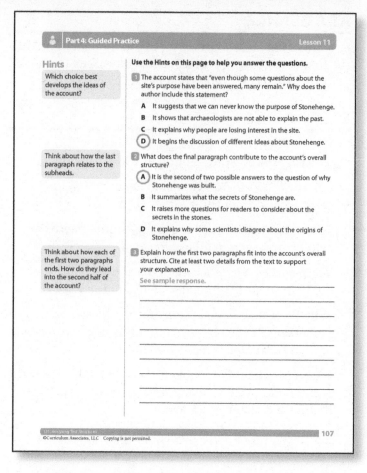

Hints

Which choice best develops the ideas of the account?

Think about how the last paragraph relates to the subheads.

Think about how each of the first two paragraphs ends. How do they lead into the second half of the account?

Use the Hints on this page to help you answer the questions.

1 The account states that "even though some questions about the site's purpose have been answered, many remain." Why does the author include this statement?

A It suggests that we can never know the purpose of Stonehenge.

B It shows that archaeologists are not able to explain the past.

C It explains why people are losing interest in the site.

D It begins the discussion of different ideas about Stonehenge.

2 What does the final paragraph contribute to the account's overall structure?

A It is the second of two possible answers to the question of why Stonehenge was built.

B It summarizes what the secrets of Stonehenge are.

C It raises more questions for readers to consider about the secrets in the stones.

D It explains why some scientists disagree about the origins of Stonehenge.

3 Explain how the first two paragraphs fit into the account's overall structure. Cite at least two details from the text to support your explanation.

See sample response.

_____

_____

_____

_____

_____

_____

_____

_____

Integrating Standards

Use these questions to further students' understanding of "Secrets in the Stones."

1 Summarize the main idea and key details from "Secrets in the Stones," using information from the account. **(RI.6.2)**

Stonehenge is a mysterious stone structure in southern England that dates back more than 5,000 years. Scientists have studied the structure and artifacts around it for years, trying to determine how and why it was built. Two theories are that it was built as a burial ground or to track the seasons.

2 What artifacts or discoveries did the scientists find that helped them determine that Stonehenge might have been used as a burial site? **(RI.6.1)**

Scientists discovered burial mounds and pits full of ashes, which helped them surmise that the site may have been used as a burial and cremation site.

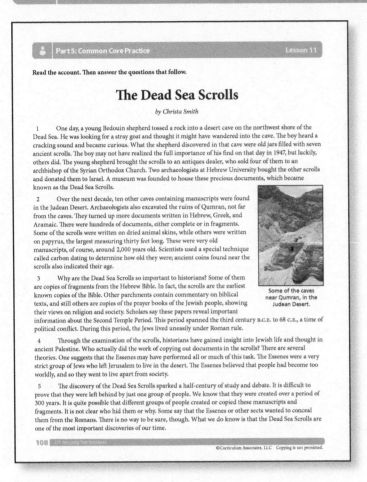

Read the account. Then answer the questions that follow.

The Dead Sea Scrolls

by Christa Smith

1   One day, a young Bedouin shepherd tossed a rock into a desert cave on the northwest shore of the Dead Sea. He was looking for a stray goat and thought it might have wandered into the cave. The boy heard a cracking sound and became curious. What the shepherd discovered in that cave were old jars filled with seven ancient scrolls. The boy may not have realized the full importance of his find on that day in 1947, but luckily, others did. The young shepherd brought the scrolls to an antiques dealer, who sold four of them to an archbishop of the Syrian Orthodox Church. Two archaeologists at Hebrew University bought the other scrolls and donated them to Israel. A museum was founded to house these precious documents, which became known as the Dead Sea Scrolls.

2   Over the next decade, ten other caves containing manuscripts were found in the Judean Desert. Archaeologists also excavated the ruins of Qumran, not far from the caves. They turned up more documents written in Hebrew, Greek, and Aramaic. There were hundreds of documents, either complete or in fragments. Some of the scrolls were written on dried animal skins, while others were written on papyrus, the largest measuring thirty feet long. These were very old manuscripts, of course, around 2,000 years old. Scientists used a special technique called carbon dating to determine how old they were; ancient coins found near the scrolls also indicated their age.

3   Why are the Dead Sea Scrolls so important to historians? Some of them are copies of fragments from the Hebrew Bible. In fact, the scrolls are the earliest known copies of the Bible. Other parchments contain commentary on biblical texts, and still others are copies of the prayer books of the Jewish people, showing their views on religion and society. Scholars say these papers reveal important information about the Second Temple Period. This period spanned the third century B.C.E. to 68 C.E., a time of political conflict. During this period, the Jews lived uneasily under Roman rule.

4   Through the examination of the scrolls, historians have gained insight into Jewish life and thought in ancient Palestine. Who actually did the work of copying out documents in the scrolls? There are several theories. One suggests that the Essenes may have performed all or much of this task. The Essenes were a very strict group of Jews who left Jerusalem to live in the desert. The Essenes believed that people had become too worldly, and so they went to live apart from society.

5   The discovery of the Dead Sea Scrolls sparked a half-century of study and debate. It is difficult to prove that they were left behind by just one group of people. We know that they were created over a period of 300 years. It is quite possible that different groups of people created or copied these manuscripts and fragments. It is not clear who hid them or why. Some say that the Essenes or other sects wanted to conceal them from the Romans. There is no way to be sure, though. What we do know is that the Dead Sea Scrolls are one of the most important discoveries of our time.

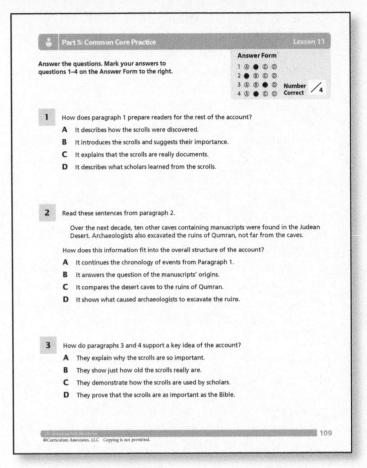

Some of the caves near Qumran, in the Judean Desert.

Part 5: Common Core Practice   Lesson 11

Answer the questions. Mark your answers to questions 1–4 on the Answer Form to the right.

Answer Form

1 Ⓐ ● Ⓒ Ⓓ
2 ● Ⓑ Ⓒ Ⓓ
3 Ⓐ Ⓑ ● Ⓓ   **Number** ⁄4
4 Ⓐ ● Ⓒ Ⓓ   **Correct**

1   How does paragraph 1 prepare readers for the rest of the account?

   A   It describes how the scrolls were discovered.

   B   It introduces the scrolls and suggests their importance.

   C   It explains that the scrolls are really documents.

   D   It describes what scholars learned from the scrolls.

2   Read these sentences from paragraph 2.

> Over the next decade, ten other caves containing manuscripts were found in the Judean Desert. Archaeologists also excavated the ruins of Qumran, not far from the caves.

How does this information fit into the overall structure of the account?

   A   It continues the chronology of events from Paragraph 1.

   B   It answers the question of the manuscripts' origins.

   C   It compares the desert caves to the ruins of Qumran.

   D   It shows what caused archaeologists to excavate the ruins.

3   How do paragraphs 3 and 4 support a key idea of the account?

   A   They explain why the scrolls are so important.

   B   They show just how old the scrolls really are.

   C   They demonstrate how the scrolls are used by scholars.

   D   They prove that the scrolls are as important as the Bible.

AT A GLANCE

Students independently read a longer account and answer questions in a format that provides test practice.

STEP BY STEP

- Tell students to use what they have learned about reading closely and analyzing text structure to read the account on page 108.

- Remind students to underline or circle important details and ideas that help determine the structure of the account.

- Tell students to answer the questions on pages 109 and 110. For questions 1–4, they should fill in the correct circle on the Answer Form.

- When students have finished, use the Answer Analysis to discuss correct responses and the reasons for them. Have students fill in the Number Correct on the Answer Form.

ANSWER ANALYSIS

1   Choice B is correct. The paragraph sets up the account to describe the discovery's importance. Choice A is incorrect because the main purpose of the paragraph is to highlight the scrolls' importance. Choice C is incorrect because this is only one detail contained in the paragraph. Choice D is incorrect because paragraph 1 does not explain what scholars have learned from the scrolls. **(DOK 2)**

2   Choice A is correct. It tells that more caves with scrolls were found. Choice B is incorrect because it does not discuss the scrolls' origin. Choice C is incorrect because no comparisons are made in paragraph 2. Choice D is incorrect because it does not explain why archaeologists excavated the ruins. **(DOK 2)**

Theme Connection

- How do all the accounts in this lesson relate to the theme of ancient civilizations?

- What is one fact or idea you learned about ancient civilizations from each account in this lesson?

3 Choice C is correct. These paragraphs describe what scholars and historians are learning from the scrolls. Choices A and B are incorrect because the paragraphs tell more than that the scrolls are important and that they are old. The paragraphs also explain what scholars have learned from the documents. Choice D is incorrect. No comparison is made between the scrolls and the Bible. *(DOK 2)*

4 Choice B is correct. The text structure of "The Dead Sea Scrolls" primarily follows a cause-and-effect structure. When the shepherd boy finds the scrolls, that discovery becomes the cause of a great many effects. These effects include archaeological digs in the region, scholarly debates, new historical insights into Jewish life in ancient Palestine, and so on. Choices A, C, and D are incorrect. The text does not use structures based in comparison, persuasion, or clear sequence to present its information. *(DOK 2)*

5 Sample response: Paragraph 5 brings the reader up to date in the events following the discovery of the scrolls. It completes the chronology that began in paragraph 1. It also leaves room for future discoveries that may answer some of the questions about the scrolls. *(DOK 3)*

Inset page:

4 Which graphic **best** represents the structure of the informational text "The Dead Sea Scrolls"?

A   Both   B
A

Opinion → Reason 1, Reason 2, Reason 3
C

Cause → Effect → Effect
B

Step 1 → Step 2 → Step 3
D

5 Explain why the author includes paragraph 5 in the account. Use at least **three** details from the text to show how this paragraph fits into the overall structure of the account.

See sample response.

_____
_____
_____
_____
_____
_____
_____
_____
_____

✓ **Self Check** *Go back and see what you can check off on the Self Check on page 94.*

110   L11: Analyzing Text Structures   ©Curriculum Associates, LLC   Copying is not permitted.

Integrating Standards

Use these questions and tasks as opportunities to interact with "The Dead Sea Scrolls."

1 What can you infer from the last sentence in paragraph 1, "A museum was founded to house these precious documents, which became known as the Dead Sea Scrolls"? *(RI.6.1)*

This sentence tells that the scrolls warranted having a museum built specifically for them. I know that things that are valuable and rare are kept in museums, so I can make an inference that these documents are very valuable and rare.

2 Why do scholars and historians think the Dead Sea Scrolls are so important? *(RI.6.1)*

These documents provide insight and clues about the lives and cultures of people that lived thousands of years ago, and they provide valuable information about human history.

3 How are the ideas about the Dead Sea Scrolls introduced in the text? *(RI.6.3)*

The anecdote at the beginning about the young shepherd introduces readers to the topic of the scrolls and helps them to understand that the ancient scrolls were discovered accidentally.

4 Summarize: Write a brief summary of the account, including key details that support the main idea. *(RI.6.2; W.6.2)*

Sample response: The account is about the Dead Sea Scrolls and how they were discovered. These scrolls are thousands of years old. They are the earliest known copies of the Hebrew Bible. These documents reveal significant historical information and have led to much study and debate.

5 Discuss in small groups: What is the author's opinion of the scrolls? What words and phrases suggest this opinion? Do you agree with the author's opinion? Why? *(SL.6.1)*

Discussions will vary. Encourage students to cite specific evidence that shows the author's opinion that the scrolls are a very important discovery.

Writing Activities

Write a Letter (W.6.4; W.6.9.b)

- Have students think about how they would feel if they discovered the terra-cotta soldiers, Stonehenge, or the Dead Sea Scrolls. What would the moment feel like when they first saw the ancient site? What would they want to tell their friends and families about their discovery?

- Have students suppose that they were the first to discover one of the ancient treasures described in this lesson. Have them write a letter to a friend or family member describing their discovery. Encourage students to be descriptive and to include details from the account to inform their audience about the discovery.

Compound Sentences (L.6.3.a)

- Tell students that compound sentences consist of two independent sentences joined by a comma and a conjunction, such as *and, but,* or *or.* Point out the last sentence of paragraph 4 in "The Dead Sea Scrolls." Explain that this sentence is a compound sentence.

- Reread the last paragraph of this account. Tell students that there are several simple sentences that could be combined to form compound students. Have students write two compound sentences from the sentences in paragraph 4. Invite volunteers to share their compound sentences with the class.

LISTENING ACTIVITY (SL.6.1)

Listen Closely/Describe Text Structure

- Have students work in pairs to review "The Dead Sea Scrolls." Have students first reread the account.

- One student then describes in his or her own words the function of paragraph 1 in developing the account's main idea. The other student listens and then elaborates on the student's answer by explaining how paragraph 2 develops the main idea.

- Students continue until they have discussed each paragraph in the account.

DISCUSSION ACTIVITY (SL.6.1)

Talk in Groups/Discuss Symbols

- Discuss with students how the discovery of Stonehenge gave insight into what life and culture were probably like 5,000 years ago for the people who built that structure.

- Have students form small groups to discuss how discoveries provide information about ancient civilizations. Encourage students to talk about the discoveries mentioned in this lesson as well as other discoveries with which they are familiar.

MEDIA ACTIVITY (RI.6.7)

Be Creative/Write a Caption

- Have students find a photograph of the terra-cotta soldiers they read about in "Terra-Cotta Army Protects First Emperor's Tomb."

- Have students print the photo and write a caption that describes the soldiers. Then ask students to discuss how seeing a picture of the soldier gives them a more complete understanding of this discovery.

RESEARCH ACTIVITY (W.6.7; SL.6.4)

Research and Present/Give a Presentation

- Have students use the information in this lesson's accounts as a starting point for a report about archaeological discoveries.

- Have students research another important discovery, such as the pyramids of Egypt, the cliff dwellings in Mesa Verde, the Mayan ruins in Mexico, or King Tut's tomb.

- Have students research their selected discovery and write a report about it. Ask students to present their findings to the class. Encourage students to use visual aids to show what the discovery looks like and where it was found.

Determining Point of View

LESSON OBJECTIVES

- Determine an author's purpose for writing informational text.

- Determine an author's point of view about the topic of informational text.

- Cite evidence to explain how the author's point of view is conveyed in a text.

THE LEARNING PROGRESSION

- **Grade 5:** CCLS RI.5.6 asks students to analyze the point of view in multiple texts related to the same topic.

- **Grade 6: CCLS RI.6.6 builds on the Grade 5 standard by requiring students to focus on using evidence to describe the point of view.**

- **Grade 7:** CCLS RI.7.6 requires students to analyze how an author distinguishes his or her position from that of others.

PREREQUISITE SKILLS

- Identify the author's point of view or purpose in a text.

- Recognize statements and word choices that make clear the text is expressing the author's point of view.

- Explain how word choice and tone help establish an author's perspective and bias.

TAP STUDENTS' PRIOR KNOWLEDGE

- Tell students they will be working on a lesson about determining the author's purpose and point of view. Remind them that an author's purpose is his or her reason for writing. Have students give examples of authors' purposes. (*to persuade, inform, or entertain*)

- Display two different informational texts that students have read recently. Discuss the authors' purposes for writing each text. Point out that the purpose of many informational texts is to inform the reader about a topic or persuade the reader.

- Then ask what an author's point of view is. (*his or her feelings, opinions, or beliefs about a topic*) Ask students to share their opinion about a popular song or movie. Tell them that the opinion they expressed is their point of view.

- Point out that not everyone shares the same point of view about a topic. Authors often try to convince readers to agree with their point of view by using persuasive words, such as *best, worst,* or *amazing,* to help convince readers to agree with their ideas.

- Remind students that looking for words and phrases such as *I think* or *I believe* can help them identify the author's point of view.

- Point out that recognizing an author's purpose and point of view in a text will help students to better understand what they read.

Ready *Teacher Toolbox*   *teacher-toolbox.com*

	Prerequisite Skills	RI.6.6
Ready Lessons	✓	✓
Tools for Instruction	✓	
Interactive Tutorials		✓

CCLS Focus

RI.6.6 Determine an author's point of view or purpose in a text and explain how it is conveyed in the text.

ADDITIONAL STANDARDS: **RI.6.1, RI.6.2, RI.6.4, RI.6.5; W.6.2, W.6.4, W.6.7, W.6.11.c; SL.6.1, SL.6.4, SL.6.5; L.6.4.a, L.6.4.b, L.6.5.a, L.6.5.c** (*See page A39 for full text.*)

AT A GLANCE

Through an illustration, students explore how to recognize point of view. They learn to analyze evidence to determine the point of view

STEP BY STEP

• Read the first paragraph, which includes the definitions of *author's purpose* and *author's point of view*. Discuss examples of words that authors use to express positive and negative points of view, such as *best*, *great*, *awful*, and *dreadful*.

• Have students study the illustration. Ask them to look for and circle any clues in the illustration that help them figure out each judge's point of view.

• Explain that the chart shows the process of analyzing evidence to determine points of view.

• Read the first two columns of the chart. Ask students to compare the evidence listed in the chart with the evidence they circled.

• Review the third column and discuss how the word *perfect* and the first judge's smile suggest a positive point of view, while the second judge's frown and the word *awful* suggest a negative point of view. Finally, read the point of view column with students. Help them understand how the evidence they identified conveys the judges' points of view.

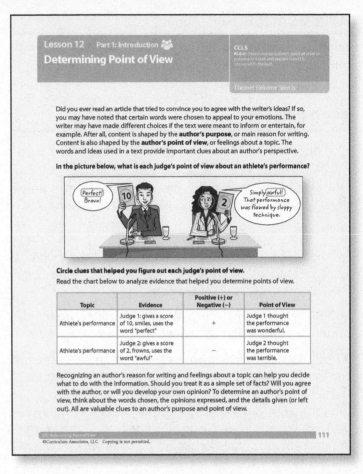

• Reinforce how recognizing an author's purpose and point of view is an important part of being an active reader. Share a recent book or movie review that you have read and explain whether you agreed with the author or developed your own point of view.

Genre Focus

Informational Texts: Editorials

Tell students that in this lesson they will read an editorial. Explain that an editorial is a short essay that is often written by a newspaper or magazine's editor. Discuss the following characteristics of editorials with students:

• expresses an opinion about a topic

• tries to persuade readers to agree with a certain opinion about a topic

• may encourage readers to take action

Based on these characteristics, have students name some examples of editorials they have read. Ask them if an article in a reference text, such as an encyclopedia, would be an editorial. Why or why not? Discuss the similarities and differences between informational articles and editorials.

Explain that "Climbing Ice!" is an essay that gives information about the sport of ice climbing. "Worth the Risk?" is an editorial about the risks involved in the sport of ice climbing. "Just for the Thrill of It" is an essay that describes what attracts people to extreme sports such as whitewater rafting and bungee jumping. "Flying Above the Water" gives information about kitesurfing, one of the newest extreme sports. Review that knowing a text's genre will help students determine the author's purpose and point of view.

AT A GLANCE

Students identify the author's point of view in an essay and support it with evidence from the text, including text details and word choices.

STEP BY STEP

- Invite volunteers to tell what they learned on the previous page about identifying point of view.

- Tell students that in this lesson they will learn how to identify the author's point of view in an essay.

- Read aloud "Climbing Ice!"

- Then read the questions: "What is the author's point of view about ice climbing? What words, phrases, or sentences reveal this viewpoint?"

- Now tell students you will use a Think Aloud to demonstrate a way of answering the question.

Think Aloud: The essay has clues to help me figure out the author's point of view. The author uses the words *dangerous*, *unique thrill*, and *deadly fall* to describe ice climbing. *Dangerous* and *deadly fall* suggest a negative point of view, but *unique thrill* is positive. These words support the idea that the author believes ice climbing is dangerous, but the danger is what makes the sport rewarding to enthusiasts.

- Direct students to the chart and explain that it shows a way of determining the author's point of view.

- Point out the evidence supporting ice climbing and how it shows both positive and negative feelings.

Think Aloud: Now I'll look for words the author uses to describe ice climbing speed competitions. I see negative phrases such as "rush of danger" and positive phrases such as "coupled with the excitement." The author has both positive and negative opinions about speed competitions. Again, she thinks that the sport is dangerous, but the danger is what makes it exciting.

- Have students fill in the third column of the chart. Then have them write the author's point of view in the last column.

- Finally, have students answer the question at the bottom of the page. Invite volunteers to share their answers. (*Sample response: The author wrote the essay to inform readers about the excitement, thrill, and potential dangers of ice climbing.*)

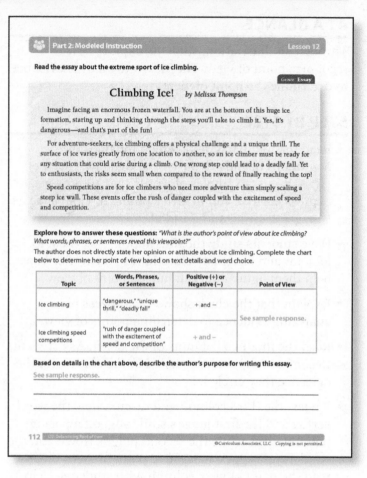

Tier Two Vocabulary: *Varies*

- Direct students to the word *varies* in paragraph 2. Tell students that the word *varies* is formed from the Latin root word *vari* meaning "different; changing." Have students use this root information, along with the context of the sentences, to tell what the word *varies* means. Guide students to understand that *varies* means "differs; changes." (***RI.6.4; L.6.4.a; L.6.4.b***)

- Have students work in pairs to list other words related to *varies*. (*variety, variable, variation*)

AT A GLANCE

Students read an editorial about ice climbing. They answer a multiple-choice question and analyze the evidence that helped them select the correct answer.

STEP BY STEP

- Tell students they will read an editorial about ice climbing.

- Close Reading helps students focus on the title and the words that the author uses to help them understand the author's point of view. The Hint will help them analyze how the words chosen and opinions expressed reveal the author's feelings about ice climbing.

- Have students read the passage and circle words and phrases that help them understand the author's point of view, as directed by Close Reading.

- Ask volunteers to share the words and phrases they circled. Have them explain how each helped them understand the author's point of view.

- Have students circle the answer to the question. Then have them review the words and phrases they circled before responding to the Show Your Thinking. Guide them to understand that words and phrases such as *worth the risk*, *high-risk*, and *great expense* suggest a negative point of view about ice climbing.

ANSWER ANALYSIS

Choice A is incorrect. The author does not admire ice climbers. Rather, he thinks they are foolish.

Choice B is incorrect. The author says that proper training and equipment are essential, but he does not believe they are enough to make the sport safe.

Choice C is correct. The author says, "Are such costs worth a few hours of excitement?"

Choice D is incorrect. The author emphasizes, not downplays, the high costs and serious risks.

ERROR ALERT: Students who did not choose C may not have recognized the author's point of view. Point out that all the choices are points of view that others may have about ice climbing, but only C tells how the author feels about it.

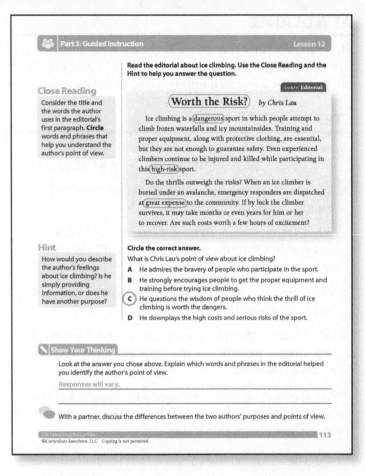

Tier Two Vocabulary: *Protective*

- Point out the word *protective* in paragraph 1. Work with students to identify the root word and suffix in *protective* and use them to determine the meaning of *protective*. Ask students to reread the sentence to make sure their definition makes sense. **(RI.6.4; L.6.4.b)**

- Write the word *protection* on the board. Discuss with students some contexts in which this related word might appear.

AT A GLANCE

Students read an essay twice about extreme sports. After the first reading, you will ask three questions to check your students' comprehension of the essay.

STEP BY STEP

- Have students read the essay silently without referring to the Study Buddy or Close Reading text.

- Ask the following questions to ensure students' comprehension of the text:

  What are most experienced participants willing to admit about training and equipment? (*They are necessary but don't guarantee safety.*)

  What are two high-risk activities? (*whitewater rafting and bungee jumping*)

  What attracts people to extreme sports? (*the need for that adrenaline rush and the satisfaction of meeting a personal challenge*)

- Ask students to reread paragraph 1 and look at the Study Buddy think aloud. What does the Study Buddy help them think about?

> **Tip:** The Study Buddy suggests that students pause at the end of each paragraph and restate it in their own words. Summarizing each paragraph will help them check their understanding. Tell students to look for the author's main idea in each paragraph.

- Have students read the rest of the essay. Tell them to follow the directions in the Close Reading.

> **Tip:** For Close Reading, guide students to look for strong, emotional words that express the author's feelings. Point out that the final sentence of a paragraph often sums up the author's overall opinion or idea.

- Finally, have students answer the questions on page 115. Use the Answer Analysis to discuss correct and incorrect responses.

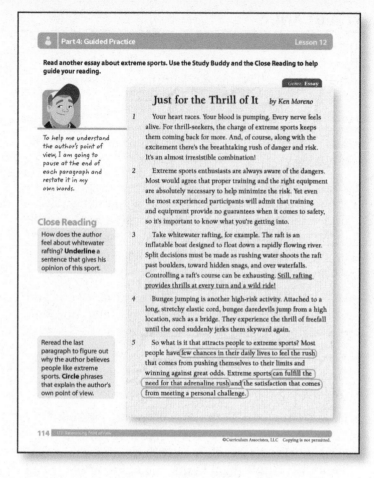

ELL Support: Compound Words

- Explain to students that a compound word is made up of two smaller words. They can look at the two smaller words to figure out the meaning of the compound word.

- Point out the word *whitewater* in paragraph 3. Guide students to identify the two smaller words in this compound word. (white *and* water) Talk about the meanings of *white* and *water*, using visuals to clarify as needed. Now ask students what they think *whitewater* means. (*"water that is moving so fast it looks white"*)

- Then have students find other compound words in the essay: *daredevil* and *freefall*. Have partners work together to write definitions of each word. (**RI.6.4; L.6.4.b**)

STEP BY STEP

- Have students read questions 1–3, using the Hints to help them answer those questions.

Tip: If students have trouble answering question 1, point out that the question is asking them which choice best states the author's point of view. Ask, "Does the author have a positive or negative feeling about extreme sports? Which tells how he feels?"

- Discuss with students the Answer Analysis below.

ANSWER ANALYSIS

1   The correct choice is A. The author says extreme sports fulfill the need for that adrenaline rush. Choice B is incorrect. The author says proper training does not guarantee safety. Choice C is incorrect. The author does not compare whitewater rafting to bungee jumping. Choice D is incorrect. The author emphasizes the thrill and excitement of extreme sports, not the exhaustion and hard work.

2   The correct choice is C. The author thinks rafting is a thrilling, wild ride. Choice A is incorrect. It describes the raft, not the author's opinion of the sport. Choice B is incorrect. It gives information about the sport. Choice D is incorrect. The author says controlling the raft can be exhausting, but he says rafting still provides thrills at every turn.

3   Sample response: The author believes that people pursue the thrill and excitement of extreme sports because they "have few chances in their daily lives to feel the rush that comes from pushing themselves to their limits and winning against great odds." The author's point of view is that extreme sports provide people with a way to escape the boredom of everyday life.

RETEACHING

Use a chart to answer to question 3. Draw the chart below, and work with students to fill in the boxes. Sample responses are provided.

Topic	Evidence	Point of View
extreme sports	breathtaking rush of excitement and danger; fulfill need for adrenaline rush	Extreme sports provide people with a way to escape boredom.

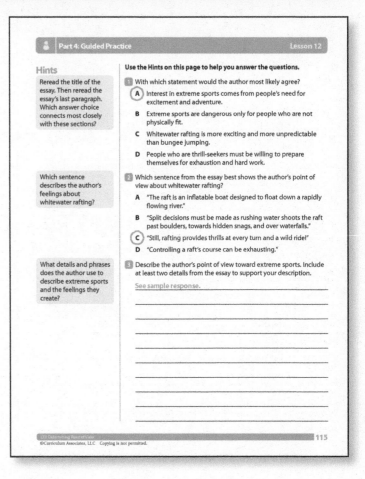

Integrating Standards

Use these questions to further students' understanding of "Just for the Thrill of It."

1   Explain how paragraphs 3 and 4 contribute to the development of the author's idea. **(RI.6.5)**

The paragraphs give examples of extreme sports and help readers visualize the excitement, thrill, and danger that comes with these kinds of sports.

2   What inference can you make about most people's everyday lives, based on paragraph 5? Give text evidence to support your inference. **(RI.6.1)**

Most people's everyday lives are boring. The author says that most have few chances in their everyday life to feel the rush that comes from pushing themselves to the limit.

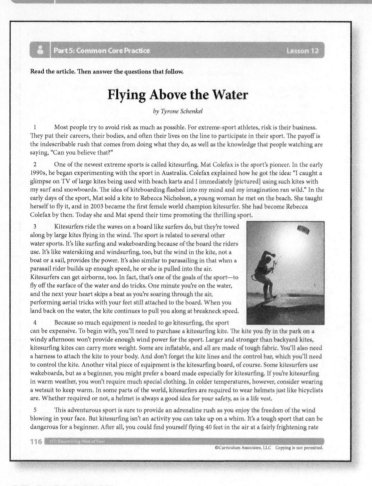

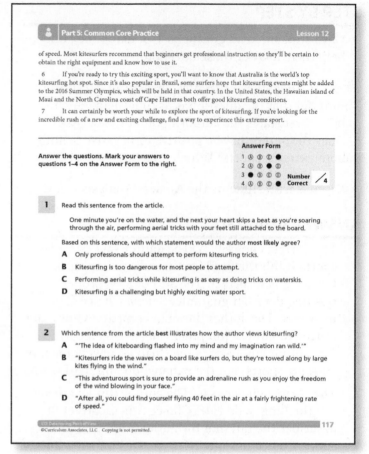

AT A GLANCE

Students independently read a longer article and answer questions in a format that provides test practice.

STEP BY STEP

- Tell students to use what they have learned about reading closely and analyzing an author's point of view to read the article on pages 116 and 117.

- Remind students to underline or circle examples of words, opinions, and details that express the author's point of view.

- Tell students to answer the questions on pages 117 and 118. For questions 1–4, they should fill in the correct circle on the Answer Form.

- When students have finished, use the Answer Analysis to discuss correct responses and the reasons for them. Have students fill in the Number Correct on the Answer Form.

ANSWER ANALYSIS

1 Choice D is correct. The words *heart skips a beat* suggest excitement and *performing aerial tricks* shows that it is challenging. Choices A and B are incorrect. The sentence shows that kitesurfing is exciting and challenging, not that it is only for professionals or too dangerous for most people. Choice C is incorrect. The sentence does not mention waterskiing. **(DOK 3)**

2 Choice C is correct. The author thinks kitesurfing is exciting and challenging. Choice A is incorrect. It tells how Mat Colefax got the idea for kiteboarding. Choices B and D are incorrect. They describe what kitesurfing is like and what could happen while kitesurfing, not the author's view. **(DOK 3)**

Theme Connection

- How do all the passages in this lesson relate to the theme of extreme sports?

- How are all the sports alike?

3 Choice A is correct. The author gives details and examples that describe the appeals and challenges of kitesurfing. Choice B is incorrect. The author explains the expenses of kitesurfing, but it is not his main purpose. Choice C is incorrect. The comparisons help readers picture the sport, but they are not the main purpose. Choice D is incorrect. The author does not encourage readers to take action to make kiteboarding an Olympic sport. ***(DOK 3)***

4 Choice D is correct. The author tells readers who are looking for "the incredible rush of a new and exciting challenge" to "find a way to experience this extreme sport." That's another way of saying that the thrills to be had in the sport are worth the difficulties of learning it. Choice A is incorrect because it only supports the idea that the sport is expensive. Choice B supports the notion that the sport is dangerous, but not that the excitement is worth the risk. Choice C supports the idea that the sport is exciting, not that it's worth pursuing. ***(DOK 2)***

5 Sample response: The author shows readers what they are getting into by explaining the expenses and challenges of the sport. He says, "Because so much equipment is needed to go kitesurfing, the sport can be expensive." He also says, "It's a tough sport that can be dangerous for a beginner. After all, you could find yourself flying 40 feet in the air at a fairly frightening rate of speed." These details help readers more fully understand the expenses and risks of the sport before attempting it. ***(DOK 3)***

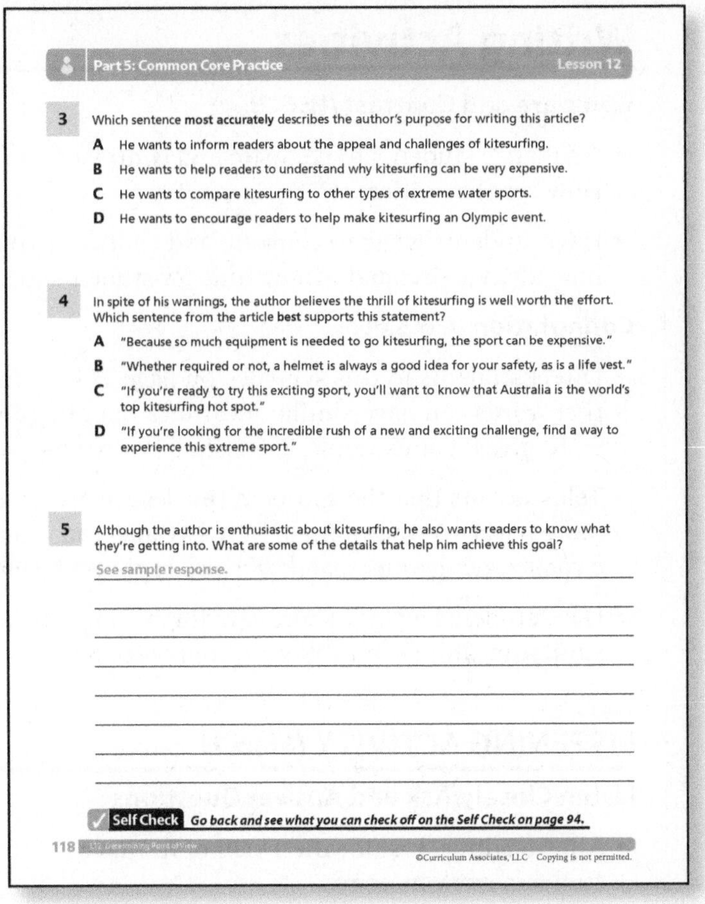
Part 5: Common Core Practice Lesson 12

3 Which sentence **most accurately** describes the author's purpose for writing this article?

A He wants to inform readers about the appeal and challenges of kitesurfing.

B He wants to help readers to understand why kitesurfing can be very expensive.

C He wants to compare kitesurfing to other types of extreme water sports.

D He wants to encourage readers to help make kitesurfing an Olympic event.

4 In spite of his warnings, the author believes the thrill of kitesurfing is well worth the effort. Which sentence from the article **best** supports this statement?

A "Because so much equipment is needed to go kitesurfing, the sport can be expensive."

B "Whether required or not, a helmet is always a good idea for your safety, as is a life vest."

C "If you're ready to try this exciting sport, you'll want to know that Australia is the world's top kitesurfing hot spot."

D "If you're looking for the incredible rush of a new and exciting challenge, find a way to experience this extreme sport."

5 Although the author is enthusiastic about kitesurfing, he also wants readers to know what they're getting into. What are some of the details that help him achieve this goal?

See sample response.

Self Check *Go back and see what you can check off on the Self Check on page 94.*

118 L12: Determining Point of View

©Curriculum Associates, LLC Copying is not permitted.

Integrating Standards

Use these questions and tasks as opportunities to interact with "Flying Above the Water."

1 How does paragraph 3 help the author develop his ideas about kitesurfing? ***(RI.6.5)***

The paragraph helps readers picture an unfamiliar sport by comparing it to other water sports. It describes what the kitesurfing is like. Descriptions such as "heart skips a beat," "soaring through the air," and "breakneck speed" support the author's idea that kitesurfing is a thrilling, risky sport.

2 In paragraph 3, what does the expression "your heart skips a beat" mean? ***(RI.6.4; L.6.5.a)***

It means you feel nervous and excited. It describes the slightly breathless feeling you have when you are doing something dangerous or thrilling.

3 Summarize: Write a summary of this passage. ***(RI.6.2; W.6.4)***

Summaries will vary. Sample response: Kitesurfing is an extreme sport that combines elements of many water sports, such as surfing and parasailing. It can be expensive, tough, and dangerous, but it is also exciting and challenging.

4 Discuss in small groups: Why do you think the author chose to include information about the expense and danger of kitesurfing if he wants people to try it? Does this information affect your desire to try kitesurfing? If so, how? ***(SL.6.1)***

Discussions will vary. Encourage students to consider why they might need to know about the costs and risks of windsurfing before trying it. Why is this information important, even if it discourages some people from participating? Tell students to return to the text to support their own opinions about kitesurfing with evidence.

Writing Activities

Compare and Contrast *(W.6.2)*

- Challenge students to compare and contrast two of the extreme sports they read about. How are they alike? How are they different?

- Have students write to compare and contrast two extreme sports, using transition words and phrases to show how ideas are related. Allow time for students to share their writing with the class.

Connotation *(L.6.5.c)*

- Direct students to this sentence on page 114: "Controlling a raft's course can be exhausting." Tell students that words can have similar meanings but different connotations. Explain that connotation is the feeling a word gives. For example, *exhausting* is a stronger word than *tiring*. It suggests that something is very tiring.

- Tell students that the sports in this lesson are described as both *risky* and *dangerous*. Ask: Which word has a more negative connotation? Why? (Dangerous *has a more negative connotation.* Risky *sounds like you are taking a chance;* dangerous *sounds like you might get seriously injured.*)

- Have students write a short paragraph about an extreme sport, using at least one pair of words that have similar meanings but different connotations.

LISTENING ACTIVITY *(SL.6.1)*

Listen Closely/Ask and Answer Questions

- After reading "Just for the Thrill of It," have students work in pairs.

- Have one student ask two questions about kitesurfing that can be answered from the text, and have the other student answer them.

- Have partners switch roles and repeat the activity.

DISCUSSION ACTIVITY *(SL.6.1)*

Talk in a Group/Talk About Extreme Sports

- Ask students to recall what they learned about participating in extreme sports. (*Extreme sports are dangerous, expensive, exciting, and challenging.*) Point out that extreme sports have pros and cons, or positives and negatives.

- Have small groups of students make a two-column chart that lists pros and cons associated with participating in extreme sports. Tell them to use their charts to help them decide if they think participating in extreme sports is a good or bad decision and why.

- Allow 10 to 15 minutes for discussion. Then have each group share its results with the class.

MEDIA ACTIVITY *(SL.6.5)*

Be Creative/Make a Video Presentation

- Have students work in groups to choose an extreme sport, such as kitesurfing. Ask them to conduct an Internet search to find video footage of an athlete participating in that sport.

- Tell students to use what they learned about the sport to record audio narration describing what viewers are seeing the athlete do. They should describe the overall sport, as well as the risks and necessary equipment. Have them present their audio and video to the class.

RESEARCH ACTIVITY *(W.6.7; SL.6.4)*

Research and Present/Give a Presentation

- Have students choose an extreme sport from one of the passages and use the description in the passage to write a brief report.

- Ask students to research the sport further to find information about noted athletes in the sport, competitions, and risks and dangers.

- Encourage students to include their point of view about the sport in their report.

- Have students present their reports to the class.

SCORING GUIDE AND ANSWER ANALYSIS

Informational Passage Answer Analysis

1A Ⓐ Ⓑ Ⓒ ●	4 ● Ⓑ Ⓒ Ⓓ
1B Ⓐ Ⓑ ● Ⓓ	5 Ⓐ Ⓑ ● Ⓓ
2 Ⓐ Ⓑ ● Ⓓ	6 Ⓐ Ⓑ Ⓒ ●
3 ● Ⓑ Ⓒ Ⓓ	

1   **Part A:** Choice D is correct. It closely matches the phrase "charted the course." The sentence with this phrase explains how the first presidents planned for the future by establishing important laws.

Choice A is incorrect. The sentence with this phrase was about how presidents shaped American history. Choice B is incorrect. The sentence with this phrase is about how presidents helped America become a strong nation. Choice C is incorrect. The sentence with the phrase does not refer to anyone moving to the country. *(RI.6.4; DOK 2)*

Part B: Choice C is correct. The phrase "guide citizens for years to come" best suggests planning for the future. Choices A, B, and D don't suggest planning for the future. *(RI.6.4; DOK 2)*

2   Choice C is correct. In the article, the author describes how Madison "oversaw the Louisiana Purchase." Despite that, "most people give credit" to Jefferson. This is one of several examples where the author compares the fame and credit awarded to Jefferson's accomplishments to how Madison has been remembered.

Choices A and B are incorrect. Both mention Madison and Jefferson but do not support the idea that Madison's accomplishments were underrated. Choice D is incorrect. It does not refer to one of Madison's accomplishments. *(RI.6.6; DOK 2)*

3   Choice A is correct. It fits the meaning of the sentence, which is about how Madison helped the United States during the War of 1812. The people of the country were able to "endure," or live through, the war because of Madison's leadership.

Choice B is incorrect. It does not fit in the sentence because the author has stated that the United States was in the war. The target sentence is mostly about the United States during and after the war. Choice C is incorrect. Madison encouraged soldiers to fight in the war, but this phrase does not fit the meaning of the word "endure" as used in the sentence. Choice D does not fit in the sentence because it tells about Madison's brave deeds. It would not have been brave of Madison to help citizens escape from the War of 1812. *(RI.6.4; DOK 2)*

4   Choice A is correct. These sentences compare how much time Madison and Jefferson spent with the congress. They suggest that Madison accomplished more than Jefferson did during this time.

Choice B is incorrect. While these sentences do refer to critical decisions, they do not describe the decisions. Choice C is incorrect. The sentences do compare leaders, but both leaders lived long ago. The sentences do not mention the leaders of today. Choice D is incorrect. These sentences say that Madison and Jefferson were friends, but that is not the sentences' main point. *(RI.6.6; DOK 3)*

5   Choice C is correct. The last paragraph summarizes the key ideas and restates the belief that Madison should be praised for his accomplishments.

Choice A is incorrect. The last paragraph is meant to remind readers of what they have read, not introduce new arguments. Choice B is incorrect. The author explains his own ideas and opinions in this paragraph. The paragraph does not present an alternative view of these ideas and opinions. Choice D is incorrect. The article does compare different people, but the last paragraph does not contain any comparisons. *(RI.6.5; DOK 3)*

6   Choice D is correct. The passage gives information about Madison primarily in chronological order, from his early days as a state representative through the challenges he faced as President.

Choice A is incorrect. While the passage may present some causes and their effects, that's not the overall structure. The graphic in Choice B might be a useful device for making comparisons between Madison and his friend Jefferson, but it doesn't represent the text's structure nearly as well as Choice D. Choice C is incorrect. While Madison's rise to the presidency may seem to reflect the graphic in one respect, the text does not use anything like the narrative plot structure so common in fiction to tell his story. *(RI.6.5; DOK 2)*

SAMPLE RESPONSES

Short Response (See 2-Point Rubric—Short Response on page A46 for scoring.)

7 This sentence begins developing the idea that Madison always wanted to protect people's rights. The author writes that Madison helped pass laws to give the colonists freedom of religion in Virginia when he first entered politics. This sentence establishes the idea that Madison would try to protect freedom throughout his life. Later in the passage, the author explains that Madison wrote the Bill of Rights, which helped preserve the rights of citizens, and that he helped in the fight against slavery. All of these details show that Madison worked hard to protect citizens' rights from the start of his career. *(RI.6.5; DOK 3)*

8 This sentence helps to develop the idea that Madison was a very important figure in United States history. The fact that Madison became known as the Father of the Constitution establishes the idea that he did a lot to help create this important document. In the next paragraph, the author explains that Madison wrote the Bill of Rights, a key piece of the Constitution, and that he helped write *The Federalist Papers*, which encouraged leaders across the country to support the Constitution. By including this sentence, the author introduces the idea that Madison's work helped shape the newly formed democratic government. *(RI.6.5; DOK 3)*

9 In paragraph 9, the author explains why people should not remember Madison primarily for the tragic events that occurred during the War of 1812. The author includes this paragraph because he wants people to know that Madison was actually a brave leader during the war. Madison assisted in the fight against the British and then helped the country rebuild once the war ended. The author adds that the challenges Madison faced during this time were even greater than the challenges faced by presidents who came before him. This paragraph shows that the author believes the president did his best during a difficult time. *(RI.6.6; DOK 3)*

Performance Task (See New York State Grade 6–8 Expository Writing Evaluation Rubric on pages A47 and A48 for scoring.)

10 This passage is mostly about James Madison, but the author makes many comparisons between Madison and Thomas Jefferson. The author explains that these men were alike in many ways. Madison and Jefferson met while representing the Virginia colony. They were both Founding Fathers who participated in the Continental Congress. Later, they worked together on the Louisiana Purchase, and they both served as president.

However, the author makes a point of explaining that Madison and Jefferson were different in many ways as well. The author explains that Jefferson became legendary for his deeds, but Madison did not receive the same sort of admiration for his hard work. The author believes that this is unfair to Madison. He feels that more people remember Jefferson's Declaration of Independence, even though Madison's work on the Constitution is probably more important today. Madison served in the Continental Congress, wrote *The Federalist Papers*, and helped to gain support for the Constitution, yet he is often overshadowed by his friend Jefferson. Madison was important in making the Louisiana Purchase, but most people give credit for the deal to Jefferson.

The author's comparison is very important to the passage. It shows readers that Madison was a great leader who helped make the United States what it is today. The comparison also shows that the author believes it is unfair when people are too critical of Madison or give too much credit to others, such as Jefferson. The author uses the comparison to support his belief that people should give Madison the praise and honor he deserves for all the great things he did. *(RI.6.6; DOK 3)*

Determining Word Meanings: Figurative and Connotative

LESSON OBJECTIVES

- Identify different types of figurative language.

- Determine the figurative or connotative meaning of words and phrases in a literary text.

THE LEARNING PROGRESSION

- **Grade 5:** CCLS RL.5.4 asks students to determine the figurative meaning of words and phrases used in literary texts.

- **Grade 6: CCLS RL.6.4 broadens the Grade 5 standard to include determining the connotative meaning of words and phrases.**

- **Grade 7:** CCLS RL.7.4 expands to include sound devices such as rhyme and repetition.

PREREQUISITE SKILLS

- Understand that figurative language compares one thing to another.

- Identify examples of similes and metaphors and recognize the comparison made.

- Understand the meaning suggested by similes and metaphors.

TAP STUDENTS' PRIOR KNOWLEDGE

- Tell students they will be working on a lesson about the figurative meaning of words and phrases. Remind them that figurative language is used to compare things. The figurative meaning of the language is different from the meaning of the individual words.

- Tell students that they hear figurative language every day. For example, when parents tell them that their room looks like a tornado hit it, they are using figurative language. Ask students what they think of when they hear the word *tornado*. (*a violent whirlwind that leaves a path of destruction behind it*)

- Explain that the parent doesn't really think a tornado hit the room. Ask students what this figurative language means. (*The room is untidy.*)

- Explain to students that they will also learn in this lesson about the connotative meanings of words. Explain that connotative meaning refers to the feeling suggested by a word or phrase.

- Tell students the words *brisk* and *frigid* refer to cold temperatures; but *brisk* has a positive connotation associated with feeling energized and invigorated, whereas *frigid* has a negative connotation of feeling so cold you can't wait to get back inside.

- Remind students that writers use figurative language and words that have a certain connotation in order to create vivid mental pictures for readers.

Ready *Teacher Toolbox*   teacher-toolbox.com

	Prerequisite Skills	RL.6.4
Ready Lessons	✓	✓
Tools for Instruction	✓ ✓	✓ ✓
Interactive Tutorials		✓

CCLS Focus

RL.6.4 Determine the meaning of words and phrases as they are used in a text, including figurative and connotative meanings ....

ADDITIONAL STANDARDS: **RL.6.1, RL.6.2, RL.6.5, RL.6.7; W.6.3, W.6.4; SL.6.1, SL.6.2, SL.6.4; L.6.4.a, L.6.4.b, L.6.5.a** (See page A39 for full text.)

AT A GLANCE

Through an illustration, students learn to recognize figurative language. They learn about different types of figurative language and their purposes in literary texts.

STEP BY STEP

- Read the first paragraph that includes the definition of *connotative meaning*. Discuss examples of similar words with different connotations, such as *smell/fragrance, proud/vain,* and *snoop/investigate.* Have students tell what feelings or images the words bring to mind. You might have them pantomime actions to convey their idea of each word's connotation.

- Then read the second paragraph, which includes the definition of *figurative language.* Direct students to look at the illustration and read the caption. Tell them to determine what is being compared and circle those words in the caption.

- Explain that the chart defines three types of figurative language commonly used in literary texts.

- Read the first two columns of the chart. Then use the first example to model how to analyze figurative language. Ask what is being compared. *(a smile and sunshine)* Have students suggest ways smiles and sunshine are similar. *(often described as bright; associated with happy feelings)* Explain that just as sunshine brightens a day, a smile brightens a face.

- Have students tell the meaning of the second and third examples. *(The man is large—tall and broad;*

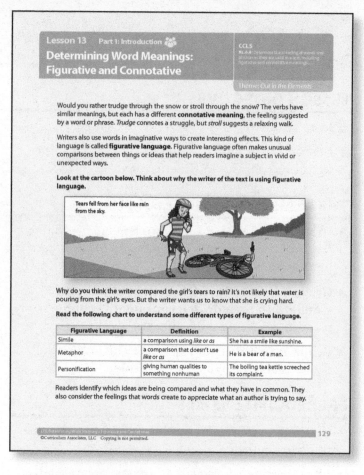

The boiling tea kettle sounded like a whining or complaining person.)

- Reinforce how figurative language makes stories and poems come alive by creating vivid images in a reader's mind.

Genre Focus

Literary Texts: Realistic Fiction

Tell students that in this lesson they will read realistic fiction. Explain that realistic fiction is literary text with characters, settings, and situations that are believable but a story that is made up. Discuss these characteristics of realistic fiction with students:

- interesting, believable characters

- details that clearly establish a setting

- plot events that could really happen

- language that paints vivid mental images

Based on these characteristics, have students name some examples of realistic fiction they have read. Ask

them if the *Harry Potter* or *Hunger Games* stories are realistic fiction. Why or why not? Discuss the similarities and differences between types of fiction, such as historical fiction, science fiction, and fantasy.

Explain that "The Gold Watch" is a short realistic fiction story about finding treasure in an unexpected place. Another realistic story in this lesson is an excerpt from "To Build a Fire" by Jack London. It is a gripping portrait of a man caught out in below-zero weather, faced with a life-threatening situation. "A Thunder-Storm" by Emily Dickinson is a poem that uses figurative language to describe an approaching thunderstorm.

AT A GLANCE

Students identify and analyze figurative language in a short passage of realistic fiction.

STEP BY STEP

• Invite volunteers to tell what they learned on the previous page about figurative language and how to determine what a figurative expression means.

• Tell students that in this lesson they will learn how to analyze figurative language in a story.

• Read aloud "The Gold Watch."

• Then read the question: "To what does the author compare the electrical cord, and how does this make you imagine the coffee maker?"

• Now tell students you will use a Think Aloud to demonstrate a way of answering the question.

Think Aloud: The author is comparing the cord to a tail, which gives the coffee maker the qualities of an animal. The word *like* tells me that this is a simile. The comparison makes me picture the coffee maker as a cat with a tail that drags along the ground.

• Direct students to the chart and explain that it shows a way of determining what an example of figurative language means.

Think Aloud: In the last sentence, the pocket watch is compared to the sun: "a pocket watch as golden as a tiny sun." How are the watch and the sun alike? They are both golden in color, and the sun and gold objects are both bright and shiny.

• Have students fill in the second column of the chart to tell how the watch and the sun are alike.

Think Aloud: Now I'll think about what this comparison means. I think the author wants me to understand that the watch is bright gold and shines in the light.

• Have students complete the third column of the chart to tell the meaning in their own words.

• Finally, have students answer the question at the bottom of the page. Invite volunteers to share their answers with the class. (*Sample response: The author uses the simile to show Gabriel's feelings about the watch. Words such as* golden, tiny, *and* sun *have a positive connotation, so the simile helps readers*

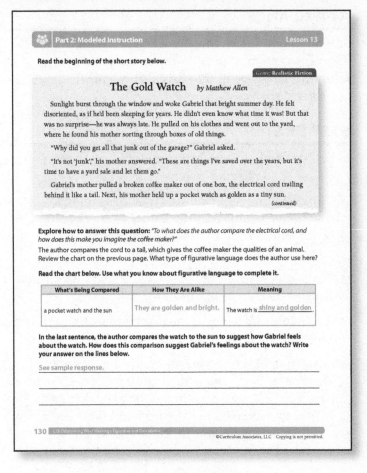

understand that the watch is special.)

Tier Two Vocabulary: *Disoriented*

• Direct students to the word *disoriented* in paragraph 1. Point out the prefix *dis-*, meaning "not," and the base word *orient*.

• Ask students what context clue in the sentence might help them figure out the meaning of *disoriented*. (*"sleeping for years"*)

• Ask students to imagine how someone might feel waking up after a very, very long sleep. (*confused, not sure where they were or what day it was*)

• Based on the clue and the prefix *dis-*, ask students what they think *disoriented* means. (*"confused, not able to tell what your position is in relation to your surroundings"*) **(RL.6.4; L.6.4.a)**

AT A GLANCE

Students continue reading about Gabriel and the watch. They answer a multiple-choice question and analyze the figurative language in the story that helped them select the correct answer.

STEP BY STEP

- Tell students they will continue reading about Gabriel and the gold watch.

- Close Reading will help students focus on the descriptive details that the author uses. The Hint will help them analyze the effect of the words and phrases on the passage's meaning.

- Have students read the passage and mark up positive and negative descriptions of the watch.

- Ask volunteers to share the descriptions they circled and boxed and the feeling each description conveys.

- Have students circle the answer to the question. Then have them review the definition of metaphor on page 129 before responding to the Show Your Thinking. Guide them to understand that "had a new treasure" is a metaphor in which the watch is compared to treasure.

ANSWER ANALYSIS

Choice A is correct. The last sentence shows that Gabriel thinks of the watch as a new treasure.

Choice B is incorrect. It is Gabriel's mother, not Gabriel, who expresses the opinion that some people would think the watch is worthless.

Choice C is incorrect. A heartbeat is not how Gabriel thinks of the watch. Rather, this description conveys the idea of the sound of the watch as comforting and dependable—like a steady heartbeat.

Choice D is incorrect. As in B, it is Gabriel's mother, not Gabriel, who describes the watch as a "familiar friend."

ERROR ALERT: Students who did not choose A may have confused Gabriel's feelings about the watch with his mother's. Point out that all the choices are words that someone might use to describe an old watch, but only A tells how Gabriel feels about it.

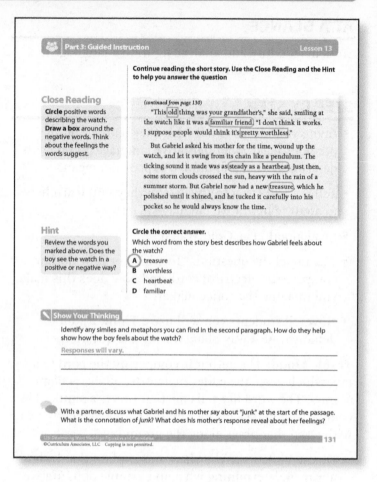

ELL Support: Suffixes

- Explain to students that a suffix is a group of letters added to the end of a word to change the word's meaning. Some common suffixes are *-ful* (meaning "full of," as in *helpful*) and *-able* (meaning "can be," as in *dependable*). Another suffix is *-less*, which means "without." Tell students that knowing the meanings of suffixes can help them figure out the meanings of unfamiliar words.

- Direct students to the word *worthless* in paragraph 1. Guide them to identify the suffix (*-less*) and the base word (*worth*). Then ask them to use what they know about the suffix *-less* to tell what this word means. (*"without worth or value"*)

- Have students check this meaning in the sentence to be sure it makes sense. Reinforce that it makes sense that some people might think an old watch has no value. *(RL.6.4; L.6.4.b)*

AT A GLANCE

Students read a poem about a storm twice. After the first reading, you will ask three questions to check your students' comprehension of the poem.

STEP BY STEP

- Have students read the poem silently without referring to the Study Buddy or Close Reading text.

- Ask the following questions to ensure students' comprehension of the text:

Who is the "he" referred to in line 3 of the poem? *(the wind)* What are the "tunes"? *(the sounds of the wind)*

What do you think the poet means by saying the lightning "showed" a beak and a claw? *(The jagged lightning was in the shape of a beak and a claw.)*

Describe the progress of the storm in order, according to the poem. *(First, the wind began to blow, scattering leaves and dust everywhere. Next, thunder and lightning occurred. Then the rain came in torrents.)*

- Ask students to reread the first stanza and look at the Study Buddy think aloud. What does the Study Buddy help them think about?

Tip: The Study Buddy suggests that students underline words with connotations that suggest the power of the coming storm. Guide them to look in the last four stanzas for words that convey a feeling of danger. The first stanza provides models.

- Have students read the rest of the poem. Tell them to follow the directions in the Close Reading.

Tip: The Close Reading asks students what they think is meant by the line "The birds put up the bars to nests." To understand what the poet means, tell students to think about why people sometimes board up their windows when severe weather is forecast.

- Finally, have students answer the questions on page 133. Use the Answer Analysis to discuss correct and incorrect responses.

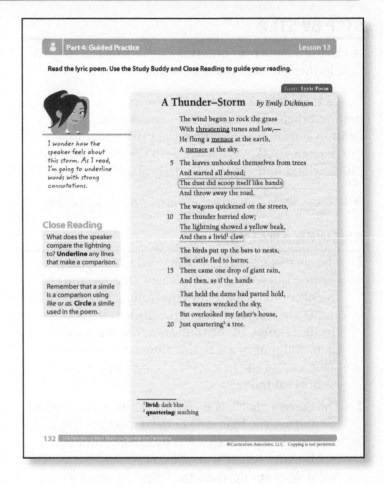

Read the lyric poem. Use the Study Buddy and Close Reading to guide your reading.

Genre: **Lyric Poem**

A Thunder–Storm   *by Emily Dickinson*

The wind begun to rock the grass
With <u>threatening</u> tunes and low,—
He flung a <u>menace</u> at the earth,
A <u>menace</u> at the sky.
5   The leaves unhooked themselves from trees
And started all abroad;
The dust did scoop itself like hands
And throw away the road.

The wagons quickened on the streets,
10   The thunder hurried slow;
The lightning showed a yellow beak,
And then a livid[1] claw.

The birds put up the bars to nests,
The cattle fled to barns;
15   There came one drop of giant rain,
And then, as if the hands

That held the dams had parted hold,
The waters wrecked the sky,
But overlooked my father's house,
20   Just quartering[2] a tree.

I wonder how the speaker feels about this storm. As I read, I'm going to underline words with strong connotations.

Close Reading

What does the speaker compare the lightning to? **Underline** any lines that make a comparison.

Remember that a simile is a comparison using *like* or *as.* **Circle** a simile used in the poem.

[1] **livid:** dark blue
[2] **quartering:** reaching

132   L13: Determining Word Meanings: Figurative and Connotative   ©Curriculum Associates, LLC   Copying is not permitted.

Tier Two Vocabulary: *Hurried*

- Read lines 9 and 10 of the poem with students. Ask what the author is trying to convey here. *(People traveling on the roads rushed to get out of the storm.)*

- Ask students what *hurried* means. *("rushed or moved quickly")* Guide them to identify context clues that help them understand this meaning. *("quickened")* **(RL.6.4; L.6.4.a)**

STEP BY STEP

- Have students read questions 1–3, using the Hints to help them answer those questions.

Tip: If students have trouble answering question 1, remind them that writers use certain words to convey a feeling or idea they want the reader to understand. Ask, "What words in the poem help you understand how the speaker feels about the storm?"

- Discuss with students the Answer Analysis below.

ANSWER ANALYSIS

1 The correct choice is A. The word "threatening" in the line is a strong context clue to the meaning of "menace" in the two lines that follow. Choices B, C, and D are incorrect. All of the lines contribute to the description of the thunderstorm, but none of them add to it in a way that illustrates the threat, or "menace," of the first stanza being carried out in the events that follow.

2 The correct choice is B. The writer uses a metaphor to compare the lightning to the dangerous features of living birds. Choices A is incorrect. Although nearby lines mention wagons, nests, and barns, the poem does not describe the lightning as striking them. Choice C is too literal a reading of the imagery. Choice D is incorrect because the poem does not mention eagles or hawks.

3 Sample response: The speaker says the dust scoops "like hands," so this is a simile. She also says that it "throws away" the road, which is personification. It means that the wind has carried so much dust into the air that the road cannot be seen.

RETEACHING

Use the chart to answer question 3. Draw the chart below, and have students fill in the boxes. Sample responses are provided.

What's Being Compared?	How Are They Alike?	Meaning
dust and hands	perform the action of scooping	The wind caused dust to swirl up.
dust and the ability to throw	can throw	The wind covers the road in dust.

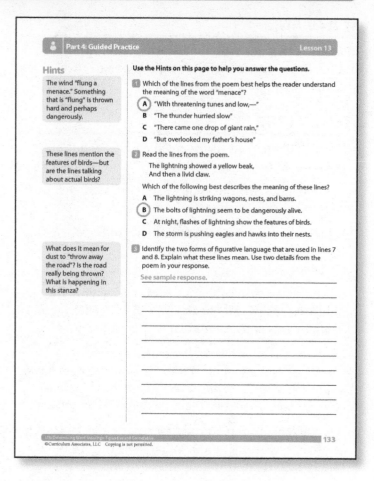

 Part 4: Guided Practice Lesson 13

Hints

The wind "flung a menace." Something that is "flung" is thrown hard and perhaps dangerously.

These lines mention the features of birds—but are the lines talking about actual birds?

What does it mean for dust to "throw away the road"? Is the road really being thrown? What is happening in this stanza?

Use the Hints on this page to help you answer the questions.

1 Which of the lines from the poem best helps the reader understand the meaning of the word "menace"?

A "With threatening tunes and low,—"

B "The thunder hurried slow"

C "There came one drop of giant rain,"

D "But overlooked my father's house"

2 Read the lines from the poem.

The lightning showed a yellow beak,
And then a livid claw.

Which of the following best describes the meaning of these lines?

A The lightning is striking wagons, nests, and barns.

B The bolts of lightning seem to be dangerously alive.

C At night, flashes of lightning show the features of birds.

D The storm is pushing eagles and hawks into their nests.

3 Identify the two forms of figurative language that are used in lines 7 and 8. Explain what these lines mean. Use two details from the poem in your response.

See sample response.

L13: Determining Word Meanings: Figurative and Connotative
©Curriculum Associates, LLC   Copying is not permitted.
133

Integrating Standards

Use these questions to further students' understanding of "A Thunder-Storm."

1 What is the theme of "A Thunder-Storm"? Use details from the poem in your answer. **(RL.6.2)**

The theme of the poem is that weather has the power to thrill and excite and to affect all living things. The description of the approaching storm as "threatening" and "a menace" conveys drama, and the images of animals and people seeking shelter show the power of the storm over all living things.

2 Explain how the third stanza contributes to the development of the theme. **(RL.6.5)**

The third stanza tells of people in wagons trying to escape the approaching storm, which makes its presence known by the sound of thunder and menacing images created by jagged streaks of lightning. These vivid images build on the sense of drama and excitement created by the powerful descriptions of the wind in the first two stanzas.

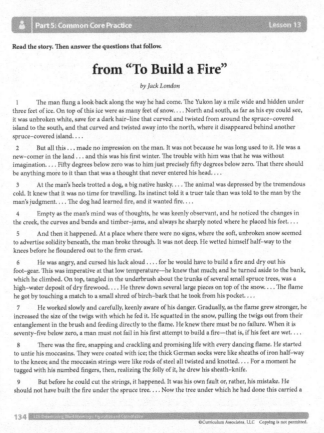

Part 5: Common Core Practice Lesson 13

Read the story. Then answer the questions that follow.

from "To Build a Fire"

by Jack London

1   The man flung a look back along the way he had come. The Yukon lay a mile wide and hidden under three feet of ice. On top of this ice were as many feet of snow.... North and south, as far as his eye could see, it was unbroken white, save for a dark hair–line that curved and twisted from around the spruce–covered island to the south, and that curved and twisted away into the north, where it disappeared behind another spruce–covered island....

2   But all this ... made no impression on the man. It was not because he was long used to it. He was a new–comer in the land ... and this was his first winter. The trouble with him was that he was without imagination.... Fifty degrees below zero was to him just precisely fifty degrees below zero. That there should be anything more to it than that was a thought that never entered his head....

3   At the man's heels trotted a dog, a big native husky.... The animal was depressed by the tremendous cold. It knew that it was no time for travelling. Its instinct told it a truer tale than was told to the man by the man's judgment.... The dog had learned fire, and it wanted fire....

4   Empty as the man's mind was of thoughts, he was keenly observant, and he noticed the changes in the creek, the curves and bends and timber–jams, and always he sharply noted where he placed his feet....

5   And then it happened. At a place where there were no signs, where the soft, unbroken snow seemed to advertise solidity beneath, the man broke through. It was not deep. He wetted himself half–way to the knees before he floundered out to the firm crust.

6   He was angry, and cursed his luck aloud .... for he would have to build a fire and dry out his foot–gear. This was imperative at that low temperature—he knew that much; and he turned aside to the bank, which he climbed. On top, tangled in the underbrush about the trunks of several small spruce trees, was a high–water deposit of dry firewood.... He threw down several large pieces on top of the snow.... The flame he got by touching a match to a small shred of birch–bark that he took from his pocket....

7   He worked slowly and carefully, keenly aware of his danger. Gradually, as the flame grew stronger, he increased the size of the twigs with which he fed it. He squatted in the snow, pulling the twigs out from their entanglement in the brush and feeding directly to the flame. He knew there must be no failure. When it is seventy–five below zero, a man must not fail in his first attempt to build a fire—that is, if his feet are wet....

8   There was the fire, snapping and crackling and promising life with every dancing flame. He started to untie his moccasins. They were coated with ice; the thick German socks were like sheaths of iron half–way to the knees; and the moccasin strings were like rods of steel all twisted and knotted.... For a moment he tugged with his numbed fingers, then, realizing the folly of it, he drew his sheath–knife....

9   But before he could cut the strings, it happened. It was his own fault or, rather, his mistake. He should not have built the fire under the spruce tree.... Now the tree under which he had done this carried a

134   L13: Determining Word Meanings: Figurative and Connotative
©Curriculum Associates, LLC   Copying is not permitted.

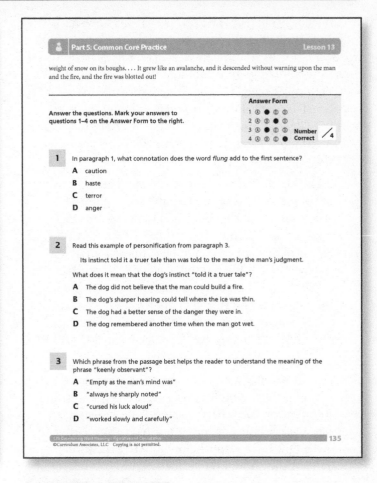

Part 5: Common Core Practice Lesson 13

weight of snow on its boughs.... It grew like an avalanche, and it descended without warning upon the man and the fire, and the fire was blotted out!

Answer the questions. Mark your answers to questions 1–4 on the Answer Form to the right.

Answer Form
1 Ⓐ ● Ⓒ Ⓓ
2 Ⓐ Ⓑ ● Ⓓ
3 Ⓐ ● Ⓒ Ⓓ   **Number** /4
4 Ⓐ Ⓑ Ⓒ ●   **Correct**

1   In paragraph 1, what connotation does the word *flung* add to the first sentence?

A   caution

B   haste

C   terror

D   anger

2   Read this example of personification from paragraph 3.

> Its instinct told it a truer tale than was told to the man by the man's judgment.

What does it mean that the dog's instinct "told it a truer tale"?

A   The dog did not believe that the man could build a fire.

B   The dog's sharper hearing could tell where the ice was thin.

C   The dog had a better sense of the danger they were in.

D   The dog remembered another time when the man got wet.

3   Which phrase from the passage best helps the reader to understand the meaning of the phrase "keenly observant"?

A   "Empty as the man's mind was"

B   "always he sharply noted"

C   "cursed his luck aloud"

D   "worked slowly and carefully"

L13: Determining Word Meanings: Figurative and Connotative   135
©Curriculum Associates, LLC   Copying is not permitted.

AT A GLANCE

Students independently read a longer story and answer questions in a format that provides test practice.

STEP BY STEP

- Tell students to use what they have learned about reading carefully and analyzing figurative and connotative meanings to read the story on pages 134 and 135.

- Remind students to underline or circle examples of figurative language and words with strong connotations.

- Tell students to answer the questions on pages 135 and 136. For questions 1–4, they should fill in the correct circle on the Answer Form.

- When students have finished, use the Answer Analysis to discuss correct responses and the reasons for them. Have students fill in the Number Correct on the Answer Form.

ANSWER ANALYSIS

1   Choice B is correct. The word *flung* indicates that the man looks hastily over his shoulder. Choice A is incorrect. The story does not suggest he looked with caution. Choices C and D are incorrect. The beginning of the passage does not suggest the man is afraid or angry. Rather, the text says the severe cold meant nothing to the man. **(DOK 2)**

2   Choice C is correct. The text says the dog "knew it was no time for travelling." Choice A is incorrect. The story says, "The dog had learned fire," which implies it had seen the man build a fire before. Choices B and D are incorrect. The passage doesn't say the dog had an ability to sense thin ice or that it remembered another time the man got wet. **(DOK 3)**

Theme Connection

- How do all the texts in this lesson relate to the theme of being out in the elements?

- Describe the role weather plays in each text.

3 Choice B is correct. The phrase "always he sharply noted" describes what a "keenly observant" person does. Choices A and C are incorrect. Neither phrase in contributes to an understanding of the phrase in question. Choice D, "worked slowly and carefully," suggests some qualities that would go along with being "keenly observant," but it does not give strong context clues to an exact meaning of the phrase. **(DOK 2)**

4 Choice D is correct. The socks and laces are not really made of metal. This figurative language helps the reader understand that the frigid temperatures had turned the wet clothing into solid ice. Choice A is incorrect. The man could not have made a fire if his feet were stuck in the ground. Choice B is incorrect because the problem is not the man's strength but his numbed fingers and frozen clothes. Choice C rephrases the figurative language used in the story. It does not explain what the figurative language means. **(DOK 3)**

5 Sample response: This is an example of personification. Snow is not human, so it cannot really advertise, which means "to make public" or "call attention to." There was nothing, no sign such as snow with holes or indentations, to show that the snow might have water below it. All indications were that the snow was perfectly solid, as indicated by the text "soft, unbroken snow." **(DOK 3)**

Part 5: Common Core Practice   Lesson 13

4 Read this sentence from the story.

They were coated with ice; the thick German socks were like sheaths of iron half–way to the knees; and the moccasin strings were like rods of steel all twisted and knotted. . . .

What do the two similes in this sentence show?

A The man's feet are stuck in the frozen ground.
B The man is too weak to remove his own socks.
C The man's socks and laces are made of metal.
D The man's wet clothes have frozen solid.

5 In paragraph 5, the author says that "the soft, unbroken snow seemed to advertise solidity beneath." State what type of figurative language is this, and explain what it means. Support your answer with at least **two** details from the story.

See sample response.

✓ **Self Check** Go back and see what you can check off on the Self Check on page 128.

136   L13 Determining Word Meanings: Figurative and Connotative   ©Curriculum Associates, LLC   Copying is not permitted.

Integrating Standards

Use these questions and tasks as opportunities to interact with "To Build a Fire."

1 Using details from the passage, how would you describe the man? **(RL.6.1)**

He is a man "without imagination" and seems not to have realized the danger of being out in severely cold weather. He is also described as "keenly observant," and he is not without survival skills. He looks for signs of thin ice, and he knows how to make a fire. Most important, he knows he might not survive if he doesn't dry his wet clothes quickly.

2 What probably caused the "avalanche" that buried the man's fire? **(RL.6.1)**

The man built the fire under a tree with a lot of snow on its boughs. The heat from the fire would have warmed the snow, causing it to melt. I know that when snow melts, it expands and gets heavier. The weight of the melting snow probably caused it to slip off the tree boughs and onto the fire.

3 Summarize: Write a summary of this passage. **(RL.6.2; W.6.4)**

Sample response: A man and a dog are traveling along the Yukon River in subzero weather. The dog senses it is too cold for traveling, but the man seems unaware of the potential danger. Suddenly, the man falls through the snow into icy water. He makes a fire to dry out his clothes as quickly as possible, but snow from the tree above it falls into the fire and puts it out.

4 Discuss in small groups: Why do you think the author chose not to tell the name of the man? Does this affect your understanding or appreciation of the passage? If so, how? **(SL.6.1)**

Discussions will vary. Encourage students to consider the roles of the dog and the elements in the story. They are not named, but they are important characters too, aren't they? Is there any significance to the namelessness of the characters?

Writing Activities

Another Point of View *(W.6.3)*

- Challenge students to think about how the dog would describe the man and the events of the passage. Would the dog express opinions or simply state the facts?

- Have students write about the events of the passage from the dog's point of view. Allow time for students to share their stories with the class.

Figurative Language *(L.6.5.a)*

- Direct students to this sentence on page 134: "There was the fire, snapping and crackling and promising life with every dancing flame." Ask students what type of figurative language this sentence is an example of. *(personification)* Review that personification gives human qualities to nonhuman things.

- Ask what are the two qualities being attributed here to fire. *(the ability to promise and the ability to dance)* Discuss with students the meaning of the phrase. *(The flickering flames of the fire may save the man's life by giving him a chance to dry his clothes.)*

- Have students write a short paragraph about one of the elements of nature, using at least one example of personification.

LISTENING ACTIVITY *(SL.6.2)*

Listen Closely/Conveying Meaning

- Have student pairs review "A Thunder-Storm."

- Have one student read aloud the poem, using his or her voice to convey its meaning. For example, the student might use a low, quiet voice to convey the danger of the approaching storm. Listeners then describe what they heard.

- Have partners switch roles and repeat the activity.

DISCUSSION ACTIVITY *(SL.6.1)*

Talk in a Group/Discuss Connotations

- Have students list the elements described in "To Build a Fire." *(cold, snow, water, ice, fire)* Point out that these elements may have positive and negative aspects—instances when they are critical to survival and other times when they can be extremely destructive forces of nature.

- Have small groups of students make a chart that lists words associated with each element. Challenge them to include words that convey positive connotations and negative connotations.

- Allow 10 to 15 minutes for discussion. Then have each group share its results with the class.

MEDIA ACTIVITY *(RL.6.7)*

Be Creative/Depict Figurative Language

- Have students review the illustration on page 129. Ask them to describe how the illustration helps viewers better understand the figurative language.

- Encourage students to choose an example of figurative language from "To Build a Fire." Then have them enhance the figurative language example through a different format. They may choose to draw an illustration or to act out the meaning through pantomime.

RESEARCH ACTIVITY *(W.6.4; SL.6.4)*

Research and Present/Severe Weather Alert

- Have students choose a type of weather from one of the passages and use the description in the passage to write a weather alert.

- Ask students to research weather reports about their chosen topic to determine the kind of scientific information they might include as well as the potential effects of the weather.

- Encourage students to include figurative language in their alerts.

- Have students present their alerts to the class.

Analyzing Word Choice

LESSON OBJECTIVES

- Understand tone and mood in literary text.
- Analyze the impact of word choice on meaning and tone.

THE LEARNING PROGRESSION

- **Grade 5:** CCLS RL.5.4 asks students to determine the meaning of figurative language.

- **Grade 6: CCLS RL.6.4 builds on the Grade 5 standard by requiring students to determine the connotative meaning of words and phrases and to understand the relationship between word choice and the overall meaning and tone of a text.**

- **Grade 7:** CCLS RL.7.4 requires students to go beyond figurative language to analyze how other devices, such as rhyme, repetition, and alliteration, shape meaning.

PREREQUISITE SKILLS

- Understand that some words have positive and negative connotations.
- Understand the meaning suggested by figurative language.

TAP STUDENTS' PRIOR KNOWLEDGE

- Tell students they will be working on a lesson about how a writer's choice of words affects the meaning of a text and also sets an overall tone or mood. Tell them that tone is the attitude of the narrator or speaker, and mood refers to the atmosphere or feeling in a story or poem.

- Ask students what attitude, or tone, they would try to set if they wanted to convince a reluctant parent to let them have a pet. (*a serious tone that would convey how responsible and trustworthy they are*)

- Next, ask them how they would create the right mood if they were going to tell a ghost story. (*turn out the lights or gather by a fire, speak in an ominous or whispery voice*)

- Tell students that good writers do the same thing with words. By choosing just the right words, they can convey an attitude about something or create a certain mood. Recognizing these word choices will help students enjoy and appreciate what they read.

Ready *Teacher Toolbox*   teacher-toolbox.com

	Prerequisite Skills	RL.6.4
Ready Lessons		✓
Tools for Instruction	✓ ✓	✓
Interactive Tutorials	✓	✓

CCLS Focus

RL.6.4 … analyze the impact of a specific word choice on meaning and tone.

ADDITIONAL STANDARDS: **RL.6.1, RL.6.5, RL.6.7; W.6.3, W.6.7, W.6.11.c; SL.6.1, SL.6.4, SL.6.6; L.6.1, L.6.2.a, L.6.4.a, L.6.4.b** (*See page A39 for full text.*)

AT A GLANCE

Through a short poem, students are introduced to the idea of paying careful attention to a writer's choice of words in order to understand a text's meaning, tone, and mood. They learn to analyze words by thinking about whether they convey positive or negative feelings.

STEP BY STEP

- Read the definitions of *tone* and *mood*. Then have students read the poem carefully and think about the words the writer chose. Ask, "What feelings do the words convey?"

- After students have finished reading the poem, point out the change in tone as the words go from negative to positive. Tell students to go back and circle the words in each line that show how the speaker feels.

- Explain that the chart lists some descriptive adjectives and exact verbs from the poem. Read the words and discuss how they clearly and vividly convey the gloom of a Monday morning and how that gloom is transformed by a sweet smile.

- Discuss with students how poems can convey happy, sad, funny, or silly moods. Have students share the titles of poems they have read and enjoyed.

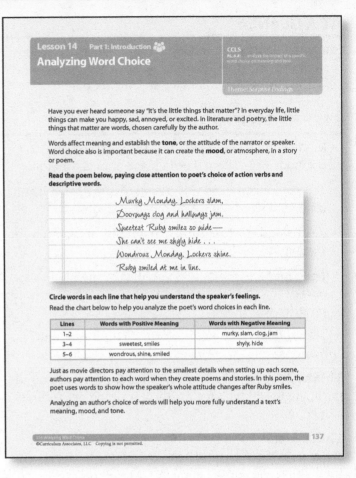

Genre Focus

Literary Texts: Mystery

Tell students that in this lesson they will read a mystery. Remind them that a mystery is a fiction story with characters who try to solve a crime or some unexplained event.

Explain that one of the characteristics of mysteries is the element of suspense. Discuss the definition of *suspense* and how suspense can range from the stomach-churning anticipation of a scary roller-coaster ride, to a hint of the supernatural that raises the hair on the back of your neck, to a rising feeling of panic that comes with the threat of bodily harm.

Discuss with students how authors create a suspenseful mood. Ask, "What part does the setting play?" "What settings are suited to mysteries and why?" (*nighttime, a dark forest, a storm, an old, abandoned house*) "How is the conflict or problem often set up?" (*someone is alone, lost, powerless, unaware of hidden danger*)

Have students name some suspenseful mysteries they have read. Ask them to tell how the author created a suspenseful mood.

- Tell students that "A Fright in the Night" is a story that has some familiar characteristics of suspense—a nighttime setting and an unexplained noise.

AT A GLANCE

Students identify the mood of a short story about a girl who is awakened by a strange noise. They think about how the author's word choice sets the mood.

STEP BY STEP

- Invite volunteers to tell what they learned on the previous page about word choice, mood, and tone.

- Tell students that in this lesson they will analyze the impact of word choice on mood and tone.

- Read aloud the first three paragraphs of "A Fright in the Night."

- Then read the prompt: "Describe the mood of this part of the story. Identify specific words that help to produce this mood."

- Tell students you will perform a Think Aloud to demonstrate a way of answering the question.

Think Aloud: In this story, a girl is woken by a sound in the night. I'll look for words describing her feelings and actions.

Think Aloud: In the first line, *squinted* suggests that she fears what she might see through the window. It tells that she doesn't open her eyes all the way.

- Point out the chart. Explain that it is made to hold words from the story and the feelings they convey.

- Have students reread the story. Tell them to consider how specific words are meant to convey feelings.

Think Aloud: In the second paragraph, the author uses the words *pounded* and *sweaty*. When my chest pounds and my palms are sweaty, I know I am nervous.

- Guide students to fill in the rest of the chart with other words from the story.

Think Aloud: Look at the "Feelings the Words Convey" column. What do these feelings have in common? How do they add up to a mood, or overall feeling?

- Finally, have students write paragraphs describing the mood of the story so far. Invite volunteers to share their answers with the class. (*Sample response: The overall mood of the story is tense and frightening. For example, the phrase "more snakelike than serene" suggests that the shadows are scary. Descriptions such as these help readers understand why Carmen feels uneasy in her room.*)

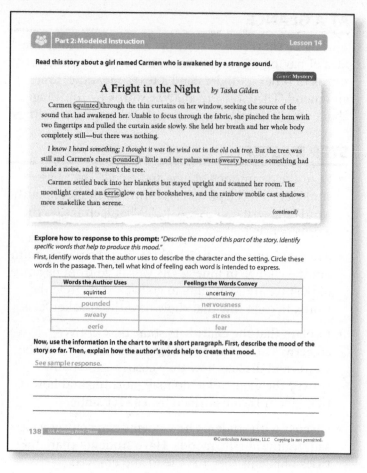

Tier Two Vocabulary: *Scanned*

- Point out the word *scanned* in the last paragraph. Ask students what context clues in the paragraph can help them figure out what *scanned* means. (*"stayed upright," "the moonlight created a glow," "the mobile cast shadows"*).

- Explain that the descriptions of the moonlight on the bookshelves and the shadows of the mobile indicate that Carmen's eyes are open and she is looking around her room, checking to make sure things are as they should be. Now ask students what *scanned* means. (*to look over quickly and systematically*) (**RL.6.4; L.6.4.a**)

AT A GLANCE

Students continue reading about Carmen. They answer a multiple-choice question and analyze the details that helped them select the correct answer.

STEP BY STEP

- Tell students they will continue reading about Carmen and the nighttime interruption.

- Point out the two features to the left of the passage. Remind students that good readers pay attention to an author's word choice. The Close Reading helps students focus on the mood of the story. The Hint will help them understand how a few well-chosen words can completely change the mood of a story.

- Have students read the passage and underline words and phrases that convey the mood, as directed by the Close Reading.

- Ask volunteers to share the words and phrases they underlined. Have them explain the mood that the words convey. If necessary, ask: "Do the words express positive or negative feelings?"

- Have students respond to Show Your Thinking. (*Sample response: The mood so far in the story has been suspenseful. The word laugh suggests humor.*)

ANSWER ANALYSIS

Choice A is incorrect. When Carmen swallows the lump in her throat, this continues the suspenseful mood established at the start of the story.

Choice B is correct. This group of words reflects the change in mood created by the story's surprise ending.

Choice C is incorrect. These words let the reader know how the noise was made but do not change the mood.

Choice D is incorrect. Carmen's concern for her cat comes after her laugh of relief, so the change in mood has already occurred by the time she talks to her cat.

ERROR ALERT: Students who did not choose B may not have understood the question. Point out that it asks for the words that reflect the change in mood. All the choices are from the ending. Only B shows how the mood changes from suspenseful to funny.

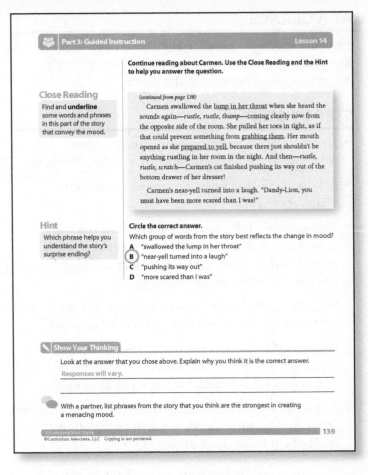

ELL Support: Irregular Past-Tense Verbs

- Remind students that some verbs do not follow the rules for forming the past tense. These verbs are called irregular verbs, and students must remember their past-tense forms.

- Ask students to find an irregular past-tense verb in the first sentence. (*heard*) Ask what the present tense form of the verb is. (*hear*)

- Display these sentences and help students fill in the blanks with the proper form of the verb *hear*:

  Carmen _____ a noise last night.

  Do you _____ that noise? **(L.6.1)**

AT A GLANCE

Students read a poem twice about two boys. After the first reading, you will ask three questions to check students' comprehension of the poem.

STEP BY STEP

- Have students read the poem silently without referring to the Study Buddy or Close Reading text.

- Ask the following questions to ensure students' comprehension of the text:

  The poet says Bill "would fracture each rule" at school and at play. What does "fracture each rule" mean? *(Bill broke all the school's rules and also the rules of any games or sports he played.)*

  What happened to the two boys when they grew up? *(Jim achieved honor and fame. Bill ended up in jail.)*

  What do you think is the main message of "Those Two Boys"? *(The way you behave in childhood is a good sign of how you will turn out when you grow up.)*

- Ask students to reread the first stanza and look at the Study Buddy think aloud. What does the Study Buddy help them think about?

Tip: The Study Buddy reminds students to pay attention to the poet's word choice. Have students think about whether the poet uses words with positive or negative connotations to describe Bill.

- Have students read the rest of the poem. Tell them to follow the directions in the Close Reading.

Tip: Point out to students that a reader could interpret the poem's tone in different ways. Is the tone light-hearted? Stern? Joking? Have students point to clues in the poem that suggest the tone. The bouncy rhythm and phrases such as "naught but a blot" and "fracture each rule" create a comic effect. How would a different interpretation of the poem's tone affect how a reader understands the poem's message? The last line of the poem suggests it might be poking fun at the idea that "good" and "bad" children reverse roles as adults.

- Finally, have students answer the questions on page 141. Use the Answer Analysis to discuss correct and incorrect responses.

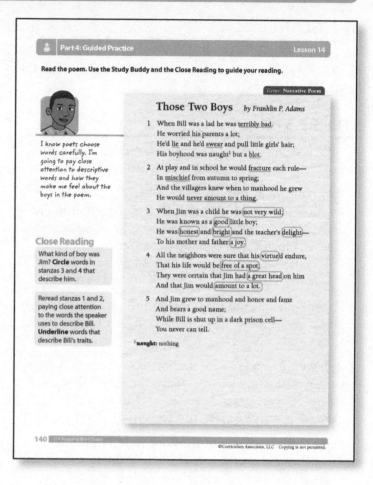

Tier Two Vocabulary: *Mischief*

- Read the first two lines of Stanza 2. Ask, "Who is the poet telling about here?" *(Bill)* "How do you know?" *(Bill is the bad boy described in Stanza 1. Breaking rules is something a bad boy would do.)*

- Ask students how the context of the first six lines of the poem helps them understand what the word *mischief* means. *(It must have something to do with behaving badly all year.)*

- Tell students another clue is the prefix *mis-*, which means "bad" or "wrong," as in *misbehave.*

- Based on these clues, ask students what *mischief* means. *("annoying or bad behavior")* **(RL.6.4; L.6.4.a; L.6.4.b)**

- Then ask students what other words would make sense in place of *in mischief* (*in trouble, behaving badly*).

STEP BY STEP

- Have students read questions 1–3, using the Hints to help them answer those questions.

Tip: If students are having trouble answering question 1, have them reread line 4. Point out that this is a metaphor—figurative language that compares two things. Have students tell what the metaphor is comparing and what the comparison means.

- Discuss with students the Answer Analysis below.

ANSWER ANALYSIS

1 The correct choice is A. The poem says Bill's boyhood was nothing but a blot, a metaphor suggesting there was nothing good about Bill. Choice B is incorrect. Bill's misdeeds such as lying and swearing didn't happen by accident. Choice C is incorrect because people are usually not considered criminals until they are adults. Choice D is a valid conclusion, but the metaphor is only about Bill's boyhood, not his life.

2 The correct choice is B. All these words are used to describe what people thought of Jim. Choices A and C are incorrect. Words such as *child* and *mother* do not help readers understand what Jim is like. Choice D is incorrect. These isolated words are misleading without the rest of the descriptions they are part of—"not very wild" and "free of a spot."

3 Sample response: The poet creates a judgmental tone by using harsh words to describe Bill and glowing words to describe Jim. The second stanza, which tells about Bill, ends with the line "He would never amount to a thing." Jim, on the other hand, is called "honest and bright" and gains "honor and fame."

RETEACHING

Use a chart to verify the answer to question 3. Draw the chart below, and have students fill in the boxes. Sample responses are provided.

Boy	Words Suggesting Judgmental Tone
Bill	would never amount to a thing
Jim	would amount to a lot

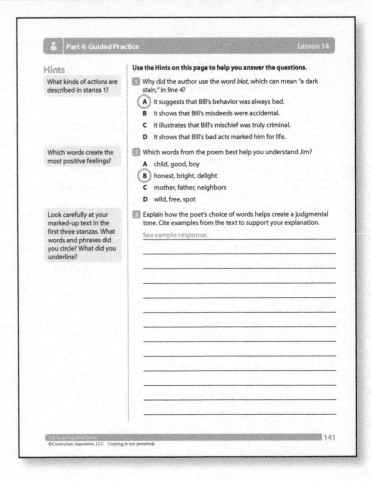

 Part 4: Guided Practice   Lesson 14

Hints

What kinds of actions are described in stanza 1?

Which words create the most positive feelings?

Look carefully at your marked-up text in the first three stanzas. What words and phrases did you circle? What did you underline?

Use the Hints on this page to help you answer the questions.

1 Why did the author use the word *blot*, which can mean "a dark stain," in line 4?

  A It suggests that Bill's behavior was always bad.
  B It shows that Bill's misdeeds were accidental.
  C It illustrates that Bill's mischief was truly criminal.
  D It shows that Bill's bad acts marked him for life.

2 Which words from the poem best help you understand Jim?

  A child, good, boy
  B honest, bright, delight
  C mother, father, neighbors
  D wild, free, spot

3 Explain how the poet's choice of words helps create a judgmental tone. Cite examples from the text to support your explanation.

  See sample response.

L14: Analyzing Word Choice
©Curriculum Associates, LLC   Copying is not permitted.   141

Integrating Standards

Use these questions to further students' understanding of "Those Two Boys."

1 Compare and contrast lines 4 and 14. Tell why you think the poet included them. **(RL.6.1)**

The lines are similar because they both include words that can mean a stain—blot and spot. But the difference is that Bill's life is judged as nothing but a stain, whereas Jim's life is predicted to be free of any stain. I can infer that the poet is using the same image, in a positive and a negative way, to connect the two boys but also to emphasize how different they are.

2 What does the poet mean when he says that "Jim had a great head on him"? **(RL.6.4)**

The next line says that Jim would amount to a lot. Usually, you don't amount to a lot unless you are smart. Your brain is in your head, so I think "great head" means smart. The poet is saying that people thought Jim was very smart.

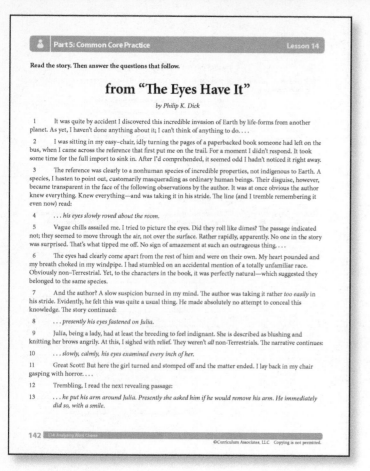

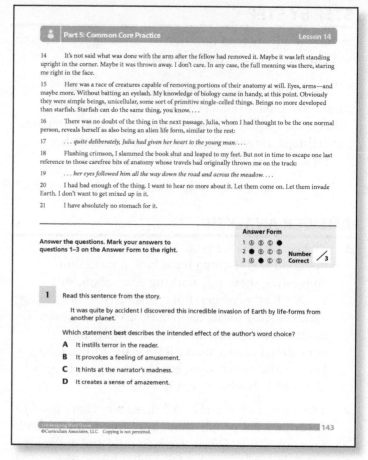

AT A GLANCE

Students independently read a longer story and answer questions in a format that provides test practice.

STEP BY STEP

- Tell students to use what they have learned about reading carefully and analyzing word choice to read the story on pages 142 and 143.

- Remind students to circle or underline words that help them understand the meaning and tone of the passage.

- Tell students to answer the questions on pages 143 and 144. For questions 1–3, they should fill in the correct circle on the Answer Form.

- When students have finished, use the Answer Analysis to discuss the correct responses and the reasons for them. Have students fill in the Number Correct on the Answer Form.

ANSWER ANALYSIS

1 Choice D is correct. The word *incredible* creates a sense of amazement. Choices A and B are incorrect. These lines do not suggest terror or amusement. Choice C is incorrect. The narrator recognizes that the idea of alien life-forms invading Earth is hard to believe, so the lines do not suggest madness. **(DOK 3)**

2 Choice A is correct. The lines from the book show that the narrator does not recognize figurative language when he reads it. Choices B, C, and D are incorrect because they all assume the narrator is correct in his literal interpretation of the book. **(DOK 3)**

Theme Connection

- How do all the stories in this lesson relate to the theme of surprise endings?

- How would you describe the tone of each passage?

3 Choice B is correct. The words "my heart pounded" and "my breath choked" most strongly convey a sense of growing fear in the narrator. Choice A is incorrect. It describes the narrator's realization — a totally false one — that he is reading about strange horrors. But the words themselves do not convey fear. In choice C, the "slow suspicion" gradually growing in the narrator also has to do with his false fears, but the sentence itself has a calm quality to it. Choice D also has more to do with the narrator's faulty reasoning than his emotions and is incorrect. **(DOK 2)**

4 Sample response: All along, the narrator has interpreted figurative language literally. When he reads about eyes roving or a heart being given to someone, he thinks these organs disengage from the body and move on their own. He says, "Here was a race of creatures capable of removing portions of their anatomy at will." Clear evidence of an alien race, he concludes. Nevertheless, the tone of the passage changes to humorous at the end when the narrator himself uses figurative language without realizing it. By saying he has "no stomach for it," he is referring to his stomach as a thing separate from his body. **(DOK 3)**

---

2 Throughout the story, the narrator includes excerpts from the book he is reading. How are these excerpts **most likely** intended to affect your understanding of the story?

   A They show that the narrator is wrong about the alien invasion.

   B They add tension as the narrator finds more proof of the aliens.

   C They tell a separate story about Julia's romance with an alien.

   D They demonstrate the narrator's ability to find hidden messages.

3 Which of the following sentences from the story **best** conveys the narrator's growing sense of fear in the text?

   A "It took some time for the full import to sink in."

   B "My heart pounded and my breath choked in my windpipe."

   C "A slow suspicion burned in my mind."

   D "In any case, the full meaning was there, staring me right in the face."

4 In the last sentence from the story, the narrator states, "I have absolutely no stomach for it." Explain how the author's word choice adds a humorous meaning to the story. Use text evidence to support your answer.

   See sample response.

   _____

   _____

   _____

   _____

   _____

   _____

   ✓ **Self Check** Go back and see what you can check off on the Self Check on page 128.

144 · L14 Analyzing Word Choice   ©Curriculum Associates, LLC   Copying is not permitted.

Integrating Standards

Use these questions and tasks as opportunities to interact with "The Eyes Have It."

1 The narrator says, "The reference was clearly to a nonhuman species of incredible properties, not indigenous to Earth." Use context clues to figure out the meaning of *indigenous*. **(RL.6.4; L.6.4.a)**

The narrator says that the species is "nonhuman" with "incredible properties," clearly a life form not from Earth, so indigenous *means "native."*

2 How does paragraph 16 contribute to the development of the plot of the passage? **(RL.6.5)**

Up to this point, the narrator thinks that Julia is a normal human. In Paragraph 16, the narrator is shocked to read that she, too, seems able to remove a body part—her heart. This is the climax of the passage and seems to resign the narrator to the fact that Earth has indeed been invaded.

3 Using details from the passage, how would you describe the narrator? **(RL.6.1)**

The narrator is naive and gullible. He is too quick to take what he reads literally, and he jumps to conclusions. He uses sophisticated vocabulary, though, and the passage says he has a knowledge of biology. Perhaps his inability to recognize and analyze figurative language is because he has not read much fiction, only science. Also, he resigns himself to the invasion, rather than doing something about it. Maybe he has little experience of the world.

4 Discuss in small groups: Why do you think the author chose to write the story in the first person? How would it be different if it was written in the third person? **(SL.6.1)**

Discussions will vary. Encourage students to consider how the story would sound if written in the third person. Would it be as engaging? Would the narrative be as smooth? Would readers have to use their imaginations as much if the third person was used? Would it make any difference at all?

Writing Activities

What If...? *(W.6.3)*

- Ask students: What if the narrator of "The Eyes Have It" is right, and Earth is being invaded? What if the narrator, rather than being resigned, takes action? What might he do, or not do?

- Have students write what happens next in the story as if Earth has been invaded by a "nonhuman species of incredible properties," and only the narrator knows that the invasion has happened.

Using Dashes *(L.6.2.a)*

- Display this sentence from paragraph 3 of "The Eyes Have It": "Knew everything—and was taking it in his stride." Point out the dash and tell students that a dash can be used to set off an afterthought or a sudden change of thought. Explain that another use of the dash is to mean "in other words."

- Ask students to find two other examples of the use of a dash in the passage and tell how it is being used. (*Paragraph 6: "—which suggested they belonged to the same species"; to mean "in other words"; Paragraph 15: "—and maybe more"; an afterthought*)

- Have partners write sentences about an alien life form using a dash both ways.

LISTENING ACTIVITY *(RL.6.7; SL.6.6)*

Listen Closely/Recite a Poem

- Have pairs recite "Those Two Boys," with one reading the stanzas about Bill, the other reading the stanzas about Jim.

- Encourage students to create a distinct "voice" for each boy and to use appropriate rate and expression when they read. Remind students to listen respectfully and comment constructively on the oral readings.

- Then have students compare the experience of listening to the poem to reading it to themselves.

DISCUSSION ACTIVITY *(SL.6.1)*

Talk in a Group/Discuss Suspense

- Remind students of the elements of suspense. Ask students to think about each of the three passages and how they achieved, or didn't achieve, a feeling of suspense.

- Have students form small groups to discuss how to create suspense and which passage in the lesson was most successful at creating suspense.

- Allow 10 to 15 minutes for discussion. Then have each group share its results with the class.

MEDIA ACTIVITY *(RL.6.7)*

Be Creative/Interpret a Scene

- Invite students to illustrate a scene from one of the passages. They can do a straightforward rendering based on the passage's details, or they can add other characters or objects to the scene. Encourage them to convey a tone, such as scary or humorous.

- Invite students to explain their illustrations.

- Discuss how a picture compares with what students "saw" in their minds when they read the scene. Does the picture add a new dimension to their understanding or appreciation of the story?

RESEARCH ACTIVITY *(W.6.7; SL.6.4)*

Research and Present/Give a Presentation

- Tell students that Philip K. Dick was a famous science fiction writer and Franklin P. Adams a well-known writer and newspaper columnist.

- Have students research biographical information about one of these authors and how he achieved fame. Encourage students to use print and digital resources to locate information.

- Allow time for students to present their research to the class.

Analyzing the Structure of a Poem

LESSON OBJECTIVES

- Analyze how lines and stanzas fit into the overall structure of a poem and contribute to the development of the theme.

THE LEARNING PROGRESSION

- **Grade 5:** CCLS RL.5.5 requires students to think about how the parts of a text provide the structure.

- **Grade 6: CCLS RL.6.5 builds on the Grade 5 standard by requiring students to consider how a particular part of the text fits into the structure and how it contributes to the theme, setting, or plot.**

- **Grade 7:** CCLS RL.7.5 focuses on how a drama's or poem's structure contributes to its meaning.

PREREQUISITE SKILLS

- Identify a text's theme, setting, and plot.

- Recognize the general structure of a text.

- Explain how a particular sentence, chapter, scene, or stanza functions within a larger text.

TAP STUDENTS' PRIOR KNOWLEDGE

- Tell students they will be learning about the structure of a poem and how it contributes to the poem's theme. Ask students how poems are different from other texts. (*Poems are usually written in groups of lines called stanzas, rather than paragraphs; they may use rhyme, rhythm, and repetition; they may not use punctuation in the same ways as other texts.*)

- Share a short poem that students are familiar with. As appropriate, discuss elements of the poem such as rhyme, rhythm, repetition, punctuation, and figurative language.

- Have students recall what they have learned about theme. (*A theme is a lesson or message the author wants readers to learn.*) Ask students to describe the theme of the poem you shared.

- Tell students they will analyze how the structure of a poem can help them figure out the theme. Recognizing a poem's theme will help make the poetry they read more enjoyable and help them understand how the text connects to their own lives.

Ready *Teacher Toolbox*

teacher-toolbox.com

	Prerequisite Skills	RL.6.5
Ready Lessons	✓	✓
Tools for Instruction	✓	
Interactive Tutorials	✓	✓

CCLS Focus

RL.6.5 Analyze how a particular sentence, chapter, scene, or stanza fits into the overall structure of a text and contributes to the development of the theme, setting, or plot.

ADDITIONAL STANDARDS: **RL.6.1, RL.6.2, RL.6.4, RL.6.7; W.6.3, W.6.4, W.6.6, W.6.7, W.6.11.b, W.6.11.c; SL.6.1, SL.6.4, SL.6.9; L.6.4.a, L.6.4.c, L.6.4.d** (*See page A39 for full text.*)

AT A GLANCE

By reading a poem, students explore how to identify themes in poetry. They learn that recognizing the structure of a poem can help them figure out its theme.

STEP BY STEP

- Read the definitions of *structure* and *theme*. Then read the poem with students. Encourage them to note the structure. Ask: How are the lines of the poem organized? (*They are organized in three-line stanzas with each stanza expressing a different thought.*) Have students think about what each stanza means.

- Explain that the chart shows a way to visualize the organization of the poem. Breaking down the structure of the poem to identify the main ideas will help students figure out the theme.

- Read aloud the main idea of each stanza and have students compare it to the meaning they determined from reading that stanza. Point out how, like chapters in a book, the stanzas in a poem build toward a theme that the speaker is trying to express. Discuss the theme expressed in this poem. Point out that all the stanzas as a whole lead the reader to understand that the speaker has fond, pleasant memories of summer and misses the fun and peacefulness of July.

- Ask students to give examples of other poems they have read and share the themes expressed.

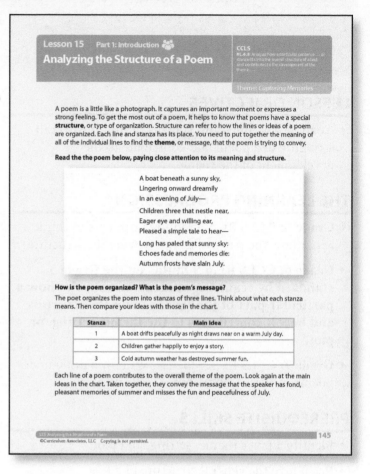

- Share a theme from a poem you have read. Explain how being able to recognize the theme helped make the poetry more enjoyable.

Genre Focus

Literary Texts: Poetry

Tell students that in this lesson they will read poetry. Explain that a poem uses language in an unusual way to express emotions, ideas, or experiences. Two types of poems are lyric poems, which express personal thoughts or feelings, and narrative poems, which tell a story. Common features of poems include:

- stanzas, or groups of lines that form a pattern.

- rhyme, the use of repeated sounds at the ends of words.

- rhythm, the pattern of beats or stressed syllables.

- figurative language, which speaks to the senses.

Based on these characteristics, ask students to tell about poems they have read or heard. Invite students to recite any poems they know. Did the poem have an obvious rhyme or rhythm? What was the poem about? What did they visualize when they read (or heard) the poem? How did the poem make them feel?

Tell students that three poems they will read in this lesson are lyric poems. "Motto" tells how the speaker feels about getting along with others. "The Heart of a Woman" expresses the speaker's thoughts on being a woman. "I Sit and Think" describes the speaker's thoughts about time, both past and future. "Brennan on the Moor" is a ballad about an important outlaw figure in the shared cultural memory of a people.

AT A GLANCE

Students read a poem and recognize how the poem's structure contributes to the poem's theme.

STEP BY STEP

- Invite volunteers to tell what they learned on the previous page about analyzing a poem's structure.

- Tell students that in this lesson they will practice analyzing the structure of poems.

- Read aloud the poem "Motto."

- Then read the question: "What do you notice about the structure, or organization, of this poem?"

- Tell students you will use a Think Aloud to help demonstrate a way of answering this question.

Think Aloud: As I read the poem, I notice the way the lines are organized. There are two stanzas, or groups of lines. Each stanza has its own main idea.

- Direct students to the chart and ask where they've seen a similar chart. Review that it shows the way the poem is organized and the main ideas.

Think Aloud: I'll determine the main idea of each stanza to figure out how the ideas in the poem build to a theme. In stanza 1, I think that "I play it cool and dig all jive" means the speaker is relaxed and gets along with people. "That's the reason I stay alive" indicates that the speaker thinks this is the key to life.

- Point out the main idea of stanza 1 in the chart.

Think Aloud: I think the main idea of stanza 2 is that the speaker has found that if he respects and is kind to others, then others will respect and be kind to him.

- Have students discuss what they think the main idea of stanza 2 is. Ask them to write this main idea in the chart.

Think Aloud: Now I'll use these main ideas to think about the theme of the poem. Because the title of the poem is "Motto" and the main ideas have to do with getting along with people, I think the theme has to do with a philosophy or guiding principle about interacting with people.

- Have students complete the chart by writing the theme of the poem. Ask volunteers to share their answers with the class.

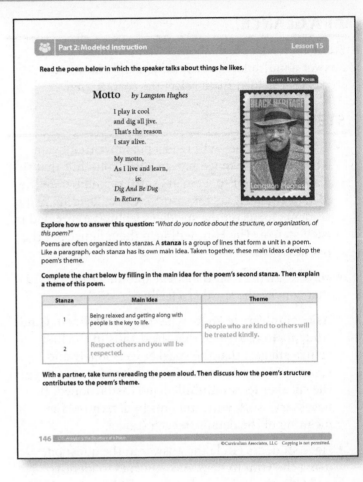

Tier Two Vocabulary: *Motto*

- Direct students to the word *motto* in the title of the poem. Say, "'Live every day to the fullest' is my motto." Ask students to tell what a *motto* is (*a short statement of beliefs, or words to live by*). Suggest students consult a dictionary to verify the meaning.

- Ask students to share mottos they know; for example, "Live and let live." If appropriate, point out familiar business mottos or government mottos students may recognize. **(RL.6.4; L.6.4.d)**

AT A GLANCE

Students read a poem about a woman's heart. They answer a multiple-choice question and analyze the words that helped them select the correct answer.

STEP BY STEP

- Tell students they will read a poem written by an African American woman in 1918. Point out that this was a time prior to women's suffrage and before the idea of equal rights for women. Close Reading helps students focus on the speaker's feelings expressed in each stanza. The Hint will help them figure out the poem's theme.

- Have students read the poem and underline details that convey the speaker's feelings.

- Ask volunteers to share what they underlined. Guide students to recognize that the details in the first stanza suggest that the speaker feels lonely and restless while the details in the second stanza suggest the speaker feels unfulfilled and disillusioned. If necessary, work with students to determine the meaning of the details in each stanza.

- Have students circle the answer to the question, using the Hint to help. Ask students to identify words in the answers that are similar in meaning to words in the poem, such as "trapped" and "cage."

ANSWER ANALYSIS

Choice A is incorrect. The first stanza compares the heart to a bird "soft winging so restlessly on." This conveys an image of something frail, not strong.

Choice B is correct. The poet describes the heart as a restless, roaming figure in search of adventure.

Choice C is incorrect. The poet describes the heart trying "to forget it has dreamed of the stars." This does not suggest it is happy.

Choice D is incorrect. Only the second stanza conveys dark images like a night sky.

ERROR ALERT: Students who did not choose B may not have understood the concept of theme. Point out that although the other choices describe things that may be true about the heart of a woman, only B is supported by the details in the poem.

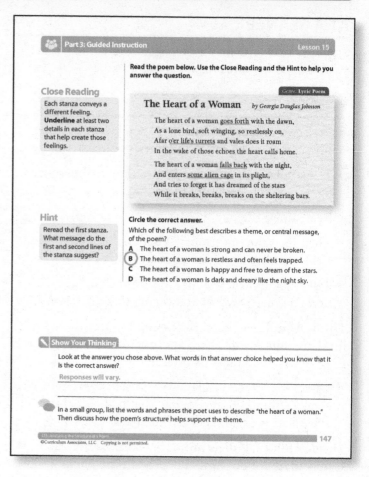

ELL Support: Multiple-Meaning Words

- Explain to students that some words have more than one meaning and are called multiple-meaning words. Tell students that they can use other words or phrases in a sentence to help them know which meaning of a multiple-meaning word is being used.

- Point out the word *echoes* in line four. In this line, does *echoes* mean "a repetition of sound" or "a remnant"? (*a remnant*)

- Ask, "What context clues help you figure out which meaning is intended?" Guide students to see how the words *go forth, roam,* and *wake* describe going out looking for adventure, leaving behind the remnants of home.

- Similarly, help students determine the meaning of *alien* in line 6. ("*unfamiliar or strange*") **(RL.6.4; L.6.4.a)**

AT A GLANCE

Students read a poem twice about the passage of time. After the first reading, you will ask three questions to check your students' comprehension of the poem.

STEP BY STEP

• Have students read the poem silently without referring to the Study Buddy or Close Reading text.

• Ask the following questions to ensure students' comprehension of the text:

How can you tell that the speaker of the poem is an older person? (*The speaker says, "I … think of all that I have seen," "in summers that have been," "in autumns that there were."*)

What does the speaker recall seeing in his lifetime? (*"meadow-flowers and butterflies," "yellow leaves and gossamer," "morning mist and silver sun and wind upon my hair"*)

What does the speaker imagine when he thinks about the future? (*He imagines what the world will be like after he has passed.*)

• Ask students to reread the poem and look at the Study Buddy think aloud. What does the Study Buddy help them think about?

• Tell students to follow the directions in the Close Reading.

Tip: The Study Buddy helps students identify clues that relate to time. Close Reading helps students identify details that show what times the speaker is thinking about and how the speaker feels about the future. Explain to students that when they read poems, they can mark details as they read, just as they do when they read other literary texts. Then they can review the details to help them think about the poem and its theme. They may also use a dictionary to look up unfamiliar words.

• Finally, have students answer the questions on page 149. Use the Answer Analysis to discuss correct and incorrect responses.

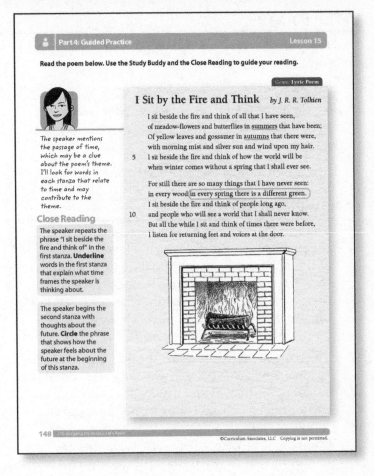

ELL Support: Compound Words

• Review with students that a compound word is made up of two smaller words and that you can look at the two smaller words to figure out the meaning of the compound word.

• Point out the word *butterflies* in line 2. Guide students to identify the two smaller words and talk about their meanings. Explain that some compound words mean something different from the two smaller words. *Butterflies*, for example, does not mean "insects made of butter."

• Tell students it is important to check the meaning of a compound word by looking at clues in the surrounding text. Ask, "What context clues help you figure out that butterflies are flying insects?" (*meadow-flowers, summers*) **(RL.6.4; L.6.4.a)**

STEP BY STEP

- Have students read questions 1–3, using the Hints to help them answer those questions.

Tip: If students have trouble answering question 2, have them reread the poem, looking for words and phrases that relate to time. Tell them to think about the time order.

- Discuss with students the Answer Analysis below.

ANSWER ANALYSIS

1 The correct choice is C. The speaker says he thinks "of all that I have seen," which refers to the past, and that he thinks about "a spring that I shall never see." Choice A is incorrect. The speaker thinks of the past fondly, not regretfully. Choices B and D are incorrect. The speaker wonders about when he is no longer alive, not about what he will do in the future.

2 The correct choice is A. The speaker thinks of "people long ago," "people who will see a world that I shall never know," and listens "for returning feet and voices." Choice B is incorrect. The speaker thinks of "all that I have seen," which is the past. Choice C is incorrect. The speaker thinks of "autumns that were." Choice D is incorrect. The speaker listens for "returning feet" in the present.

3 Sample response: As we get older and approach the "winter" of our lives, we think about our past and about a future we may not see. The final sentence relates to this theme because the speaker seems to decide to focus on the past ("times that were before") and the "feet and voices" in the present.

RETEACHING

Use a chart to answer question 3. Draw the chart below, Have students fill in the boxes.

Stanza	Main Idea	Theme
1	As we get older, we think about the past and wonder about the future.	We don't know what the future holds, but we can focus on our past and our present.
2	There are things in the future we may never do, but we can focus on our memories and live in the present.	

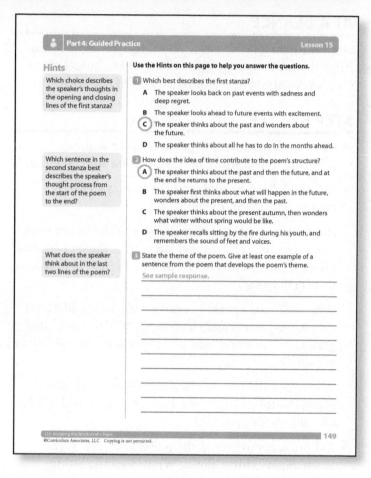

 Part 4: Guided Practice   Lesson 15

Hints

Which choice describes the speaker's thoughts in the opening and closing lines of the first stanza?

Which sentence in the second stanza best describes the speaker's thought process from the start of the poem to the end?

What does the speaker think about in the last two lines of the poem?

Use the Hints on this page to help you answer the questions.

1 Which best describes the first stanza?

   A The speaker looks back on past events with sadness and deep regret.

   B The speaker looks ahead to future events with excitement.

   C The speaker thinks about the past and wonders about the future.

   D The speaker thinks about all he has to do in the months ahead.

2 How does the idea of time contribute to the poem's structure?

   A The speaker thinks about the past and then the future, and at the end he returns to the present.

   B The speaker first thinks about what will happen in the future, wonders about the present, and then the past.

   C The speaker thinks about the present autumn, then wonders what winter without spring would be like.

   D The speaker recalls sitting by the fire during his youth, and remembers the sound of feet and voices.

3 State the theme of the poem. Give at least one example of a sentence from the poem that develops the poem's theme.

See sample response.

L15: Analyzing the Structure of a Poem   149
©Curriculum Associates, LLC Copying is not permitted.

Integrating Standards

Use these questions to further students' understanding of "I Sit by the Fire and Think."

1 What does the speaker mean by "when winter comes without a spring that I shall ever see"? **(RL.6.1)**

The speaker is wondering about a time when he is no longer alive. Spring naturally follows winter. The reason the speaker will not see the spring is that he died before spring came.

2 Summarize this poem in your own words. **(RL.6.2)**

Sample response: The speaker reflects upon his life: things he's done and seen, and people he's known. He wonders about the future when life will go on without him. He decides to focus his thoughts on his memories of the past and on the present.

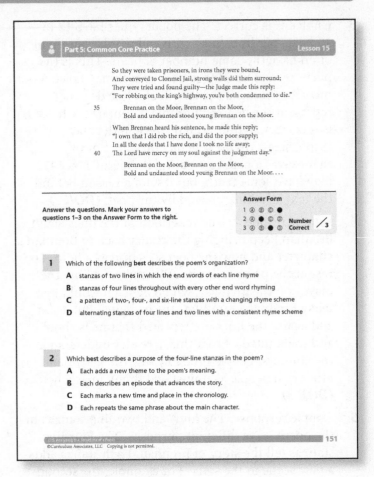

AT A GLANCE

Students independently read a ballad and answer questions in a format that provides test practice.

STEP BY STEP

- Tell students to use what they have learned about reading carefully and analyzing the structure of a ballad to read the poem on pages 150 and 151.

- Remind students to underline or circle important details that help them understand the theme.

- Tell students to answer the questions on pages 151 and 152. For questions 1–3, they should fill in the correct circle on the Answer Form.

- When students have finished, use the Answer Analysis to discuss correct responses and the reasons for them. Have students fill in the Number Correct on the Answer Form.

ANSWER ANALYSIS

1 Choice D is correct. It is the only choice that correctly describes the structure of the entire poem. Choice A describes only the two-line chorus, not the four-line stanzas. Choice B does not mention the two-line chorus. Choice C is simply incorrect. **(DOK 2)**

2 Choice B is correct. Each four-line stanza tells about an event that moves the story forward. Choice A is incorrect because each new four-line stanza does not represent a new theme. Choice C is incorrect because several stanzas describe Brennan robbing the mayor on the highway; the time and place of those episodes is the same. Choice D is incorrect because it describes only the two-line stanzas. **(DOK 2)**

Theme Connection

- How do all the poems in this lesson relate to the theme of capturing memories?

- Which poem did you like the best? Why?

3 Choice C is correct. The poem's lines have 12 to 15 beats per line; lines with end words that rhyme often have the same number of beats. This is the poet's way of keeping a steady rhythm. Choice A is incorrect because the length of a line does not represent the degree of drama it contains. Choice B is incorrect. While similar line lengths may emphasize a rhyme scheme, they are not in themselves a path to creating rhymes. Choice D may have some truth, but it's not a reason behind the text structure created by the poet. **(DOK 2)**

4 Sample response: The repetition of the lines about Brennan keep bringing the reader back to Brennan's character and how the poet sees him as a hero. The rest of the poem tells about Brennan robbing the mayor on the highway, which by itself would just make Brennan seem like "the bad guy." But again and again, the lines are repeated that he is "bold and undaunted." From this, a reader understands the common people probably saw the mayor and other rich people as unjust and Brennan as a hero. **(DOK 3)**

5 Sample response: The four- and two-line stanzas in the poem serve different purposes. The four-line stanzas tell the story of Brennan. Each stanza adds a new scene to the story. For example, the second four-line stanza tells about Brennan meeting the mayor on the highway, and how the mayor wants to take him in. In the third four-line stanza, Brennan's wife gives him a gun, and in the fourth, he robs the

mayor. In contrast, the two-line stanzas are all repetitions of the same line. Basically, these lines tell the reader how many people of the time viewed Brennan. **(DOK 3)**

Integrating Standards

Use these questions and tasks as opportunities to interact with "Brennan on the Moor."

1 Use details from the first stanza to explain what kind of man Willy Brennan was. **(RL.6.1)**

Wild and intimidating: "...he commenced his wild career;" "...many a wealthy gentleman before him shook with fear."

2 In line 19, the speaker says that "One hundred pounds were offered for [Brennan's] *apprehension* there." What does *apprehension* mean in this context? Use a dictionary to find the precise meaning. **(RL.6.4; L.6.4.d)**

In this context, apprehension *means "capture."*

3 Summarize the poem's main events. **(RL.6.2; W.6.4)**

One day, a highwayman named Willy Brennan crosses paths with the Mayor of Cashel who plans to arrest Brennan for his crimes. When Brennan sees his wife in town, he asks for money. She hands him a firearm, which Brennan uses to rob the Mayor of his gold and escape. A reward is set on Brennan's head, so he retreats to the mountains. Eventually he is caught, tried, found guilty, and sentenced to death.

4 Discuss: Was Willy Brennan's fate fair? **(SL.6.1)**

Discussions will vary but should reflect Brennan's history as an outlaw. Students may cite details from the poem that outline Brennan's violent tendencies or his personal defense after being tried.

Writing Activities

Creative Rewrites (W.6.3; W.6.4)

- Have students review the structure of the poems in this lesson. Then ask them to rewrite a familiar story using another structure. For example, ask students to use a familiar plot or character to create a poem written in stanzas.

- Conversely, reread one of the poems and ask students to use another structure to convey the content of the poem (a narrative, for example).

- Allow time for students to share their writing with the class.

Consult Reference Materials (L.6.4.c)

- Direct students to the word *o'er* in line 3 of "The Heart of a Woman." Write the word on the board and explain that it means "over." Explain that people today don't generally use this word in their speech, but it may be used in poetry.

- Tell students they can use a print or online dictionary to determine the pronunciation of *o'er*. Have students find the phonetic spelling in a print or online dictionary and an audio pronunciation online. Then have volunteers say the word aloud. Ask students to look up other unfamiliar words from this lesson's poems.

LISTENING ACTIVITY (SL.6.4)

Listen Closely/Recite with a Partner

- Invite students to work in pairs to recite "Motto" or "I Sit by the Fire and Think." Have partners decide who will start, and then take turns reading, switching readers after each stanza.

- Have partners reread the poem several times to practice reading with accuracy and appropriate expression, and at an understandable pace.

- Partners should listen carefully and give one another constructive feedback.

DISCUSSION ACTIVITY (SL.6.1; SL.6.9)

Talk in a Group/Compare Poems

- Have students form small groups to compare and contrast "I Sit by the Fire and Think" with "Brennan on the Moor."

- If necessary, share these prompts with the groups: How are the poems' structures and their themes similar? How are they different?

- Appoint one member of each group to take notes. Allow 10 to 15 minutes for discussion.

- Have each group share its results with the class.

MEDIA ACTIVITY (RL.6.7)

Be Creative/Create an Album Cover

- Select one of the poems in this lesson and discuss some images the poet creates in the reader's mind.

- Tell students to imagine one of the poems is going to be set to music and their job is to design the album cover. Invite students to create a visual to appear on the album cover.

- Have students exchange visuals and discuss how they relate to images in the poem.

RESEARCH ACTIVITY (W.6.6; W.6.7; SL.6.4)

Research and Present/Give a Presentation

- Have students use "Motto" as a starting point for an oral presentation on the Harlem Renaissance.

- Ask students to use print and digital sources to research literature, art, and music or writers, artists, and musicians associated with that time.

- Students should take notes and write a brief report for an oral presentation. Suggest they include audio recordings of music or samples of art downloaded from the Internet to accompany their presentation.

Analyzing the Structure of Stories

LESSON OBJECTIVES

- Analyze how sentences, chapters, or scenes fit into the overall structure of a text and contribute to the development of the theme.

THE LEARNING PROGRESSION

- **Grade 5:** CCLS RL.5.5 requires students to think about how the parts of a story create its structure.

- **Grade 6: CCLS RL.6.5 builds on the Grade 5 standard by requiring students to consider how part of the story fits into the structure and how it contributes to the theme, setting, or plot.**

- **Grade 7:** CCLS RL.7.5 focuses on how a drama's or poem's structure contributes to its meaning.

PREREQUISITE SKILLS

- Identify a text's theme, setting, and plot.

- Recognize the general structure of a text.

- Explain how a particular sentence, chapter, scene, or stanza functions within a larger text.

- Describe how a particular sentence or scene contributes to a text's theme, setting, or plot.

TAP STUDENTS' PRIOR KNOWLEDGE

- Tell students they will be learning about the structure of a story and how all the elements of the story contribute to the theme.

- Ask students what a plot is (*what happens in a story*) and what they recall about these elements of a plot: exposition (*introduces the characters and setting*), rising action (*events in which a conflict is introduced and problems increase*), climax (*point of highest excitement*), falling action (*events that lead to solving the conflict*), and resolution (*the final outcome*). Ask what setting is (*when and where the story takes place*).

- Ask students to think about a story they have read in class. What is the setting? Who are the characters? What happens in the story? What problems must the characters solve? Discuss how the plot relates to the story's setting and problem.

- What is the theme of a story? (*The theme is a lesson or message the author wants readers to learn.*) What lesson about life or human behavior did you learn from this story?

- Ask students why the theme is important. (*It is the message the author wants to get across to the reader.*) Explain that analyzing how story elements work together will help students better understand the theme of a story.

▣ Ready *Teacher Toolbox*   *teacher-toolbox.com*

	Prerequisite Skills	RL.6.5
Ready Lessons	✓	✓
Tools for Instruction		✓
Interactive Tutorials		✓

CCLS Focus

RL.6.5 Analyze how a particular sentence, chapter, scene, or stanza fits into the overall structure of a text and contributes to the development of the theme, setting, or plot.

ADDITIONAL STANDARDS: RL.6.1, RL.6.2, RL.6.3, RL.6.4, RL.6.11.b; W.6.1, W.6.7, W.6.9.a, W.6.11.a, W.6.11.c; SL.6.1, SL.6.1.c, SL.6.4; L.6.1.a, L.6.2.a, L.6.4.a, L.6.4.c, L.6.4.d (*See page A39 for full text.*)

AT A GLANCE

Through a cartoon, students build an understanding of how paying attention to details in every sentence or paragraph of a text will help them comprehend how these details contribute to theme, setting, and plot.

STEP BY STEP

- Read the first two paragraphs, focusing particularly on the definitions of *structure*.

- Then have students study the cartoon and describe what is happening in each frame. Ask them to make notes identifying the hikers' problems.

- Read the chart and discuss each box. Have volunteers tell what they learn from the first picture about the setting and plot. Then, discuss how setting and plot function in the second picture.

- Have students complete the chart. Discuss how analyzing details of setting and plot leads to an understanding of the conflict (the problem) the characters face. By understanding the conflict, students can consider the theme, or what the characters (and readers) learn from the dilemma.

- Read the paragraph below the chart. Reinforce the importance of paying attention to story elements.

- Call on volunteers to share a story they have read, focusing on the events and details that lead to a better understanding of the setting, the plot, or the theme.

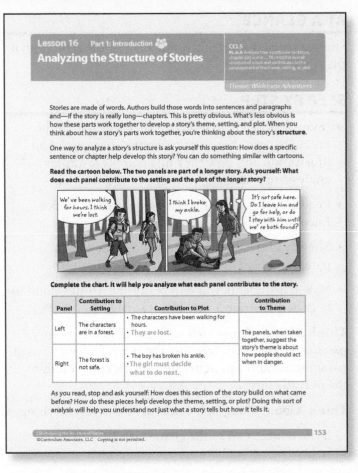

- Share an example of how you have analyzed story elements when reading in order to understand the conflict and ultimately determine the theme. Explain how using this skill helped you better understand the story.

Genre Focus

Literary Texts: Adventure

Tell students that in this lesson they will read adventures. Explain that an adventure is a fiction story in which the characters often face a challenging situation or are on some kind of action-oriented quest. The plot of an adventure relates to the characters facing the challenge or following the quest. Adventures often share the following characteristics:

- Most stories have a strong main character or characters.

- The main character often uses wits to survive.

- Sometimes the adventure turns out successfully but not always.

Based on these characteristics, ask students to share adventure stories they have read. What challenging situation(s) did the character(s) face? What, if any, kind of action-oriented quest were the characters on? How did the adventure turn out? What did students like about reading an adventure?

Explain that the three stories in this lesson are all adventures. "A Moose Encounter" is an adventure about encountering an animal in the wild. *Tracker* is an excerpt of an adventure story about a boy who is out alone, looking for a deer. The third story, *Hatchet*, is an excerpt of an adventure novel about a boy who is stranded in the wilderness after surviving a plane crash.

AT A GLANCE

Students read a short story and analyze the structure of the story.

STEP BY STEP

- Invite volunteers to tell what they learned on the previous page about analyzing the structure of an illustration and how they might apply a similar analysis to a story.

- Read aloud the first two paragraphs of "A Moose Encounter."

- Then read the question: "What role does each paragraph play in helping to develop the story?"

- Now tell students you will perform a Think Aloud to help demonstrate a way of answering the question.

Think Aloud: I know that each paragraph of a story plays some role in developing the story. I'll look at each paragraph and try to figure out what it contributes to the overall story.

Think Aloud: Paragraph 1 accomplishes several things:

It introduces two of the characters, Jill and her father.

It introduces the setting: a cool, fall morning in the Minnesota woods.

And it initiates the plot: Jill wants to see a moose so badly that she disobeys her father to go see one.

- Now direct students to the chart. Tell them that it contains information about setting and plot (but not character).

- Tell students to reread the second paragraph of the story and then complete the second row of the chart. Remind students that each paragraph will serve specific functions in a story to move that story along.

- Have volunteers share how they complete the chart.

- Finally, have students pair up and discuss what a possible theme for the story might be and the roles each paragraph plays in developing that theme. *(Possible theme: Listen to the advice of one's elders. Possible roles of each paragraph in developing such a theme: Paragraph one introduces the advice that Jill's father gave her. Paragraph two introduces the danger Jill might be in because she disregarded her father's advice.)*

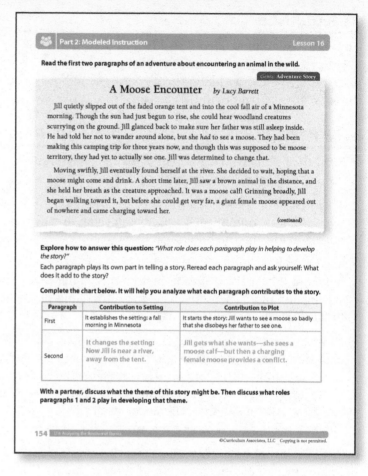

Tier Two Vocabulary: *Wander*

- Direct students to the word *wander* in paragraph 1. Ask students to tell what *wander* means in this sentence (*to walk way from a place*). Have them check the meaning in a dictionary and then confirm that it makes sense in this context.

- Work with students to name some related words (*stray, depart, roam*) and to understand that all the words have something to do with moving away from a location. **(RL.6.4; L.6.4.d)**

AT A GLANCE

Students continue reading about the moose encounter. They answer a multiple-choice question and explain how specific paragraphs and sentences contribute to the story's theme.

STEP BY STEP

- Tell students they will continue to read about the moose encounter.

- Close Reading helps students identify details that tell what happened to solve the conflict. The Hint reminds them of what falling action, climax, and resolution are to help them answer the question.

- Have students read the text and circle the details that show what happens to Jill after the calf's mother runs toward her, as directed by Close Reading.

- Then have students circle the answer to the question and respond to Show Your Thinking. Encourage students to describe how the first sentence in the second paragraph contributes to the story's plot and theme. Possible response: This paragraph describes what happens to Jill after the moose charges. This moves the plot forward and tells that Jill put herself in danger.

ANSWER ANALYSIS

Choice A is incorrect. Details of the story's turning point come in the first paragraph, when a petrified Jill watches the mother moose coming toward her. Also, the story never says Jill's father scolds her.

Choice B is incorrect. There is no new problem presented in the second paragraph.

Choice C is incorrect. The story says Jill learned to always listen to her father in the third paragraph, and this is part of the resolution.

Choice D is correct. The second paragraph describes how Jill's father saves her and Jill is relieved. This sets up the resolution in the next paragraph.

ERROR ALERT: Students who did not choose D might not have focused on the correct paragraph. Call students' attention to the second paragraph. Have them summarize what it says. Point out that it describes the falling action.

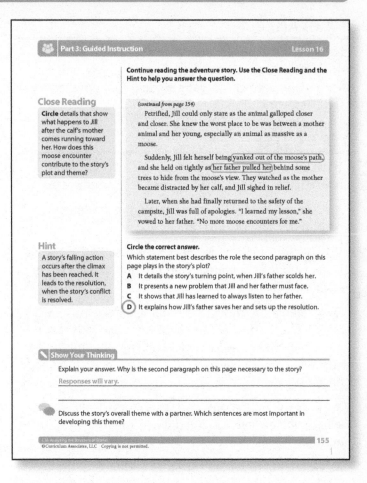

Continue reading the adventure story. Use the Close Reading and the Hint to help you answer the question.

Close Reading

Circle details that show what happens to Jill after the calf's mother comes running toward her. How does this moose encounter contribute to the story's plot and theme?

(continued from page 154)

Petrified, Jill could only stare as the animal galloped closer and closer. She knew the worst place to be was between a mother animal and her young, especially an animal as massive as a moose.

Suddenly, Jill felt herself being yanked out of the moose's path, and she held on tightly as her father pulled her behind some trees to hide from the moose's view. They watched as the mother became distracted by her calf, and Jill sighed in relief.

Later, when she had finally returned to the safety of the campsite, Jill was full of apologies. "I learned my lesson," she vowed to her father. "No more moose encounters for me."

Hint

A story's falling action occurs after the climax has been reached. It leads to the resolution, when the story's conflict is resolved.

Circle the correct answer.

Which statement best describes the role the second paragraph on this page plays in the story's plot?

A It details the story's turning point, when Jill's father scolds her.

B It presents a new problem that Jill and her father must face.

C It shows that Jill has learned to always listen to her father.

D It explains how Jill's father saves her and sets up the resolution.

Show Your Thinking

Explain your answer. Why is the second paragraph on this page necessary to the story?

Responses will vary.

Discuss the story's overall theme with a partner. Which sentences are most important in developing this theme?

L16: Analyzing the Structure of Stories
©Curriculum Associates, LLC   Copying is not permitted.
155

Tier Two Vocabulary: *Petrified*

- Point out the word *petrified* in paragraph 1. Ask students to look at the surrounding words and concepts and tell what *petrified* means (*paralyzed with fear*). Work with students to help them understand which other words helped them figure out the definition. (*"Jill could only stare as the animal galloped closer."*)

- Suggest that students look up *petrified* in a dictionary or thesaurus to find synonyms. Ask: What are some words that could be used in place of *petrified*? (*terrified, horrified*) **(RL.6.4; L.6.4.a; L.6.4.c)**

AT A GLANCE

Students read an adventure twice about a boy who is looking for a deer. After the first reading, you will ask three questions to check your students' comprehension of the passage.

STEP BY STEP

- Have students read the passage silently without referring to the Study Buddy or Close Reading text.

- Ask the following questions to ensure students' comprehension of the text:

  Why is John looking for deer by himself? (*He always hunts with his grandfather, but his grandfather is dying of cancer.*)

  How does John know that the noise he hears comes from a deer? (*He discovers a deer bed and feels that it is warm. Then he sees deer tracks and figures that the deer heard him and ran away, hitting the willow, which made the noise.*)

  What is the main conflict in this story? (*John cannot stop thinking about his grandfather, who is dying of cancer.*)

- Ask students to reread the story and look at the Study Buddy think aloud. What does the Study Buddy help them think about?

- Tell students to follow the directions in the Close Reading.

Tip: The Study Buddy calls students' attention to details about the deer that contribute to the plot. The Close Reading helps students recognize clues that suggest the story's setting and details about an event that point to the theme. Discuss how all of these work together to create the story. Review fundamental reading strategies, such as making inferences and summarizing, that will help students understand these elements and how they all contribute to the story.

- Finally, have students answer the questions on page 157. Use the Answer Analysis to discuss correct and incorrect responses.

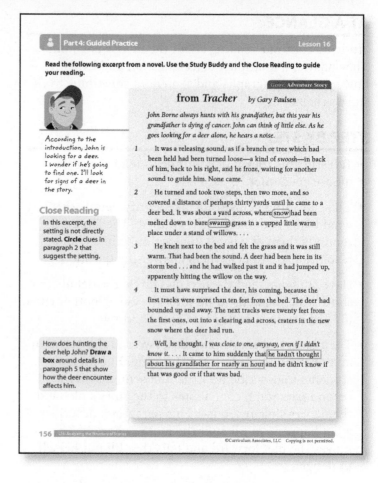

ELL Support: Possessives

- Review that possessives are words that show who or what owns something. To make a singular noun a possessive noun, add an apostrophe and an *s*. (*boy's*) To make a plural noun a possessive noun, add only an apostrophe. (*boys'*) Explain that the pronouns *my, his, her, their,* and *its* also show possession.

- Have students read the first sentence of paragraph 4 and point out the words *his coming*. Have students identify the possessive. (*his*) Explain that in this sentence, *coming* is a noun meaning "an arrival or approach." Have students tell whose approach surprised the deer. (*John's*) **(RL.6.4; L.6.1.a)**

STEP BY STEP

- Have students read questions 1–3, using the Hints to help them answer those questions.

Tip: If students have trouble answering question 2, have them look back at the text they circled in the story. Ask what each word or phrase suggests about the setting.

- Discuss with students the Answer Analysis below.

ANSWER ANALYSIS

1 The correct choice is D. It creates suspense because it doesn't say what caused the sound. Choice A is incorrect. Anybody hunting could hear a sound and freeze like John did. Choice B is incorrect. The story's theme is not about the thrill of deer hunting. Choice C is incorrect. The story is not about a conflict John has with the deer.

2 The correct choice is A. Paragraph 2 contains the phrases "snow" and "swamp grass." Choice B is incorrect. How far John has walked is a plot detail, not a setting detail. Choice C is incorrect. Paragraph 3, not 2, gives more information about what a deer bed is. Choice D is incorrect because the paragraph doesn't give any information about the time of day.

3 Sample response: The sentence shows that John is beginning to overcome his problem. It says, "he hadn't thought about his grandfather." But he hasn't fully solved his problem, because he's not sure "if that was good or if that was bad."

RETEACHING

Use a chart to verify the answer to question 3. Draw the chart below, and have students fill in the boxes. Sample responses are provided.

Event	Details	Conflict
John goes looking for a deer by himself.	John's grandfather can't hunt with him because he is dying of cancer.	John can't stop thinking of his grandfather.

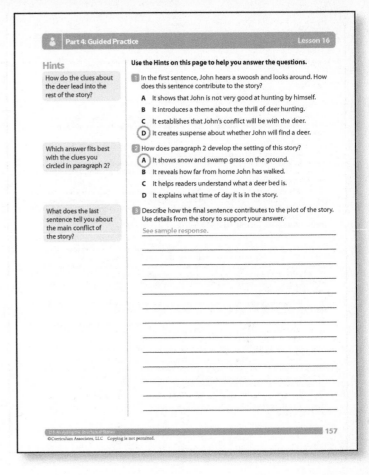

Integrating Standards

Use these questions to further students' understanding of *Tracker*.

1 Why can't John stop thinking about his grandfather? Cite evidence from the text in your response. *(RL.6.1)*

"John Borne always hunts with his grandfather, but this year his grandfather is dying of cancer."

2 What is the theme of the story? What details help convey the theme? *(RL.6.2)*

Sample response: The theme is that concentrating on a task can help distract you from a problem. In the introduction, readers learn that John is upset because his grandfather is dying. In the paragraphs that follow, he is fully focused on the deer. In the last paragraph, he realizes that "he hadn't thought about his grandfather for nearly an hour."

Read the following excerpt from a novel. Then answer the questions that follow.

from *Hatchet*

by Gary Paulsen

Thirteen-year-old Brian Robeson is stranded in the Canadian wilderness after a plane crash, and now he must study his environment to survive. In this part of the novel, he has been dreaming of his father. Now he dreams of his friend Terry.

1 He was not gesturing to Brian but was sitting in the park at a bench looking at a barbecue pit and for a time nothing happened. Then he got up and poured some charcoal from a bag into the cooker, then some starter fluid, and he took a flick type of lighter and lit the fluid. When it was burning and the charcoal was at last getting hot he turned, noticing Brian for the first time in the dream. He turned and smiled and pointed to the fire as if to say, see, a fire.

2 But it meant nothing to Brian, except that he wished he had a fire. He saw a grocery sack on the table next to Terry. Brian thought it must contain hot dogs and chips and mustard and he could think only of the food. But Terry shook his head and pointed again to the fire, and twice more he pointed to the fire, made Brian see the flames, and Brian felt his frustration and anger rise and he thought, All right, all right. I see the fire but so what? I don't have a fire. I know about fire; I know I need a fire.

3 I know that.

4 His eyes opened and there was light in the cave, a gray dim light of morning. He wiped his mouth and tried to move his leg, which had stiffened like wood. There was thirst, and hunger, and he ate some raspberries from the jacket. They had spoiled a bit, seemed softer and mushier, but still had a rich sweetness. He crushed the berries against the roof of his mouth with his tongue and drank the sweet juice as it ran down his throat. A flash of metal caught his eye and he saw his hatchet in the sand where he had thrown it at the porcupine in the dark.

5 He scootched up, wincing a bit when he bent his stiff leg, and crawled to where the hatchet lay. He picked it up and examined it and saw a chip in the top of the head.

6 The nick wasn't too large, but the hatchet was important to him, was his only tool, and he should not have thrown it. He could keep it in his hand, and make a tool of some kind to help push an animal away. Make a staff, he thought, or a lance, and save the hatchet. Something came then, a thought as he held the hatchet, something about the dream and his father and Terry, but he couldn't pin it down.

7 "Ahhh . . ." He scrambled out and stood in the morning sun and stretched his back muscles and his sore leg. The hatchet was still in his hand, and as he stretched and raised it over his head it caught the first rays of the morning sun. The first faint light hit the silver of the hatchet and it flashed a brilliant gold in the light. Like fire. That is it, he thought. What they were trying to tell me.

8 Fire. The hatchet was the key to it all. When he threw the hatchet at the porcupine in the cave and missed and hit the stone wall it had showered sparks, a golden shower of sparks in the dark, as golden with fire as the sun was now.

158 L16: Analyzing the Structure of Stories ©Curriculum Associates, LLC Copying is not permitted.

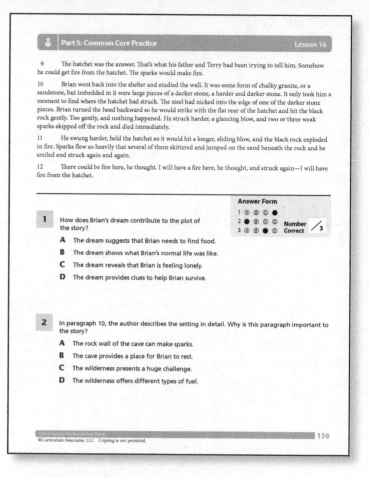

9 The hatchet was the answer. That's what his father and Terry had been trying to tell him. Somehow he could get fire from the hatchet. The sparks would make fire.

10 Brian went back into the shelter and studied the wall. It was some form of chalky granite, or a sandstone, but imbedded in it were large pieces of a darker stone, a harder and darker stone. It only took him a moment to find where the hatchet had struck. The steel had nicked into the edge of one of the darker stone pieces. Brian turned the head backward so he would strike with the flat rear of the hatchet and hit the black rock gently. Too gently, and nothing happened. He struck harder, a glancing blow, and two or three weak sparks skipped off the rock and died immediately.

11 He swung harder, held the hatchet so it would hit a longer, sliding blow, and the black rock exploded in fire. Sparks flew so heavily that several of them skittered and jumped on the sand beneath the rock and he smiled and struck again and again.

12 There could be fire here, he thought. I will have a fire here, he thought, and struck again—I will have fire from the hatchet.

1 How does Brian's dream contribute to the plot of the story?

Answer Form
1 Ⓐ Ⓑ Ⓒ ●
2 ● Ⓑ Ⓒ Ⓓ Number Correct /3
3 Ⓐ Ⓑ ● Ⓓ

A The dream suggests that Brian needs to find food.

B The dream shows what Brian's normal life was like.

C The dream reveals that Brian is feeling lonely.

D The dream provides clues to help Brian survive.

2 In paragraph 10, the author describes the setting in detail. Why is this paragraph important to the story?

A The rock wall of the cave can make sparks.

B The cave provides a place for Brian to rest.

C The wilderness presents a huge challenge.

D The wilderness offers different types of fuel.

L16: Analyzing the Structure of Stories ©Curriculum Associates, LLC Copying is not permitted. 159

AT A GLANCE

Students independently read a longer adventure story and answer questions in a format that provides test practice.

STEP BY STEP

- Tell students to use what they have learned about reading carefully and analyzing the structure of stories to read the passage on pages 158 and 159.

- Remind students to underline or circle important points.

- Tell students to answer the questions on pages 159 and 160. For questions 1–3, they should fill in the correct circle on the Answer Form.

- When students have finished, use the Answer Analysis to discuss correct responses and the reasons for them. Have students fill in the Number Correct on the Answer Form.

ANSWER ANALYSIS

1 Choice D is correct. Although Brian is puzzled by the dream at first, he realizes that Terry is trying to explain how to make a fire—something he needs to survive. Choice A is incorrect. The food Brian imagines in the sack may suggest that Brian needs food, but in the dream Terry points to the fire, suggesting Brian needs fire to survive, not food. Choice B is incorrect because, although seeing Terry make a barbecue might reflect something in Brian's normal life, it doesn't contribute to the plot, which is about Brian's survival. Choice C is incorrect. Dreaming about Terry may reveal that Brian is lonely, but it doesn't contribute to the plot. **(DOK 2)**

Theme Connection

- How do all the stories in this lesson relate to the theme of wilderness adventures?

- Which of the adventures you read did you find most exciting? Why?

2   Choice A is correct. The story is about Brian's survival in the wilderness. He needs fire to survive. The description of the rock wall shows how Brian discovers he can strike the wall with his hatchet to make fire. Choices B, C, and D are incorrect. Although they may be true statements about the cave, they are not supported by details in the text. **(DOK 2)**

3   Choice C is correct. The climax is the story's turning point. The rock exploding in fire is a turning point that begins to solve Brian's problem of needing fire. Choice A is incorrect. The resolution tells what happens after the conflict is solved, and it hasn't been solved yet. Choice B is incorrect. The sentence describes the conflict getting better, not worse. Choice D is incorrect. The falling action is described after this sentence when Brian realizes he will have a fire in the cave. **(DOK 2)**

4   Sample response: The theme of the story is to never give up. These paragraphs describe how Brian realizes the hatchet is the key to his survival because throwing it against the stone wall creates sparks that can lead to a fire. It doesn't work the first few times Brian tries, but he doesn't give up. After many tries Brian succeeds and realizes, "I will have a fire here." **(DOK 3)**

Part 5: Common Core Practice   Lesson 16

3   Read this sentence from paragraph 11.

> He swung harder, held the hatchet so it would hit a longer, sliding blow, and the black rock exploded in fire.

What does this sentence contribute to the plot?

A   It is the resolution, because Brian has solved his problem, ending the conflict.

B   It represents the rising action, because the problem is becoming even worse.

C   It serves as the climax, because after this Brian begins to solve the problem.

D   It is part of the falling action, because it is the solution to Brian's problem.

4   Describe how paragraphs 8 through 12 contribute to the development of the story's theme. Use details from the text to support your answer.

See sample response.

✓ **Self Check**   *Go back and see what you can check off on the Self Check on page 128.*

160   L16: Analyzing the Structure of Stories   ©Curriculum Associates, LLC   Copying is not permitted.

Integrating Standards

Use these questions and tasks as opportunities to interact with *Hatchet*.

1   What does Terry do in Brian's dream to help his friend? Cite details from the text. **(RL.6.1)**

Terry lights a charcoal fire. Then he looks at Brian and "pointed to the fire as if to say, see, a fire."

2   When Brian wakes up, what leads him to realize what Terry was trying to tell him? **(RL.6.3)**

The sun hits the hatchet and it shines a light like fire. Brian realizes Terry is trying to tell him that he could use the hatchet to get fire.

3   In paragraph 4, the author says Brian's leg "had stiffened like wood." What does this figure of speech mean? **(RL.6.4; L.6.4.a)**

Wood is stiff, or hard; you cannot bend it. "Stiffened like wood" means Brian's leg cannot easily be bent.

4   Write about how Brian's feelings change throughout the story. **(W.6.9.a)**

Sample response: In his dream, Brian feels frustrated and angry. When Brian wakes up he is thirsty, hungry, and in pain. At the end of the story, he is determined and happy that he's going to have a fire.

5   Discuss in small groups: What do you predict will happen to Brian? Use text evidence to support your predictions. **(SL.6.1)**

Discussions will vary. Students might mention paragraph 12, where Brian thinks, "I will have fire from the hatchet." They may predict that he will build a fire that will help him survive until he is rescued. Remind students to make comments that contribute to the issue under discussion.

Writing Activities

Argumentative Essay *(W.6.1)*

• Have students review "A Moose Encounter," *Tracker*, and *Hatchet*. Ask them to think about the stories and which character faced the most challenging situation.

• Challenge students to write an argument to support their opinion. Remind them to state their claim clearly and provide clear reasons and relevant evidence to support it.

• Allow students to share their writing with the class.

Dashes and Nonrestrictive Elements *(L.6.2.a)*

• Have students read the first sentence of paragraph 1 in *Tracker*. Point out the phrase *a kind of swoosh* and the dashes used to separate it from the rest of the sentence.

• Explain that *a kind of swoosh* is an example of a nonrestrictive phrase. It is not essential to the sentence, but it adds relevant information. Explain that dashes and commas are used to separate a nonrestrictive element from the rest of a sentence.

• Have students write a sentence that includes a nonrestrictive element and uses appropriate punctuation.

LISTENING ACTIVITY *(SL.6.1)*

Listen Closely/Pose a Question

• Have a student read aloud "A Moose Encounter," while the class listens closely and takes notes on details they hear.

• After reading, ask students to write a question based on their notes, such as "What time of day does the story take place?" or "Where is Jill's father when she slips out of the tent?"

• Have pairs pose their questions to each other and answer them using evidence from the story.

DISCUSSION ACTIVITY *(SL.6.1)*

Talk in a Group/Discuss Adventures

• Ask students to recall the characteristics of an adventure and think about how the stories in this lesson conform to the genre.

• Have students form small groups to discuss the stories in the lesson as well as other adventures they have read. Encourage them to talk about what makes a great adventure.

• Appoint one member of each group to take notes. Allow 10 to 15 minutes for discussion, and then have students present their ideas to the class.

MEDIA ACTIVITY *(RL.6.2)*

Be Creative/Produce a Movie Trailer

• Invite students to watch the movie trailer for *A Cry in the Wild,* a movie based on the book *Hatchet*. Discuss how the trailer shows some of the adventure but doesn't give away the whole story.

• Tell students to imagine that one of the other stories they read in this lesson has been made into a movie and they get to create the movie trailer.

• Have partners create a storyboard to plan what they will show, or make an actual video.

• Allow time for pairs to share their trailers.

RESEARCH ACTIVITY *(W.6.7; SL.6.4)*

Research and Present/Give a Presentation

• Point out that *Tracker* and *Hatchet* are written by the same author, Gary Paulsen.

• Have students research information to use in an oral presentation about this author. They might include biographical facts, details about how his writing reflects his life, and summaries of the books he has written.

• Students should take notes and write a brief report for their presentations.

Explaining Point of View

LESSON OBJECTIVES

- Identify the narrator's point of view in a story.
- Recognize how the description of events in a story or poem are influenced by the narrator or speaker.

THE LEARNING PROGRESSION

- **Grade 5:** CCLS RL.5.6 emphasizes that students need to understand the different kinds of narrative point of view in a text and how the different points of view affect what the reader learns.

- **Grade 6: CCLS RL.6.6 builds on the Grade 5 standard by focusing on the way that the author develops the point of view of the narrator or speaker.**

- **Grade 7:** CCLS RL.7.6 emphasizes that students need to both identify point of view and recognize how authors present different points of view through characters or narrators.

PREREQUISITE SKILLS

- Understand the literary concept of point of view.
- Identify the narrator or speaker in a literary text.
- Recognize that narrators or speakers have distinct points of view.
- Understand how the narrator's point of view affects the description of a story's events.

TAP STUDENTS' PRIOR KNOWLEDGE

- Tell students that they will be working on a lesson about explaining the point of view of a narrator or speaker in a story. Ask students to tell who a narrator or speaker is. (*the person telling the story*) Explain that point of view is how the narrator or speaker feels about a situation. The way the narrator describes events in a story is determined by his or her feelings about the events. Authors use point of view to develop their characters.

- Have students think about a familiar story that has several characters. For example, retell "The Three Little Pigs," telling the story from the point of view of the third little pig—the one that builds a strong house out of bricks.

- Then ask students to think about how the story would be different if told from the point of view of a different character, such as the wolf. Have volunteers share the story from the wolf's point of view. Then ask students to share the story as told by one of the "lazy" pigs. Point out that the details of the story sound different when told from different narrators' points of view.

- Explain that in this lesson they will look at different stories and learn about how each narrator's point of view affects how the story is told. Recognizing point of view in a story will help students understand how an author develops the characters' attitudes, feelings, and beliefs.

Ready *Teacher Toolbox*   teacher-toolbox.com

	Prerequisite Skills	RL.6.6
Ready Lessons	✓	✓
Tools for Instruction		✓
Interactive Tutorials		✓

CCLS Focus

RL.6.6 Explain how an author develops the point of view of the narrator or speaker in a text.

ADDITIONAL STANDARDS: **RL.6.1, RL.6.2, RL.6.3, RL.6.4, RL.6.6.a; W.6.3, W.6.7, W.6.9.a, W.6.11.b, W.6.11.c; SL.6.1, SL.6.2.a, SL.6.4; L.6.1, L.6.4.a, L.6.4.c, L.6.5.a** (*See page A39 for full text.*)

AT A GLANCE

Through an illustration, students are introduced to the idea of point of view and how an event is described differently when told from the different point of view of each character in the scene.

STEP BY STEP

- Read the first paragraph, which includes the definitions of *point of view* and *narrator*. Then have students study the illustration. Ask them to think about how a narrator would describe the scene from the boy's point of view and then from the woman's point of view. Guide them to look for evidence in the illustration.

- Explain that the chart shows evidence from the picture that suggests each character's point of view. Read the chart and discuss with students why each point of view seems reasonable based on the evidence from the illustration. Then ask students to explain how the two characters would describe the event from their point of view. How would the descriptions be different? Explain that the point of view of the narrator will affect how the details of the story are told.

- Reinforce that as students read, they should think about who is telling the story and what point of view, or perspective, the narrator or speaker has about the story. The point of view of the narrator will shape how the author portrays the characters and events.

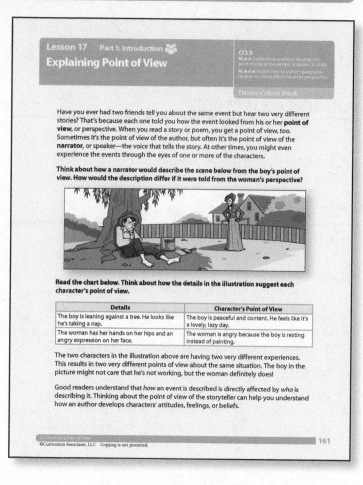

Genre Focus

Literary Texts: Historical Fiction

Tell students that in this lesson they will read literary texts. One type of literary text is historical fiction, which is a fiction story set in the past. Historical fiction may be about real people who lived in the past, real events that happened in the past, or both. Historical fiction includes:

- A setting that accurately and authentically portrays a specific historical time period.

- Details that are realistic for the time period.

- Real or fictional characters that are realistic for the historical time period.

Based on these characteristics, ask students to name examples of historical fiction that they have read. Examples may include *The Watsons Go to Birmingham—1963*, *Little House on the Prairie*, or *Sign of the Beaver*. Point out that these stories are about made-up characters but the historical settings and events are accurate and authentic.

Explain that "The Settlers" is a historical fiction story about a Native American boy's experience with white settlers. "Landing at Ellis Island" is a historical fiction story about a Russian immigrant girl's experience as she arrives in America. The last story, an excerpt from *A Jar of Dreams*, is historical fiction about a Japanese-American girl's experience in America in 1935.

AT A GLANCE

Students read a historical fiction story and explain how the narrator's point of view affects the readers' understanding of the events.

STEP BY STEP

- Invite volunteers to tell what they learned on the previous page about using evidence in an illustration to determine characters' points of view.

- Tell students that in this lesson they will use evidence from a text to determine the character's point of view in the story.

- Read aloud "The Settlers."

- Then read the question: "The narrator describes the scene from Little Bear's point of view. What do you find out as a result?"

- Now tell students you will use a Think Aloud to demonstrate a way of answering the question.

Think Aloud: The narrator doesn't specifically state how Little Bear feels about the white settlers. However, I can use words and phrases in the text as clues to understand how Little Bear feels. I'll underline these words in the text: *He creeps close to the wagon trail; he's never seen white people before; Little Bear had heard all the warnings, but he still wanted to see what they looked like.* These words tell me that Little Bear is curious about the white settlers but not really afraid of them.

- Direct students to the chart and ask where they've seen a similar chart before. Review the chart with students and show how evidence from the text connects to the narrator's point of view.

- Have students write the evidence from paragraph 1 that suggests Little Bear's point of view about the white settlers.

Think Aloud: In paragraph 3, words such as *froze, crouched into a small ball* and *heart drumming in his ears* tell me that Little Bear becomes afraid of the settlers when he hears the rifle shot.

- Have students complete the chart from Little Bear's point of view.

- Then have students respond to the directive at the bottom of the page. Invite volunteers to share their responses with the class.

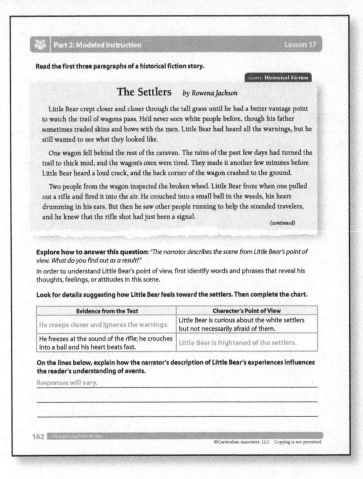

👥 Part 2: Modeled Instruction Lesson 17

Read the first three paragraphs of a historical fiction story.

Genre: **Historical Fiction**

The Settlers   *by Rowena Jackson*

Little Bear crept closer and closer through the tall grass until he had a better vantage point to watch the trail of wagons pass. He'd never seen white people before, though his father sometimes traded skins and bows with the men. Little Bear had heard all the warnings, but he still wanted to see what they looked like.

One wagon fell behind the rest of the caravan. The rains of the past few days had turned the trail to thick mud, and the wagon's oxen were tired. They made it another few minutes before Little Bear heard a loud crack, and the back corner of the wagon crashed to the ground.

Two people from the wagon inspected the broken wheel. Little Bear froze when one pulled out a rifle and fired it into the air. He crouched into a small ball in the weeds, his heart drumming in his ears. But then he saw other people running to help the stranded travelers, and he knew that the rifle shot had just been a signal.

(continued)

Explore how to answer this question: *"The narrator describes the scene from Little Bear's point of view. What do you find out as a result?"*

In order to understand Little Bear's point of view, first identify words and phrases that reveal his thoughts, feelings, or attitudes in this scene.

Look for details suggesting how Little Bear feels toward the settlers. Then complete the chart.

Evidence from the Text	Character's Point of View
He creeps closer and ignores the warnings.	Little Bear is curious about the white settlers but not necessarily afraid of them.
He freezes at the sound of the rifle; he crouches into a ball and his heart beats fast.	Little Bear is frightened of the settlers.

On the lines below, explain how the narrator's description of Little Bear's experiences influences the reader's understanding of events.

Responses will vary.

162 L17: Explaining Point of View   ©Curriculum Associates, LLC Copying is not permitted.

Tier Two Vocabulary: *Vantage*

- Direct students to the word *vantage* in sentence 1. Have students explain what they think *vantage* means. (*"a place or position from which to view something"*) Ask them to describe the context clues in the surrounding words that helped them determine this meaning. (*Clues may include "crept closer," "better...point," and "to watch."*) **(RL.6.4; L.6.4.a)**

- Ask volunteers to use the word *vantage* in a complete sentence to demonstrate understanding.

AT A GLANCE

Students continue reading about Little Bear and then complete a chart to explain Little Bear's point of view at the end of the story.

STEP BY STEP

- Tell students that they will continue reading about Little Bear.

- Close Reading helps students identify evidence in the text that signals Little Bear's point of view about the settlers at this point in the story. The Hint will help them compare how Little Bear felt at the beginning of the story to how he now feels about the settlers.

- Have students circle words and phrases in the last paragraph that indicate Little Bear's attitude toward the white settlers, as directed by Close Reading. If necessary, ask: "What words provide clues about how Little Bear feels? Does he still feel afraid? Does he feel threatened by the settlers? How do you know?"

- Ask volunteers to share the words and phrases they circled. Discuss what these words and phrases indicate about how Little Bear feels about the settlers.

- Then have students complete the chart. Have volunteers share their responses.

- Then have students respond to the Show Your Thinking. Have students work with a partner to discuss how the author reveals Little Bear's changing point of view during the story. (*Sample response: The author reveals three different attitudes toward the white settlers. At first, Little Bear is curious and wants to see them up close. Then he is afraid and hides in the weeds. Finally, after his brother arrives, he wishes them well because he is concerned.*)

ERROR ALERT: Students may have difficulty determining evidence that shows how Little Bear's point of view about the white settlers changed throughout the story from being curious and then afraid to being sympathetic and caring. Help students review the text to identify the words and phrases that show how Little Bear's feelings changed as he observed the settlers.

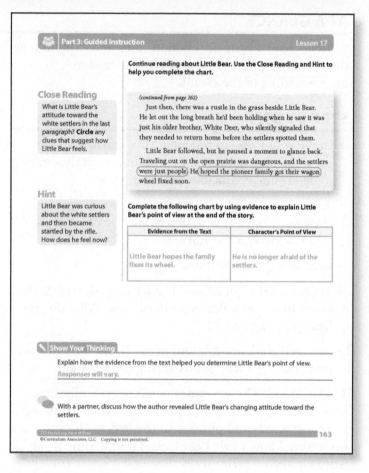

ELL Support: Comparatives and Superlatives

- Explain to students that comparatives are words that compare two things, and superlatives are words that compare three or more things.

- Point out the word *older* in sentence 2. Tell students that this is a comparative word. Have them tell what the word compares. (*the ages of the two brothers*) Explain that if three or more brothers were being compared, the superlative form *oldest* would be used.

- Write the words *small, smaller,* and *smallest* on the board. Then pick three classroom objects that vary in size. Work together with students to use the words *small, smaller,* and *smallest* to describe the objects. (Example: *This book is smaller than this desk. This pencil is the smallest of them all.*) **(L.6.1)**

AT A GLANCE

Students will read a passage twice about a young immigrant arriving at Ellis Island. After the first reading, you will ask three questions to assess students' comprehension of the text.

STEP BY STEP

- Have students read the story silently without referring to the Study Buddy or the Close Reading text.

- Ask the following questions to assess students' comprehension of the passage:

  Where is Anya from? *(Russia)*

  Why is she on a boat arriving at Ellis Island? *(Her family is immigrating to the United States in search of a new life full of opportunities.)*

  Why is Anya not happy to arrive in Ellis Island? *(She doesn't know the language or the customs in America, and she misses her home in Russia.)*

- Then have students reread paragraph 1 and look at the Study Buddy think aloud. What does the Study Buddy help them think about?

Tip: The Study Buddy points out that this passage is in the form of a diary and guides students to underline details about the narrator's perspective. Tell students that underlining details will help them determine Anya's point of view about arriving in America. Explain that details related to a narrator's point of view include details about the narrator's attitudes, feelings, and motivations.

- Have students reread the rest of the passage. Tell them to follow the directions in the Close Reading.

Tip: The Close Reading helps students identify the character's thoughts, attitudes, and emotions. Review with students that authors develop their characters by revealing what the character thinks, says, and does. Looking for evidence about the narrator will help students better explain the narrator's point of view and better understand the text.

- Finally, have students answer the questions on page 165. When students have finished, use the Answer Analysis to discuss correct and incorrect responses.

Tier Two Vocabulary: *Bustling*

- Direct students to the word *bustling* in paragraph 4. Point out that the *-ing* ending changes the verb *bustle* to an adjective. Ask students to explain what this word describes. *(the city)*

- Then work with students to determine the meaning of *bustling* in this sentence. Explain that they can use a dictionary or thesaurus to help them determine the word's meaning. They can then find other words that are similar in meaning that would also make sense in this sentence. Have students tell what *bustling* means. *("full of activity")* **(RL.6.4; L.6.4.c)**

STEP BY STEP

- Have students read questions 1–3, using the Hints to help them answer these questions.

> **Tip:** If students have trouble answering question 3, point out the dates of the second and third diary entries. Explain that these dates provide a clue that many days have passed between the entries, allowing time for Anya's feelings to change.

- Discuss with students the Answer Analysis below.

ANSWER ANALYSIS

1   The correct choice is A. Paragraph 1 provides evidence that Anya is angry about leaving her home. Choice B is incorrect. The story does not state that Anya is nervous about learning English, only that she doesn't speak English. Choices C and D are incorrect because paragraph 1 indicates that Anya is not excited about coming to America and is not interested in new opportunities.

2   The correct choice is C. The word *terrifying* indicates that Anya felt afraid. Choice A is incorrect. The five-hour wait indicates tedium, not fear. Choice B is incorrect because this indicates that Anya is healthy, which should not make her feel afraid. Choice D is incorrect. The word *impatient* indicates that Anya didn't like the man but does not indicate that she is afraid.

3   Sample response: Anya's thoughts and actions in the first two paragraphs suggest that she is fearful and angry about moving to America. By the end of the story, however, she feels hopeful about her new life. She reveals that her family is living with other Russian immigrants, that her parents are doing well, and that she has a new friend.

RETEACHING

Use a graphic organizer to verify the correct answer to question 2. Draw the chart below. Work with students to complete the boxes. Sample responses are provided.

Evidence	Point of View
"where we waited five hours to be processed thundered with strange voices and terrifying faces."	Anya feels afraid during her day at Ellis Island.

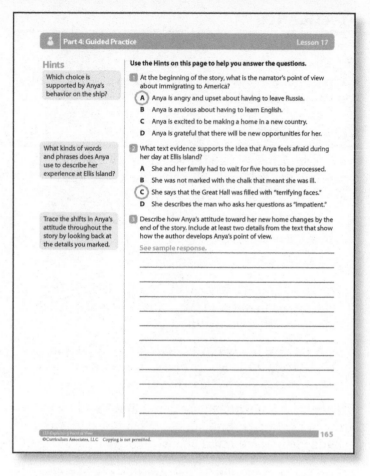

Integrating Standards

Use these questions to further students' understanding of "Landing at Ellis Island."

1   Why is Anya angry with her parents at the beginning of the story? **(RL.6.1)**

She blames her parents for making her leave her home in Russia to come to America.

2   Do you think Anya wants to return home to Russia at the end of the story? Why or why not? **(RL.6.3)**

Anya will probably not want to go back to Russia because she has begun enjoying her new life in America. She has made a new friend, her parents are happy, and she thinks New York can be her new home, which means that she no longer thinks of Russia as her home.

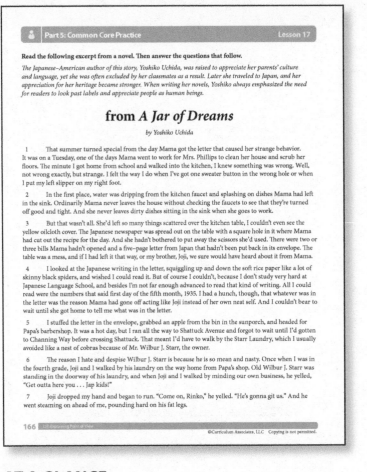

Part 5: Common Core Practice Lesson 17

Read the following excerpt from a novel. Then answer the questions that follow.

The Japanese-American author of this story, Yoshiko Uchida, was raised to appreciate her parents' culture and language, yet she was often excluded by her classmates as a result. Later she traveled to Japan, and her appreciation for her heritage became stronger. When writing her novels, Yoshiko always emphasized the need for readers to look past labels and appreciate people as human beings.

from *A Jar of Dreams*

by Yoshiko Uchida

1   That summer turned special from the day Mama got the letter that caused her strange behavior. It was on a Tuesday, one of the days Mama went to work for Mrs. Phillips to clean her house and scrub her floors. The minute I got home from school and walked into the kitchen, I knew something was wrong. Well, not wrong exactly, but strange. I felt the way I do when I've got one sweater button in the wrong hole or when I put my left slipper on my right foot.

2   In the first place, water was dripping from the kitchen faucet and splashing on dishes Mama had left in the sink. Ordinarily Mama never leaves the house without checking the faucets to see that they're turned off good and tight. And she never leaves dirty dishes sitting in the sink when she goes to work.

3   But that wasn't all. She'd left so many things scattered over the kitchen table, I couldn't even see the yellow oilcloth cover. The Japanese newspaper was spread out on the table with a square hole in it where Mama had cut out the recipe for the day. And she hadn't bothered to put away the scissors she'd used. There were two or three bills Mama hadn't opened and a five-page letter from Japan that hadn't been put back in its envelope. The table was a mess, and if I had left it that way, or my brother, Joji, I'm sure would have heard about it from Mama.

4   I looked at the Japanese writing in the letter, squiggling up and down the soft rice paper like a lot of skinny black spiders, and wished I could read it. But of course I couldn't, because I don't study very hard at Japanese Language School, and besides I'm not far enough advanced to read that kind of writing. All I could read were the numbers that said first day of the fifth month, 1935. I had a hunch, though, that whatever was in the letter was the reason Mama had gone off acting like Joji instead of her own neat self. And I couldn't bear to wait until she got home to tell me what was in the letter.

5   I stuffed the letter in the envelope, grabbed an apple from the bin in the sunporch, and headed for Papa's barbershop. It was a hot day, but I ran all the way to Shattuck Avenue and forgot to wait until I'd gotten to Channing Way before crossing Shattuck. That meant I'd have to walk by the Starr Laundry, which I usually avoided like a nest of cobras because of Mr. Wilbur J. Starr, the owner.

6   The reason I hate and despise Wilbur J. Starr is because he is so mean and nasty. Once when I was in the fourth grade, Joji and I walked by his laundry on the way home from Papa's shop. Old Wilbur J. Starr was standing in the doorway of his laundry, and when Joji and I walked by minding our own business, he yelled, "Get outta here you . . . Jap kids!"

7   Joji dropped my hand and began to run. "Come on, Rinko," he yelled. "He's gonna git us." And he went steaming on ahead of me, pounding hard on his fat legs.

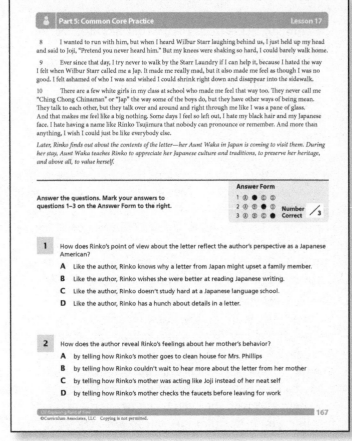

Part 5: Common Core Practice Lesson 17

8   I wanted to run with him, but when I heard Wilbur Starr laughing behind us, I just held up my head and said to Joji, "Pretend you never heard him." But my knees were shaking so hard, I could barely walk home.

9   Ever since that day, I try never to walk by the Starr Laundry if I can help it, because I hated the way I felt when Wilbur Starr called me a Jap. It made me really mad, but it also made me feel as though I was no good. I felt ashamed of who I was and wished I could shrink right down and disappear into the sidewalk.

10   There are a few white girls in my class at school who made me feel that way too. They never call me "Ching Chong Chinaman" or "Jap" the way some of the boys do, but they have other ways of being mean. They talk to each other, but they talk over and around and right through me like I was a pane of glass. And that makes me feel like a big nothing. Some days I feel so left out, I hate my black hair and my Japanese face. I hate having a name like Rinko Tsujimura that nobody can pronounce or remember. And more than anything, I wish I could just be like everybody else.

Later, Rinko finds out about the contents of the letter—her Aunt Waka in Japan is coming to visit them. During her stay, Aunt Waka teaches Rinko to appreciate her Japanese culture and traditions, to preserve her heritage, and above all, to value herself.

Answer the questions. Mark your answers to questions 1–3 on the Answer Form to the right.

Answer Form
1 Ⓐ ● Ⓒ Ⓓ
2 Ⓐ Ⓑ ● Ⓓ   Number /3
3 Ⓐ Ⓑ Ⓒ ●   Correct

1   How does Rinko's point of view about the letter reflect the author's perspective as a Japanese American?

   A   Like the author, Rinko knows why a letter from Japan might upset a family member.

   B   Like the author, Rinko wishes she were better at reading Japanese writing.

   C   Like the author, Rinko doesn't study hard at a Japanese language school.

   D   Like the author, Rinko has a hunch about details in a letter.

2   How does the author reveal Rinko's feelings about her mother's behavior?

   A   by telling how Rinko's mother goes to clean house for Mrs. Phillips

   B   by telling how Rinko couldn't wait to hear more about the letter from her mother

   C   by telling how Rinko's mother was acting like Joji instead of her neat self

   D   by telling how Rinko's mother checks the faucets before leaving for work

AT A GLANCE

Students independently read a longer passage and answer questions in a format that provides test practice.

STEP BY STEP

• Tell students to use what they have learned about reading closely and explaining point of view to read the story on pages 166 and 167.

• Remind students to underline clues that help them figure out the narrator's point of view, or perspective, throughout the story.

• Tell students to answer the questions on pages 167 and 168. For questions 1–3, they should fill in the correct circle on the Answer Form.

• When students have finished, use the Answer Analysis to discuss correct and incorrect responses. Have students fill in the Number Correct on the Answer Form.

ANSWER ANALYSIS

1   The correct choice is B. Rinko says she wishes she could read the Japanese writing in the letter. The author was raised to appreciate her parents' language. Choice A is incorrect. The text does not say that Rinko knew why a letter from Japan might upset her mother. Choices C and D are incorrect. There is no evidence that the author studied at a Japanese language school or that the author had a hunch about details in the letter. **(DOK 3)**

Theme Connection

• How do all the stories in this lesson relate to the theme of culture shock?

• What is one idea you learned about cultures from each passage in this lesson?

2 Choice C is correct. The author tells how Rinko feels when she sees the mess her mother left behind, and she compares this mess to one that her brother, Joji, might have left. Choices A and D are incorrect because these details reveal nothing about Rinko's feelings. Choice B is incorrect because it describes Rinko's excitement about the letter but does not reveal her feelings about her mother. **(DOK 2)**

3 Choice D is correct. Rinko describes being talked over and through by the girls at school like she was "a pane of glass." This develops the point of view that Rinko feels left out. Choices A and B do not indicate that Rinko feels left out, only that there are things she does not understand. Choice C indicates that Rinko demonstrates pride and courage in the face of taunts, which is a positive feeling that has little to do with the negative one of feeling left out. **(DOK 2)**

4 Sample response: Yoshiko Uchida grew up as a Japanese American, so she knew what it was like to be treated differently. Rinko's descriptions of being picked on, excluded, and humiliated might be similar to what Yoshiko experienced. Like Rinko, Yoshiko likely had feelings about wanting to be like her classmates. Maybe she even hated her name and face, just like Rinko. Yoshiko was able to use her own experiences to develop Rinko's point of view. **(DOK 3)**

Integrating Standards

Use these questions and tasks as opportunities to interact with "A Jar of Dreams."

1 Why do you think the author wrote this story from the point of view of a young Japanese-American girl? **(RL.6.1)**

Yoshiko Uchida, the author, wrote this story from Rinko's point of view because she had similar experiences when she was a young girl, facing exclusion from her classmates and learning to appreciate her Japanese heritage. She could write about Rinko's experiences in an authentic way.

2 Why did Rinko hold her head up and walk away, instead of running, when Wilbur Starr taunted her and her brother? **(RL.6.3)**

She held her head proudly and walked, despite her fear, because she did not want to give Starr the satisfaction of seeing her run away.

3 What does Rinko mean when she says that the other girls "talk over and around and right through me like I was a pane of glass"? **(RL.6.4; L.6.4.a)**

She means that the girls acted as though she was not even there and ignored her as if she were invisible.

4 Summarize: Write a brief summary of the story. **(RL.6.2; W.6.9.a)**

Summaries will vary. Rinko comes home to a mess left behind by her mother, who is usually neat. She walks to the laundromat and thinks about how the owner taunted her and how her classmates treat her badly because she is Japanese-American.

5 Discuss in small groups: How would you describe Rinko's personality? Use evidence from the text. **(SL.6.1)**

Discussions will vary. Remind students that a character's personality is revealed through the character's thoughts, feelings, attitudes, and motivations. Encourage students to follow discussion rules.

Writing Activities

Write Diary Entries *(W.6.3)*

- Have students reread "Landing at Ellis Island," paying attention to the dates of the diary entries. Explain that each diary entry discusses Anya's recollections of the events from that day. Point out that Anya describes her feelings in each diary entry, which gives the reader insight into her point of view.

- Have students write two new diary entries for Anya, for dates following the September 9 entry. They may choose to write entries for one week later, one month later, or one year later. Encourage students to think about what kinds of experiences Anya might have as she adjusts to her new life in New York City. Remind students to describe Anya's feelings and emotions as they write each entry.

Similes *(L.6.5.a)*

- Tell students that a simile compares two things using the words *like* or *as*. Read aloud the simile in sentence 1 of paragraph 4 in *A Jar of Dreams*. Ask students what two things are being compared in this simile and what they have in common. *(Japanese letters are compared to black spiders; both are squiggly.)*

- Then point out the simile in sentence 3 of paragraph 10. Discuss with students what is being compared. *(Rinko is compared to a pane of glass. Both can be seen through.)* Have students write three original similes.

LISTENING ACTIVITY *(SL.6.1; SL.6.4)*

Listen Closely/Summarize

- Have small groups of students read aloud individual paragraphs from *A Jar of Dreams*.

- Ask students to listen closely as each student reads a paragraph. Then have listeners paraphrase what they heard. They should be able to name at least two details they heard.

DISCUSSION ACTIVITY *(SL.6.1)*

Talk in a Group/Discuss a Theme

- Ask students to review each of this lesson's passages and then think about how they might feel if their family were to emigrate to another country. Would they be excited? Scared? Upset?

- Have students form small groups to discuss how they might feel if they were to emigrate to another country. Ask them to choose what country they would like to emigrate to, and why they would choose this country. Have them discuss what kinds of experiences they might have in this new country.

- Appoint one member of each group to take notes. Allow 10 to 15 minutes for discussion, and then have each group share with the class.

MEDIA ACTIVITY *(RL.6.2)*

Be Creative/Draw an Illustration

- Have students review the illustration on page 161. Point out that the illustration shows two characters, each with a different point of view.

- Ask students to create their own illustration of an event, showing two characters with different points of view. They may choose characters based on real people or made-up characters.

- Have students exchange illustrations and discuss each character's point of view.

RESEARCH ACTIVITY *(W.6.7; SL.6.4)*

Research and Present/Cultural Backgrounds

- Discuss how Yoshiko Uchida's cultural background impacted Rinko's point of view.

- Have small groups research other books by Uchida, such as *Journey to Topaz* or *The Bracelet*. Have students write a report to compare and contrast the main character's perspective with Rinko's point of view. Have students include information about how Uchida's cultural background is reflected in her characters.

SCORING GUIDE AND ANSWER ANALYSIS

Literature Passage Answer Analysis

1A ● Ⓑ Ⓒ Ⓓ   5 Ⓐ Ⓑ ● Ⓓ

1B Ⓐ Ⓑ Ⓒ ●   6 Ⓐ ● Ⓒ Ⓓ

3 Ⓐ Ⓑ Ⓒ ●   7 ● Ⓑ Ⓒ Ⓓ

4 Ⓐ Ⓑ ● Ⓓ

1 Part A: Choice A is correct. The squirrels are storing up fruit as it falls from the trees in autumn. Choices B and C are incorrect because the squirrels would not store branches or rain. Choice D is incorrect because night cannot be stored or later dug up by swine. **(RL.6.4; DOK 2)**

Part B: Choice D is correct. The word describes the fruit of a tree, even acorns, particularly for the squirrels whose diet it comprises. Choices A and C describe parts of the squirrels' homes, not what is falling. Choice B is what the squirrels do, so it is not a clue to the unknown word. **(RL.6.4; DOK 2)**

3 Choice D is correct. The last paragraph explains the lesson the narrator learns ("there are some things even a seasoned woodsman should fear") and how it makes him change his point of view.

Choice A is incorrect. This paragraph does not help the reader understand how dangerous grizzly bears can be. Choice B is incorrect. The last paragraph does not summarize the problem and solutions. Choice C is incorrect. The reader doesn't know how the rangers know where to look for the men. **(RL.6.5; DOK 2)**

4 Choice C is correct. This sentence best shows the narrator's great confidence in his and Tom's abilities to camp and survive in the wilderness.

Choices A and B are incorrect. Each of these gives a description of what the men are doing, but these sentences do not do much in themselves to establish a point of view. Choice D is also incorrect. The sentence describes what the narrator is doing and may add to the reader's impressions of the man, but it does not directly support the conclusion about how the author develops point of view. **(RL.6.6; DOK 3)**

5 Choice C is correct. The most important of these events is the campers' decision to spend the night in a remote area of the forest, where they are exposed to wild animals.

Choice A is incorrect. Although the fire from the campsite might have attracted the bear, the most important event is that the campers choose a spot far from the protection of the lodge. Choice B is incorrect. While the noise of an engine that heralds the arrival of the park rangers is important, it is more significant that the campers choose an isolated spot to spend the night. Choice D is also incorrect. Most of these sounds are pleasant. It is really the campers' decision to pitch their tent in the heart of the wilderness that is important to the plot development. **(RL.6.5; DOK 2)**

6 Choice B is correct. The connotation of the words as they are used here is "something menacing."

Choice A is incorrect. The connotation of the words is not something unusual, but something full of menace. Choice C is incorrect. Although a possible connotation is a lack of vitality, in this case the words mean "something menacing." Choice D is also incorrect. Sometimes the word *shadow* connotes something that is not really there. But in this context, the word means "something menacing." **(RL.6.4; DOK 3)**

7 Choice A is correct. The metaphor of the scuttling crab conveys the panic of the frightened campers as they move as fast as they can to get away from the bear.

Choice B is incorrect. There is little humor in the flight of people from a grizzly bear. The metaphor of the scuttling crab conveys the men's panic. Choice C is incorrect. The men are not clumsy, although it is difficult to flee from a tent. The impact of the metaphor is that it shows the panic of the campers. Choice D is also incorrect. "To scuttle" may seem cowardly, but the comparison shows the men in a state of panic because of a real danger. **(RL.6.4; DOK 3)**

SAMPLE RESPONSES

Short Response (See 2-Point Rubric—Short Response on page A46 for scoring.)

2 The poem is structured into six stanzas. The first three describe a peaceful scene, with the squirrels living in their own "town" in the woods. Then the tone of the poem changes abruptly in the last three stanzas. An element of danger is introduced with the coming of the "hungry wild swine" that are digging up and eating the squirrels' food. The squirrels are forced to "flee" or move some place else and look for food. The structure illustrates the theme that nature is unpredictable, and animals must adapt and respond quickly to survive. *(RL.6.5; DOK 3)*

8 The narrator's attitude changes from self-confident to more humble. As the story begins, the narrator explains that he is a seasoned woodsman who has been a Scout leader for more than ten years. He thinks only "less seasoned" hikers would stay in the lodge. When the bear threatens the safety of the narrator and his friend, they know what to do, but it is partly luck that saves them. By the end of the story, the narrator realizes that even experienced woodsmen need to observe caution in the woods and that staying in the lodge might not be so bad. *(RL.6.6; DOK 3)*

Performance Task (See New York State Grade 6–8 Expository Writing Evaluation Rubric on pages A47 and A48 for scoring.)

9 The setting of "The Campsite" determines the problems that Tom and the narrator will face during the course of a summer night in the state park. The area is described as a mountain forest. The two men select a campsite in a clearing deep in the woods because it is near a stream where they can get fresh water. They also choose a campsite that is far from the lodge where other people are staying.

Choosing the isolated campsite is key to the plot of the story. The real conflict comes about when the men have to escape the grizzly bear. They have to run from the tent and climb pine trees before the bear attacks them. Their actions save them from a possible attack. At last, they are driven to civilization by two park rangers who point out that the campers have not made a wise choice in choosing a campsite far from the lodge. *(RL.6.5; DOK 3)*

Evaluating an Argument

LESSON OBJECTIVES

- Identify the claims, reasons, and evidence an author uses to develop an argument.

- Evaluate an argument's effectiveness by determining whether its specific claims are supported by reasons and evidence from the text.

THE LEARNING PROGRESSION

- **Grade 5:** CCLS RI.5.8 focuses on having students identify reasons and evidence that support particular points made by the author.

- **Grade 6: CCLS RI.6.8 expands on earlier learning while introducing students to the structure of an argument. Further, students learn how to evaluate an argument by focusing on whether or not the author's claims are supported by reasons and evidence.**

- **Grade 7:** CCLS RI.7.8 requires students to analyze whether the reasoning or evidence that supports an author's claims is relevant and sufficient.

PREREQUISITE SKILLS

- Identify the author's point of view or purpose in a text.

- Recognize statements and word choices that make clear the text is expressing the author's point of view.

- Explain how word choice and tone help to reveal an author's perspective and biases.

- Explain how an author uses reasons and evidence to support particular points in a text.

TAP STUDENTS' PRIOR KNOWLEDGE

- Tell students they will be working on a lesson about evaluating an argument. Explain that an argument expresses a person's position (opinion) about a topic and presents claims to convince others that the position is valid. An effective argument does not appeal to emotions or rely on someone's popularity. Instead, it supplies sound reasons and evidence to prove each claim.

- Clarify this point by providing contrasting claims about a topical issue. For example, discuss these claims for the argument that a student should go on a field trip to a museum: 1) Everybody else is going. 2) The trip will be educational. Note that claim 1 may be emotionally appealing but isn't reasonable. Claim 2 is based on sensible thinking, and reasons or evidence can be used to support it. Ask volunteers to suggest convincing support for the second claim.

- Ask volunteers to describe times when they have needed to provide a convincing argument to friends or family. Then point out that, in most instances, sensible, logical reasons and sound evidence make their argument stronger and more convincing.

- Stress that understanding how claims are supported by reasons and evidence will help students determine whether or not an author has made a strong and convincing argument.

Ready *Teacher Toolbox* — teacher-toolbox.com

	Prerequisite Skills	*RI.6.8*
Ready Lessons	✓	✓
Tools for Instruction	✓	✓
Interactive Tutorials		✓

CCLS Focus

RI.6.8 Trace and evaluate the argument and specific claims in a text, distinguishing claims that are supported by reasons and evidence from claims that are not.

ADDITIONAL STANDARDS: **RI.6.2, RI.6.4, RI.6.5, RI.6.6, RI.6.7, RI.6.9.a; W.6.1, W.6.4, W.6.9, W.6.11.c; SL.6.1, SL.6.2.a, SL.6.3, SL.6.5; L.6.1, L.6.3.a, L.6.4.a, L.6.4.d** (See page A39 for full text.)

AT A GLANCE

Through a cartoon, students are introduced to the process of identifying and evaluating an argument. They learn how an argument is supported by claims, reasons, and evidence.

STEP BY STEP

- Read the first two paragraphs, which include the definitions of *argument, evaluate, claims, reasons,* and *evidence.* Then have students study the cartoon and think about the argument that the girl is making.

- Explain that the chart reflects the structure of an argument. It shows the girl's argument and then gives two claims that explain why she should have a dog. Discuss her first claim and the proof she gives in the cartoon to support it. Have students add the evidence below the first claim.

- Explain that Claim 2 on the chart gives an additional claim that the girl makes later, after the events shown in the cartoon. Discuss reasons or evidence that could be used to support the statement. Then have students add a sensible example that supports her second claim.

- Review the completed chart. Then ask students to explain why having good reasons and evidence is key to a well-supported argument.

- Read and discuss the last paragraph, which gives questions to help students evaluate the effectiveness of an argument. Guide students in evaluating the argument the girl presents to her mother.

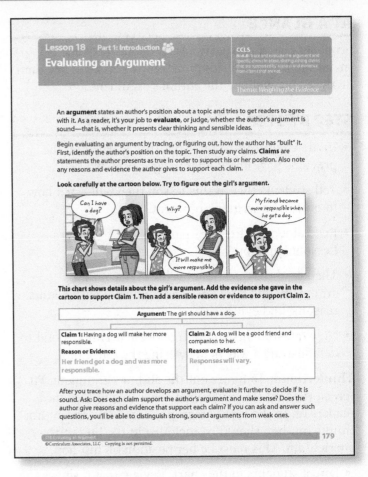

- Reinforce how evaluating the effectiveness of an argument is an important part of reading essays and other persuasive writing. Note that when a claim is made, it must be supported with reasons and evidence to help develop a solid argument.

Genre Focus

Informational Texts: Persuasive Essay

Tell students that in this lesson they will read one type of informational text known as a persuasive essay, which presents an argument. A persuasive essay has the following characteristics:

- It is a short opinion piece in which the writer presents an argument that expresses his or her position about a topic.

- It provides reasons and facts, examples, or other evidence to prove why his or her position is correct.

- It is meant to convince readers to agree with the writer's position or opinion.

Ask students to share any persuasive essays they have read or written. What subjects or issues are often addressed in persuasive essays? Who writes persuasive essays? Explain to students that persuasive essays are often published in magazines and newspapers. They may also appear on websites related to the topic of the essay.

Ask students to consider writing a persuasive essay and what argument they would like to make. Perhaps they would try to bring about change in the school or at home. Encourage students to brainstorm sources for evidence, such as books, scientists, officials, and other experts. Point out that authors of persuasive essays follow the same steps.

AT A GLANCE

Students read a persuasive essay about the value of including hip-hop lyrics in literature classes. They then analyze and evaluate the author's argument.

STEP BY STEP

- Invite volunteers to tell what they learned on the previous page about analyzing arguments.

- Tell students that in this lesson they will learn how to evaluate a written argument.

- Read aloud the first two paragraphs of "Today's Lesson: Hip-Hop."

- Then read the question: "What is the author's argument, and how does she support it with claims, reasons, and evidence?"

- Now tell students you will perform a Think Aloud to demonstrate a way of answering the question.

Think Aloud: To figure out the author's argument, I'll reread the text to decide what she wants to convince readers of. In the first paragraph, I read that the author thinks hip-hop should be included in the literature curriculum. This must be her position on hip-hop.

- Direct students to the chart. Review that it shows the structure of an argument. Have students restate the author's argument and write it in the chart. Then read and discuss the first claim.

Think Aloud: How does the author support Claim 1 about hip-hop? . . . In paragraph 2, sentence 3, she offers proof to support her claim. She explains that hip-hop has rhyme, rhythm, and meter, just like other poetry. And poetry is already part of the curriculum.

- Read and discuss the evidence the author gives to support Claim 2. Then use a Think Aloud to guide students in identifying the claim it supports.

Think Aloud: In paragraph 2, sentence 4 names heartache and growing up as themes dealt with in hip-hop lyrics and other poetry. They support her claim that hip-hop deals with important themes.

- Have students add Claim 2 to the chart. Then have partners evaluate the author's argument. Suggest that they refer to the questions in the last paragraph on page 179 for guidance. Allow time for volunteers to share their evaluations with their classmates.

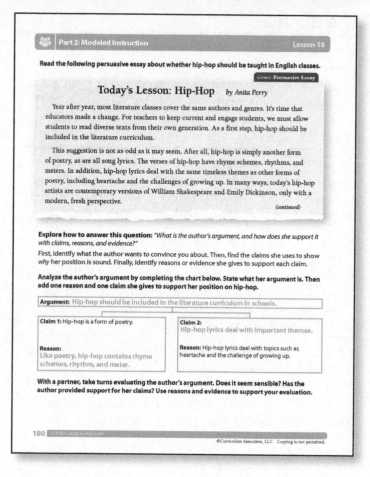

Tier Two Vocabulary: *Contemporary*

- Direct students to the word *contemporary* in paragraph 2. Remind them that they can use context clues to help them determine the meaning of a word. Point out that synonyms, or words that are similar in meaning, are one type of context clue.

- Have students identify synonyms and other context clues that help them understand the meaning of *contemporary*. (*modern, fresh perspective*) Then ask students to define *contemporary* in their own words. (*in the present day*)

- Have students verify that their definition makes sense by checking it in context. (*RI.6.4; L.6.4.a; L.6.4.d*)

AT A GLANCE

Students continue reading the persuasive essay about using hip-hop lyrics in the literature curriculum. They answer a multiple-choice question and evaluate how well the author supports her reasons with evidence.

STEP BY STEP

- Tell students they will continue reading the essay about hip-hop lyrics in the literature curriculum.

- Close Reading guides students to look for another claim that supports the author's argument. The Hint will help them locate the claim and select the best answer for the question.

- Have students read the passage and underline the claim the author provides in the first paragraph of page 181, as directed by Close Reading.

- Ask volunteers to share the sentence they underlined. Discuss how that sentence further supports the author's argument that hip-hop songs should be taught in literature class.

- Have students circle the answer to the question, and then write a response for Show Your Thinking. (*Sample response: The author does not support her argument well. While she gives some reasons as support for her claims, she provides no facts or concrete evidence as proof.*)

ANSWER ANALYSIS

Choice A is incorrect. It is an opinion, not a claim that supports the author's argument.

Choice B is incorrect. The author does not make this point in this part of the text.

Choice C is correct. It gives another claim to support the idea that teachers should use hip-hop lyrics in literature class.

Choice D is incorrect. The author does not mention students learning to write hip-hop lyrics.

> **ERROR ALERT:** Students who did not select C may have chosen an answer that is not a claim. The question asks for an additional claim to support the argument. Only C provides a claim the author presents as true.

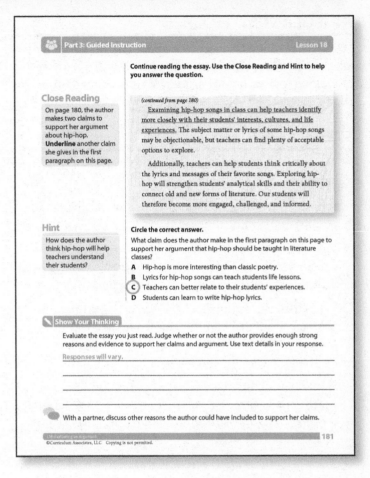

ELL Support: Possessives

- Explain to students that possessives are words that show who or what owns something. To make a singular noun a possessive noun, add an apostrophe and an *s*, as in the example *duck's*. To make a plural noun a possessive noun, add only an apostrophe, as in the example *ducks'*.

- Point out the plural possessive noun *students'* in paragraph 1. Ask them to identify what belongs to the students. (*interests, cultures, and life experiences*) Then have students form the singular possessive form of this noun. (*student's*)

- Also tell students that the pronouns *my, his, her, their,* and *its* show possession. Have students identify possessive pronouns used in this passage (*their*). **(L.6.1)**

AT A GLANCE

Students read a passage twice about the censorship of yearbooks. After the first reading, you will ask three questions to check your students' comprehension of the passage.

STEP BY STEP

- Have students read the editorial silently without referring to the Study Buddy or Close Reading text.

- Ask the following questions to ensure students' comprehension of the text:

What does the author say teachers are doing to censor yearbooks? (*Teachers are removing things from yearbooks that they think are not appropriate.*)

Why does the author feel the First Amendment protects students' right to put what they want into their yearbooks? (*The First Amendment includes the right to freedom of expression.*)

How do students use creative expression to make yearbooks? (*They use creativity when putting together yearbooks. It allows them to capture their experiences in an interesting way.*)

- Then ask students to reread paragraph 1 and look at the Study Buddy think aloud. What does the Study Buddy help them think about?

Tip: The Study Buddy tells students to think about the author's claims and to look for reasons and evidence as they read. Thinking about and looking for the claims, reasons, and evidence that support an argument are important to understanding it.

- Have students reread the rest of the editorial. Tell them to follow the directions in the Close Reading.

Tip: The Close Reading assists students in locating the author's claims, reasons, and evidence. Students first need to determine these details before they can take the next step, which is to decide how well the author has developed the argument.

- Finally, have students answer the questions on page 183. Use the Answer Analysis to discuss correct and incorrect responses.

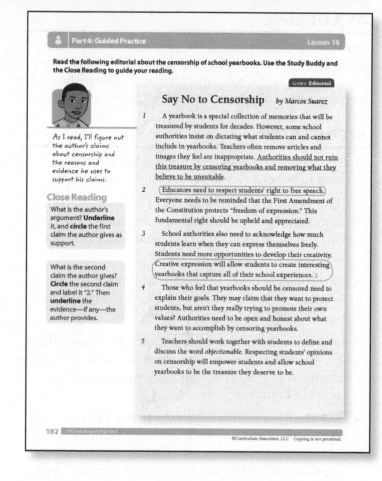

Tier Two Vocabulary: *Censorship*

- Point out the word *censorship* in the title and paragraph 1. Ask students to use the context clues in the paragraph to help them understand what *censorship* means. What examples of censorship does the author include? (*"remove articles and images they feel are inappropriate"*)

- Then work with students to define *censorship* (*"reviewing and not allowing content"*). **(RI.6.4; L.6.4.a)**

STEP BY STEP

- Have students read questions 1–3, using the Hints to help them answer those questions.

Tip: If students have trouble answering question 2, remind them that the First Amendment plays an important role in the author's argument. It describes a right that is protected by the Constitution for the United States of America.

- Discuss with students the Answer Analysis below.

ANSWER ANALYSIS

1   The correct choice is D. The author believes that students should be allowed the freedom to use creative expression to develop their yearbooks. Choices A and B are incorrect because they contradict the author's argument. Choice C is incorrect. The author doesn't make this point.

2   The correct choice is B. The First Amendment protects the right to expression. It supports the reasoning that students have a right to express themselves. Choice A does not agree with the author's ideas. Choice C is incorrect. Censorship is controversial, but this does not explain why the author refers to the First Amendment. Choice D is incorrect. The idea of objectionable school materials contradicts the intent of the amendment.

3   Sample response: The editorial does not present a sound argument about why yearbooks should not be censored. Only one of the author's claims is well supported; he points to students' right to free speech and uses the First Amendment as support. His second claim about student creativity leading to "interesting yearbooks," however, is not supported by solid evidence. Also, his answer to a claim made by the opposing side is not strong or convincing.

RETEACHING

Use a graphic organizer to verify the answer to question 1. Draw the graphic organizer below, and have students complete it. Sample responses are provided.

Argument: Authorities should not censor yearbooks.	
Claim: Students have a right to express themselves.	**Claim:** Students should be allowed to be creative.

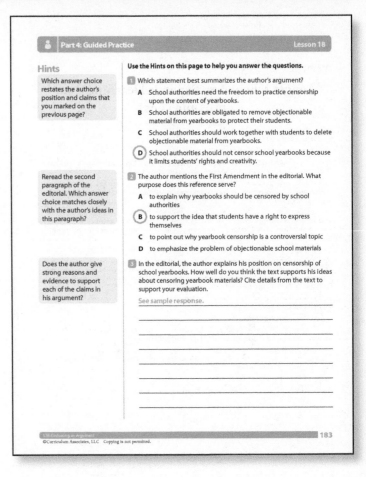

Part 4: Guided Practice Lesson 18

Hints

Which answer choice restates the author's position and claims that you marked on the previous page?

Reread the second paragraph of the editorial. Which answer choice matches closely with the author's ideas in this paragraph?

Does the author give strong reasons and evidence to support each of the claims in his argument?

Use the Hints on this page to help you answer the questions.

1   Which statement best summarizes the author's argument?

   A   School authorities need the freedom to practice censorship upon the content of yearbooks.

   B   School authorities are obligated to remove objectionable material from yearbooks to protect their students.

   C   School authorities should work together with students to delete objectionable material from yearbooks.

   D   School authorities should not censor school yearbooks because it limits students' rights and creativity.

2   The author mentions the First Amendment in the editorial. What purpose does this reference serve?

   A   to explain why yearbooks should be censored by school authorities

   B   to support the idea that students have a right to express themselves

   C   to point out why yearbook censorship is a controversial topic

   D   to emphasize the problem of objectionable school materials

3   In the editorial, the author explains his position on censorship of school yearbooks. How well do you think the text supports his ideas about censoring yearbook materials? Cite details from the text to support your evaluation.

   See sample response.

L18: Evaluating an Argument
©Curriculum Associates, LLC   Copying is not permitted.   183

Integrating Standards

Use these questions to further students' understanding of "Say No to Censorship."

1   What purpose does the first sentence serve in this editorial? **(RI.6.5)**

   The author informs the reader that yearbooks are created for students to enjoy for years to come. This sets up the author's argument by explaining why yearbooks are important before the author tells why yearbooks should not be censored by teachers.

2   What do you think is the author's purpose in writing this editorial? **(RI.6.6)**

   His purpose is to convince school authorities that they should not allow censorship of yearbooks at their schools.

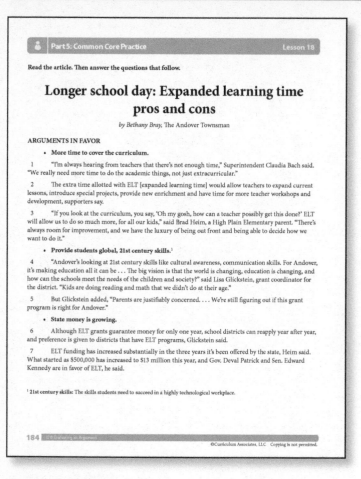

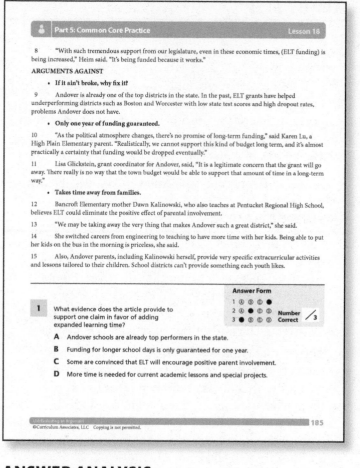

AT A GLANCE

Students independently read a longer article and answer questions in a format that provides test practice.

STEP BY STEP

- Tell students to use what they have learned about reading carefully and evaluating an argument to read the passage on pages 184 and 185.

- Remind students to underline or circle important claims, reasons, and evidence.

- Tell students to answer the questions on pages 185 and 186. For questions 1–3, they should fill in the correct circle on the Answer Form.

- When students have finished, use the Answer Analysis to discuss correct responses and the reasons for them. Have students fill in the Number Correct on the Answer Form.

ANSWER ANALYSIS

1 Choice D is correct. The first claim for the argument in favor of expanded learning time (ELT) points to the need by teachers for more time to cover the curriculum, which includes academic lessons and special projects. Choices A and B are incorrect because each lists evidence used to oppose ELT. Choice C is incorrect; the point was not used as evidence to support the argument in favor of ELT. **(DOK 2)**

Theme Connection

- How do all the articles in this lesson relate to the theme of weighing the evidence?

- What is one fact you learned from each article?

2 Choice B is correct. This fact shows that ELT programs are well-funded and successful. Choice A is incorrect; the grants are meant to fund ELT programs, not to raise money for Andover. Choice C is incorrect. Increased funding suggests that Andover will not have to be the sole support of the program. Choice D is incorrect. Current increases to grants does not guarantee funding in the future. **(DOK 3)**

3 Choice A is correct. It includes all of the main claims in the argument against lengthening the school day. Choices B, C, and D are incorrect because each lists only a single claim from the argument against implementing ELT in the town. **(DOK 2)**

4 Sample response: In both sections of the article, the author notes that future funding of an ELT program is uncertain. In the "pros" section, she writes that "ELT grants guarantee money for only one year." While supporters of the program note increasing state funds for ELT, that doesn't change the fact that the grants must be renewed each year. In the "cons" section, the author quotes a parent as saying "there's no promise of long-term funding." She also quotes a grant coordinator as saying, "It's a legitimate concern that the grant will go away." While the writer covers both sides of the story, she clearly intends to show funding is a major issue. **(DOK 3)**

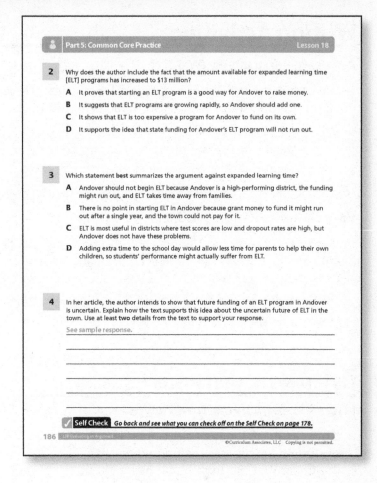

Integrating Standards

Use these questions and tasks as opportunities to interact with "Longer school day."

1 How does the arrangement of the opposing sides of the ELT issue help make each argument clearer? **(RI.6.5)**

The claims for both sides of this argument are clear because they are divided up into two sections and labeled under headings. The main points are also bulleted and in bold, which makes it easy to see what is most important.

2 Briefly summarize the arguments presented for and against expanded learning time. **(RI.6.2)**

The arguments in favor of ELT are that it gives teachers more time to cover the curriculum; it provides students with global, 21st-century skills; and state ELT funding is growing. The arguments against ELT are that the current program doesn't need to be fixed, only one year of funding is guaranteed, and ELT may take time away from families.

3 What does the phrase "expanded learning time" mean? **(RI.6.4; L.6.4.a)**

Expanded learning time is an extension of the school day that is used by some school systems.

4 Write a paragraph to explain the author's purpose in writing this article. **(RI.6.6; W.6.4)**

In this article, the author's purpose is to inform readers about both sides on the ELT issue. She summarizes each group's argument by explaining their claims and the evidence used as support.

5 Discuss in small groups: Which side do you think has presented the more effective argument about adding ELT in the Andover schools? Explain why, using text evidence. **(SL.6.1)**

Discussions will vary. Encourage students to use the questions on page 179 to help them evaluate the arguments in the article objectively. Then have groups share their personal opinions about which side has presented a more convincing argument.

Writing Activities

Advocate Persuasively (W.6.1)

- Have students review the arguments for and against Andover schools switching to a longer school day. Which claims do they agree with most? Which claims are best supported by strong evidence?

- Challenge students to write a persuasive essay that is either for or against adopting extended learning time for schools in their community. Encourage students to use evidence from the text to support their claims. Suggest that they also present a claim given by the opposing side and explain why it is less convincing.

- Allow time for students to share their essays with the class.

Vary Sentence Patterns (L.6.3.a)

- Have a volunteer read aloud the second paragraph of "Today's Lesson: Hip-Hop" on page 180. Discuss with students how the variation in sentence patterns helps maintain readers' interest. For example, the author uses some longer sentences and some shorter sentences. Also, she also begins several sentences with an introductory phrase that is set off with a comma, which adds even more variety.

- Have students reread their persuasive essays and revise them to add more variety to their sentence patterns.

LISTENING ACTIVITY (SL.6.1; SL.6.3)

Listen Closely/Summarize a Viewpoint

- After reading "Today's Lesson: Hip-Hop," ask pairs of students to discuss their opinions about the argument that hip-hop should be taught in literature class. Have students take turns stating their opinions while their partners listen.

- Then have students explain to the class their partner's viewpoint on the issue, without interjecting their own opinion.

DISCUSSION ACTIVITY (SL.6.1)

Talk in a Group/Debate an Argument

- Ask students to review the arguments in "Say No to Censorship."

- Have students work in small groups to discuss whether or not they think this argument also applies to other school materials. Should students be allowed to publish whatever they like in the school newspaper or in a newsletter that goes home to family members? Why or why not?

- Have groups discuss arguments for both sides of the issue. Allow 10 to 15 minutes for discussion. Then have groups present their ideas to the class.

MEDIA ACTIVITY (RI.6.7)

Be Creative/Act It Out

- Have students review the girl's argument shown in the chart on page 179.

- Then ask students to work in pairs to create a script for the rest of the conversation between the girl and her mother. Encourage them to include other reasons the girl might use, as well as the argument the mother might present in response. Remind students to include clear conclusions in their scripts.

- Have students practice their scripts and then act them out for the class.

RESEARCH ACTIVITY (W.6.9; SL.6.5)

Research and Present/Give a Presentation

- Ask students to use the claims, reasons, and evidence in "Today's Lesson: Hip-Hop" as a basis for an argument that literature classes should use song lyrics from all genres of music.

- Ask students to create visual displays using lyrics from songs to show how they are worthwhile for analysis in literature class.

- Have students present their work to the class.

Comparing and Contrasting Texts

LESSON OBJECTIVES

- Recognize the difference between facts and opinions.

- Compare and contrast texts by different authors about the same topic or event.

- Identify how an author's purpose for writing influences the focus of the text and the details presented.

THE LEARNING PROGRESSION

- **Grade 5:** CCLS RI.5.9 requires students to integrate information from several texts on the same topic in order to write or speak about the subject knowledgeably.

- **Grade 6: CCLS RI.6.9 builds on the Grade 5 standard by having students compare and contrast one author's presentation of events with that of another. Students compare and contrast texts on the same events, not simply the same subject.**

- **Grade 7:** CCLS RI.7.9 requires students to analyze how two or more authors writing about the same topic shape their presentations of key information by emphasizing different evidence or advancing different interpretations of facts.

PREREQUISITE SKILLS

- Identify the central idea and topic of a text.

- Compare and contrast different aspects of nonfiction texts.

- Identify an author's point of view and purpose for writing.

TAP STUDENTS' PRIOR KNOWLEDGE

- Tell students they will be working on a lesson comparing and contrasting different texts about the same topics and events. Remind students of the different purposes authors have for writing. (*to inform, entertain, persuade*)

- Ask students why it is important to determine the author's purpose while reading. (*Depending on the author's purpose, he or she might present only some of the important details. Readers might not get the whole picture or all of the information.*)

- Have students think about the difference between facts and opinions. (*A fact is information that can be proved to be true. An opinion is what someone thinks, feels, or believes.*)

- Then have students think about the difference between first-person and third-person accounts. (*A first-person account, such as an autobiography, tells about events from someone who was there to experience them. A third-person account, such as a biography, relates facts about events from someone who wasn't there when they happened.*)

- Explain to students that they should always pay attention to the author's purpose for writing. It helps them not only better understand the text but also interpret the information that is provided.

Ready *Teacher Toolbox*   teacher-toolbox.com

	Prerequisite Skills	RI.6.9
Ready Lessons	✓	✓
Tools for Instruction	✓ ✓	
Interactive Tutorials		✓

CCLS Focus

RI.6.9 Compare and contrast one author's presentation of events with that of another (e.g., a memoir written by and a biography on the same person).

ADDITIONAL STANDARDS: **RL.6.11.a, RI.6.1, RI.6.2, RI.6.3, RI.6.4, RI.6.6, RI.6.7, RI.6.8; W.6.1, W.6.2, W.6.4, W.6.8; SL.6.1, SL.6.2.a, SL.6.4; L.6.1, L.6.2.a, L.6.4.a, L.6.4.b, L.6.4.c, L.6.4.d, L.6.5.a** (*See page A39 for full text.*)

AT A GLANCE

By reading two historical accounts of the same event, students practice comparing and contrasting texts.

STEP BY STEP

- Remind students that authors have different purposes for writing. Writing can be entertaining, educational, persuasive, or personal. Explain that two authors can write about the same event but with a different purpose for writing.

- Read the first paragraph and review the meanings of *biography* and *autobiography*. Have students compare and contrast the features of each.

- Have students read the two historical accounts. Then have them determine each author's purpose for writing. What is the same about the two accounts? What is different?

- To help students compare and contrast the two accounts, have them circle information that is the same or similar between the two paragraphs. Then have them underline details that are in one account but not the other.

- Discuss with students the information they marked. Then read the paragraph at the bottom of the page and have students compare the details they circled and underlined to the information in the paragraph.

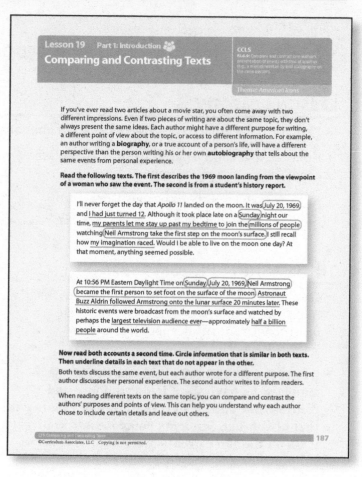

Genre Focus

Informational Texts: Memoir

Explain to students that a memoir is a form of autobiographical writing in which the writer shares details of his or her life with readers. Memoirs are often informal or intimate in tone.

Remind students that an autobiography is an informational text about the events in the author's life. Autobiographies includes facts and details about the person's life. They are usually written by famous people who have achieved great things, but they can be written by anyone. Often, an autobiography will focus on the reflections and important memories a person has about his or her life.

A memoir is slightly different from other autobiographies in that it usually relates very personal thoughts and feelings. It is more personal in nature. An autobiography is written to keep the writer's memories alive, but a memoir is written to keep the writer's feelings and emotions alive.

Point out that diaries can sometimes be a form of memoir. Cite the example of *The Diary of a Young Girl* by Anne Frank. She wrote it as a personal diary, but it was later published as a personal memoir of an important person during a significant time in history.

Have students share examples of other memoirs and autobiographies with which they are familiar.

AT A GLANCE

Students read a short biography of Amelia Earhart and then determine how the author's purpose influences the focus of the text.

STEP BY STEP

- Invite volunteers to tell what they learned on the previous page about comparing and contrasting two texts about the same event.

- Tell students that they will read a short biography of Amelia Earhart. They will determine the author's purpose for writing and how that purpose influences the focus of the text.

- Read aloud "Born to Fly." Then read the question: "How does the author's purpose influence the focus of the text and the details presented?"

- Tell students you will use a Think Aloud to demonstrate a way of answering the question.

Think Aloud: This is a biography, so the author's purpose for writing is to inform. She wants the reader to learn more about Amelia Earhart and her life. The author wants to explain how and why Earhart learned to love flying.

- Have students circle or underline details that help the reader understand how and why Amelia Earhart learned to love flying.

Think Aloud: The second paragraph talks about how Frank Hawks took her for her first flight and how she took flying lessons five days later. This is important. It shows that Earhart was immediately in love with flying and wanted to learn how to do it herself.

- Have students respond to the prompt with other facts from the text. (*Sample response: The author writes to inform readers about Earhart's early career and how she decided she wanted to be a pilot. For example, the text mentions her first flight with Frank Hawks and how she took flying lessons five days later.*)

- Then have partners discuss the question at the bottom of the page. (*Sample response: The author respects and admires Amelia Earhart. She includes positive language such as "fearless," "born to fly," and "flying was truly in her blood." The author included this language and the specific facts that she chose in order to show readers Earhart's greatness.*)

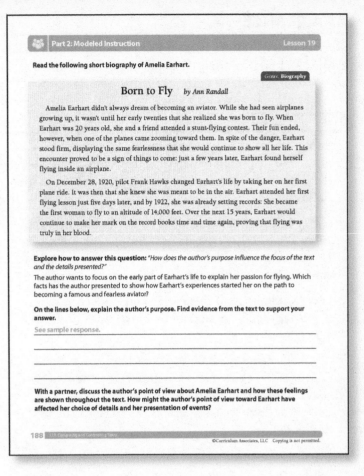

Part 2: Modeled Instruction   Lesson 19

Read the following short biography of Amelia Earhart.

Genre: **Biography**

Born to Fly   *by Ann Randall*

Amelia Earhart didn't always dream of becoming an aviator. While she had seen airplanes growing up, it wasn't until her early twenties that she realized she was born to fly. When Earhart was 20 years old, she and a friend attended a stunt-flying contest. Their fun ended, however, when one of the planes came zooming toward them. In spite of the danger, Earhart stood firm, displaying the same fearlessness that she would continue to show all her life. This encounter proved to be a sign of things to come: just a few years later, Earhart found herself flying inside an airplane.

On December 28, 1920, pilot Frank Hawks changed Earhart's life by taking her on her first plane ride. It was then that she knew she was meant to be in the air. Earhart attended her first flying lesson just five days later, and by 1922, she was already setting records: She became the first woman to fly to an altitude of 14,000 feet. Over the next 15 years, Earhart would continue to make her mark on the record books time and time again, proving that flying was truly in her blood.

Explore how to answer this question: *"How does the author's purpose influence the focus of the text and the details presented?"*

The author wants to focus on the early part of Earhart's life to explain her passion for flying. Which facts has the author presented to show how Earhart's experiences started her on the path to becoming a famous and fearless aviator?

On the lines below, explain the author's purpose. Find evidence from the text to support your answer.

See sample response.

With a partner, discuss the author's point of view about Amelia Earhart and how these feelings are shown throughout the text. How might the author's point of view toward Earhart have affected her choice of details and her presentation of events?

188   L19: Comparing and Contrasting Texts   ©Curriculum Associates, LLC Copying is not permitted.

ELL Support: Contractions

- Explain to students that a contraction is two words that have been joined together and shortened. When the words are joined, letters are dropped. An apostrophe is added to take the place of any dropped letters.

- Work with students to identify the two words in a contraction. Point out the word *didn't* in paragraph 1. Explain that it is made up of the words *did* and *not*. Tell students that the letter *o* in *not* has been dropped, and an apostrophe has been put in its place.

- Next, point out the word *wasn't* in paragraph 1 and *Earhart's* in paragraph 2. Have students identify which word is a contraction (*wasn't*) and tell what two words are in it (*was* and *not*). Point out that *Earhart's* is a possessive noun that shows ownership. **(L.6.1)**

AT A GLANCE

Students read another biographical article about Amelia Earhart. They then identify details to help them compare and contrast each text.

STEP BY STEP

- Tell students they will read another biographical article about Amelia Earhart. They should read for details that are similar to and different from the first biography.

- Close Reading helps students identify details about Earhart's life that this author chose to include. The Hint will help students recognize the different ways that authors can use facts and details.

- Have students read the article and underline important facts about Amelia Earhart, as directed by Close Reading.

- Ask volunteers to share the facts they underlined. Discuss why these facts are important and whether they are different from the facts used in "Born to Fly." If necessary, ask, "What was Earhart the first to do?"

- Have students fill in the chart with information from both articles.

- Then have partners respond to the prompts in Show Your Thinking. (*Sample response: Both name her as a famous, fearless aviator who set records. The first biography focuses on Earhart's early life and what motivated her to become a famous aviator. The second was written to show her accomplishments on behalf of all women.*)

ANSWER ANALYSIS

Refer to the annotations provided on the facsimile page at right.

ERROR ALERT: Students who had difficulty completing the chart may not have understood similarities between the two articles. Have them ask themselves: "What do I learn about in the first article that I then read about in the second article?"

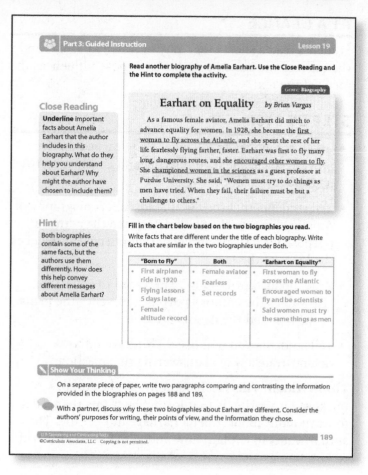

Tier Two Vocabulary: *Championed*

- Direct students to the word *championed*. Remind them that they can look for other words in the text that have a similar meaning, or are synonyms, to help them understand an unfamiliar word. Ask them to identify synonyms and other context clues that help them understand the meaning of *championed*. ("*encouraged*," "*challenge*") Then have them define *championed* in their own words. ("*supported*")

- Encourage students to use a thesaurus to identify synonyms of *championed* as it is used in this text. **(RI.6.4; L.6.4.a; L.6.4.c)**

AT A GLANCE

Students read a memoir by Helen Keller twice. After the first reading, you will ask three questions to check your students' comprehension of the passage.

STEP BY STEP

- Have students read the memoir silently without referring to the Study Buddy or Close Reading text.

- Ask the following questions to ensure students' comprehension of the text:

  Why are many of the words in this passage spelled out with letters? (*Helen is showing that she was learning everything had a name and those names are spelled with letters.*)

  How does Helen feel after she breaks the doll? (*She feels good. She is happy that she has gotten rid of something that was bothering her and causing her problems.*)

  How does Helen finally learn the word *water*? (*She feels cool water rush over her hand as it is pumped from a well.*)

- Ask students to reread the passage and look at the Study Buddy think aloud. What does the Study Buddy help them think about?

Tip: The Study Buddy asks students to identify details that reveal Helen's emotions and how they influence her writing. This is the very nature of the author's purpose for writing. Students should repeatedly practice this as they read memoirs.

- Have students answer the questions and follow the directions in the Close Reading.

Tip: The Close Reading asks students to analyze Helen's purpose for writing. Be sure students are familiar with the differences between biographies (such as those about Amelia Earhart) and autobiographies and their differing purposes.

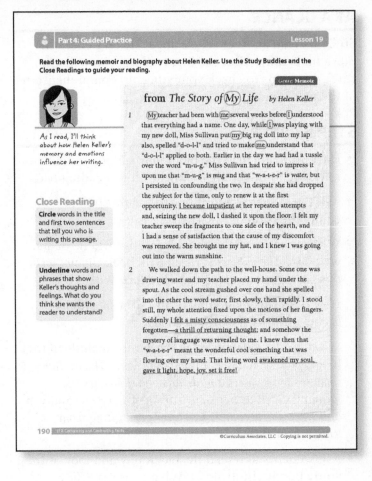

Read the following memoir and biography about Helen Keller. Use the Study Buddies and the Close Readings to guide your reading.

Genre: **Memoir**

from *The Story of My Life*   *by Helen Keller*

As I read, I'll think about how Helen Keller's memory and emotions influence her writing.

Close Reading

Circle words in the title and first two sentences that tell you who is writing this passage.

Underline words and phrases that show Keller's thoughts and feelings. What do you think she wants the reader to understand?

1   My teacher had been with me several weeks before I understood that everything had a name. One day, while I was playing with my new doll, Miss Sullivan put my big rag doll into my lap also, spelled "d-o-l-l" and tried to make me understand that "d-o-l-l" applied to both. Earlier in the day we had had a tussle over the word "m-u-g." Miss Sullivan had tried to impress it upon me that "m-u-g" is *mug* and that "w-a-t-e-r" is *water*, but I persisted in confounding the two. In despair she had dropped the subject for the time, only to renew it at the first opportunity. I became impatient at her repeated attempts and, seizing the new doll, I dashed it upon the floor. I felt my teacher sweep the fragments to one side of the hearth, and I had a sense of satisfaction that the cause of my discomfort was removed. She brought me my hat, and I knew I was going out into the warm sunshine.

2   We walked down the path to the well-house. Some one was drawing water and my teacher placed my hand under the spout. As the cool stream gushed over one hand she spelled into the other word *water*, first slowly, then rapidly. I stood still, my whole attention fixed upon the motions of her fingers. Suddenly I felt a misty consciousness as of something forgotten—a thrill of returning thought; and somehow the mystery of language was revealed to me. I knew then that "w-a-t-e-r" meant the wonderful cool something that was flowing over my hand. That living word awakened my soul, gave it light, hope, joy, set it free!

190   L19 Comparing and Contrasting Texts   ©Curriculum Associates, LLC   Copying is not permitted.

Tier Two Vocabulary: *Confounding*

- Point out the word *confounding* in paragraph 1. Have students identify the part of speech (*verb*). Then encourage them to use context clues to determine the meaning of this word. If students need to, they may also use a dictionary to find the definition of the word as it is used in this context. (*"mixing up or confusing two things"*)

- Have students give examples of other related words that would make sense in this context. (*confusing, mixing up*) **(RI.6.4; L.6.4.a; L.6.4.d)**

AT A GLANCE

Students read another article about Helen Keller, this one a biography. After the first reading, you will ask three questions to check your students' comprehension of the text.

STEP BY STEP

- Have students read the biography silently without referring to the Study Buddy or Close Reading text.

- Ask the following questions to ensure students' comprehension of the text:

Who is the subject of this biography? Did he or she write it? (*The subject is Helen Keller. She did not write this passage; it is a biography by Mary Wilkes.*)

How does this biography begin? (*The biography begins with Helen's birth in 1880.*)

What kinds of details does the author include in this biography? What are some examples? (*The author includes many facts and details about Helen's life. Examples include her time learning from Anne Sullivan and what she accomplished after graduating from Radcliffe in 1904.*)

- Ask students to reread the biography and look at the Study Buddy think aloud. What does the Study Buddy help them think about?

Tip: The Study Buddy helps students look for clues that point to the author's purpose for writing. This will be different from the memoir. Students should recognize and understand that both texts are about the same topic, but they have different purposes.

- Have students answer the questions and follow the directions in the Close Reading.

Tip: The Close Reading guides students to look for similarities and differences. Encourage students to think about how details that are unique to this text reveal the author's purpose for writing. This will help them better understand what they read.

- Finally, have students answer the questions on page 192. Use the Answer Analysis to discuss correct and incorrect responses.

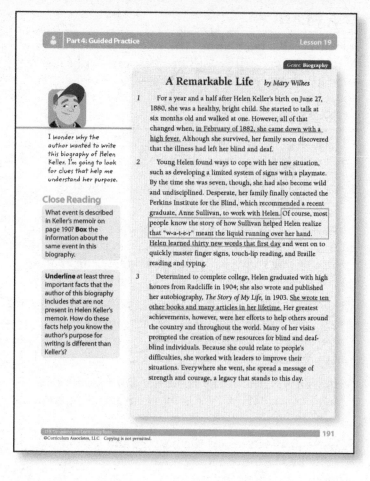

Genre: Biography

A Remarkable Life *by Mary Wilkes*

I wonder why the author wanted to write this biography of Helen Keller. I'm going to look for clues that help me understand her purpose.

Close Reading

What event is described in Keller's memoir on page 190? **Box** the information about the same event in this biography.

Underline at least three important facts that the author of this biography includes that are not present in Helen Keller's memoir. How do these facts help you know the author's purpose for writing is different than Keller's?

1   For a year and a half after Helen Keller's birth on June 27, 1880, she was a healthy, bright child. She started to talk at six months old and walked at one. However, all of that changed when, in February of 1882, she came down with a high fever. Although she survived, her family soon discovered that the illness had left her blind and deaf.

2   Young Helen found ways to cope with her new situation, such as developing a limited system of signs with a playmate. By the time she was seven, though, she had also become wild and undisciplined. Desperate, her family finally contacted the Perkins Institute for the Blind, which recommended a recent graduate, Anne Sullivan, to work with Helen. Of course, most people know the story of how Sullivan helped Helen realize that "w-a-t-e-r" meant the liquid running over her hand. Helen learned thirty new words that first day and went on to quickly master finger signs, touch-lip reading, and Braille reading and typing.

3   Determined to complete college, Helen graduated with high honors from Radcliffe in 1904; she also wrote and published her autobiography, *The Story of My Life*, in 1903. She wrote ten other books and many articles in her lifetime. Her greatest achievements, however, were her efforts to help others around the country and throughout the world. Many of her visits prompted the creation of new resources for blind and deaf-blind individuals. Because she could relate to people's difficulties, she worked with leaders to improve their situations. Everywhere she went, she spread a message of strength and courage, a legacy that stands to this day.

L19: Comparing and Contrasting Texts
©Curriculum Associates, LLC Copying is not permitted.   191

ELL Support: Prefixes

- Explain to students that many English words have prefixes. A prefix is a group of letters that is added to the beginning of a word to change the word's meaning.

- Direct students to the word *undisciplined* on this page. Write the word on the board and circle the prefix. (*un-*) Then point out the base word. (*discipline*)

- Encourage students to read the sentence aloud and try to determine the meaning of the word and prefix. Then have students think of or find other words with prefixes. (**L.6.4.b**)

STEP BY STEP

- Have students read questions 1–3, using the Hints to help them answer those questions.

> **Tip:** Question 3 requires students to compare and contrast the passages about Helen Keller. Students should have already identified much of this information as they read those texts. Remind students to pay attention to the authors' purposes.

- Discuss with students the Answer Analysis below.

ANSWER ANALYSIS

1 The correct choice is C. The memoir includes more personal feelings and reflections on her life. The biography includes more facts and is intended to inform. Choice A is incorrect because Helen doesn't want simply to inform people about her life. She wants to share some personal experiences. Choice B is incorrect because Helen doesn't attempt to explain her actions, and the biographer never calls Helen's childhood "wild." Choice D is incorrect because neither text is written to entertain.

2 The correct choice is B. Both passages mention the event when Helen realized that "w-a-t-e-r" meant cool liquid, or water. Choices A, C, and D are incorrect because those events are not mentioned in both texts—only in the biography.

3 Sample response: Both texts tell about how Sullivan helped Helen learn about the names for things. The memoir describes the events in detail, along with Helen's thoughts and feelings. The biography gives less detail about the event itself, but it describes other important events in her life in a factual way.

RETEACHING

Use a chart to organize details from the texts to answer Question 3. Draw the chart below, and have students fill in the boxes. Sample responses are provided.

The Story of My Life	Both	"A Remarkable Life"
• lots of detail • includes thoughts and feelings	• Anne Sullivan helped Helen learn about the names of things.	• not much detail • describes other events

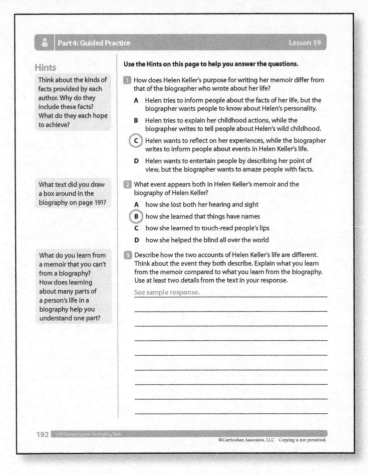

Integrating Standards

Use these questions to further students' understanding of the two texts.

1 What can you infer from the memoir about Helen's attempts to learn that everything has a name? *(RI.6.1)*

Helen says she "persisted in confounding" different words. She also describes her impatience and discomfort. I can infer that this was a very difficult process for her, and she was easily frustrated while she was trying to learn. Once she learns that "w-a-t-e-r" means water, she says the realization "awakened my soul ... set it free."

2 How does the biography introduce the event when Helen learns that words name things? *(RI.6.3)*

The event is quickly referenced as something "most people know." It is used as an example of the obstacles Helen had to overcome.

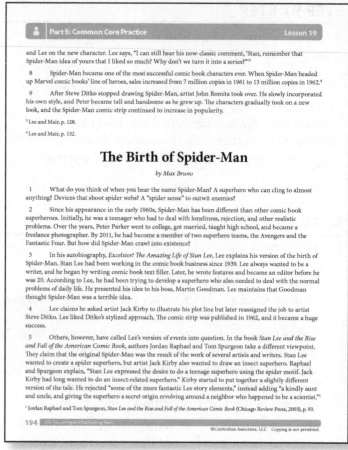

AT A GLANCE

Students independently read two longer passages and answer questions in a format that provides test practice.

STEP BY STEP

- Tell students to use what they have learned about analyzing the author's purpose and how it affects the focus of a text to read the passages on pages 193–195.

- Remind students to underline or circle important points.

- Tell students to answer the questions on pages 195 and 196. For questions 1–3, they should fill in the correct circle on the Answer Form.

- When students have finished, use the Answer Analysis to discuss correct responses and the reasons for them. Have students fill in the Number Correct on the Answer Form.

ANSWER ANALYSIS

1   Choice A is correct. The first article focuses on Stan Lee and his involvement in the creation of Spider-Man. The author includes Lee's point of view about the events. The second article includes other points of view and different versions of the same events. Choice B is incorrect because neither article focuses on the popularity of Stan Lee or Spider-Man; they are about the history of the character. Choice C is not the best choice because the second article does not include many details about Lee's career. Choice D is incorrect because the second article includes more points of view than Jack Kirby's. **(DOK 3)**

Theme Connection

- How do all the texts in this lesson relate to the theme of American icons?

- What is one fact or idea you learned about American icons from each article in this lesson?

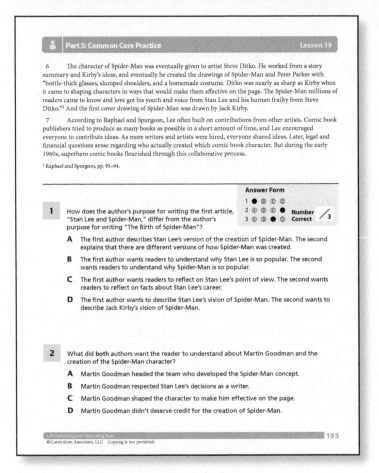

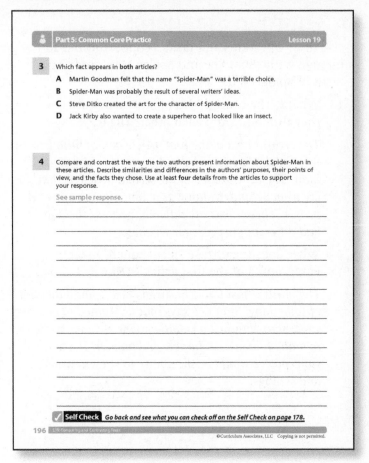

2 Choice D is correct. The first article says that Goodman hated Lee's idea and felt that "a superhero couldn't be a teenager with personal problems." The second article also says that Goodman thought Spider-Man was "a terrible idea." Choices A, B, and C are incorrect because none of them are supported by evidence in the texts. Martin Goodman was Stan Lee's boss, but there are no details in either text to suggest he developed the character or respected Lee as a writer. **(DOK 3)**

3 Choice C is correct. This fact appears in Paragraph 7 of the first article and in Paragraphs 4 and 6 of the second article. Choice A is not correct because Goodman hated the entire idea of Spider-Man, not just the name. Choices B and D are facts that appear only in the second article. **(DOK 2)**

4 Sample response: Both articles tell about the creation of the comic book character Spider-Man. The first article explains Stan Lee's version of how he came to create the character. The author quotes from Lee's own memoir to describe how ideas about the character came to him over time. The second article claims that the Spider-Man character was the result of the collaboration of many artists, as much from Jack Kirby and Steve Ditko as from Stan Lee. Some information in the second article contradicts what Lee wrote in his memoir. The second author writes that Spider-Man "got his youth and voice from Stan Lee [but] his human frailty from Steve Ditko." The author describing Lee's memoir suggests that Lee himself was the key force behind creating the popular hero. **(DOK 3)**

Integrating Standards

Use these questions and tasks as opportunities to interact with "Stan Lee and Spider-Man" and "The Birth of Spider-Man."

1 What is the central idea of both articles? How are they different from each other? (**RI.6.2**)

The central idea of the first article is that Stan Lee was the driving force behind the creation of Spider-Man. The central idea of the second article is that the creation of Spider-Man was a joint effort by several people. These ideas are different because the authors had different purposes for writing.

2 What does the phrase "just a touch" mean in Paragraph 3 of the first article? (**RI.6.4; L.6.5.a**)

The phrase "just a touch" means just a small amount of something. Stan Lee says that he wanted to create a superhero with just a small amount of super strength to make him more relatable and human. His main superpower would be the ability to stick to walls and ceilings.

3 What is the second author's point of view? How is it conveyed in the article? (**RI.6.6**)

The second author's point of view is that Spider-Man was created by several different people. He disputes Stan Lee's version of events and introduces evidence to support his own view. He says, "Lee often built on contributions from other artists" and "Lee encouraged everyone to contribute ideas."

4 Write a summary of the two articles and how they differ from each other. How do the purposes for writing affect the texts? (**RI.6.2; W.6.2**)

Summaries will vary.

5 Discuss in small groups: Think about creativity and the creation of new ideas. Are new ideas usually from one person, or are they the result of several people's thinking? (**SL.6.1**)

Discussions will vary. Remind students to use details from the text to support their ideas. They should also paraphrase other students' perspectives.

Writing Activities

Write an Argument *(W.6.1)*

- Have students think about the characteristics of memoirs and autobiographies. Do authors have a bias to present themselves in a certain way? How might this style of writing influence the facts and details the author chooses to include? Can they be believed?

- Ask students to write an argument either for or against the validity of memoirs. Students can take either side of the issue, but they should support their claims with clear reasons and relevant evidence.

Nonrestrictive Elements *(L.6.2.a; W.6.4)*

- Explain to students that nonrestrictive elements are words, phrases, or dependent clauses that provide additional, but not essential, information to a sentence. These elements are usually set off with commas.

- Direct students to paragraph 3 of "The Birth of Spider-Man." Point out that the title of Stan Lee's autobiography is set off with commas. This sentence would be fine without this title, but it provides additional information for the reader.

- Have students find other examples of nonrestrictive elements in this lesson's articles. Then have students write two or three sentences with nonrestrictive elements set off by commas.

LISTENING ACTIVITY *(SL.6.4)*

Listen Closely/Present Claims and Findings

- Have small groups of students reread the articles about Spider-Man. Then have them orally present the claims from each text. They should sequence their ideas logically and use relevant facts and details to support the claims.

- Students must listen closely to the oral arguments. They should be able to summarize what they hear and explain how these claims are a result of the authors' purpose for writing.

DISCUSSION ACTIVITY *(RI.6.8; SL.6.1)*

Talk in a Group/Evaluate Arguments

- Ask students to compare and contrast the information presented in two articles about the same topic from this lesson.

- Have students evaluate the claims made in each. Which are based in fact? Which are based in personal experience? Students should be able to identify claims that are supported by evidence.

- Appoint one member of each group to take notes. Allow 10 to 15 minutes for discussion, and then have each group share its results with the class.

MEDIA ACTIVITY *(RI.6.7)*

Be Creative/Read a Graphic Novel

- Direct students to several appropriate graphic novels featuring the character of Spider-Man. If possible, provide different versions of the same event, such as Spider-Man's origin.

- Students should read the graphic novels and compare and contrast how they each portray the same event. Have them pay attention to the art, dialogue, and tone of each piece.

RESEARCH ACTIVITY *(W.6.8; SL.6.4)*

Research and Present/Research Amelia Earhart

- Ask students to research more about the life of Amelia Earhart. What important events in her life were not mentioned in either of this lesson's passages? What else did she do that was interesting or significant?

- Remind students to assess the credibility of each source they choose and quote or paraphrase their conclusions.

- Students should present their findings orally to the class. Have them create a bibliography or references list that includes all their sources.

LESSON OBJECTIVES

- Compare and contrast nonfiction articles on the same topic by two different authors.
- Analyze an extended response writing prompt.
- Identify and analyze textual evidence for an informative essay.
- Organize ideas for an informative essay.
- Evaluate and revise text for an informative essay.
- Draw evidence and synthesize ideas from two texts.
- Write coherently using textual evidence.
- Understand the steps and process of writing an extended response essay.

AT A GLANCE

The opening page introduces students to an effective process they can use when responding to an extended-response question on a test. Students learn a five-step process, along with the specific actions each step entails.

STEP BY STEP

- Together, read the paragraphs at the top of the page. Tell students that extended-response questions will often require them to write several paragraphs.
- Make sure students understand what an essay is. Define an essay as a type of short nonfiction writing in which the writer discusses a specific topic or supports an opinion.
- Tell students that the chart lists steps they should follow when they write an essay in response to a prompt on a test. Review the five-step process with the class. Explain that this process is designed to work in the short time frame of a testing situation.

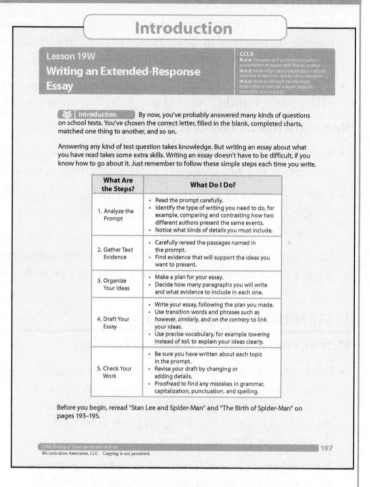

- Direct students to reread the articles "Stan Lee and Spider-Man" and "The Birth of Spider-Man" on pages 193–195 of the student book. Explain that the activities in this lesson are based on these articles.

Ready *Teacher Toolbox*   Teacher-Toolbox.com

	Prerequisite Skills	RI.6.9, W.6.2, W.6.9
Ready Lessons	✓	

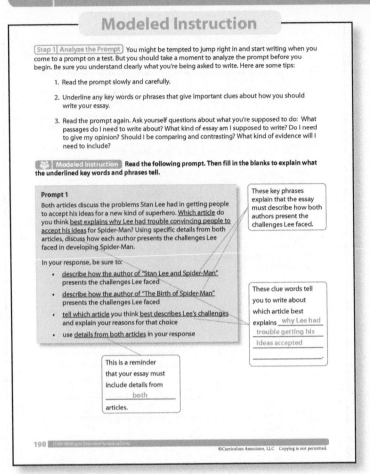

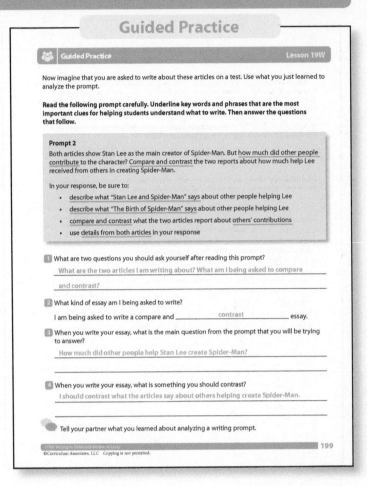

AT A GLANCE

Students learn techniques for analyzing a writing prompt. They identify key words and phrases in a prompt to determine what form their essay should take.

STEP BY STEP

- Tell students that the first step in writing a response to a test question is to carefully analyze the prompt.

- Ask a volunteer to read the information at the top of page 198. Discuss with students the three steps in analyzing a test prompt.

- Emphasize to students the importance of asking themselves basic questions about the prompt before they begin writing.

- Read aloud the activity directions. Model the process of analyzing a prompt by thinking aloud.

Think Aloud: When I read this prompt, the key phrase "Which article" tells me that I need to write an essay that compares the two articles. The next key phrase,

"best explains why Lee had trouble convincing people to accept his ideas," tells me that I will need to decide which article best explains the problem Lee faced.

- Continue modeling how to analyze the prompt. Have students record information to complete the sentences on page 198.

- Next, have students apply what they have learned by completing the **Guided Practice** activity.

Tip: Be sure students understand the key terms *compare* and *contrast*. Explain that when writers compare, they tell how things are alike. When they contrast, they tell how things are different.

- Support students' analysis of the prompt by asking questions that focus their attention on key words and phrases, for example: *Which words tell the type of writing students should do? Which words explain what the essay should compare?*

- Have students pair up to complete the activity at the bottom of the page.

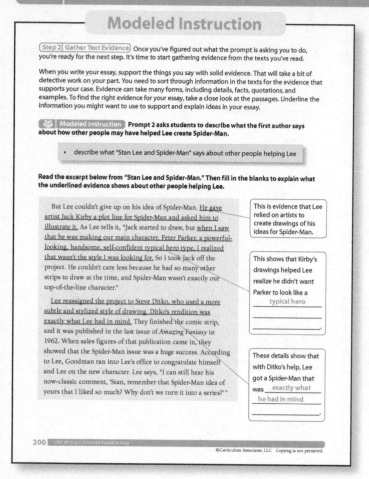

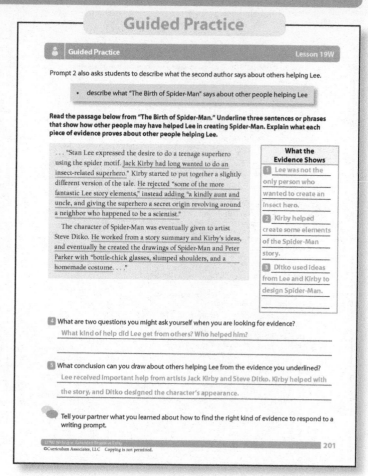

AT A GLANCE

Students practice identifying and analyzing text evidence that can be used to support ideas in a written response to a test prompt. They explore methods for selecting relevant evidence from an informative article.

STEP BY STEP

- Tell students that the next step in responding to a test prompt is gathering evidence from the passages they've read.

- Together, read the paragraphs at the top of page 200. Make sure that students understand that the types of evidence they might find in a passage can take several forms. These forms include facts, definitions, examples, and quotations. Ask volunteers to give examples of each kind of evidence noted in the instruction.

- Read aloud the activity directions. Model how to identify evidence in a passage by thinking aloud.

Think Aloud: To write a complete response to this prompt, I will need to describe what the author of "Stan Lee and Spider-Man" says about other people helping Lee. The sentence "He gave artist Jack Kirby a plot line for Spider-Man and asked him to illustrate it" tells me that Lee relied on artists to draw pictures of his ideas.

- Continue modeling how to evaluate the evidence by thinking aloud. Have students record details to complete the sentences on page 200. Discuss how each piece of underlined evidence relates to the prompt.

- Next, have students apply what they have learned by completing the **Guided Practice** activity.

- Before students begin looking for evidence in the passage from "The Birth of Spider-Man," Ask: *What kind of evidence will you look for? Why?*

- Have students pair up to complete the activity at the bottom of the page.

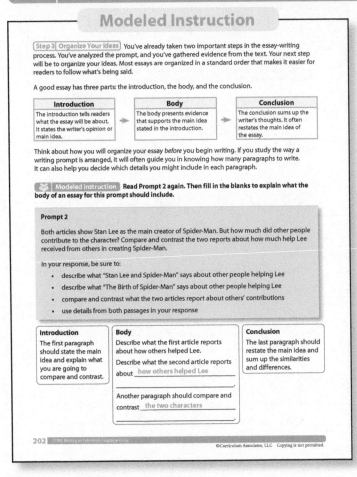

Modeled Instruction

Step 3 | Organize Your Ideas You've already taken two important steps in the essay-writing process. You've analyzed the prompt, and you've gathered evidence from the text. Your next step will be to organize your ideas. Most essays are organized in a standard order that makes it easier for readers to follow what's being said.

A good essay has three parts: the introduction, the body, and the conclusion.

Introduction	**Body**	**Conclusion**
The introduction tells readers what the essay will be about. It states the writer's opinion or main idea.	The body presents evidence that supports the main idea stated in the introduction.	The conclusion sums up the writer's thoughts. It often restates the main idea of the essay.

Think about how you will organize your essay *before* you begin writing. If you study the way a writing prompt is arranged, it will often guide you in knowing how many paragraphs to write. It can also help you decide which details you might include in each paragraph.

Modeled Instruction Read Prompt 2 again. Then fill in the blanks to explain what the body of an essay for this prompt should include.

Prompt 2

Both articles show Stan Lee as the main creator of Spider-Man. But how much did other people contribute to the character? Compare and contrast the two reports about how much help Lee received from others in creating Spider-Man.

In your response, be sure to:
- describe what "Stan Lee and Spider-Man" says about other people helping Lee
- describe what "The Birth of Spider-Man" says about other people helping Lee
- compare and contrast what the two articles report about others' contributions
- use details from both passages in your response

Introduction	**Body**	**Conclusion**
The first paragraph should state the main idea and explain what you are going to compare and contrast.	Describe what the first article reports about how others helped Lee. Describe what the second article reports about ___how others helped Lee___ Another paragraph should compare and contrast ___the two characters___	The last paragraph should restate the main idea and sum up the similarities and differences.

202 L19W: Writing an Extended-Response Essay ©Curriculum Associates, LLC Copying is not permitted.

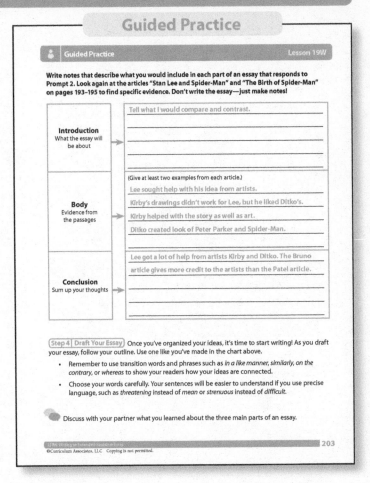

Guided Practice

Guided Practice Lesson 19W

Write notes that describe what you would include in each part of an essay that responds to Prompt 2. Look again at the articles "Stan Lee and Spider-Man" and "The Birth of Spider-Man" on pages 193–195 to find specific evidence. Don't write the essay—just make notes!

Introduction
What the essay will be about
→ Tell what I would compare and contrast.

Body
Evidence from the passages
(Give at least two examples from each article.)
→ Lee sought help with his idea from artists.
→ Kirby's drawings didn't work for Lee, but he liked Ditko's.
→ Kirby helped with the story as well as art.
→ Ditko created look of Peter Parker and Spider-Man.

Conclusion
Sum up your thoughts
→ Lee got a lot of help from artists Kirby and Ditko. The Bruno article gives more credit to the artists than the Patel article.

Step 4 | Draft Your Essay Once you've organized your ideas, it's time to start writing! As you draft your essay, follow your outline. Use one like you've made in the chart above.
- Remember to use transition words and phrases such as *in a like manner, similarly, on the contrary,* or *whereas* to show your readers how your ideas are connected.
- Choose your words carefully. Your sentences will be easier to understand if you use precise language, such as *threatening* instead of *mean* or *strenuous* instead of *difficult.*

Discuss with your partner what you learned about the three main parts of an essay.

L19W: Writing an Extended-Response Essay 203 ©Curriculum Associates, LLC Copying is not permitted.

AT A GLANCE

Students learn how ideas and evidence can be organized within a standard model to plan their essay.

STEP BY STEP

- Tell students that the next step in the process will be to organize their evidence into an effective plan.

- With the class, read the information at the top of page 202. Review the three main parts of an essay and discuss the purpose of each.

- Read aloud the activity directions. Use Think Alouds to model how the wording of a prompt can suggest a way to organize an essay that thoroughly responds to all aspects of the prompt.

Think Aloud: When reading a prompt, I look for details that tell me how I might organize my response. I ask myself: *How many paragraphs do I need to write to respond to the entire prompt? What information belongs in each paragraph?*

Think Aloud: The first part of the prompt says the essay should compare and contrast the two authors' reports about how much help Stan Lee received from others in creating Spider-Man. This clue tells me my introduction should explain what I am going to compare and contrast.

- Continue modeling, having students record details to complete the sentences on page 202.

- Next, have students apply what they have learned as they complete the **Guided Practice** activity. Ask volunteers to share which details they chose for each part of the essay and explain why.

- Finally, discuss what writers do as they draft. Be sure students understand that when they draft, they will turn their notes into complete sentences.

- Have students pair up to complete the activity at the bottom of the page.

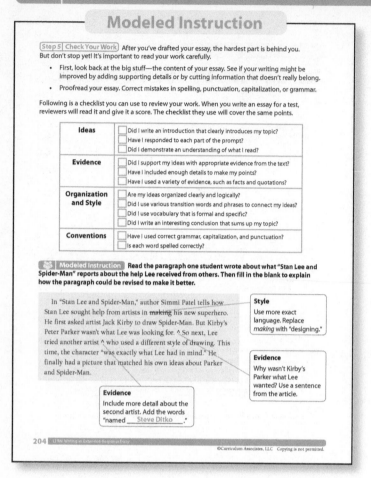

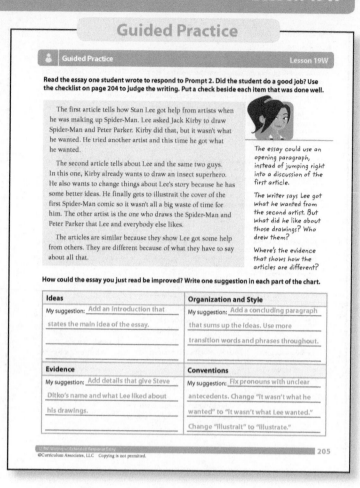

AT A GLANCE

Students are introduced to the specific criteria that will be used to score their test essays. They evaluate a sample response to a prompt and then suggest edits that will correct and improve the essay.

STEP BY STEP

- Discuss with students the importance of carefully and systematically checking their work after completing their draft. Tell students that a good method is to read their draft twice: once to review the overall content and make revisions, and a second time to check for mistakes in spelling, grammar, and mechanics.

Tip: Use the Language lessons on pages 239–274 to develop students' understanding of formal English grammar and mechanics.

- As a class, read the instruction at the top of page 204. Ask students to explain each item mentioned in the checklist in their own words.

- Read aloud the activity directions. Use Think Alouds to model evaluating a paragraph.

Think Aloud: The first thing I notice is that the word *making* is vague. I would change *making* to "designing" because that paints a much clearer picture for readers of what Lee was seeking help with, as described in the details of the article.

- Continue modeling how to assess the paragraph, having students complete the sentence on page 204.

- Next, have students apply what they have learned by completing the **Guided Practice** activity. Write the prompt from page 202 on the board so students can refer to it easily as they work.

Tip: Use the Study Buddy's comments to help students identify three ways the student essay could be improved. Then ask partners to discuss more ways to make the essay stronger.

AT A GLANCE

Students evaluate a single paragraph from the student essay they have been reviewing. They rewrite and revise the text to more clearly and completely respond to elements in the prompt.

STEP BY STEP

- Together, read the activity directions and sample paragraph.

- Ask students to revise the paragraph using the various techniques for responding to a prompt that they have learned earlier in the lesson.

- Point out that the student essay on the previous page did not have a conclusion. Explain that students will write a paragraph that addresses the bullet points from the prompt, *not* a concluding paragraph.

- After students have paired up to discuss their rewrites, ask several volunteers to share their revised paragraphs, as well as some of the reasons behind their changes, with the class.

> **Tip:** Remind students that extended-response essays are evaluated using a checklist similar to the one on page 204 of the student book. A thorough, honest, point-by-point review of their essay will help them achieve their best score on a test. Have students refer to the checklist as you discuss the essay.

ANSWER ANALYSIS

Sample response:

The articles are similar in discussing the help Lee got from the two artists. But they differ in describing how important that help was to Lee. In the Patel article, Kirby's drawings just showed Lee what he didn't want, while Ditko's drawings aren't really described at all. In contrast, Bruno's article gives Kirby and Ditko far more credit. He tells how Kirby helped with story ideas as well as art, and he describes how Ditko created Spider-Man's famous look of "human frailty."

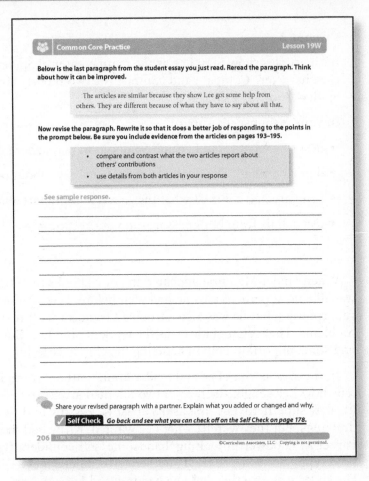

WRITING ACTIVITY

- Photocopy or project the essay on page 188 of the teacher resource book.

- Explain to students that it is an example of a four-point response to Prompt 2. Say that you will review the essay together to understand what makes it a four-point response.

- Remind students that they already analyzed Prompt 2 on page 199. They determined that the prompt requires a compare and contrast essay that explains how others helped Stan Lee create Spider-Man and describes how the two articles differ on this point.

- Use the essay to review the essential points of the lesson, including text evidence, organization, drafting, and proofreading. Use the comments provided with the essay to generate discussion.

- Ask students to compare the essay to the checklist on page 204. Point out how each point of the checklist is fulfilled by examples in the text.

- Encourage students to think about other ways the writer could have addressed the prompt.

Prompt 2

Both articles show Stan Lee as the main creator of Spider-Man. But how much did other people contribute to the character? Compare and contrast the two reports about how much help Lee received from others in creating Spider-Man.

In your response, be sure to:

- describe what "Stan Lee and Spider-Man" says about other people helping Lee
- describe what "The Birth of Spider-Man" says about other people helping Lee
- compare and contrast what the two articles report about others' contributions
- use details from both passages in your response

When Spider-Man first appeared in comic books in 1962, he was like no superhero anyone had seen before. Peter Parker had superpowers, but he was also a troubled teenager with real life problems. That original idea was the work of Stan Lee. But Lee had some important help in bringing his character to life.

In the article "Stan Lee and Spider Man," author Simmi Patel tells how Lee sought the help of two talented artists in developing his new superhero. Lee first asked artist Jack Kirby to do some drawings, but they weren't what Lee wanted. Kirby had drawn Parker as "a powerful-looking, handsome, self-confident typical hero type." So next Lee tried another artist named Steve Ditko. His style "was exactly what Lee had in mind."

In the article "The Birth of Spider-Man," author Max Bruno describes how Kirby "wanted to draw an insect-related superhero" even before Lee approached him. Kirby also helped develop the story, including the idea of giving Parker "a kindly aunt and uncle." While Kirby drew the first Spider-Man cover, it was Ditko who created the look that "readers came to know and love." Ditko drew Spider-Man with "a homemade costume" and Parker as a teenager with "bottle thick glasses" and "slumped shoulders."

The articles are similar in discussing the help Lee got from the two artists. But they differ in describing how important that help was to Lee. In the Patel article, Kirby's drawings just showed Lee what he didn't want, while Ditko's drawings aren't really described at all. In contrast, Bruno's article gives Kirby and Ditko far more credit. He tells how Kirby helped with story ideas as well as art, and he describes how Ditko created Spider-Man's famous look of "human frailty."

In conclusion, both articles describe a team effort behind the creation of Spider-Man. But however much help Lee got from others, he was still the one with the idea for a "new kind of superhero." Fifty years later, people still enjoy Spider-Man. The story of a super-human hero with human problems never gets old.

The essay has a clear introduction. It tells readers that the essay will be about the creation of Spider-Man, and about how Stan Lee got important help from others in developing his famous character.

The prompt asks what the first article says about other people helping Lee. The paragraph provides evidence in the form of details from the article, including names, events, and quotations.

This paragraph responds to the part of the prompt that asks what the second article says about people helping Lee. It presents ideas in a logical order that follows the text, and it supports those ideas with a variety of evidence.

In this paragraph, the writer compares and contrasts the two articles, using details from both articles. This directly addresses the third and fourth bulleted points of the prompt.

Transition words and phrases such as *while*, *but*, *first*, *so*, *next*, and *in contrast* are used throughout to help connect ideas.

The conclusion sums up the information in the essay and adds some of the writer's own thoughts about the topic.

SCORING GUIDE AND ANSWER ANALYSIS

Informational Passage Answer Analysis

1 Ⓐ Ⓑ Ⓒ ●   3 Ⓐ ● Ⓒ Ⓓ

2 Ⓐ ● Ⓒ Ⓓ   4 Ⓐ Ⓑ Ⓒ ●

1 Choice D is correct. The inability of farmers to earn much money under the state system is evidence that the rural farm collectives were not managed well during the Cultural Revolution.

Choice A is incorrect. This statement simply refers to the Five-Year Plans and does not show whether collectives were managed well or poorly. Choice B refers to the time before the Cultural Revolution and offers no evidence about the management of the farm collectives. Choice C is incorrect because the statement about how private land became collectivized does not offer any evidence about the management of the collectives during the Cultural Revolution. *(RI.6.8; DOK 2)*

2 Choice B is correct. The author states that Mao and his followers benefited politically from keeping the upper classes down, but does not provide sufficient evidence for this claim.

Choice A is incorrect. This statement is supported by details explaining how those who owned or managed property often were blamed and victimized during the Cultural Revolution. Choice C is incorrect. This statement about improving China by sweeping out the old ways is supported by the explanation of the fourolds and why they were dismissed. Choice D is incorrect. The statement that the Chinese had gained a voice and some power is supported by details about collectives, local government, and education. *(RI.6.8; DOK 3)*

3 Choice B is correct. The fact that some peasants successfully broke away from the feudal system to work for their own gain is evidence that the feudal system might have ended even without the Cultural Revolution.

Choice A is incorrect. The fact that the peasants had to pay rent, taxes, and fines before the Cultural Revolution might lead some students to think that the peasants rebelled against the system, but that is not stated in the text. Choice C is incorrect. The fact that millions of agricultural workers lived in poverty does not suggest that the feudal system might have ended even without the Cultural Revolution. Choice D is incorrect. The fact that most rural peasants worked for a wealthy landowner is not evidence that the feudal system might have ended even without the Cultural Revolution. Rather, the evidence is that some peasants successfully broke away from the feudal system to work for their own gain. *(RI.6.8; DOK 2)*

4 Choice D is correct. During the Cultural Revolution, anything that represented the fourolds was forbidden, so the family had to destroy many of the family photographs.

Choice A is incorrect. The Red Guard frowns on anything that depicts a fourold, which is why Mom and Dad have to destroy some of their pictures. This had nothing to do with the Five-Year Plans. Choice B is incorrect. Families are not allowed to keep photos revealing class privilege. It's not about showing photos to others. Choice C is incorrect. Wearing wool is not fourold, so this answer is incorrect. Photos that represent something related to the past are dangerous to keep, so the family has to destroy some of their pictures. *(RI.6.8; DOK 3)*

SAMPLE RESPONSES

Short Response (See 2-Point Rubric—Short Response on page A46 for scoring.)

5 **Part A:** Students select the second choice, "Chairman Mao's Cultural Revolution drastically changed the lives of the Chinese people." The first choice tells Mao's intention for the Five-Year Plans, but the article provides much evidence that the Chinese people suffered under them. The third choice tells one of Mao's beliefs, but the article does not show that Mao proved that belief. *(RI.6.9; DOK 3)*

Part B: Choices of sentences will vary. Possible first sentence: "A farming family could own the land it worked, and education became available to the masses." Possible second sentence: "No longer did the people engage in civil wars as there were no more rival kingdoms to defend." *(RI.6.9; DOK 3)*

6 The Communist Party did not want people wearing clothing that was expensive and fancy. The new leaders also did not want anyone to wear old-fashioned clothing from before the Cultural Revolution. Anything that suggested wealth or the old way of life was frowned on. Everyone was supposed to be a worker of some kind, so clothing should make everyone look equal. *(RI.6.9; DOK 3)*

7 The author of *Red Scarf Girl* would agree with the statement that "Mao's Red Guards led a reign of terror" because she lived in a city where the Red Guards were always looking for signs that a family was wealthy or comfortable. Because her own family had nice possessions, they would have been targets of the Red Guards. These guards scared people into doing things like burning precious photographs and other objects. *(RI.6.9; DOK 3)*

Performance Task (See New York State Grade 6–8 Expository Writing Evaluation Rubric on pages A47 and A48 for scoring.)

8 Although I don't think the two authors would completely disagree with one another, there are definitely two different points of view in these passages. To begin with, the author of "China's Cultural Revolution" gives a more balanced view of what happened in that country from 1966 to 1976. That is because one writer lived through the events as a child and saw things from her own point of view, while the other person is writing based on what he has learned from history.

Joseph Vitale describes the good and the bad of the years when Mao was China's leader. He knows that the peasants had suffered from poverty and lack of education for centuries. After the Cultural Revolution began, although there were big problems with the farming collectives, gradually life improved for the peasants. From what she reveals about her home, Ji-Li Jiang was a child from an educated city family that was well off. It seems strange to her that the Red Guards would threaten people who were not doing any harm. She doesn't say anything about the poor people in the country, and she doesn't know why her family is considered an enemy.

The author of "China's Cultural Revolution" has the big picture about what happened during those years. There was violence and starvation, but there were also improvements in society. Ji-Li Jiang would not have known that as a young girl. Only the author of the nonfiction article could understand that Mao turned China into a global power with people who were better educated and who lived better lives in many cases. *(RI.6.9; DOK 3)*

Integrating Information

LESSON OBJECTIVES

- Understand different kinds of media formats and the unique benefits of each for delivering information.

- Integrate information from different media formats to develop an understanding of a topic or subject.

THE LEARNING PROGRESSION

Grade 5: CCLS RI.5.7 requires students to use print or digital sources to find "an answer to a question quickly or to solve a problem efficiently."

Grade 6: CCLS RI.6.7 builds on the Grade 5 standard by requiring students to combine information from different media formats to "develop a coherent understanding of a topic or issue." This helps prepare students for the analysis required at Grade 7.

Grade 7: CCLS RI.7.7 requires students to compare and contrast text to various media versions of the text, "analyzing each medium's portrayal of the subject."

TAP STUDENTS' PRIOR KNOWLEDGE

- Do an informal survey of the sources students use most to look up information, listing each one on the board and keeping track of the number of students who use each one. Odds are the Internet will be the overwhelming favorite.

- Point out one reason for the popularity of the Internet: you can quickly access a number of sources and find material in a variety of formats (print, video, images, and visual aids such as charts and graphs).

- Discuss the strength of sources outside of the Internet—books, magazines, documentaries, etc. (Books can be more reliable and provide information in more depth. Also, someone else has already sifted through information, chosen what he or she feels is most relevant, and organized it in a logical order.)

- Now ask students what their biggest problems are when they gather information from a variety of sources. (It can be hard to pick out and organize information.)

- Tell students they will look at four types of media formats used to deliver information—print, images, visual aids, and video—and learn the characteristics and benefits of each. They will also have an opportunity to practice integrating, or pulling together, information from numerous sources.

Ready *Teacher Toolbox*

teacher-toolbox.com

	Prerequisite Skills	RI.6.7
Ready Lessons	✓	✓
Tools for Instruction		
Interactive Tutorials		

CCLS Focus

RI.6.7 Integrate information presented in different media or formats (e.g. visually, quantitatively) as well as in words to develop a coherent understanding of a topic or issue.

ADDITIONAL STANDARDS: **W.6.2, W.6.7; SL.6.2**

AT A GLANCE

By examining different types of media formats, students will learn how to integrate information from different sources to develop a comprehensive understanding of a topic or issue.

STEP BY STEP: PAGE 215

- Ask students for examples of topics they've been interested in and wanted to learn more about, such as pets, sports teams, movies, or stories in the news. Have volunteers describe the process they went through to investigate the topic.

- Have a volunteer read the introduction on page 215 aloud to the class. Point out that today we have an almost infinite amount of information that we can access within seconds via the Internet, but that books, television, and magazines add even more possibilities. No matter what the source, though, they'll usually find information delivered in one of a few basic formats: as print, through images, through visual aids such as charts, graphs, and maps; and in videos or multimedia presentations.

- Read the lines above the chart on page 215. Be sure students understand what they will be looking at in the chart: different types of media, with varied ways of arranging or presenting information.

- **Print:** Ask students to offer more specific examples of where they find print information, e.g. newspapers, textbooks, or encyclopedias. Point out that printed information from reliable sources has usually undergone detailed fact-checking, which helps assure the accuracy of the information. This is true of many online sources, but many of those are less reliable.

- **Images:** Ask students how pictures and images help them when they read. Ask how the picture in the chart is more helpful than this definition of a leopard gecko: "a nocturnal, ground-dwelling lizard, about 8–10 inches in length, with bumpy skin." Point out that captions and labels provide additional information.

- **Visual Aids:** Confirm that students understand the visual aids listed in this section.

Chart: information usually presented in the form of a table—boxes in columns and rows

Graph: a drawing showing the relationship between two different sets of variables

Map: a labeled picture of an area of land

Diagram: simplified drawings with labels

- **Videos and Multimedia:** Point out that newscasts, TV documentaries, online videos, and multimedia presentations can bring the information we seek to life by showing us the subject or event. For example, seeing a video of a tsunami quickly tells us more about how the water floods the land than reading a description of it would.

- **Discussion:** Have small groups brainstorm questions about what they would want to know before deciding whether or not a gecko would make a good pet, and then discuss how students can use each medium to research what they need.

STEP BY STEP: PAGE 216

- Tell students that they are going to look at examples of information in three of the media formats they just learned about. They will need to integrate, or pull together and analyze, important information from each source to thoroughly understand what's involved in having a gecko as a pet.

- Read aloud the directions above the examples on page 216. Point out that students will have to separate information about the care of geckos from other interesting facts. Remind them to consider both time and expense to decide how hard it is to care for a gecko. Following are the details they might underline or circle in each box.

- **Chart:** details about diet and habitat

- **Diagram:** thermometers, light, heaters

- **Book Excerpt:** Students should circle the information about temperature, the hot and cool zones, the live food, and need to provide water and spray daily.

- **Discussion:** Have students use their annotations to make notes about what they need to create a gecko habitat. Remind them to consider facts that are the same in each source as they organize and summarize the key information. Then have them discuss whether or not they would want a leopard gecko for a pet, and how the information from the sources on page 216 might impact their answer to this question.

PICTURE THIS *(RI.6.7; W.6.7)*

After directing students to an image-specific site or search engine (like Shutterstock.com or Google Images), have them choose one of the following unusual animals and learn as much as they can about it only by searching for and looking at pictures and diagrams, along with any accompanying captions:

- blobfish
- giant coconut crab
- okapi
- aye-aye
- leafy sea dragon
- star-nosed mole
- narwhal
- helmeted hornbill

Once students have completed the activity, ask them what else they would like to learn about the creature. Have them put together a list of questions and see if they can find the answers using additional sources. Then have them integrate the information and present their findings to the rest of the class.

CHARTS, GRAPHS, AND MAPS *(SL.6.2)*

Students may not be aware of how many charts, graphs, diagrams, and other visual aids they see on a daily basis. Challenge them to find one example of each in something they would see at home or at school. To get them started, brainstorm together places to look: newspapers, assembly directions, user manuals, labels, etc. Have them display their findings in small groups, and then ask them to choose one of the samples they brought in to explain it to the others.

SITE EXPLORATION *(RI.6.7)*

Provide students with a list of safe, engaging and interesting sites; for example, the student sections of the following:

NASA

How Stuff Works

Adler Planetarium (Chicago)

The Smithsonian

The Exploratorium (San Francisco)

National Geographic Kids

NGA Kids (National Gallery of Art)

Have them explore the sites in groups of two or three, noting the different kinds of information available on each one and the formats that the information is presented in. Ask them to create a "highlights" tour for their chosen sites, and have them take turns walking other students through the site and showing them the variety of information available and the formats that are used to convey it.

NEWS SHOW RESEARCHER *(W.6.2)*

- Tell students they will be putting together notes, talking points, and image suggestions to help prepare the host of a popular news show for a feature. As researchers, students will gather as much information as possible on the latest app or groundbreaking new technology, a popular music group, or the latest fad or fashion trend.

- Students should research the topic thoroughly using print, images, graphic aids, and a video from a variety of sources. Have them use the copymaster on page 194 to record and organize their notes. Their summary must cite the sources they used.

- In small groups, ask them to discuss the benefits and drawbacks of the various sources. If they could choose only one, which would they select?

DREAM TRIP *(W.6.7)*

- Tell students to imagine they have won a contest and have three days to get ready for a week-long trip to any place in the United States.

- Challenge them to do the research that will tell them:

  - how to dress (a weather site would help)

  - what to see and do (suggest a travel guide)

  - where to stay (suggest they use a map to identify the best location)

- When they are done with their research, ask them to summarize what they've found in a travel plan.

Name_____ Date_____

DIRECTIONS: Write down a question or topic you'd like to explore in depth. Pull information from different media and different formats, and use the chart to organize the information according to type. Make your notes specific and detailed. When you are done, summarize the information in 2 to 3 paragraphs.

Topic: _____

Print	Images and Visual Aids	Video

Summary:

Comparing and Contrasting Genres

LESSON OBJECTIVES

- Identify similar themes and topics in different genres.

- Compare and contrast the authors' approaches to those themes and topics.

THE LEARNING PROGRESSION

- **Grade 5:** CCLS RL.5.9 has students focus on comparing the theme and topic of stories in the same genre.

- **Grade 6: CCLS RL.6.9 changes to cover comparing and contrasting the theme and topic in different genres and forms.**

- **Grade 7:** CCLS RL.7.9 moves away from theme, and students need to compare and contrast a fictional portrayal of a time, place, or character with a historical account of the same period.

PREREQUISITE SKILLS

- Understand that stories in the same genre can develop similar themes and topics in different ways.

- Identify the themes and topics in stories of the same genre.

- Compare and contrast how similar elements are treated in stories from the same genre.

TAP STUDENTS' PRIOR KNOWLEDGE

- Tell students that they will work on a lesson about comparing and contrasting genres. Explain that genre is a specific category of literature, such as poetry, drama, fantasy, or historical fiction.

- Students may have read both a biography and a historical fiction story about the same person. Identify these as two different types of genres.

- Ask students how the two stories are alike. (*They are both about the same person.*) Next, ask how the two stories are different. (*One is a biography that contains facts about a person's life. The other is a fiction story based on real events in history.*)

- Next, discuss the theme of a text as its larger message. Ask students to identify the themes of the fables "The Tortoise and the Hare" (*slow and steady wins the race*) and "The Boy Who Cried Wolf" (*no one believes a liar, even when he tells the truth*).

- Tell students that texts in different genres may have a common theme or similar themes. Tell students that recognizing the genre an author chooses can help them to better understand the theme of the text.

Ready *Teacher Toolbox*   *teacher-toolbox.com*

	Prerequisite Skills	*RL.6.9*
Ready Lessons	✓	✓
Tools for Instruction	✓ ✓	
Interactive Tutorials		✓

CCLS Focus

RL.6.9 Compare and contrast texts in different genres (e.g., stories and poems, historical novels and fantasy) in terms of their approaches to similar themes and topics.

ADDITIONAL STANDARDS: **RL.6.1, RL.6.2, RL.6.3, RL.6.4, RL.6.5, RL.6.6, RL.6.7, RL.6.11.a; W.6.2; SL.6.1; L.6.1, L.6.2.b, L.6.4.a, L.6.4.c, L.6.5.a** (*See page A39 for full text.*)

AT A GLANCE

By studying two illustrations, students learn how stories with different elements, such as settings and characters, can share a similar theme.

STEP BY STEP

- Read the first paragraph, which includes the definition of *genre*. Then have students study the illustrations and think about each scene's storyline. Have students look for similarities and differences in both the text and the pictures.

- Explain that the Venn diagram shows how the scenes are alike and different. Point out the headings in the left and right ovals: Story 1 and Story 2. Have students write the types of stories in these sections.

- Point out the intersection of the ovals labeled "Both." Tell students to complete this part of the diagram.

- Discuss how both stories have a similar theme, or larger message, even though the characters and settings differ.

- Ask students to share other stories they have read that had a similar theme. Students may mention a real-life story in a newspaper article or a novel.

- Provide an example of when you have identified a story's theme and connected it to a similar theme in a different story.

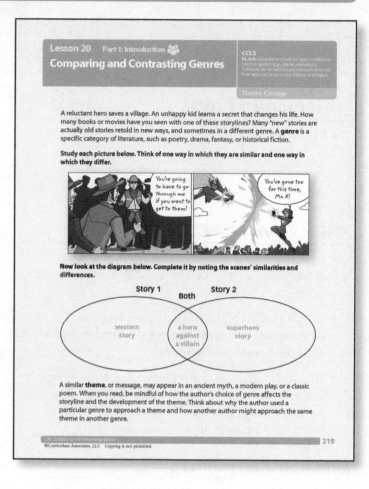

Genre Focus

Literary Texts: Fantasy

Tell students that in this lesson they will read a type of literature called fantasy. A fantasy is a fiction story with at least some characters and at least part of a setting that are not found in the real world.

A fantasy may include the following elements:

- Characters may be people, non-human creatures, talking animals, or objects that come alive.

- The setting may be a real place and time or an imaginary one.

- The plot events may be exaggerated or feature things that could not really happen to make them more dramatic.

Based on these characteristics, ask students to name fantasies they have read. Were they set in the real world or an imaginary place such as Middle Earth? What were they about? Were the characters human? Students may mention fantasy novels such as *The Lightning Thief* or *Artemis Fowl*.

Explain that "Ogel's Tear" is a fantasy story about children who are transported from the real world to the world of a comic book. This story expresses the idea that it takes courage to see past a monstrous appearance. Discuss the way that fantasy can use unusual characters and situations to make observations that apply to the real world.

AT A GLANCE

Students read a lyric poem. They identify the poem's topic and theme in preparation for comparing and contrasting the poem with a short story that has a similar topic and related theme.

STEP BY STEP

- Invite volunteers to tell what they learned on the prior page about comparing and contrasting genres.

- Tell students that they will learn how to identify the topic and theme in another type of genre, poetry.

- Read aloud the poem "To Fight Aloud Is Very Brave."

- Then read the question: "What are the topic and the theme of this poem?"

- Tell students you will use a Think Aloud to demonstrate a way of answering the questions.

Think Aloud: I can identify the topic and theme of the poem. Then I'll be able to compare and contrast the poem's theme with the theme of a text in another genre.

- Direct students to the diagram. Review that it can be used to show how two passages from different genres are alike and different.

Think Aloud: I see that the left circle in the diagram labeled "Poem" is where I can put information about the poem's topic and theme. Based on the title and the word *brave* in the first line, I think this poem's topic is bravery.

- Point out the topic in the left circle of the diagram. Have students look for other details that suggest this poem is about bravery.

Think Aloud: I notice that the poem compares the courage to face our daily struggles with the valor shown by soldiers at war. In the first stanza, the speaker notes that fighting battles against sorrow in our hearts requires more courage than it takes to "fight aloud." I think this is the main theme of the poem.

- Direct students again to the diagram's left circle and read the theme: "It takes more courage to struggle without glory." Have students connect this theme with specific words in the poem.

- Finally, tell students that they can use the diagram to compare and contrast the genre, topic, and theme of the poem to that of another text.

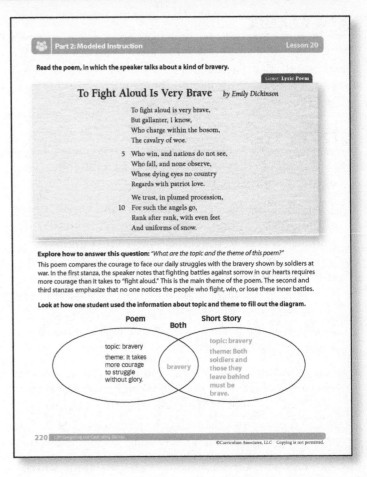

Tier Two Vocabulary: *Gallanter*

- Read the first stanza of the poem. Tell students that they can first look for context clues in nearby words and phrases that might help them figure out the meaning of *gallanter*.

- If there are no context clues, tell students they can try to take apart the word to understand its meaning. Point out the affix *-er*. Explain that it signifies a comparative adjective. Ask students what the root word is. (*gallant*)

- Have students use a dictionary to find the meaning of *gallant*. ("*brave, courageous*") Then ask students to identify the meaning of *gallanter*. ("*braver, more courageous*") **(RL.6.4; L.6.4.c)**

AT A GLANCE

Students read a short story and answer an open-ended question to identify the story's topic. They compare and contrast the story's topic and theme with those of the poem they read earlier.

STEP BY STEP

- Tell students they will read a text in a different genre, a realistic fiction story.

- Close Reading has students find a similarity between the short story and the poem. Identifying similarities and differences in different types of text prepares students for comparing and contrasting texts in different genres in terms of their approaches to similar themes and topics. The Hint focuses students on the way the story handles the topic of bravery. Students identify specific dialogue and actions that illustrate the characters' show of bravery.

- Have students read the text and underline a phrase that shows how Tasha is like the speaker in the poem, as directed by the Close Reading. If necessary, ask: "What comparison did the speaker in the poem make? How does Tasha make a similar comparison?"

- Ask volunteers to share the phrase they underlined.

- Have students answer the question, using the Hint to help them. Then have students use their answer to the question, as well as their underlined text, to complete the diagram on the previous page.

- Have students refer to their completed diagrams to answer Show Your Thinking. Students can use their diagrams as a basis for their partner discussions.

ANSWER ANALYSIS

Sample response: Tasha's dad shows bravery by speaking about his responsibility to protect the country, as well as Tasha's responsibility to be strong and brave at home. Tasha shows her bravery by holding back her tears and not showing her fear.

ERROR ALERT: Students who did not identify the common topic of the texts as "bravery" might not have understood the difference between a topic and a theme. Reinforce that the topic is the subject of the text and the theme is the text's larger message.

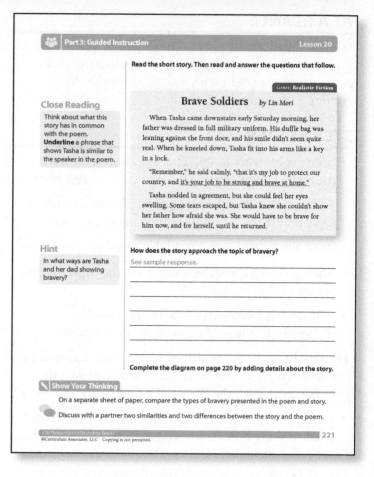

ELL Support: Regular Past Tense

- Tell students that a verb is an action word. The past tense of a verb tells that the action has already happened.

- Point out the word *kneeled* in paragraph 1. Explain that it is the past tense of the verb *kneel*. The past tense of a regular verb ends in *-ed*. Point out that the past tense *kneeled* means that the action of kneeling is finished. Identify the verb as *kneel* and the ending as *-ed*.

- Have students locate other past-tense verbs in this passage and explain how the past tense of each is formed. *(nod: add -ded; escape: add -d; return: add -ed)* **(L.6.1)**

AT A GLANCE

Students twice read a historical fiction story. After the first reading, you will ask three questions to check your students' comprehension of the passage.

STEP BY STEP

- Have students read the passage silently without referring to the Study Buddy or Close Reading text.

- Ask the following questions to ensure students' comprehension of the text:

  Who are Chief Joseph, White Feather, and Lean Elk? *(They are leaders of the Nez Perce tribe.)*

  Why did the soldiers build a fort in the canyon? *(They wanted to protect the settlers from the Nez Perce tribe.)*

  How was a battle between the Nez Perce tribe and the soldiers avoided? *(Chief Joseph led the tribe to climb up the mountain and through a ridge above the fort in order to get to the valley, instead of going through the canyon where the fort was located.)*

- Ask students to look at the Study Buddy think aloud. What does the Study Buddy help them think about?

Tip: The Study Buddy prompts students to think about the story's theme. Thinking about the theme prepares students for comparing and contrasting the theme of this historical fiction story with the theme of the text in the fantasy genre that follows.

- Have students reread the passage. Tell them to follow the directions in the Close Reading.

Tip: The Close Reading has students identify phrases that describe Chief Joseph's character, as well as words that show how the author approaches the topic of courage. Recognizing character traits and a story's topic sets the stage for students to be able to compare and contrast texts in two different genres.

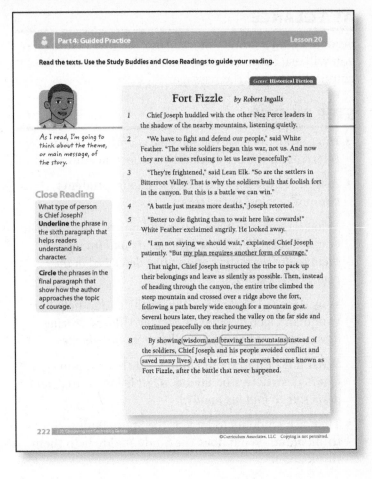

Tier Two Vocabulary: *Fizzle*

- Point out the word *fizzle* in the title and paragraph 8. Read the sentence: "And the fort in the canyon became known as Fort Fizzle, after the battle that never happened." Tell students that context clues are sometimes given in supporting phrases and that they can use these clues to help them figure out the meaning of *fizzle*.

- Have students identify the phrase that explains why the fort was named Fort Fizzle. *("after the battle that never happened")* Have students complete the following sentence: "If something does not happen, it _____." *(fizzles)*

- Ask students what *fizzle* means. *("fail to happen")* **(RL.6.4; L.6.4.a)**

AT A GLANCE

Students read a fantasy story. After the first reading, you will ask three questions to check your students' comprehension of the passage.

STEP BY STEP

- Have students read the passage silently without referring to the Study Buddy or Close Reading text.

- Ask the following questions to ensure students' comprehension of the text:

  What happens to Kate, Eli, and Juan as they read the comic book? (*A flash of light occurs and transports them to the characters and setting described in the comic book's story.*)

  Why does Gilda the Great want the trio to help her vanquish Ogel? (*Ogel is destroying villages, tearing down trees, and scaring families from their homes.*)

  What does Eli find out about Ogel that explains Ogel's destructive behavior? (*Ogel is lost, scared, and desperate to find his family.*)

- Then ask students to look at the Study Buddy think aloud. What does the Study Buddy help them think about?

Tip: The Study Buddy identifies the genre for students as fantasy and has them focus on events in the story that relate to the topic of courage. Recall that courage was the topic in the historical fiction story students just read. Students will then be able to link together in their own minds the common topic that the two stories share.

- Have students reread the passage. Tell them to follow the directions in Close Reading.

Tip: Close Reading has students identify a character trait that the fantasy character Eli shares with the historical fiction character Chief Joseph. Prompting students to think about the endings of both stories sets students up for comparing and contrasting ways that the character trait of courage can be displayed by fictional characters.

- Finally, have students answer the questions on page 224. Use the Answer Analysis to discuss correct and incorrect responses.

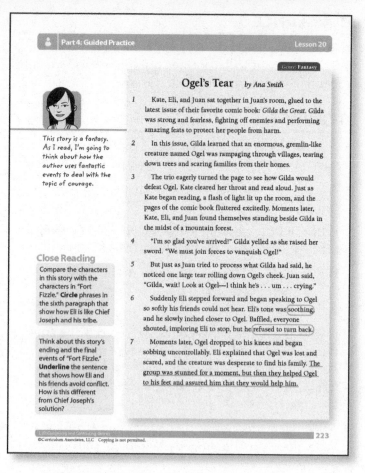

ELL Support: Multiple-Meaning Words

- Explain to students that words that have more than one meaning are called multiple-meaning words. Tell students that they can use other words or phrases in a sentence to help them know which meaning of a multiple-meaning word is being used.

- Direct students to the word *glued* in the first sentence. Discuss two meanings of *glued*: "pasted" and "gripped by."

- Ask students whether the friends are enjoying the comic book. (*yes*) Ask what clue word tells them this. (*favorite*) Then have students determine which meaning of *glued* makes sense in this context. (*"gripped by"*)

- Repeat for the words *issue* ("*edition of a magazine; matter at hand*") and *stun* ("*knock out; astound, astonish*"). **(RL.6.4; L.6.4.a)**

STEP BY STEP

• Have students read questions 1–3, using the Hints to help them answer those questions.

Tip: If students have trouble answering question 3, remind them that they can look back at the text they marked in both stories. These parts of both texts tell about courage, as well as describe how the conflict is resolved at the end of each story.

• Discuss with students the Answer Analysis below.

ANSWER ANALYSIS

1 The correct choice is A. Chief Joseph braved "the mountains instead of the soldiers." Eli refuses to turn back when approaching Ogel. Choice B is incorrect. The characters do not hide. Choice C is incorrect. Both characters understand the enemy, but their bravery comes from taking action. Choice D is incorrect. Neither character acts cowardly.

2 The correct choice is D. Chief Joseph and Eli both show bravery and kindness. Choice A is incorrect. Neither character is obedient or shy. Chief Joseph is outspoken. Eli is confident. Choice B is incorrect. Neither Chief Joseph nor Eli displays character traits of loyalty or honesty. Choice C is incorrect. Both Chief Joseph and Eli show intelligence, but neither displays a sense of humor.

3 Sample response: Both stories show a battle that the heroes cannot win, and both show that it takes bravery to avoid a fight. "Fort Fizzle" shows that walking away from a conflict is a courageous solution. "Ogel's Tear" shows that another way to solve problems is to make peace with an enemy.

RETEACHING

Use a chart to answer question 3. Draw the chart below, and have students fill in the boxes. Sample responses are provided.

"Fort Fizzle"	Both	"Ogel's Tear"
Resolution: Chief Joseph shows courage by avoiding a battle with the soldiers.	Approach to the topic: Non-violent solutions	Resolution: Eli shows courage by approaching and comforting Ogel.

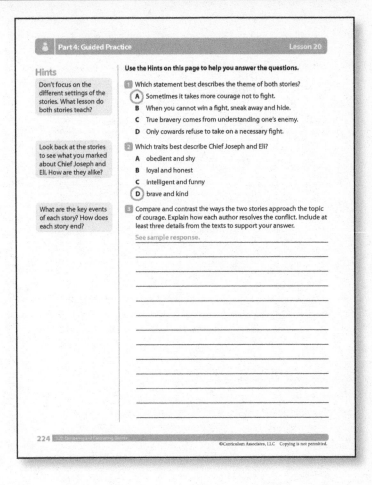

Integrating Standards

Use these questions to further students' understanding of "Fort Fizzle" and "Ogel's Tear."

1 How does paragraph 2 in "Fort Fizzle" fit into the story's structure and contribute to the development of the story's theme? *(RL.6.6)*

Sample response: White Feather's dialogue explains the conflict between the Nez Perce tribe and the settlers. By showing that a fight is imminent, it contributes to the theme of how courage can be displayed by avoiding conflict.

2 What impact does the phrase "slowly inched closer" have on the meaning and tone in "Ogel's Tear"? *(RL.6.4)*

"Slowly inched closer" shows how Eli approached Ogel, bit by bit, at a steady pace. It sets a mood of quiet anticipation.

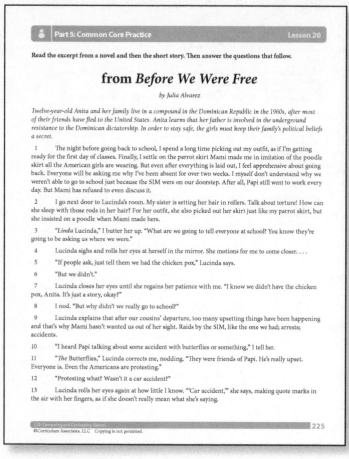

Read the excerpt from a novel and then the short story. Then answer the questions that follow.

from *Before We Were Free*

by Julia Alvarez

Twelve-year-old Anita and her family live in a compound in the Dominican Republic in the 1960s, after most of their friends have fled to the United States. Anita learns that her father is involved in the underground resistance to the Dominican dictatorship. In order to stay safe, the girls must keep their family's political beliefs a secret.

1 The night before going back to school, I spend a long time picking out my outfit, as if I'm getting ready for the first day of classes. Finally, I settle on the parrot skirt Mami made me in imitation of the poodle skirt all the American girls are wearing. But even after everything is laid out, I feel apprehensive about going back. Everyone will be asking me why I've been absent for over two weeks. I myself don't understand why we weren't able to go to school just because the SIM were on our doorstep. After all, Papi still went to work every day. But Mami has refused to even discuss it.

2 I go next door to Lucinda's room. My sister is setting her hair in rollers. Talk about torture! How can she sleep with those rods in her hair? For her outfit, she also picked out her skirt just like my parrot skirt, but she insisted on a poodle when Mami made hers.

3 "*Linda* Lucinda," I butter her up. "What are we going to tell everyone at school? You know they're going to be asking us where we were."

4 Lucinda sighs and rolls her eyes at herself in the mirror. She motions for me to come closer. . . .

5 "If people ask, just tell them we had the chicken pox," Lucinda says.

6 "But we didn't."

7 Lucinda closes her eyes until she regains her patience with me. "I know we didn't have the chicken pox, Anita. It's just a story, okay?"

8 I nod. "But why didn't we really go to school?"

9 Lucinda explains that after our cousins' departure, too many upsetting things have been happening and that's why Mami hasn't wanted us out of her sight. Raids by the SIM, like the one we had; arrests; accidents.

10 "I heard Papi talking about some accident with butterflies or something," I tell her.

11 "*The* Butterflies," Lucinda corrects me, nodding. "They were friends of Papi's. He's really upset. Everyone is. Even the Americans are protesting."

12 "Protesting what? Wasn't it a car accident?"

13 Lucinda rolls her eyes again at how little I know. "'Car accident,'" she says, making quote marks in the air with her fingers, as if she doesn't really mean what she's saying.

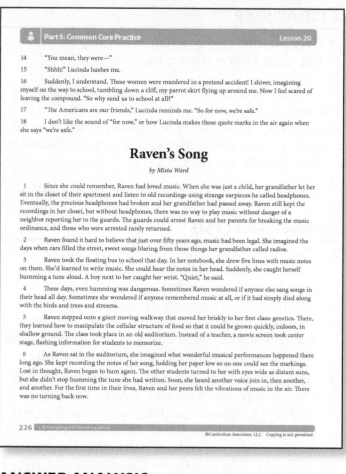

14 "You mean, they were—"

15 "Shhh!" Lucinda hushes me.

16 Suddenly, I understand. These women were murdered in a pretend accident! I shiver, imagining myself on the way to school, tumbling down a cliff, my parrot skirt flying up around me. Now I feel scared of leaving the compound. "So why send us to school at all?"

17 "The Americans are our friends," Lucinda reminds me. "So for now, we're safe."

18 I don't like the sound of "for now," or how Lucinda makes those quote marks in the air again when she says "we're safe."

Raven's Song

by Mista Ward

1 Since she could remember, Raven had loved music. When she was just a child, her grandfather let her sit in the closet of their apartment and listen to old recordings using strange earpieces he called headphones. Eventually, the precious headphones had broken and her grandfather had passed away. Raven still kept the recordings in her closet, but without headphones, there was no way to play music without danger of a neighbor reporting her to the guards. The guards could arrest Raven and her parents for breaking the music ordinance, and those who were arrested rarely returned.

2 Raven found it hard to believe that just over fifty years ago, music had been legal. She imagined the days when cars filled the street, sweet songs blaring from those things her grandfather called radios.

3 Raven took the floating bus to school that day. In her notebook, she drew five lines with music notes on them. She'd learned to write music. She could hear the notes in her head. Suddenly, she caught herself humming a tune aloud. A boy next to her caught her wrist. "Quiet," he said.

4 These days, even humming was dangerous. Sometimes Raven wondered if anyone else sang songs in their head all day. Sometimes she wondered if anyone remembered music at all, or if it had simply died along with the birds and trees and streams.

5 Raven stepped onto a giant moving walkway that moved her briskly to her first class: genetics. There, they learned how to manipulate the cellular structure of food so that it could be grown quickly, indoors, in shallow ground. The class took place in an old auditorium. Instead of a teacher, a movie screen took center stage, flashing information for students to memorize.

6 As Raven sat in the auditorium, she imagined what wonderful musical performances happened there long ago. Lost in thought, Raven began to hum again. The other students turned to her with eyes wide as distant suns, but she didn't stop humming the tune she had written. Soon, she heard another voice join in, then another, and another. For the first time in their lives, Raven and her peers felt the vibrations of music in the air. There was no turning back now.

AT A GLANCE

Students independently read two stories from different genres and answer questions in a format that provides test practice.

STEP BY STEP

- Tell students to use what they have learned about reading carefully and comparing and contrasting texts in different genres to read the stories on pages 225 and 226.

- Remind students to underline or circle important points.

- Tell students to answer the questions on pages 227 and 228. For questions 1–3, they should fill in the correct circle on the Answer Form.

- When students have finished, use the Answer Analysis to discuss correct responses and the reasons for them. Have students fill in the Number Correct on the Answer Form.

ANSWER ANALYSIS

1 The correct choice is A. Both texts address dangers of oppressive governments: Anita's family keeps their political beliefs secret to avoid notice by the dictatorial government; in Raven's world, the government arrests people who play or listen to music. Choice B is incorrect. "Raven's Song" shows how some scientific developments change society, but *Before We Were Free* does not. Choice C is incorrect. Although both texts mention school, they do not address the need to fit in with classmates. Choice D is incorrect because *Before We Were Free* does not address the importance of music in people's lives. **(DOK 3)**

Theme Connection

- How do all of the texts in this lesson relate to the theme of courage?

- Compare and contrast the ways the authors portray bravery in these texts.

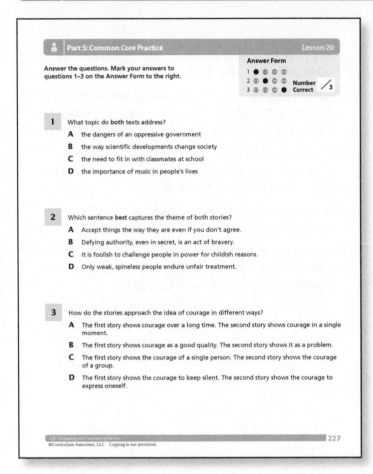

2 The correct choice is B. Anita's family's defiance of the government's authority shows a bravery that is not apparent to the outside world. Raven's listening to musical notes in her head shows her secret defiance of authority. Choice A is incorrect because neither Anita's family nor Raven accept things that they disagree with. Choice C is incorrect because Anita's father and Raven and her classmates do challenge people in power, but it is not for foolish, childish reasons. Choice D is incorrect because the characters in both stories endure unfair treatment while displaying character traits of courage and bravery, not weakness. **(DOK 3)**

3 The correct choice is D. Anita's family courageously keeps their beliefs secret, and Raven braves authority by humming in class, leading others to join her. Choice A is incorrect because, while the second story shows a moment of courage, the first story takes place in one evening, not over a long period of time. Choice B is incorrect because both stories show courage as a good quality, not as a problem. Choice C is incorrect because both stories

show the courage of a group: Anita's family in the first story and Raven and her classmates in the second story. **(DOK 3)**

4 Sample response: At first Anita is unaware of the reason her family must keep its secret, so she is not concerned or worried about keeping the secret. She wants to be able to tell her classmates the truth about being away from school. As Anita learns why her family must avoid detection by the government, she tells that she feels "scared of leaving the compound." Raven is similar to Anita in that Raven is also unconcerned about keeping secret her love of music. Raven absentmindedly hums a tune and is reprimanded by a classmate. Raven differs from Anita in that Raven does not change her attitude about keeping secret her love of music. Raven writes musical notes and hums in class, causing the entire class to join in and hum along with her. **(DOK 3)**

Integrating Standards

Use these questions and tasks as opportunities to interact with *Before We Were Free* and "Raven's Song."

1 In *Before We Were Free*, how does Anita's attitude about leaving home and going to school change? **(RL.6.3)**

Anita is carefree at the beginning of the story and eager to go back to school. By the story's end, she is fearful about leaving the family compound and concerned about her safety.

2 Why does Anita imagine herself as an accident victim? Cite evidence in the text. **(RL.6.1)**

Anita realizes that the car accident involving friends of her father's was deliberately arranged: "These women were murdered in a pretend accident!" Anita then imagines herself falling off a cliff in a similar kind of pretend accident and fears for her own safety.

3 In "Raven's Song," how does the following sentence help develop the setting: "Raven found it hard to believe that just over fifty years ago, music had been legal." **(RL.6.5)**

It shows that the society Raven lives in has declared music illegal. It also shows how a societal change has taken place over a relatively short period of time.

4 Why do you think the author uses the phrase "eyes wide as distant suns" in reference to Raven's classmates? **(RL.6.4; L.6.5.a)**

The author means to show how very wide their eyes are open in disbelief.

5 Discuss in small groups: How are the themes of *Before We Were Free* and "Raven's Song" conveyed through particular details? **(SL.6.1)**

Discussions will vary. Students might cite details given in the explanatory paragraph at the start of Before We Were Free, *as well as Raven's habit of singing songs in her head all day in "Raven's Song."*

Writing Activities

Essay Writing: Making Connections Across Narrative Texts *(W.6.2; RL.6.2; RL.6.9)*

- Have students choose and read a text that is related by theme or topic to *Before We Were Free* and "Raven's Song." Grade-appropriate texts from different genres include the following:

  Adventure: *Abel's Island* by William Steig, *Hatchet* by Gary Paulsen, *Island of the Blue Dolphins* by Scott O'Dell
  Historical: *Elephant Run* by Roland Smith, *Number the Stars* by Lois Lowry, *Weedflower* by Cynthia Kadohata
  Realistic Fiction: *The Breadwinner* by Deborah Ellis, *HUSH* by Jacqueline Woodson
  Science Fiction: *Life As We Knew It* by Susan Beth Pfeffer, *The Hunger Games* by Suzanne Collins

- Ask students to write an essay describing how their chosen text is related to one or both of the lesson texts. Students should recognize and interpret ethical and artistic connections between the texts. Students' essays may include discussion of ideas, differences in cultural perspectives and historical eras, and personal events and situations.

- Students' essays should discuss connections between the texts, the texts' shared attributes or features, and specific examples showing how a similar theme or topic is exemplified in each text. Students may include facts, concrete details, or quotations in their essays to support their approach.

LANGUAGE ACTIVITY *(L.6.2.b)*

Conventions of Standard English/Spell Correctly

- Review potentially troublesome spellings, such as *night, Chief, instructed, their/there, belongings, silently, possible.*

- Display the following sentence with misspellings: "That nihgt Cheif Joseph instruncted the tribe to pack up there beelongings and leef as silently as posible."

- Then have students review with a partner the essays they wrote and correct the spelling of any words as needed. Encourage them to use a dictionary for reference.

LISTENING ACTIVITY *(SL.6.1)*

Listen Closely/Summarize

- Have student pairs assign roles as speaker and listener.

- The speaker reads aloud from "Ogel's Tear," pausing after each paragraph. The listening partner summarizes the paragraph using his or her own words.

- Have pairs reverse roles and repeat the activity until they have summarized the entire story.

DISCUSSION ACTIVITY *(SL.6.1; RL.6.6)*

Talk in a Group/Discuss Point of View

- Have students reread *Before We Were Free*, paying attention to the character of Anita and the point of view she expresses.

- Discuss how the author's choice of words helps develop Anita's point of view.

- Have students form small groups to talk about the role of Anita's dialogue with Linda, as well as specific word choices used by Anita, that show how her point of view evolves as the story unfolds.

MEDIA ACTIVITY *(RL.6.7)*

Be Creative/Create Multimedia Poetry

- Have students create audio or video recordings of the poem "To Fight Aloud Is Very Brave."

- Allow students to practice pacing, rhythm, and rhyme of the poem before recording.

- Play selected recordings for the class. Have students compare and contrast the multimedia versions with the written version.

- Then have students discuss how the experience of seeing or hearing the poem read aloud differs from the experience of reading the text.

SCORING GUIDE AND ANSWER ANALYSIS

Literature Passage Answer Analysis

1 Ⓐ ● Ⓒ Ⓓ   3 Ⓐ ● Ⓒ Ⓓ

2 ● Ⓑ Ⓒ Ⓓ   4 Ⓐ Ⓑ ● Ⓓ

1 Choice B is correct. It says that both stories use dialogue. In both stories, the fathers use dialogue to explain the dangers of trying to handle the horses.

Choice A is incorrect. It says that both stories are set in the distant past. However, only the first story is set in the past. The second story is set in the present. Choice C is incorrect. It says that both stories could happen in real life. While the second story is realistic, and could happen in real life, the myth could not. Choice D is also incorrect. It says that both stories are told from the main character's point of view. However, only the second story is developed in this way. The first story is not told by Phaethon. **(RL.6.9; DOK 3)**

2 Choice A is correct. It says that it is important to know your limitations. In both stories, Phaethon and Sara think that they can do something that their fathers have spent years doing. They don't understand their limitations yet, and this causes some serious problems.

Choice B is incorrect. It says that it is important to spend time with family. Although both stories focus on the main characters and their fathers, this is not the common theme of both stories. Choice C is incorrect. It says that people should work hard to achieve their goals. While Sara does want to work hard to be a rodeo champion someday, and Phaethon travels very far to meet his father, this is not the theme of the stories. Choice D is also incorrect. It says that people should focus on the positive things in life. Although some positive things happen in both stories, this is not the major theme in these stories. **(RL.6.9; DOK 3)**

3 Choice B is correct. It says that Sara grew up knowing her father, and Phaethon did not. In the first story, it says that Phaethon begged his mother to tell him about his father for a long time. He did not learn about his father's true identity until he was a teenager. Sara has known her father for her whole life.

Choice A is incorrect. It says that Phaethon grew up riding horses. However, it is Sara who has been riding for almost as long as she could walk. The first story does not say that Phaethon is an experienced rider. Choice C is incorrect. It says that Sara is confident in her ability to control horses and Phaethon is not. However, both Sara and Phaethon are overconfident in their abilities to handle the horses. This is what gets the two characters into trouble. Choice D is also incorrect. It says that Phaethon feels guilty about the mistakes he made. However, it is Sara who feels bad when Hermes's leg is hurt after she tries to ride him. **(RL.6.9; DOK 3)**

4 Choice C is correct. Phaethon did get his father's permission to drive the chariot. Sara did not get her father's permission to ride Hermes. He only gave her permission to sit on the horse.

Choice A is incorrect. It says that Phaethon is afraid to drive the horses, but Sara is not. Phaethon was not afraid either. Choice B is incorrect. It says that Phaethon is successful on his ride and Sara is not. Actually neither was successful. Choice D is also incorrect. It says that Phaethon is safe during his ride but Sara is injured. Neither character was injured, although both were in serious danger. **(RL.6.9; DOK 3)**

SAMPLE RESPONSES

Short Response (See 2-Point Rubric—Short Response on page A46 for scoring.)

5 **Part A:** The words *determined* and *brave* describe Phaethon and Sara. Phaethon is "determined to meet his father," who calls him "a brave boy." Sara calls her pleading "relentless" (a synonym for determined) and she tries to imitate her father's "courageous acts." **(RL.6.9; DOK 3)**

Part B: Students' choice of sentence will vary. Sample sentence: "The trip took many months, and Phaethon often thought about turning back, but he kept going." **(RL.6.9; DOK 3)**

Part C: Students' choice of sentence will vary. Sample sentence: "One day, after another round of relentless pleading on my part, Dad agreed to let me sit on Hermes but not ride him." **(RL.6.9; DOK 3)**

6 Both stories show the importance of relationships between fathers and children. In the first story, Phaethon has never known his father. When he finally learns who his father is, he sets out on a long and difficult journey to meet him. In the second story, Sara has a great relationship with her father. The reader can tell that he is important to her, because she explains how terrific she thinks he is and how much she wants to be like him. These details show the importance of the relationship between fathers and children. **(RL.6.9; DOK 3)**

7 Both Phaethon and Sara were determined to reach their goals, and both ran into problems. Phaethon convinced his father to let him drive a chariot pulled by horses across the sky. But he was unable to control the horses and as a result he burned everything on the ground under him. His father had to step in to keep him from destroying the earth. Sara had a similar problem. When she tried to ride her father's horse she also could not control him. Her father stepped in to save her. **(RL.6.9; DOK 3)**

8 Helios and Sara's father are similar. They know that their animals are difficult to handle. Because of this, they both warn their children against trying to drive or ride the horses. Still, both men are eventually worn down by their children's pleas. However, both Phaethon and Sara have accidents while trying to handle the wild horses. Despite this, both fathers are proud of how the child handles the problem. Still, it is likely that neither Helios nor Sara's father will allow allow his child to drive or ride a horse again. **(RL.6.9; DOK 3)**

Performance Task (See New York State Grade 6–8 Expository Writing Evaluation Rubric on pages A47 and A48 for scoring.)

9 In both stories, the main characters want to win the approval of their fathers. In the first story, Phaethon has never known his father. When he learns his father is Helios, he sets out on a long journey to find him. Eager to prove he is his father's son, he begs Helios to let him drive the sun chariot, even though it is dangerous.

Sara's actions are also affected by her desire to win her father's approval. She admires him and wants to be a rodeo champion like him. She tries to win her father's approval by riding Hermes, her dad's wild stallion.

Phaethon and Sara's desire to win their fathers' approval leads them to do dangerous things. However, both are so caught up in their tasks that they don't realize they don't have control until it's too late. These experiences change the characters. Phaethon realizes he was wrong to think he had control of the horses when the ride turns into a "nightmare." Sara also says that she "foolishly" thought she could control Hermes at the beginning, but then finds out that she was mistaken. Luckily, their fathers step in just in time to save the day. In the end, both Phaethon and Sara learn a lesson about understanding their limitations. **(RL.6.9; DOK 3)**

Comparing and Contrasting Reading to Viewing

LESSON OBJECTIVES

- Identify the differences between a written story and a staged or filmed version of the story.

- Compare and contrast the experience of reading a story to seeing and hearing a filmed version of the same text.

THE LEARNING PROGRESSION

Grade 5: CCLS RL.5.7 requires students to "analyze how visual and multimedia elements contribute to the meaning" of a text.

Grade 6: CCLS RL.6.7 builds on the Grade 5 standard by requiring students to not only analyze how visual and multimedia elements contribute to text meaning, but to also "compare and contrast the experience of reading a story, drama, or poem to listening to or viewing an audio, video, or live version of the text." This helps prepare students for the analysis required at Grade 7.

Grade 7: CCLS RL.7.7 requires students to compare and contrast written and filmed versions of texts by "analyzing the effects of techniques unique to each medium."

TAP STUDENTS' PRIOR KNOWLEDGE

- Ask students what they like most about favorite stories that they've read. Interesting characters? An exciting plot? Humor? Drama? Lots of description that brings the story to life?

- Now ask what they like most about their favorite movies. Thrilling action sequences? Cool sound effects? Interesting costumes and sets? Attention-grabbing pictures on a big screen?

- Ask for examples of some well-known books that have been turned into movies (e.g., the *Harry Potter*, *Hunger Games*, *Percy Jackson*, or *Diary of a Wimpy Kid* books). Explain that each medium—print and film—tells a story differently. Then ask students how the two versions of some of the stories they mentioned were alike or different.

- Explain that the author of a book relies on words to tell his or her story over the course of a number of pages. The story can be as long as the writer wants. It can even stretch over several volumes. The movie director relies on images and sound to tell a story within a limited amount of time. These limitations affect what we read in books and see in movies and plays.

- Tell students they will look at four key parts of storytelling and learn how they are presented differently in print and on a screen.

Ready *Teacher Toolbox*		*teacher-toolbox.com*
	Prerequisite Skills	*RL.6.7*
Ready Lessons	✓	✓
Tools for Instruction	✓ ✓	
Interactive Tutorials		✓

CCLS Focus

RL.6.7 Compare and contrast the experience of reading a story... to listening to or viewing an audio, video, or live version of the text, including contrasting what they "see" and "hear" when reading the text to what they perceive when they listen or watch.

ADDITIONAL STANDARDS: **W.6.1, W.6.3, W.6.10; SL.6.5**

AT A GLANCE

By focusing on four of the most important elements of storytelling, students will compare and contrast their experience of reading a story in print versus seeing and hearing it in a movie or play.

STEP BY STEP: PAGE 227

- Before students look in their book, ask them what tools a writer uses to tell his or her story. (*dialogue and direct thought, sensory description, action; sometimes images*) Then ask students what tools a filmmaker or the director of a play uses to tell a story. (*actors, lighting, music, sets, props*) Ask students who they think has the easier job when telling a story—a writer or a director—and why.

- Have a volunteer read the introduction on page 227 aloud to the class.

- Read the lines above the chart on page 227. Be sure students understand the format of the chart. Define the terms on the left, if necessary. Then explain that the other two columns contrast the differences between how those elements are presented in print and how they are presented in movies and plays.

- **Character:** Ask students which of the bullet points in each column helps them understand a character the most. Point out that one advantage writers have over filmmakers is that they can tell the reader what the characters are thinking.

- **Setting:** Help students realize that filmmakers can quickly convey the setting of a scene on film, but a writer would need plenty of space and many words to describe that same setting.

- **Plot:** Explain to students that because films are limited in time (usually to about two hours), filmmakers often have to simplify the plot and leave out entire scenes or plot developments. Ask the class for examples of movies based on books where entire scenes or characters were omitted.

- **Mood/Tone:** Point out that the combination of images and sounds allows filmmakers to create a mood quickly; writers have to rely on their descriptive language and the imagination of the reader to create a mood. Ask students about the scariest book they've ever read and the scariest movie they've ever seen. Which frightened them the most?

Why? Then do the same with a humorous book and movie.

- For the last activity on the page, pair students and have them tell each other about a book they really liked that was made into a movie. Have students discuss how knowing the story affected the experience of watching the movie.

STEP BY STEP: PAGE 228

- Tell students that now they are going to think about how the differences between print and film stories can affect their enjoyment of the story.

- Read aloud the directions for the chart on page 228. It may help to use one familiar book/movie as an example as you discuss the bulleted items in the chart with the whole class. Point out to students that they will be asked to come up with additional Pros and Cons to add to the chart.

- **Pros:** Review the bullet points in each column. Remind students that movies can convey a lot of information in a matter of seconds through sound and images. In a book, more in-depth information and detail can be conveyed with no limit on time.

- Have students work independently to add a couple of additional Pros for each medium. Student responses should reflect an understanding of the four story elements from the chart on page 227.

- **Cons:** Review the bullet points in each column. Discuss how movies often omit entire scenes and characters from a story and how books can sometimes get bogged down in too much detail.

- Have students work independently to suggest a couple of additional Cons for each medium. Student responses should reflect an understanding of the story elements from the chart on page 227.

- After they complete the chart, have students work in pairs to compare what they've written and further discuss the differences between print and movie versions of books they know. Extend the discussion by having partners tell each other about a story they read in a book and then saw as a movie. Have each partner describe the pros and cons of the movie and book version. Remind them to use specific examples from the book and movie so their partner will understand the comparisons that are being made.

STORYBOARDING (SL.6.5)

- In small groups, have students choose a scene from a book or story they've read and create a storyboard depicting how they would film that scene. Explain to students that a storyboard is like a graphic novel—it visually tells the story to be filmed. The drawing in each frame doesn't need to be expert. Simple sketches (even stick figures) will work, along with some brief notes about each frame.

- Students should consider how much of the scene they can include in their storyboard and how much detail from the print story they will be able to include. Suggest they use the four elements of storytelling chart on page 227 of the lesson to make notes and plan out how they want to film the scene.

- When each group is finished, have them present their storyboard to the class, explaining the choices they made in the way they depicted the scene.

BE A WRITER (W.6.3)

- Have students think of a memorable scene from one of their favorite movies. It doesn't need to be a movie made from a book or story they've read— this can be any movie that's appropriate for class.

- Students will write the scene in story form. This should not be a synopsis of the scene—they should write with the goal of bringing the scene to life on the page for the reader. Students will need to include detailed information about the characters, what they're thinking, and the setting. They will also need to describe the actions of the plot in detail and convey some sense of the mood or tone of the scene.

- Have student volunteers read their story version of a movie scene to the class.

READING/VIEWING RESPONSE JOURNAL (W.6.10)

- Have students keep a Reading/Viewing Response Journal for a week. Each time they read a story, have them write a paragraph detailing a scene that inspired a distinct visual image for them. Also direct students to respond to visual images they see when they watch a story on TV or see a movie. Have them describe their reaction to a visual image

from each show or film. Tell them to keep in mind how filmmakers use images and sound to tell a story.

BE A MOVIE CRITIC (W.6.1)

- Invite students to become movie critics and review a movie based on a book or story they have read. The review should be an analysis of how successful the filmmakers were in translating the story to the big screen.

- Tell students they will need to support their opinion with specific, concrete details about plot, character, setting, and mood. Have them use the copymaster on page 210 of this book to record their thoughts.

CHARACTER COMPARISON (RL.6.7)

- Have students write a short comparison of how they imagined a character from a story they read versus how the character was depicted in the movie version.

- Students should first describe how they saw the character in their imagination when reading the story, then describe the movie depiction.

- Have students decide which version they like the best.

STAGE A SCENE (SL.6.5)

- Have groups of students perform a scene from a book or story as if it were a play. Students will need to agree on one short scene from either a book they have all read or a story the class has read. (Teachers can also simply assign the scenes to the groups based on the class readings.) They should then create a script with dialogue based on their story source.

- Students will need to assign roles and rehearse the scene, blocking out the action and determining what props (if any), music, sound effects, and other elements they will need.

- Have each group present its scene to the class.

Name_____ Date_____

DIRECTIONS: Think of a book you read that was turned into a movie. Compare the two by filling out the chart. Think about how well each storytelling element did or didn't work in each medium.

Book/Movie Title: _____

_____

	Print Version	Movie Version
Plot		
Characters		
Setting		
Mood		

How successful do you think the filmmakers were in translating this story from print to film? Explain your answer.

Cut along the dotted line.

Ready® New York CCLS Language Handbook

The *Ready New York CCLS* Language Handbook was created to help students develop proficiency with the Common Core Learning Standards for Language. Each lesson uses scaffolded instruction, beginning with an introduction and guided practice and then moving students into fully independent practice of the skills and strategies behind the Common Core.

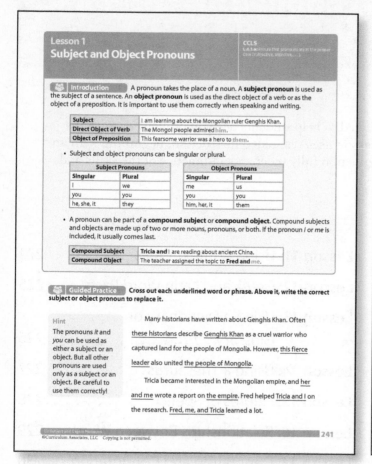

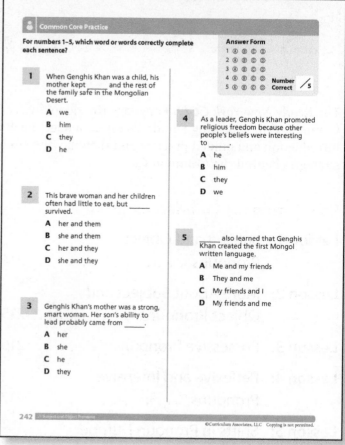

Lesson 1: Subject and Object Pronouns

Guided Practice, page 241

    Many historians have written about Genghis Khan.

          they   **him**

Often <u>these historians</u> describe <u>Genghis Khan</u> as a

cruel warrior who captured land for the people of

                           he

Mongolia. However, <u>this fierce leader</u> also united

   them

<u>the people of Mongolia</u>.

    Tricia became interested in the Mongolian

       she and I (or we)

empire, and <u>her and me</u> wrote a report on

it   **us**

<u>the empire</u>. Fred helped <u>Tricia and I</u> on the

    We (or Fred, Tricia, and I)

research. <u>Fred, me, and Tricia</u> learned a lot.

Common Core Practice, page 242

1   B

2   D

3   A

4   B

5   C

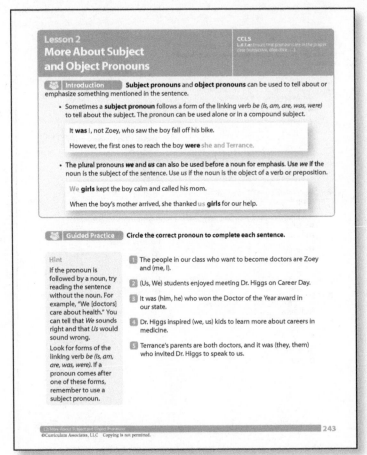

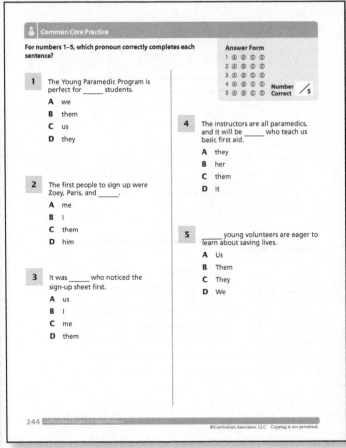

Lesson 2: More About Subject and Object Pronouns

Guided Practice, page 243

1 I

2 We

3 he

4 us

5 they

Common Core Practice, page 244

1 C

2 B

3 B

4 A

5 D

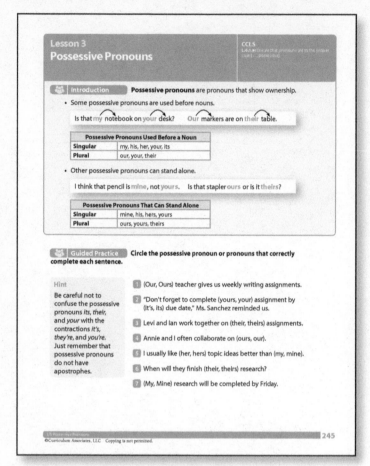

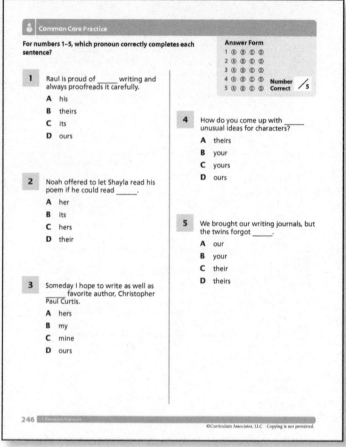

Lesson 3: Possessive Pronouns

Guided Practice, page 245

1 Our

2 your; its

3 their

4 ours

5 her; mine

6 their

7 My

Common Core Practice, page 246

1 A

2 C

3 B

4 B

5 D

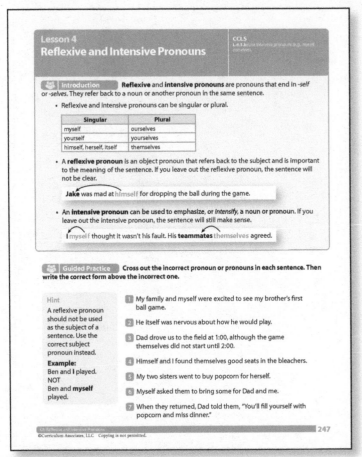

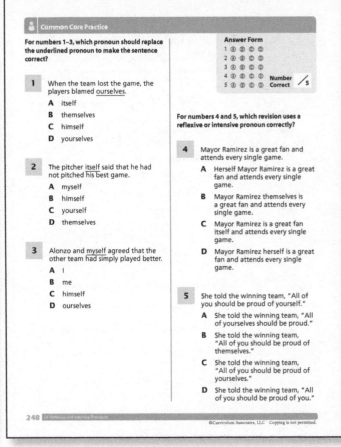

Lesson 4: Reflexive and Intensive Pronouns

Guided Practice, page 247

1 ~~myself~~: I

2 ~~itself~~: himself

3 ~~themselves~~: itself

4 ~~Himself and I~~: He and I
   ~~themselves~~: ourselves

5 ~~herself~~: themselves

6 ~~Myself~~: I

7 ~~yourself~~; yourselves

Common Core Practice, page 248

1 B

2 B

3 A

4 D

5 C

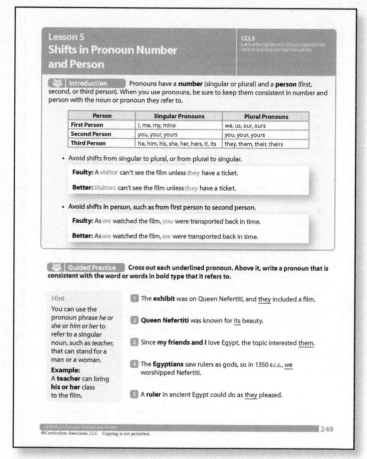

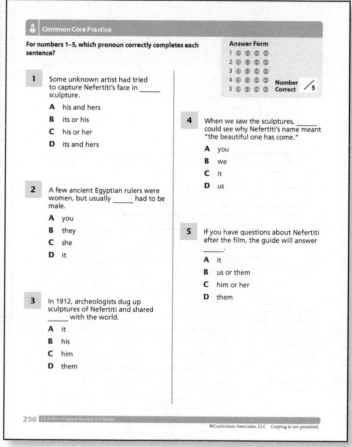

Lesson 5: Shifts in Pronoun Number and Person

Guided Practice, page 249

1 The **exhibit** was on Queen Nefertiti, and ~~they~~ *it* included a film.

2 **Queen Nefertiti** was known for ~~its~~ *her* beauty.

3 Since **my friends and I** love Egypt, the topic interested ~~them~~ *us*.

4 The **Egyptians** saw rulers as gods, so in 1350 B.C.E, ~~we~~ *they* worshipped Nefertiti.

5 A **ruler** in ancient Egypt could do as ~~they~~ *he or she* pleased. (See hint.)

Common Core Practice, page 250

1 C

2 B

3 D

4 B

5 D

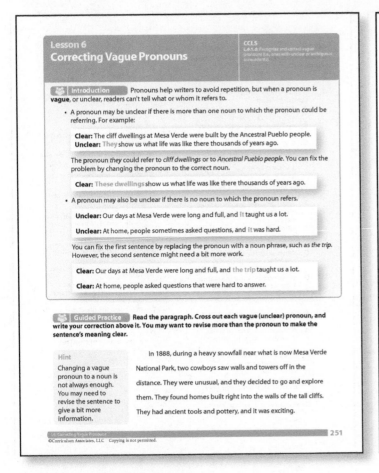

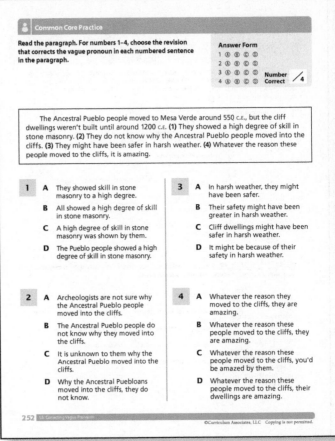

Lesson 6: Correcting Vague Pronouns

Guided Practice, page 251

Responses will vary. Sample answers:

In 1888, during a heavy snowstorm near what is

now Mesa Verde National Park, two cowboys saw

These structures
walls and towers off in the distance. ~~They~~ were

the men
unusual, and ~~they~~ decided to go and explore them.

The cowboys
~~They~~ found homes built right into the walls of the

The homes
tall cliffs. ~~They~~ had ancient tools and pottery,

the men were excited.
and ~~it was exciting~~.

Common Core Practice, page 252

1 D

2 A

3 C

4 D

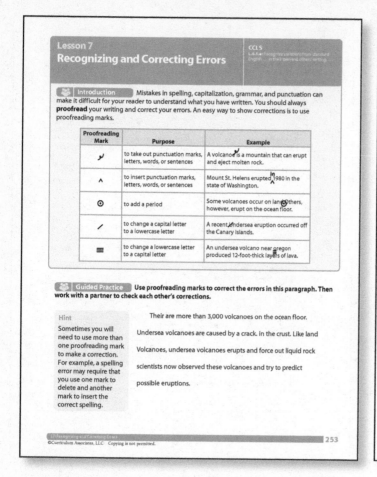

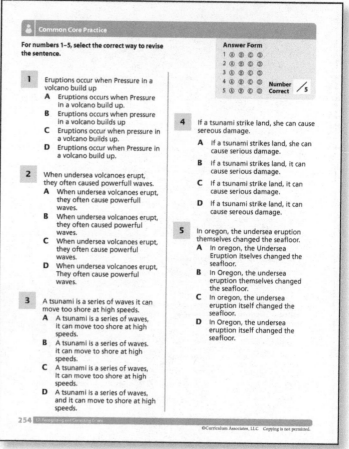

Lesson 7: Recognizing and Correcting Errors

Guided Practice, page 253

   There

Their are more than 3,000 volcanoes on the ocean

floor. Undersea volcanoes are caused by a crack in the

crust. Like land Volcanoes, undersea volcanoes erupts

and force out liquid rock scientists now observed

these volcanoes and try to predict possible eruptions.

Common Core Practice, page 254

1 C

2 C

3 D

4 B

5 D

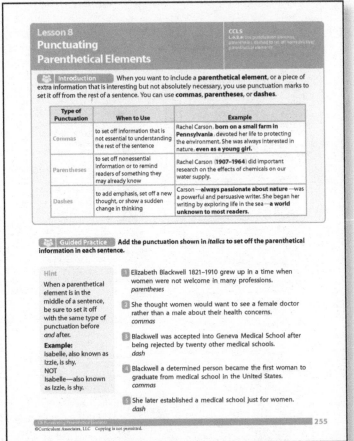

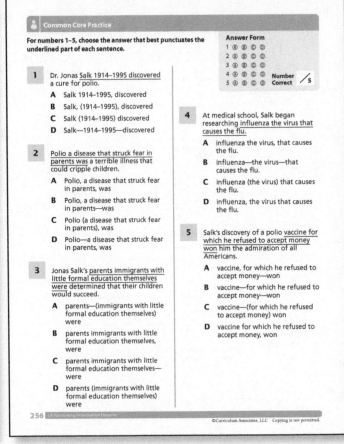

Lesson 8: Punctuating Parenthetical Elements

Guided Practice, page 255

1 Elizabeth Blackwell (1821–1910) grew up in a time when women were not welcome in many professions.

2 She thought women would want to see a female doctor, rather than a male, about their health concerns.

3 Blackwell was accepted into Geneva Medical School—after being rejected by twenty other medical schools.

4 Blackwell, a determined person, became the first woman to graduate from medical school in the United States.

5 She later established a medical school—just for women.

Common Core Practice, page 256

1 C

2 A

3 D

4 D

5 B

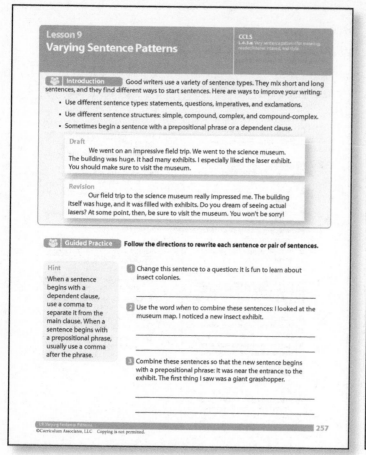

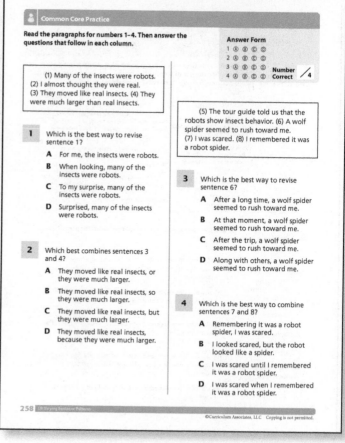

Lesson 9: Varying Sentence Patterns

Guided Practice, page 257

Responses will vary. Sample answers:

1 Wouldn't it be fun to learn about insect colonies?

2 When I looked at the museum map, I noticed a new insect exhibit.

3 Near the entrance to the exhibit, the first thing I saw was a giant grasshopper.

Common Core Practice, page 258

1   C

2   C

3   B

4   C

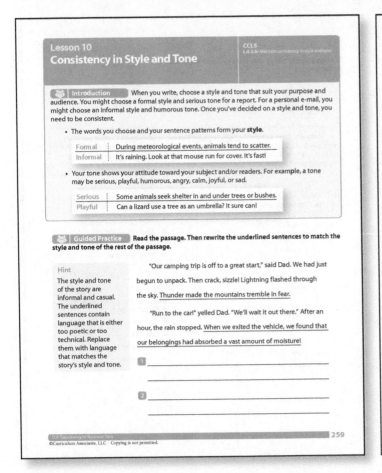

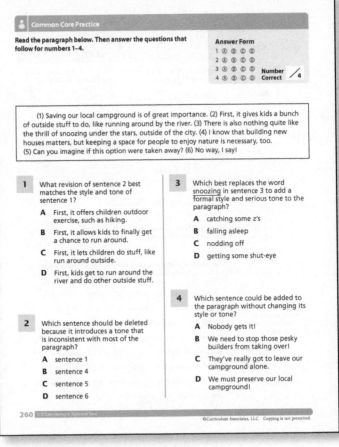

Lesson 10: Consistency in Style and Tone

Guided Practice, page 259

Responses will vary. Sample answers:

1 The thunder was so loud, we thought maybe the Fourth of July had come early.

2 It poured for an hour. When we finally got out of the car, each of our sleeping bags had soaked up a bathtub-full of water.

Common Core Practice, page 260

1 A

2 D

3 B

4 D

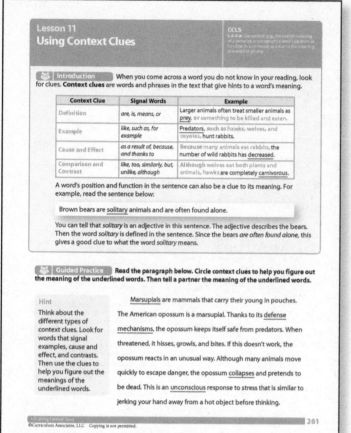

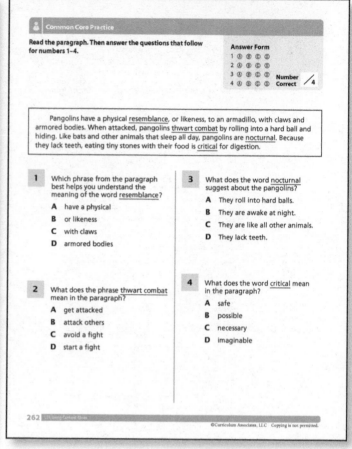

Lesson 11: Using Context Clues

Guided Practice, page 261

Context clues are underlined. Meanings provided by students will vary. Sample answers:

Marsupials: <u>are mammals that carry their young in pouches</u>. Meaning: mammals that carry their young in pouches

defense mechanisms: <u>Thanks to . . . keeps itself safe; hisses, growls, and bites.</u> Meaning: ways that one is able to protect oneself

collapses: <u>Although many animals move quickly . . . pretends to be dead.</u> Meaning: falls down

unconscious: <u>response to stress; similar to . . . before thinking.</u> Meaning: without thinking

Common Core Practice, page 262

1   B

2   C

3   B

4   C

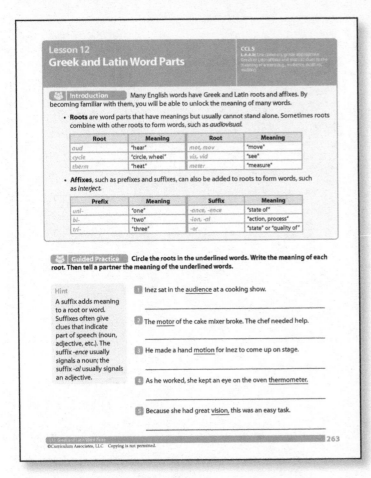

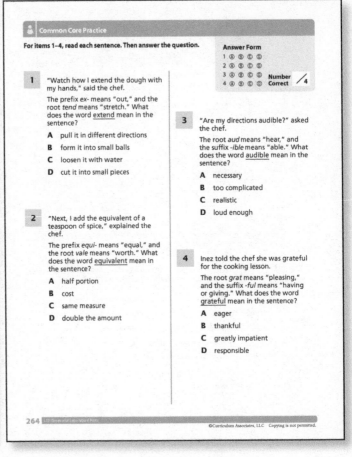

Lesson 12: Greek and Latin Word Parts

Guided Practice, page 263

Roots and their definitions are shown. Word meanings provided by students will vary. Sample answers:

1 ⟨aud⟩ience: root *aud* means "hear"; *audience* means "the state of listening"

2 ⟨mot⟩or: root *mot* means "move"; *motor* means "having the quality of movement"

3 ⟨mot⟩ion: root *mot* means "move"; *motion* means "action through a movement or gesture"

4 ⟨therm⟩o⟨meter⟩ root *therm* means "heat," root *meter* means "measure"; *thermometer* means "to measure heat"

5 ⟨vis⟩ion: root *vis* means "see"; *vision* means "process of hearing and seeing"

Common Core Practice, page 264

1 A

2 C

3 D

4 B

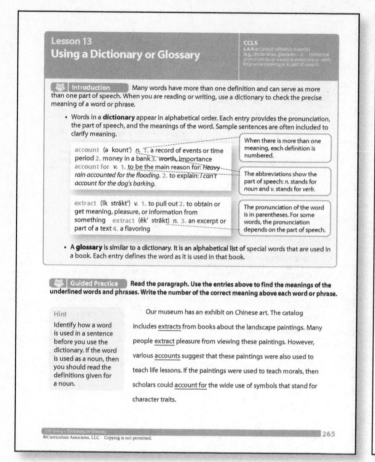

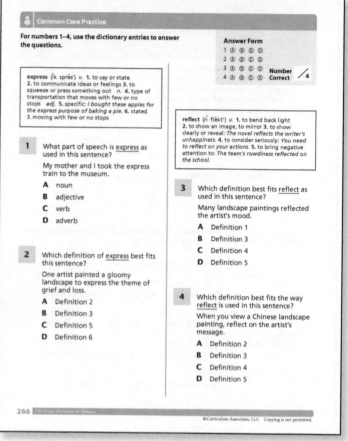

Lesson 13: Using a Dictionary or Glossary

Guided Practice, page 265

Our museum has an exhibit on Chinese art. The

catalog includes <u>extracts</u> **3** from books about the

landscape paintings. Many people <u>extract</u> **2** pleasure

from viewing these paintings. However, various

<u>accounts</u> **1** suggest that these paintings were also used

to teach life lessons. If the paintings were used to

teach morals, then scholars could <u>account for</u> **2** the wide

use of symbols that stand for character traits.

Common Core Practice, page 266

1 B

2 A

3 B

4 C

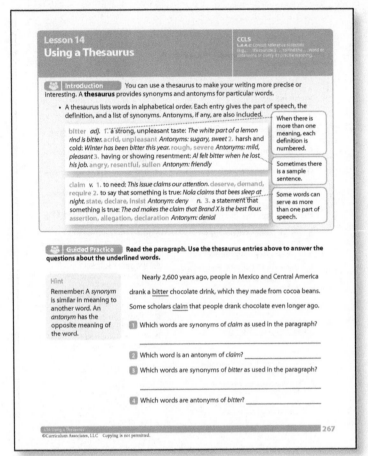

Lesson 14
Using a Thesaurus

CCLS
L.a.4.c Consult reference materials (e.g., ...thesaurus) ...to find the ... word or determine or clarify its precise meaning.

Introduction You can use a thesaurus to make your writing more precise or interesting. A **thesaurus** provides synonyms and antonyms for particular words.

- A thesaurus lists words in alphabetical order. Each entry gives the part of speech, the definition, and a list of synonyms. Antonyms, if any, are also included.

bitter *adj.* 1. a strong, unpleasant taste: *The white part of a lemon rind is bitter.* acrid, unpleasant *Antonyms: sugary, sweet* 2. harsh and cold: *Winter has been bitter this year.* rough, severe *Antonyms: mild, pleasant* 3. having or showing resentment: *Al felt bitter when he lost his job.* angry, resentful, sullen *Antonym: friendly*

> When there is more than one meaning, each definition is numbered.

> Sometimes there is a sample sentence.

claim *v.* 1. to need: *This issue claims our attention.* deserve, demand, require 2. to say that something is true: *Nola claims that bees sleep at night.* state, declare, insist *Antonym: deny* *n.* 3. a statement that something is true: *The ad makes the claim that Brand X is the best flour.* assertion, allegation, declaration *Antonym: denial*

> Some words can serve as more than one part of speech.

Guided Practice Read the paragraph. Use the thesaurus entries above to answer the questions about the underlined words.

Hint

Remember: A *synonym* is similar in meaning to another word. An *antonym* has the opposite meaning of the word.

Nearly 2,600 years ago, people in Mexico and Central America drank a <u>bitter</u> chocolate drink, which they made from cocoa beans. Some scholars <u>claim</u> that people drank chocolate even longer ago.

1 Which words are synonyms of *claim* as used in the paragraph?

_____

2 Which word is an antonym of *claim*? _____

3 Which words are synonyms of *bitter* as used in the paragraph?

_____

4 Which words are antonyms of *bitter*? _____

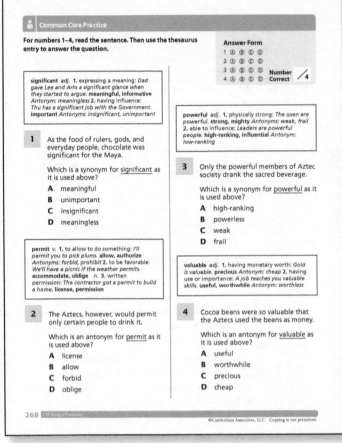

Common Core Practice

For numbers 1–4, read the sentence. Then use the thesaurus entry to answer the question.

Answer Form
1 Ⓐ Ⓑ Ⓒ Ⓓ
2 Ⓐ Ⓑ Ⓒ Ⓓ
3 Ⓐ Ⓑ Ⓒ Ⓓ   Number Correct /4
4 Ⓐ Ⓑ Ⓒ Ⓓ

significant *adj.* 1. expressing a meaning: *Dad gave Lee and Arlo a significant glance when they started to argue.* meaningful, informative *Antonym: meaningless* 2. having influence: *Thu has a significant job with the Government.* important *Antonyms: insignificant, unimportant*

1 As the food of rulers, gods, and everyday people, chocolate was significant for the Maya.

Which is a synonym for <u>significant</u> as it is used above?

A meaningful
B unimportant
C insignificant
D meaningless

permit *v.* 1. to allow to do something: *I'll permit you to pick plums.* allow, authorize *Antonyms: forbid, prohibit* 2. to be favorable: *We'll have a picnic if the weather permits.* accommodate, oblige *n.* 3. written permission: *The contractor got a permit to build a home.* license, permission

2 The Aztecs, however, would permit only certain people to drink it.

Which is an antonym for <u>permit</u> as it is used above?

A license
B allow
C forbid
D oblige

powerful *adj.* 1. physically strong: *The oxen are powerful.* strong, mighty *Antonyms: weak, frail* 2. able to influence: *Leaders are powerful people.* high-ranking, influential *Antonym: low-ranking*

3 Only the powerful members of Aztec society drank the sacred beverage.

Which is a synonym for <u>powerful</u> as it is used above?

A high-ranking
B powerless
C weak
D frail

valuable *adj.* 1. having monetary worth: *Gold is valuable.* precious *Antonym: cheap* 2. having use or importance: *A job teaches you valuable skills.* useful, worthwhile *Antonym: worthless*

4 Cocoa beans were so valuable that the Aztecs used the beans as money.

Which is an antonym for <u>valuable</u> as it is used above?

A useful
B worthwhile
C precious
D cheap

Lesson 14: Using a Thesaurus

Guided Practice, page 267

1 state, declare, insist

2 deny

3 acrid, unpleasant

4 sugary, sweet

Common Core Practice, page 268

1 A

2 C

3 A

4 D

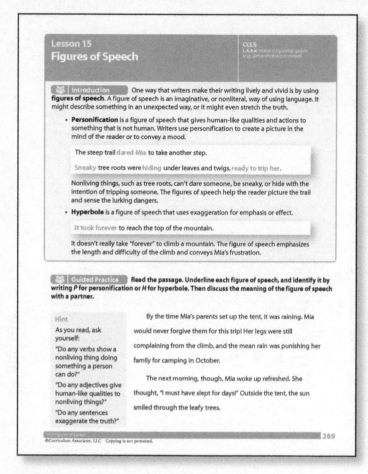

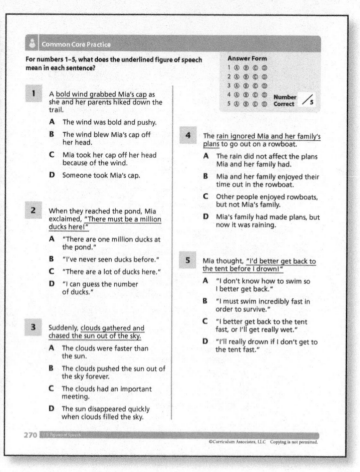

Lesson 15: Figures of Speech

Guided Practice, page 269

1 <u>Mia would never forgive them</u>; H; Mia was very angry.

2 <u>Her legs were still complaining</u>: P; Her legs still hurt.

3 <u>mean rain was punishing</u>: P; The rain made camping so unpleasant it felt like a punishment by someone mean.

4 <u>I must have slept for days</u>: H; I slept for a very long time.

5 <u>sun smiled</u>: P; The sun shone and made Mia feel happy.

Common Core Practice, page 270

1 B

2 C

3 D

4 D

5 C

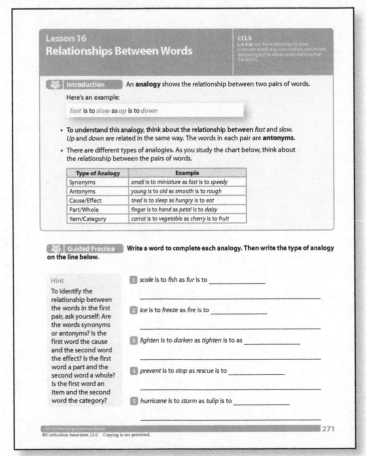

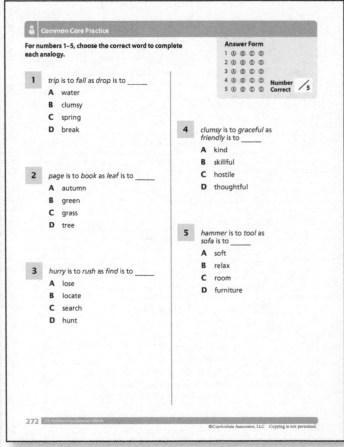

Lesson 16: Relationships Between Words

Guided Practice, page 271

Responses will vary: Sample answers:

1 mammal; part/whole

2 burn; cause/effect

3 loosen; antonym

4 save; synonym

5 flower; item/category

Common Core Practice, page 272

1 D

2 D

3 B

4 C

5 D

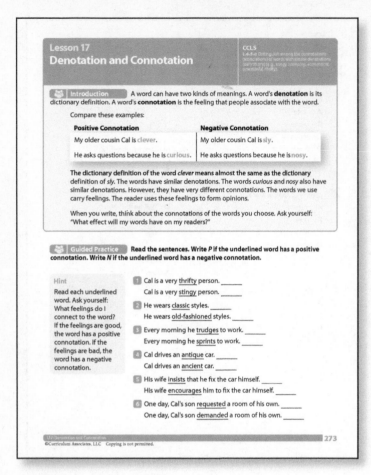

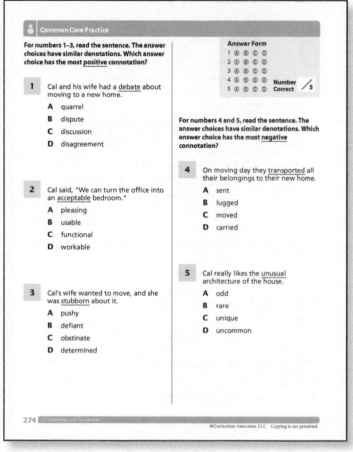

Lesson 17: Denotation and Connotation

Guided Practice, page 273

1 thrifty: P
stingy: N

2 classic: P
old-fashioned: N

3 trudges: N
sprints: P

4 antique: P
ancient: N

5 insists: N
encourages: P

6 requested: P
demanded: N

Common Core Practice, page 274

1 C

2 A

3 D

4 B

5 A